NEW YORK C
1989

Nan and Ivan Lyons frequently write travel and restaurant articles for magazines including *Bon Appétit, Travel & Leisure,* and *Food & Wine.* They are the authors of a number of novels, among them *Someone Is Killing the Great Chefs of Europe* and their latest, set in their hometown of New York City, *The President Is Coming to Lunch.*

The Business Brief in Travel Arrangements is by Sondra Snowdon, author of *The Global Edge: How Your Company Can Win in the International Marketplace.*

Maps are by Swanston Graphics.

ACKNOWLEDGMENTS

Completing this project would not have been possible without the help and support of many friends, and friends of friends, who responded to questions and questionnaires.

For service above and beyond, we want to thank Avraham Inlender, Don Cox, Frederick Lunning, and most especially Janet Rodgers and Judy Fireman for being "godmothers" who came through not only with tea and sympathy, but with shoeleather.

We are grateful to Charlotte Savidge for all her work on the nitty-gritty, to John Procopio for his computer expertise, and, as always, to Barbara Settanni.

A very special thank you to our editor, Debra Bernardi, for her unfailing good spirits and wise counsel during the writing of this book.

—Nan and Ivan Lyons

A BANTAM TRAVEL GUIDE

NEW YORK CITY

1989

Nan and Ivan Lyons

BANTAM

NEW YORK ● TORONTO ● LONDON ● SYDNEY ● AUCKLAND

NEW YORK CITY 1989

A Bantam Book / May 1989

Grateful acknowledgment is made for permission to reprint the following excerpt from "Here Is New York", copyright 1949 by E. B. White, from Essays of E. B. White *by E. B. White. Reprinted by permission of Harper & Row, Publishers, Inc.*

ISBN 0–553–34640–7

Published simultaneously in the United States and Canada

Bantam Books are published by Bantam Books, a division of Bantam Double-day Dell Publishing Group, Inc. Its trademark, consisting of the words "Bantam Books" and the portrayal of a rooster, is Registered in U.S. Patent and Trademark Office and in other countries. Marca Registrada, Bantam Books, 666 Fifth Avenue, New York, New York 10103

PRINTED IN THE UNITED STATES OF AMERICA

0 9 8 7 6 5 4 3 2 1

CONTENTS

FOREWORD

Anyone who's ever used a travel guidebook knows how addictive they become when they're good, but how annoying they are when they're bad. We at Bantam launched this new guidebook series because we honestly believed we could improve on, no, that's too weak, we believed we could *significantly* improve on the best of what's already out there. And there are some good guidebooks out there.

It was apparent to us that, unless we improved on the best of what's currently available, there was no sense in producing a new series. More to the point, there'd be no reason for you, the traveler, to buy our guidebooks. We analyzed the guidebooks already on the market, making note of their best features as well as their deficiencies. The single greatest deficiency of most guidebooks is that you have to buy something else to supplement these deficiencies. Usually you need to buy a good map or a guide to hotels or restaurants because your primary guide lacks good detailed maps, has outdated information on hotels or restaurants, or simply doesn't include such information at all—never mind whether it's up-to-date or not.

The Bantam team had one major goal—that of producing the only travel guides that both the experienced and the inexperienced traveler would ever need for a given destination. You're holding an example of how well we succeeded. Can we document this success? Let's take a look.

- One of the first things you'll notice is that **Bantam Travel Guides** include a full-color travel atlas with maps detailed enough for the most demanding travel needs.
- Upon closer scrutiny you'll find that the guide is organized geographically rather than alphabetically. Think of what this means to you. Descriptions of what's available in a contiguous geographical area make it easier to get the most out of a city neighborhood or a country region. For those who still need to locate something alphabetically we provide a detailed index.
- A real convenience is the way that restaurants and hotels in major cities are keyed into the maps so that you can locate these places easily.

- At the end of key chapters you'll find a feature called City Listings where museums, churches, major sites and shops are listed with their addresses, phone numbers and map-location code.
- Bantam guides will be revised every year. Travel conditions change and so do our guides.
- Finally, we think you'll enjoy reading our guidebooks. We've tried hard to find not only well-informed writers, but good writers. The writing is literate and lively. It pulls no punches. It's honest. Most of all it's a good read.

Still, no guidebook can cover everything that's worth seeing or doing—though we believe we come closer than anyone else. We ask you to bear in mind, too, that prices can change at any time, and that today's well-managed restaurant or hotel can change owners or managers tomorrow. Today's great service or food can be tomorrow's disappointment. We've recommended places as they are now and as we expect them to be in the future, but there are no guarantees. We welcome your comments and suggestions. Our address is Bantam Travel Guides, 666 Fifth Avenue, New York, N.Y. 10103.

Tips on Getting the Most Out of This Guide

Bantam Travel Guides are designed to be extremely user friendly, but there are a few things you should know in order to get the maximum benefit from them.

1. You'll find a special **Travel Arrangements** section, easily identified by the black-bordered pages, toward the back of the book. This section can be invaluable in planning your trip.
2. The **Priorities** chapter will insure that you see and do the most important things when you visit your destination. Whether you're spending two days or two weeks there, you'll want to make the most of your time and certainly not miss the musts.
3. Note that in addition to our main selection of important restaurants you'll also find described in the text additional places to stop for lunch or dinner, a snack or a drink.
4. To help you instantly identify restaurant and hotel writeups, whether they're in a list or mentioned in the text, we've designed the following two little versions of our friendly Bantam rooster. Miniatures of these roosters will appear at the beginning of restaurant and hotel lists and in the margin of the text whenever a restaurant or hotel is described there.

Restaurants

Hotels

1

TRAVELING IN NEW YORK, 1989

Visiting New York is like unpacking your first computer—you find yourself surrounded by lots of expensive pieces that don't seem to fit together. The parts make no sense. Nothing works unless it's hooked up to something else. That, in a nutshell, is New York.

This book is a user's manual to a complex piece of machinery (affectionately called the Big Apple) that generates more static electricity, has less memory, doesn't even try to be user-friendly, and is higher priced than any other unit in the country. New York City can get away with it because there is nothing comparable.

Repeat: There is nothing comparable. Like Atlantis and Alcatraz, Manhattan Island is one of a kind. It's Brigadoon in reverse—a hundred years go by every day while the rest of the world sleeps on. Energized by Wall Street, Broadway, the Garment Center, Madison Avenue, and the United Nations, the seven million plus who live here operate exclusive franchises for one of the world's most exciting businesses: being a New Yorker.

The key to understanding New York is first to understand New Yorkers. The typical New Yorker is either Chinese, Jewish, Black, Italian, Greek, Dutch, Irish, Protestant, German, or Ukrainian. In other words, like the unicorn, there is no such creature.

Nothing about New Yorkers is typical except their attitude. New York Attitude hangs over the city like London fog and L.A. smog. New York Attitude literally stops traffic. It can keep you from getting where you want to go. It can give you headaches, and make your blood pressure rise. Try to ignore it and, no matter how many maps you have, you won't get anywhere. Spend a few minutes understanding it, and you're on your way to conquering the city.

1

The key ingredient in New York Attitude is money. If New York had hills, the hills would be alive with the sound of money. This is the city that invented, along with power lunches, street smarts, and gridlock, the phrase "time is money." In New York City *everything* is money. It costs money just to stand still. Do you believe $10 per hour to park your car in midtown? That's why if some thug threatens, "Your money or your life," odds are he's from out-of-town. In this neck of the woods, your money *is* your life.

Being a New Yorker is something that New Yorkers do better than anyone else. It's an around-the-clock business and they work hard at it. Whatever you want to say about them, New Yorkers do their homework. It doesn't matter how much they earn or how much they're going to spend: everyone is an expert. They all know where to get the greatest hot dog in town, find the cheapest florist, which movie theater has the best sound system, and who's hot at what barbershop. Not that any two lists are ever the same. No one is supposed to agree. That would take all the fun out of it. The important thing is having an opinion. Knowing where to go and how to get there is an integral part of the New York Attitude.

Stop someone on the street and ask directions—it's as though you, a total stranger, had walked into his private office in the middle of a conference he was having with himself. New Yorkers value their privacy as fanatically as Spartans did their pecs. Of all the cities in the world, where does Greta Garbo go when she wants to be alone? Privacy is for New Yorkers what "saving face" is for Asians—a technique for survival in a crowded environment. It has nothing to do with being cold or unfriendly. (You want to know cold and unfriendly, walk into a bank on Main Street, U.S.A., and try to cash a check.) You want to see friendly New Yorkers, check into the city in the midst of a crisis (we have them all the time) and watch the zip codes interact.

It's hard being a New Yorker. On a daily basis, the city streets are littered with far more than old gum wrappers. Once upon a time you counted broken hearts by the lights on Broadway. Not anymore. After the exodus of the middle class to the suburbs, New York became a city of extremes. Extremes as unnerving as a punk rocker's hair. Like characters in a soap opera, "The Rich and the Homeless" jockey for lead-story position. The truth is that a city with all the glitz of New York can't help casting a few shadows. The homeless are a sad fact of life today, something you come upon in Paris, Rio, and Hong Kong; New York isn't alone in not knowing how best to handle the situation.

THE BAD NEWS ABOUT NEW YORK

It's noisy.
It's expensive.
People are rude.
The weather is awful.
The streets are filthy.
The traffic is impossible.
It's not safe at night in the park.
Try to find a cab when you need one.

"So what else is new?" any self-respecting New Yorker asks defensively. People have been saying these things for years and New York is still the most-visited city in the world. Like a fabulous courtesan, New York gives credence to every bad thing you've heard about it. Still, there must be something that attracts everyone. Something in New York you can't find anyplace else. There is. And that's what this book is going to tell you.

We've used a "take no prisoners" approach that sidesteps the claptrap, the guidebook filler, the astroturf that tries to be all things to all travelers. You won't find lengthy negative appraisals telling you what *not* to do. We haven't been out on the streets trying to identify villains or find crowd pleasers. We've been sifting through the thousands of things that compete for your attention—and your wallet—to find those we consider quintessential New York experiences.

It is a miracle that New York works at all. The whole thing is implausible. Every time the residents brush their teeth, millions of gallons of water must be drawn from the Catskills and the hills of Westchester. When a young man in Manhattan writes a letter to his girl in Brooklyn, the love message gets blown to her through a pneumatic tube—*pfft*—just like that. The subterranean system of telephone cables, power lines, steam pipes, gas mains, and sewer pipes is reason enough to abandon the island to the gods and the weevils. Every time an incision is made in the pavement, the noisy surgeons expose ganglia that are tangled beyond belief. By rights New York should have destroyed itself long ago, from panic or fire or rioting or failure of some vital supply line in its circulatory system or from some deep labyrinthine short circuit. Long ago the city should have experienced an insoluble traffic snarl at some impossible bottleneck. It should have perished of hunger when food lines failed for a few days. It should have been wiped out by a plague starting in its slums or carried in by ships' rats. It should have been overwhelmed by the sea that licks at it on every side. The workers in its myriad cells should have succumbed to nerves, from the fearful pall of smoke-fog that drifts over every few days from Jersey, blotting out all light at noon and leaving the high offices suspended, men groping and depressed, and the sense of world's end. It should have been touched in the head by the August heat and gone off its rocker.

Mass hysteria is a terrible force, yet New Yorkers seem always to escape it by some tiny margin: they sit in stalled subways without claustrophobia, they extricate themselves from panic situations by some lucky wisecrack, they meet confusion and congestion with patience and grit—a sort of perpetual muddling through. Every facility is inadequate—the hospitals and schools and the playgrounds are overcrowded, the express highways are feverish, the unimproved highways and bridges are bottlenecks, there is not enough air and not enough light, and there is usually either too much heat or too little. But the city makes up for its hazards and its deficiencies by supplying its citizens with massive doses of a supplementary vitamin: the sense of belonging to something unique, cosmopolitan, mighty, and unparalleled.

To an outlander a stay in New York can be and often is a series of small embarrassments and discomforts and disappointments: not understanding the waiter, not being able to distinguish between a sucker joint and a friendly saloon, riding the wrong subway, being slapped down by a bus driver for asking an innocent question, enduring sleepless nights when the street noises fill the bedroom. Tourists make for New York, particularly in summertime—they swarm all over the Statue of Liberty (where many a resident of the town has never set foot), they invade the Automat, visit radio studios, St. Patrick's Cathedral, and they window shop. Mostly they have a pretty good time. But sometimes in New York you run across the disillusioned—a young couple who are obviously visitors, newlyweds perhaps, for whom the bright dream has vanished. The place has been too much for them; they sit languishing in a cheap restaurant over a speechless meal.

—E. B. White
"Here Is New York," 1949

2

ORIENTING YOURSELF

New York City is comprised of five boroughs (independently governed local districts under the umbrella of the city government). The boroughs are Manhattan, the Bronx, Brooklyn, Queens, and Staten Island.

Ironically, it's a lot easier to find your way around Manhattan than it is to know where you're going.

All you have to do is *"think grid."*

The streets are east–west horizontally, the avenues are north–south vertically. Most streets and avenues are numbered.

The higher the number of the street, the farther north it is.

The higher the number of the avenue, the farther west.

Fifth Avenue divides midtown into east and west. Numbered Manhattan street addresses always include a designation for east or west.

There is a 41 *East* 57th Street and a 41 *West* 57th Street.

While you'll hear people refer constantly to east and west, you won't hear many New Yorkers use north and south as reference points. Instead, they'll say "uptown" for north and "downtown" for south. No one but a jogger measures distances by miles.

FYI: Twenty blocks equal one mile.

The magic of Manhattan, like the cuisine of China, lies in its infinite variety. Although the entire city is coated with a diamond-bright glare, upon closer inspection one sees that the glowing facets of the city are its neighborhoods. There are dozens of Manhattans waiting to be discovered. It all depends upon what you want and how you define excitement. (See the orientation map at the back of this book.)

A QUICK NEIGHBORHOOD TOUR

Fifth Avenue epitomizes Manhattan more than any other thoroughfare. It's not only the spine of the city—it separates east from west—but it synthesizes the glitter and the gossip that make New York hum. It's an address made famous by the Vanderbilts, Rockefeller Center, St. Patrick's Cathedral, the Empire State Building, Trump Tower, some of the world's most fashionable department stores, and the Easter Parade. Fifth Avenue at 59th Street, like Place de la Concorde and Piccadilly Circus, offers a quintessential, albeit idealized, view of the city.

Midtown East is headquarters for consumer chic. Here's where you'll find the shops and restaurants that are featured on the razor-sharp pages of slick magazines and in the syndicated scribblings of tell-it-all columnists. Madison, Park, Lexington, and Third avenues are the richest veins you're likely to find outside of the Seven Dwarfs' diamond mine. A monument to conspicuous consumption, east is the way to go when you're in the mood for immediate gratification.

Midtown West is the hooker with a heart of gold. Heading west from Fifth you still feel the fallout of East Side glitz until you reach Sixth Avenue where accountants and lawyers and everyone in the business of business gather like pin-striped tumbleweed. Although Seventh Avenue threads its way as the major artery to the Garment Center, Broadway is at the heart of the West Side. Nowhere is it more raffish or sleazy or wonderful than within walking distance of stage doors and delis that give new meaning to heartburn.

The **Upper East Side** is where all the people who shop Midtown East live. (Actually many of them secretly still shop on the Lower East Side, pushing past pickle barrels to find the bargain at the end of the rainbow.) With more per capita per capita than any other neighborhood in the city, this is museum and limo heaven, where the rich and famous ogle and mogul their way across town.

The **Upper West Side,** nourished by the reflected glory of Broadway, is where starving artists once moved when they could afford to get out of Greenwich Village. Nowadays, successful painters, writers, dancers, and musicians share Lincoln Centerish zip codes with more stars than you'll find at opening night of the Met. New York City's unofficial "yuppie" capital, the local accent is on youth.

Murray Hill is less a neighborhood than an affectation. While it once had maiden-aunt status as a section of the city, it has long since thrown in the tea towel in the battle against creeping commercialism. The townhouses that basked in the glory of the Morgan Library, the first structure in America to utilize classical Greek building techniques, are still there, but like Mr. Morgan the area is a mere shadow of its former self.

Gramercy Park, on the other hand, is a glorious holdout. It's like a Tennessee Williams heroine still waiting for her gentleman caller. You can't get into the private park without a key, and you have to live there to get a key, and, sure, it seems a colossal conceit in the 1980s. But so do the Gothic and Greek Revival façades that are enlivened with a soupçon of New Orleans fussy grillwork.

Chelsea is Gramercy Park without a park. And without Tennessee Williams. Slices of typically West Side ethnic street life are played against a movie studio backdrop of Old New York. Once a nesting place for birds of a feather migrating from the creeping commercialism of Greenwich Village or escaping the gentrification of the Upper West Side, Chelsea is fast becoming a victim of its own success: trendy boutiques and the Empire Diner.

Greenwich Village, these days, has more in common with Pompeii than Bohemia. Long gone is the bistro bourgeoisie that ruled the art world and held court in Washington Square Park. What remains is a glorious place in which to walk, if not to linger. The terrain still has much of its former charm, but the streetlife is no longer littered with the dreams of starving artists and the torn banners of protesting literati. Instead, there are scruffy computer hackers and cashmered Connecticut types who like don't understand like what all the fuss was about.

The **East Village** is where you'll find The Fuss. Block after block of hard-core tenements have been converted into smoldering ego communes where the new wave generation's idle poor have turned "kvetching" into an art form. Rebellion is everywhere—goofy restaurants and eccentric shops run the gamut from *fin-de-siècle* to Popsicle. More ethnically varied than Greenwich Village ever was, and every bit as unstable as the Weimar Republic, the East Village is the perfect shot of adrenalin after a vanilla Sunday on Fifth.

Soho-Noho-Tribeca are the winners in the sweeps for most successful new neighborhoods. Here's where you'll find all the rich and trendy "starving" artists, blue-serged brokers on their second marriages, and more types than in a printer's catalog. Proof positive that art and culture can coexist, they have matured from a series of lofty dreams into hard-working communities that celebrate individuality without compromising professionalism.

The **Lower East Side,** like **Chinatown** and **Little Italy,** is the underbelly of the city. With more restaurants on one block than many cities have per square mile, and as many opinions about which one to go to, all three areas are ghettos of high-calorie delights. You'll find bargains in clothing and housewares on the Lower East Side, as well as some of the heartiest cooking in town. Chinatown offers a tour through the many culinary styles of Chinese food as well as shops filled with all the paraphernalia and ingredients you need to wok around the clock. Little Italy is for serious eaters only. No one down here ever heard of nouvelle Italian cooking. You can spend the whole day: bagels and lox for breakfast, crab in black bean sauce for lunch, and the pasta of your dreams for dinner.

The Bowery and **Canal Street** are major arteries leading from the Lower East Side to Chinatown and Little Italy. Each has its own character: the Bowery has cleaned up its act somewhat, but there are still flophouses and doorways jammed with men passing around bottles in paper bags. But there are other doorways. The Bowery is restaurant-supply heaven as well as the address for most of the city's discount lighting stores. As you near Canal Street, there's a sprinkle of diamond dust from the below-retail jewelers. Canal Street continues west, bursting bargains onto the street as though electronics, hardware, and work clothes were going out of style.

Lower Manhattan means Wall Street, Battery Park, the World Trade Center, City Hall, and the South Street Seaport. It is, concurrently, the oldest and the newest neighborhood in town as well as one of the most important for visitors. Like **Upper Manhattan,** the harbor area has the best geography in the city. Once heading uptown, past Columbia University and Harlem, you're literally heading for the hills of Washington Heights where Fort Tryon Park offers views of the Hudson River, the George Washington Bridge, and the still unspoiled New Jersey Palisades.

The Bronx, Brooklyn, Queens, and **Staten Island** are today primarily residential areas for those working near or in Manhattan. As such, there are no World Trade Centers, international shopping complexes, or posh hotels for visitors. However, depending upon your time and interests, there are world-famous sights ranging from the Bronx Zoo to the Brooklyn Museum to Shea Stadium (home of the New York Mets) to Coney Island and City Island and Staten Island. While New York, to the visitor, means Manhattan, Manhattanites have their own cherished "out-of-borough" experiences.

3

HOTELS

The incredible thing about New York is that it has something for everyone. If you're the type who doesn't care where you hang your hat or if you're an inveterate collector of hotels, this city will take good care of you. It should be said right up front that we are not members of the "who cares where you stay/how much time do you spend in your room anyway" club. We care a lot. Whether it's after a long day in a Land Rover in Kenya or after fighting the shop-till-you-drop crowds on the rue St. Honoré or after walking miles and miles through the Kremlin Museum, a clean, well-lighted place with a few creature comforts is high on our list of priorities. When it's time to rest your weary bones, we think your bones deserve the best your money can buy.

Each of the hotels in this section has been visited and rooms inspected. We also visited a number of hotels we decided not to include for a variety of maddeningly idiosyncratic reasons that cover everything from too cold (Park Lane), too hot (Chelsea Hotel), too groupish (St. Moritz), too closed (St. Regis), too much of a good thing (Sherry-Netherland—a real class operation but it's located smack between the Plaza and the Pierre), too disappointingly unJapanese for what we expected (Kitano), too 42nd Street (Grand Hyatt—it's right atop Grand Central Station for heaven's sake), and on and on. We have been careful not to include any hotels that refused to show us their rooms (the Helmsley Palace) or those who asked not to be listed (the Carlyle and the Wales had quite enough trade, thank you very much).

You will note that generally we have avoided members of the chain gangs, however much of a security blanket they are for many people. If cost is the deciding factor on where you're going to stay, we have good news. If you're more interested in value than economy, then you, too, can relax. In the faint hope that some of you out there, like us, collect hotels as treasured travel memorabilia, sound the trumpets!

Whether or not you agree with our sins of omission, we set ourselves the task of finding hotels we would not hesitate to recommend to our friends. However, we know damn well that a few terrific places got away. Not for long, we hope.

How to Select a Hotel

1. Location, location, location. Since the easiest way to get around the city is on foot, stop and think about the pleasures of being able to walk back to your hotel after a business meeting. It's a lot simpler to deal with transportation in the evening hours. Therefore, don't book a room on the Upper West Side if you're planning to go to Wall Street on a daily basis. Check out the transportation services, if any, offered by each hotel. (There are often complimentary limos to get you to that first appointment on time.)

2. Weigh the difference in cost between the best room in a first-class hotel and a moderate room in a deluxe one. The extra deluxe dollars may pass on a wealth of services and facilities that even wind up saving you money.

3. The smaller the hotel, the better the service? Not necessarily. You are safer with the rule of thumb, "The more demanding the clientele, the better the service." Don't choose a hotel just because it succeeds with business people, couples with small children, or tour groups—all these can be exasperating in their requests, but not always sophisticated in their requirements.

4. Even if you have made the perfect choice, take a peek at some of the other hotels when you're in town. It's amazing how much you can tell just by walking into a lobby and watching the staff interact with the guests. Who knows? The next time you're planning a trip, your first choice may be booked solid.

How to Make a Reservation

Be specific about your time of arrival. No hotel is obliged to hold a reservation past the appointed hour. Therefore, it's advisable to guarantee your booking with a credit card or deposit. That's the only way you can rest assured. (Although all our hotels accept the major credit cards, unless we've noted otherwise, you should double-check to avoid any unpleasant experiences.)

Ask about special rates and weekend packages. Many hotels cut rates by half to fill up those rooms vacated by tycoons who have gone home. If you are attending a conference, there's often a special rate, even if you make your own reservation.

Tell them what you want. If you have preferences about kinds of beds, high floor or low floor, specific views, not near elevators or service areas, whatever it might be—let them know. Get your request in writing. That doesn't mean it's been guaranteed. If it's really important to you, call the front desk the day before you arrive. Ask them to check your reservation. If you have preferences and discuss them at that time, it's a request. If you wait until after you've arrived, it becomes a complaint.

The hotels below are keyed into the color maps in the back of the book, referring to the map page number and appropriate coordinates.

In descending order, by lowest price for a double room, here's a quick look at the selections discussed in depth below.

$265 / Pierre
$255 / Grand Bay Hotel
$250 / Stanhope
$230 / Westbury
$225 / Plaza
$220 / Lowell
$215 / Inter-Continental
$215 / Plaza Athénée
$210 / Drake
$210 / Mayfair Regent
$210 / Ritz-Carlton
$205 / Regency
$205 / Vista International
$205 / Parker Meridien
$190 / Waldorf-Astoria
$180 / U.N. Plaza
$175 / Doral Park Avenue
$175 / N.Y. Hilton
$170 / Morgans
$150 / Elysée
$140 / Algonquin
$130 / Manhattan East
$129 / Beverly
$110 / Wyndham
$100 / Gramercy Park
$ 95 / Empire
$ 95 / Gorham
$ 75 / Olcott

❦ THE SELECTIONS

The Algonquin

MIDTOWN WEST, p. 6, C12

59 West 44th St. (between Fifth & Sixth aves.), 10036; (212) 840-6800, 1-800-548-0345, Telex: 66532, Fax: (212) 944-1419. **Singles, $130–$140; doubles, $140–$150; suites, $260–$280.**

The Algonquin is the best anachronism in town. It is a triumph of the human spirit that this hotel has survived in a city that too often thrives on dollars rather than sense. If you have ever marched to a different drummer, the drummer probably stayed at the Algonquin.

We all know about the Round Table, the witty darlings everyone loved in an age naïve enough to worship literate people rather than beautiful ones. The Algonquin is as literate as ever. The gracefully aging lobby armchairs and the polished oak walls contribute to the genteel, club-like atmosphere. Brass bells on each table to summon the butler. Oops, the waiter.

The 165 rooms look as though they belong in a country inn rather than a few steps away from the Broadway theater. Walls are dark-green lacquer trimmed with white molding or veddy Victorian striped wallpaper or those what-the-hell cheery florals. Liberty of London fabrics and brass beds complete the picture.

But lest you get the wrong idea about the hotel in which *The New Yorker* magazine was born, there is TV—even cable TV. Concealed in a mahogany cabinet, perhaps, but it's there, as are all the other creature comforts that keep actors and writers and savvy execs coming back to this most civilized of hotels. Of note are the bars and dining rooms: the Rose Room is where the Round Table met; and the Oak Room turns itself into a supper club that offers performance levels to match the hotel's sophistication. Truly a New York landmark.

Hotel Beverly   MIDTOWN EAST, p. 7, D12
125 East 50th St. (at Lexington Ave.), 10022; (212) 753-2700, 1-800-223-0945, Telex: 66579. **Singles, $119–$129; doubles, $129–$149; suites, $129–$245.**

The Beverly is one of the best buys in town. This small family-run hotel is right opposite the Waldorf so you can share its great East Side location without having to pawn Aunt Tillie's tiara. With only 25 double rooms, the Beverly has huge junior and one-bedroom suites all with fully equipped kitchenettes. You can bring the kids, your in-laws, and even Aunt Tillie. Accommodations here are bright, newly decorated, with armoires, glass coffee tables, and antique touches. Especially welcome are locked closets in all rooms and sunny terraces in some.

The lobby is as quiet as the public library, but much prettier—palms, wood paneling, Chesterfield sofas, and crystal chandeliers. Another bonus is a very bright staff that will try to perform small miracles on request. One guest needed a bandage for his horse's leg. Coming right up!

Doral Park Avenue   MURRAY HILL, p. 7, D13
70 Park Ave. (at 38th St.), 10016; (212) 687-7050, 1-800-847-4135, Telex: 968872. **Singles, $155–$175; doubles, $175–$195; suites, $350–$650.**

There are other Dorals in the city, but this one is a particular favorite. Located in the Murray Hill section of Park Ave., the Doral is around the corner from the Pierpont Morgan Library and is in the shadow of the Empire State Building (some rooms have superb views of the ESB). The tone here is very European, from the (weather permitting) sidewalk café to the small lobby.

The 207 rooms are as warm as the welcome. Lots of pastel-flowered fabrics and soft creamy colors, the way you've imagined one of those small Parisian hotels only the French know about. Perhaps because it is on a stretch of Park that is defined by neighboring brownstones rather than by incessant traffic noises, the Doral offers a calm that is contagious, a splendid attention to detail, and a fitness center less than a block away.

The Drake Hotel   MIDTOWN EAST, p. 7, D11
440 Park Ave. (at 56th St.), 10022; (212) 421-0900, 1-800-522-5455, Telex: 147178, Fax: 212-371-4190. **Singles, $185–$215; doubles, $210–$240; suites, $380–$455.**

The symbol of the Drake is right in the middle of its brand new lobby: a huge four-faced Swiss clock. They are telling you, right up front, that everything is handled with clockwork efficiency. Now that it's run by the Swissôtel group, there are more European accents in the lobby but the rooms still draw most of their guests from the States.

Even though the hotel has over six hundred rooms, the lobby is a model of Swiss neutrality and calm. No hustle. No bustle. A quiet wood-paneled lobby bar with some nifty leather sofas and chairs placed at appropriate intervals. Upstairs, the halls are wide and bright and so are the rooms. Some are decorated in earth tones and others are all flowery, but every room is unusually large. The Swiss attention to detail is evident throughout: all rooms have fridges and safes.

A real bonus for travelers on Swissair is that luggage is routed directly from the airport to the hotel. However, even if you came by bus, everyone can enjoy the fabulous dining room, Restaurant Lafayette. The keyword here is graciousness. Amid a setting that revels in glorious Continental ambience, the Drake is a joy.

Hotel Elysée
MIDTOWN EAST, p. 7, D11

60 East 54th St. (between Madison & Park aves.), 10022; (212) 753-1066, Telex: 220373. **Singles, $135–$185; doubles, $150–$200; suites, $275–$500.**

This snug little hotel in the east fifties is a place people tend to return to because it is relaxed, low-key, and comfortable. Since 1927, the Elysée's highly personal style has catered to a very demanding trade that has included a number of big "B's": from the Barrymores and Tallulah Bankhead, to Peter "Jaws" Benchley, Marlon Brando, and Tennessee Williams (who could be any letter he wanted). The secret of success here appears to be lots of TLC mixed with a whiff of whimsey. The 98 spacious rooms are done in a cornucopia of exotic styles with no two the same. There's modern, Empire, British, and Japanese. And when was the last time your room had a name and not a number?

There is a real cheerfulness at this hotel, blatantly reflected in the ditsy-looking primates of the Monkey Bar. Definitely not "a home away from home"—which is exactly the way the owners want it to be. "What people like in a hotel is the attention they don't get at home."

Hotel Empire
UPPER WEST SIDE, p. 4, B10

44 West 63rd St. (at Broadway), 10023; (212) 265-7400, 1-800-545-7400, Telex: 428190, Fax: 212-315-0349. **Singles, $80–$120; doubles, $95–$135; suites, $300.**

Little did the owners of the Hotel Empire dream, in 1925, that it would some day be smack in the center of the city's cultural renaissance. If they had, surely the architects would have added a few ruffles and flourishes to the façade. But, the Empire did strike back by undergoing a $12 million overhaul that restored its original marble and mirror status, while upstairs has been completely redecorated in pastel greens, blues, and mauves with shiny cherrywood furniture. There are five hundred rooms, with queen-size, double, or twin beds and cozy curl-up chairs. While on the small side, the final effect is one of intimacy rather than feeling cramped. Cramped? How could anyone feel cramped with a view of Lincoln Center.

Corporate clients (read: those on expense accounts and paying $110 to $125 for singles and doubles) are given free membership in the nearby Lincoln Racquet Club and Fitness Center. But everyone staying at the Empire gets the best location in town for culture vultures.

The Gorham
MIDTOWN WEST, p. 6, C11
136 West 55th St. (between Sixth & Seventh aves.), 10019; (212) 245-1800, Telex: 286863. **Singles, $75–$95; doubles, $95–$105; suites, $100 up.**

One block from the Hilton and within sniffing distance of the Carnegie Deli is one of the city's best values. Smack in the middle of midtown, the Gorham has the good sense to offer a fully equipped kitchenette in every room (there are 350 available for guests), which is particularly handy for families. As a matter of fact, everything about the place is handy: the location, a warm and helpful management, and some surprisingly large rooms. From the small, wood-paneled lobby to the cheerfully decorated suites, the Gorham plans a super-overhaul that will upgrade all accommodations to luxury status—except in price. Most guests are European and South American travelers who share the management's goal of "luxury for less."

Gramercy Park Hotel
GRAMERCY PARK, p. 7, D14
2 Lexington Ave. (at 21st St.), 10010; (212) 475-4320, 1-800-221-4083, Telex: 668755. **Singles, $95–$105; doubles, $100–$110; suites, $135–$235.**

Overlooking Gramercy Park, one of the leafiest pockets of civilization in the city, lots of execs doing business downtown come here for some of nature's green stuff after working all day with the other kind. The hotel has an old-world residential feeling, 150 rooms comfortably furnished with antique reproductions that include a velvet settee here, a marble fireplace there. Colors are soft, no trendy kumquat-tones—this is an address for grown-ups. Do your best to reserve a room overlooking the park.

Grand Bay Hotel
MIDTOWN WEST, p. 6, C11
152 West 51st St. (at Seventh Ave.), 10019; (212) 765-1900, 1-800-237-0990, Telex: 147156, Fax: 212-541-6604. **Singles, $235–$265; doubles, $255–$285; suites, $345–$900.**

Located in the heart of Midtown West, the Grand Bay opened in 1987 as part of a ripple-effect neighborhood upgrade that began with the Equitable Center across the street. However, unlike other new hotels in the area, this one looks as though it's been around for years. Within easy walking distance of the theater district and Rockefeller Center, you enter the lobby and are greeted with an atmosphere of European posh: cool, gray marble, deep-cushion couches, accents of brass.

It is even more luscious upstairs. This is one of those no-two-rooms-are-alike places. Details change with every set of keys. In one, you'll find a country-French sleigh bed and pale floral drapes. In another, it's sleek Art Deco with lacquered furniture. All 178 rooms have spa-size marble baths with mini-TV's. Live plants and flowers are everywhere, as is the sense that you are being pampered outrageously. A few examples: an on-request packing and unpacking service at no additional charge, free limo service to Wall Street for corporate clientele, a "guest-beeper" to keep you in touch with the concierge for messages.

Hotel Inter-Continental

MIDTOWN EAST, p. 7, D12

111 East 48th St. (between Park & Lexington aves.), 10017; (212) 755-5900, 1-800-327-0200, Telex: 968677. **Singles, $215; doubles, $245; suites, $300–$500.**

What was once the stiff-upper-lip Barclay has blossomed under Inter-Continental's lighter touch. The hotel has been spruced up and polished to a fine shine. The lobby is huge in the true old-world style of grand spaces: heroic floral arrangements, English Chesterfield sofas, and a gleaming latticed-brass birdcage filled with tropical tweeters. All this under a Federal-style Tiffany skylight. FYI: guests at the old Barclay were allowed to board their birds.

The spaciousness of the lobby travels. Most of the 758 rooms upstairs are outfitted with king-size or two double beds and there is still enough room left over for a handsome armoire to hide a color TV and mini-bar, not to mention floor space for a few brocade chairs and a glass table for an intimate breakfast. Other accents are country floral quilted headboards and swashbuckling drapes. You may even find yourself in a bamboo fourposter bed with touches of Orientalia around the room. Bathrooms are more Victorian than victorious, but who's got time for marble withdrawal symptoms with Caswell-Massey in charge of the amenities? Besides, the rooms have earned a Designers Circle Award for "excellence in luxury guest-room renovation," and there's complimentary limo service to Wall Street.

The Lowell

UPPER EAST SIDE, p. 5, D1

28 East 63rd St. (between Madison & Park aves.), 10021; (212) 838-1400, Telex: 275750 LOWL/UR. **Singles, $190–$220; doubles, $220–$240; suites, $310–$540.**

There's a small hotel (without a wishing well, but with just about everything else) that's lavish and sophisticated enough to look as though it might have been moved, lock, stock, and high tea from London and dropped into New York's best zip code. Not so. Before the Lowell turned into a beautiful butterfly it was a motley residential hotel that, in better days, had been home to Scott and Zelda, Dorothy Parker, Noel Coward, and Walter Lippman. Now it's a highbrow hangout for museum curators, musicians, and entertainers. Kiri Te Kanawa, Ginger Rogers, and Shelley Long on the guest list.

There are only eight double rooms, the rest are one- and two-bedroom apartments. Most have wood-burning fireplaces and are furnished with an eye toward fine fabrics, Chinese porcelains, lacquered tables, books, fresh flowers, and plants. Fully equipped kitchenettes are stocked with snacks in the event you need a little something before having tea in the Pembroke Room, a traditionally English tearoom. Let's face it, you've got to love them for having a lunch menu that offers both Beluga caviar and a Lowell Burger. Almost makes you wonder if we made the right decision fighting for our independence from the British.

Manhattan East Suite Hotels

505 East 75th St., 10021; (212) 772-2900, 1-800-ME-SUITE, Telex: 284061.

Imagine that wealthy friends have offered you their apartment while you're in New York. The "home away from home" theory is what makes this group of properties one of the best accommodations options. Studio, one-, two-, and even three-bedroom suites are available in top locations around town for what you'd pay for a double room. The Manhattan East group of hotels are run with first-class attention that makes them a spectacular value for visitors. Prices vary slightly depending upon location, but you'll find the same large rooms, fully equipped kitchens, and sophisticated furnishings that make the accommodations ideal for families and business travelers. (Note: Single rates are lower than those given below.)

Beekman Tower
MIDTOWN EAST, p. 7, E12

3 Mitchell Place (49th St. & First Ave.); (212) 355-7300. **Studios, $160–$170; 1–2 bedroom suites, $190–$220/ $270–$290.**

Dumont Plaza
MURRAY HILL, p. 7, D13

150 East 34th St. (at Lexington Ave.); (212) 481-7600. **Studios, $175–$195; 1–2 bedroom suite, $200–$230/ $290–$330.**

Eastgate Tower
MURRAY HILL, p. 7, D13

222 East 39th St. (between Second & Third aves.); (212) 687-8000. **Studios, $170–$190; 1–2 bedroom suites, $200–$220/$280–$320.**

Lyden Gardens
UPPER EAST SIDE, p. 5, D10

215 East 64th St. (between Second & Third aves.); (212) 355-1230. **Studios, $160–$180; 1–2 bedroom suites, $190–$210/$325–$375.**

Lyden House
MIDTOWN EAST, p. 7, E11

320 East 53rd St. (between First & Second aves.); (212) 888-6070. **Studios, $160–$180; 1 bedroom suites, $180–$200.**

Plaza Fifty
MIDTOWN EAST, p. 7, D12

155 East 50th St. (at Third Ave.); (212) 751-5710. **Studios, $150–$170; 1–2 bedroom suites, $190–$220/$295–$325.**

Shelburne Murray Hill
MURRAY HILL, p. 7, D13

303 Lexington Ave. (at 37th St.); (212) 689-5200. **Studios, $160–$185; 1–2 bedroom suites, $185–$210/$300–$340.**

Southgate Tower
MIDTOWN WEST, p. 6, C13

371 Seventh Ave. (at 31st St.); (212) 563-1800. **Studios, $145–$165; 1 bedroom suites, $175–$195.**

Surrey Hotel
UPPER EAST SIDE, p. 5, D9

20 East 76th St. (at Madison Ave.); (212) 288-3700. **Studios, $175–$195; 1–2 bedroom suites, $225–$270/$350–$400.**

The Mayfair Regent

UPPER EAST SIDE, p. 5, D10

610 Park Ave. (at 65th St.), 10021; (212) 288-0800, 1-800-545-4000, Telex: 236257. **Singles/doubles, $210–$270; suites, $320–$1,200.**

How can you not fall in love with a hotel that offers room service from Le Cirque? But that's just for starters. The Mayfair Regent happens to be in tune as one of the best of the baby grands. It is not coincidental that manager Dario Mariotti is an alumnus of the Gritti in Venice and the Grand in Rome. The staff here functions as though they'd invented *la dolce vita*.

The luxurious lobby lounge, a designer's dream of sculpted archways, pillars, and pastels, corniced ceilings, and antique furniture, hums with Euro-speak. Aside from its glittering Italian delegation (Sophia Loren, the Fendis, and the Missonis), the hotel has played host to Nancy Reagan, Barbra Streisand, King Juan Carlos, and most of the international fashion set.

But man does not live by lobby alone. The two hundred ultra-plush rooms are peachy. And light gray. Some have butler pantries with fridges and sinks. Some have fireplaces, but all have walk-in closets, marble bathrooms, make-up lights, and lots of amenities. Billing itself as "a hotel for people who don't like hotels," the primary commitment here is to service. "Service is everything," according to Mariotti. "It's no use putting the chocolate on the pillow if the operator does not wake you up in the morning on time."

Morgans

MURRAY HILL, p. 7, D13

237 Madison Ave. (at 37th St.), 10016; (212) 686-0300, 1-800-334-3408, Telex: 288908. **Singles, $155–$190; doubles, $170–$190; suites, $270–$380. On weekends, singles and doubles are $120; suites $165.**

The minimalist lobby with its textured opalescent glass walls and stark leather furniture envelops you with a sleek demanding style. You are either going to fall in love with this place or run screaming for the nearest medieval tapestry. Imagine yourself in a movie made in the 1930s. That's Morgans.

It is no mere oversight that the word "hotel" is omitted on all printed material. The staff would sooner turn in their charcoal gray suits, gray shirts, and gray ties than utter such a filthy word. The theory is that Morgans, a tradition-breaker from start to finish, is a home away from home where nothing is impossible. Let's face it: room service at Morgans is whatever you want from any restaurant in town. There are rooms with VCRs, a library of over two hundred videos, and free hot popcorn. The motto here is "just tell me what you want."

You want to talk exclusive, there isn't even a name outside to let you know you've arrived. The theory being, no doubt, that everyone who stays at Morgans has already arrived: i.e., the likes of Cher, Billy Joel, Giorgio Armani.

Everything but the nothing-is-too-much attitude has been designed by French minimalist designer Andrée Putman: rooms are in tones of gray and beige with a polyester-be-damned philosophy that has resulted in comforters covered with Brooks Brothers cotton oxford cloth, down pillows, upholstered window seats, bird's-eye maple wall units, and even all-natural shampoo in the supernatural bathrooms. What a joy they are: black and white checked tile walls, stainless-steel sinks, and huge glassed-in showers just meant for sharing. Founders Steve Rubell and Ian Shrager were determined to create as homey an atmosphere as possible. They have. But you still can't help wondering how sophisticated their homes could have been.

The New York Hilton   MIDTOWN WEST, p. 6, C11
1335 Ave. of the Americas (between 53rd & 54th sts.), 10019; (212) 586-7000, 1-800-HILTONS, Telex: 238492, Fax: (212) 757-7423. **Singles, $150–$195; doubles, $175–$220; Executive Tower: singles, $210; doubles, $235; suites, $385–$510.**

Everything about the Hilton is big—it has the largest number of rooms (2,121), it has a brand-new lobby that looks like an elegantly carpeted football field (they just spent over $80 million redesigning rooms), it has a staff that speaks thirty languages, and it has a larger-than-life Wall Street Journal Business Center that's operated by Dow Jones. Yet, for all its size, and the fact that 60 percent of its guests are here on business, the Hilton has acquired some 8,500 pieces of original art to soothe the soul, has added some antique touches to soften the chrome and brass, and has a lobby bar guarded by two huge marble sphinxes sculpted in the 1860s.

Rooms are comfortable in size, most done in soft grays, mauves, or pale blues, with mahogany furniture, deep-upholstered chairs, quilted bedspreads, and drapes that add up to a clean modern feeling. The wall-to-wall windows are tinted pale blue and angled to give each room more of the cityscape. The Executive Tower is operated as a hotel within a hotel, offering 39th-floor check-in, a private lounge for complimentary breakfast, cocktails, and hors d'oeuvres (not all at once). Rooms here are larger, more elegantly put together with sleek Italian lacquer furniture to bring out the wheeler-dealer in you. Brilliantly located, and always filled with those who depend upon Hilton as their beacon of light, the hotel has ranked as the best in the United States according to overseas-business-traveler surveys.

Hotel Olcott   UPPER WEST SIDE, p. 4, B9
27 West 72nd St. (between Central Park West & Columbus Ave.), 10023; (212) 877-4200. **Singles, $65 ($390 weekly); doubles, $75 ($430 weekly); suites $95 ($550 weekly).** No credit cards.

One of the best bargains in town, the Olcott is on the Upper West Side—right down the street from the fabulous Dakota apartment house and a mere boutique's throw from pulsatingly trendy Columbus Ave. As a special bonus, Central Park is only a few steps away, and you can be at Lincoln Center in a hop, skip, and a jump. Which is why the Olcott checks in performers from the Royal Ballet, the Metropolitan Opera, and even some South American diplomats who are in the audience.

The lobby here is solid: black marble and a bank of elevators with brass-carved doors. Most of the hotel is residential, but there are about 25 studios and suites that are comfortably, if somewhat eclectically, furnished. Never mind. The big news here (aside from the rates and location) is the size of the rooms.

Some of them are two to three times bigger than standard hotel accommodations, and they all come equipped with full kitchens. Okay. But not with TVs. However, with the money you save, you can easily afford to rent one at $3 per day, $15 per week.

Le Parker Meridien

MIDTOWN WEST, p. 6, C11

119 West 56th St. (between Sixth & Seventh aves.), 10019; (212) 245-5000, 1-800-543-4300, Telex: 6801134 PARK MR, Fax: 212-307-1776. **Singles, $180–$240; doubles, $205–$265; suites, $260–$650.**

The French, having captured Broadway with *Les Misérables,* have planted the flag again, this time on 57th St. at the Parker Meridien, where they answer the phone with a bright *"Bonjour!"* Now, it may not be Paris on the Hudson, but it's about as close as you can get in these parts. After entering from the street through a narrow mirrored walkway, you step into a soaring atrium that is flooded with light to show off the marble walls and pale peach columns in a small but elegant lobby in which the *accents grave* fly faster than the Concorde.

Right off the lobby is the Maurice, a critically acclaimed restaurant that helped pave the way for a renaissance in New York hotel dining, with dishes such as lobster with vanilla sauce and roast pigeon with endive braised in brown sugar. Bubbling on the front burner is *cuisine courante,* which retains the spirit of nouvelle cuisine without sacrificing experimentation. To be sure, nothing has been sacrificed here. The seven hundred guest rooms upstairs all have that sink-in, sink-down comfort with grays, beiges, and muted celadon blues for a calming influence. Gray marble baths are outfitted with an array of goodies from Hermès.

The Parker Meridien has a full-service athletic club that offers complimentary membership, including use of the rooftop indoor pool, sundecks, an outdoor jogging track, squash and racquetball courts, plus all the usual press and stress hardware.

The Pierre

FIFTH AVENUE, p. 7, D11

2 East 61st St. (at Fifth Ave.), 10021; (212) 838-8000, 1-800-332-3442, Telex: 127426. **Singles from $240–$330; doubles from $265–$355; suites, $475–$700.**

Stepping into the lobby of the Pierre is like boarding a fabulous luxury liner. You can almost hear the gentle hum of a staff accustomed to smooth sailing. Aside from being one of the most luxurious hotels in the city, the Pierre has been one of its top cooperative residences since many of its suites were turned into apartments in the sixties. Clark Gable had an apartment here, and the hotel still has stars in its eyes: Karl Lagerfeld, Jane Fonda, and Sophia Loren always ask for their favorite suites.

The brainchild of restaurateur Charles Pierre and an investment group that included Otto Kahn, E. F. Hutton, and Walter Chrysler, the Pierre opened in 1930 with the great Escoffier potting around in the kitchen as guest chef. The two hundred rooms upstairs are large and airy with spectacular views of Central Park. Fitness buffs may take advantage of the hotel's agreement with the Atrium Club.

The Café Pierre is one of the swankiest rooms in town, with an extravagant menu to match the tone of the decor. One welcome compromise is the inclusion of reduced-calorie dishes that allow for a sinfully delicious dinner without the sin. Another favorite is having tea in The Rotunda, an oval-shaped sumptuous space with floor-to-ceiling murals of courtly garden scenes. If you look carefully, you may notice that the woman peeking out from behind the trellises and bushes bears a striking resemblance to Jacqueline Onassis. Indeed, the artist did use her face as the woman around the room. In later years, the features were blurred a bit at her request, but she's still there if you look close. So is the Pierre. Its devotion to understated comfort offers great security in a disposable and sometimes harsh world.

The Plaza
FIFTH AVENUE, p. 7, D11

769 59th St. (at Fifth Ave.), 10019; (212) 759-3000, 1-800-228-3000, Telex: 620-179 or 236-978, Fax: 212-759-3167. **Singles, $150–$450; doubles, $225–$450; suites, $500–$1,340.**

New York's grandest European-style hotel, the Plaza is where Frank Lloyd Wright lived from 1953 to 1959 during the construction of the Guggenheim Museum. Small wonder. This hotel looks as good from the outside as it does from within. Declared an official landmark, it was built in 1907 along the lines of a French Renaissance château by the same architect responsible for another New York landmark, the Dakota, a fabled apartment house on the Upper West Side. The first guest to check in was Alfred Gwynne Vanderbilt, and then decades later there was Robert Redford in *The Way We Were,* the entire cast of Neil Simon's *Plaza Suite,* and "Crocodile" Dundee himself.

The Plaza, always larger than life, was recently purchased by Donald Trump for $390 million. He intends to "upgrade" it into "the most luxurious hotel in the world." Not that it's exactly been a bed-and-breakfast. The Plaza has just undergone complete restoration—the gold-leaf moldings glow from the ceilings, and both the Oak and Edwardian rooms have been returned to their original splendor. But, one of the Trump cards here will be to install onyx in the bathrooms. And why not? The Plaza's bathrooms are Old World luxurious with floral murals on the ceiling. (No two bathroom ceilings are the same.) Bedrooms are filled with antiques and crystal chandeliers—and bedside lamps that light up when you touch them. If you're an aficionado of high ceilings, ask for a room on a low floor (there are about eight hundred rooms to choose from). Try for the park side.

The public rooms at the Plaza—the Oak Bar, the very clubby Oak Room, the romantic kitsch of the Palm Court with its piano and violin accompaniment for tea and after-theater snacks, and the heroic plush of the Edwardian Room with some of the best window seats in town—have always belonged every bit as much to New Yorkers themselves as to those visiting the city. Under no circumstance should you leave without at least stopping by for a drink.

Hotel Plaza Athénée
UPPER EAST SIDE, p. 5, D10

37 East 64th St. (between Madison & Park aves.), 10021; (212) 734-9100, 1-800-CALL-THF, Telex: 6973900-PLAZATH, Fax:

212-772-0958. **Singles/doubles from $215; deluxe from $285; suites $550–$795.**

A pocket of Right Bank elegance on an East Side tree-lined street. Like its Parisian counterpart, it reeks *par excellence.* Take three steps down to enter the lobby and from the moment you plant your tootsies on the gleaming black and white tiled floor, you inhale the sweet smell of success. Tapestry-covered walls and leather-upholstered elevators help you rise to the occasion: two hundred rooms of uncommon comfort with king-size beds, plush velvets, lush brocades, and sumptuous accessories (robes by Porthault) in pale-pink-marble bathrooms. Attention to detail is a way of life here. Each room has a small pantry and a fridge that's stocked with Evian water. Home turf to Fortune 500 CEOs as well as such *enfants du paradis* as Elizabeth Taylor, Joan Collins, and Farrah Fawcett, when in town.

The downstairs bar is accented with Brazilian mahogany, deep sofas, and marble tables. It puts you in a mood, all right, but nothing can prepare you for Le Regence, possibly the most romantic dining room in town. Mirrored, tiny alcoves, a sky blue ceiling with nothing but cloud nines overhead, designed by Valerian Rybar. Welcome to the perfect answer to "whatever happened to *belle epoque?* " But the gorgeousness here is more than skin deep. The kitchen is managed on a rotating basis by the celebrated Rostang family, a father and two sons who run two two-star restaurants in France. This is one of those rare hotels that's almost reason enough for making the trip.

The Regency Hotel UPPER EAST SIDE, p. 5, D10

540 Park Ave. (at 61st St.), 10021; (212) 759-4100, 1-800-243-1166, Telex: 147180, Fax: 212-826-5674, ext. 219. **Singles, $185–$245; doubles, $205–$265; suites, $350–$675.**

Not only is this the hotel that started the "power breakfast" perking for native New Yorkers, but it has become one of the official homes away from home for heads of state and wheeler-dealers. One enters the Regency to find antique Flemish tapestries on travertine marble walls. Satin settees. Not a clue that in the Regency Lounge empires are being swapped at the drop of a bagel.

After a $15 million renovation, the seven hundred rooms upstairs have taken on the patina of a fine old Park Avenue home. The mahogany gleams and the silks and brocades add a luxury to which everyone would like to become accustomed.

But don't be misled. Not everything is set up for sybarites. The Regency has its own fitness center to keep you mean and lean, as well as an obliging chef who will plan your personal "spa" menu. Nicknamed "Hollywood East" because it attracts so many people from the entertainment industry, the hotel is a haven for sophisticated travelers who expect the kind of professional service that guarantees security and privacy.

The Ritz-Carlton MIDTOWN WEST, p. 6, C11

112 Central Park South (between Sixth & Seventh aves.), 10019; (212) 757-1900, 1-800-223-6800, Telex: 971534. **Singles, $180–$300; doubles, $210–$330; suites, $450–$900.**

Is this New York or London? If ever a hotel were to the "manor house" born, this is it. With an English country home interior designed by internationally famous Sister Parish, the Ritz-Carlton is one of those rare hotels that is gracious and intimate without ever losing its cool.

Soft pastel bedrooms are decked out in flowered chintz and carved English oak furniture, including four-poster beds. Lots of English prints and touches of Chinoiserie in the 230 rooms to make you feel part of a crown colony. Rooms with views of Central Park are prime property for those who want a sight for their sore eyes. There is no better one to be had. But tear yourself away long enough to soak in the atmosphere of your luxurious marble bathroom. Other guests who've taken tubbies here include President Ford, Bette Davis, and Warren Beatty.

The glorious yellow pine paneling that greets you in the lobby is repeated in the posh Jockey Club restaurant and bar. The key design premise here was to create a space that looked as though it had always been there, a public place that was private and permanent. The very clubby restaurant even has three fireplaces for extra personal warmth.

The Stanhope
FIFTH AVENUE, p. 5, D8

995 Fifth Ave. (at 81st St.), 10028; (212) 288-5800, 1-800-828-1123, Telex: 6720662, Fax: 212-517-0088. **Singles and doubles, $250–$300; suites, $350–$950.**

Gilded moldings, gilded chandeliers, and very gilded clientele are what you find at this new, improved, more elegant version of the Stanhope. The renovation here has made the hotel sparkle like the brilliant prisms from the crystal fantasies that hang from the ceiling. This Upper Fifth Ave. outpost is as exclusive as the French Foreign Legion. Devoted to old world grand hotel excellence, the Stanhope experience begins with a top-hatted doorman to greet you as you throw a casual glance over your shoulder at the Metropolitan Museum of Art directly across the street. The concierge is dressed in a cutaway and striped trousers—a man who lives to make your every wish his command. On a table near the elevators, a discreet bowl of pink silk roses.

Upstairs, the elegance continues with 117 generous rooms (80 percent are suites) filled with period furniture instead of furniture, period. There are king-size beds and enough velvet, plush, and brocade to satisfy the crankiest of potentates. The "touches" around the room are as extravagant as the fabrics—leather-bound books (a note informs guests that if they haven't finished it they may return the book at their convenience), silk-moire-covered walls, chaises, and even some canopy beds. Well, what do you expect when even at breakfast, jackets and ties are a must? Not to worry. The Stanhope is sophisticated enough not to bat an eye when guests wander in for a morning cuppa still wearing tuxedos and gowns.

There are limos to take you to midtown, and at night, to Lincoln Center, the theater district, or Carnegie Hall. They have to do something or else people would never leave.

In Memory of the St. Regis Hotel: Birthplace of the Bloody Mary

Just prior to press time, the venerable St. Regis closed its doors for a one to two-year period of renovation. We look forward to its reopening and to ensure it's not forgotten wish to share this bit of lore with you.

A French bartender named Fernand Petiot is credited with being the first to add tomato juice to vodka in 1920. He brought the recipe with him to the St. Regis's King Cole bar in 1934. The original recipe called for half vodka and half tomato juice. An American entertainer named Roy Barton is credited with calling the drink a Bloody Mary, although other theories are that it was named for the English queen, Mary Tudor. Still others say that Ernest Hemingway or George Jessel devised it. St. Regis's owner Vincent Astor disapproved of the name, Bloody Mary, since the word bloody was considered British slang. And so, Petiot revised his recipe and called it the Red Snapper, the name under which it was served at the St. Regis. Here's the recipe:

Red Snapper

2 dashes each salt, black pepper, cayenne pepper
3 dashes Worcestershire sauce
1 dash lemon juice
1 ½ oz. vodka
2 oz. tomato juice
Add the salt, pepper, Worcestershire,
and lemon juice to a shaker glass.
Then add ice, vodka, tomato juice.
Shake, pour into highball glass.

United Nations Plaza Hotel

MIDTOWN EAST, p. 7, E12

One United Nations Plaza (44th St. and First Ave.), 10017; (212) 355-3400, 1-800-228-9000, Telex: 126803 HHCHUNA, Fax: (212) 702-5051. **Singles/doubles, $180–$235; suites, $400–$1,100.**

Picture this: green-marble columns inlaid with mirrors. Then more mirrors on the ceiling to cap off a brilliant kaleidoscopic entrance to a hotel where the staff speaks a couple of dozen languages—every day. An elegantly designed glass tower, the U.N. Plaza faces its namesake and is its unofficial watering hole. Wander into the Ambassador Grill for a drink after a U.N. session to learn what "international" really means.

The 444 guest rooms don't start until the 28th floor, making views from the top spectacular. The decor is sleek and uncluttered, a pale pink wall behind the bed, soft colors for fabrics and carpeting. The emphasis is on airy space and an open view that also fills the generous size rooms with lots of light. The hotel's health and swim club is truly Olympian with floor-to-ceiling windows to make sure you don't work off the view. There's even an indoor tennis court.

Located as far east as one can be, the hotel offers free one-way limousine service to Seventh Ave., Wall St., and, in the evenings, to the theater. Another bonus here is the dining room: the Ambassador Grill's prix fixe lunches and dinners are exceptional values—especially because the kitchen features superb Gascon cooking by famous French chefs from the region.

Vista International Hotel

LOWER MANHATTAN, p. 8, C19

3 World Trade Center, 10048; (212) 938-9100, Telex: 661130 VISTA NY. **Singles, $180–$245; doubles, $205–$270; suites, $510–$645.**

The vista in the lobby is one of high-powered executives rushing back and forth to meetings, while the vista from your room upstairs is of Lower Manhattan, the Statue of Liberty, and New York Harbor stretched out under your window as far as the eye can see. Whatever your personal perspective, this Hilton International humdinger puts you right in the middle of the most historic part of New York—within walking distance of City Hall, Trinity Church, Wall St., Battery Park, and the South St. Seaport. This end of the island is one of the best for visitors.

Business and pleasure are coupled here with real flair: the lobby opens directly onto the World Trade Center but retains a vibrant sense of style with walls covered in sleek red suede. A hotel for achievers, the 329 upstairs rooms are plush nests in which to unwind. They are large, well designed, and filled with light from the 360-degree open space around the hotel. No matter where you face, there's a spectacular view of the city.

The increasingly popular concept of executive floors has been adopted by the Vista, providing movers and shakers with their private lounge for complimentary breakfast, drinks, and hors d'oeuvres. There's an executive business center that links you to your offices and clients, and offers a complete catalog of business services. Making life even easier for execs on the run is the Vista's fitness center.

The Waldorf-Astoria

MIDTOWN EAST, p. 7, D12

301 Park Ave. (between 49th and 50th sts.), 10022; (212) 355-3000, Telex: WUI 666747, Fax: 212-758-9209. **Singles, $165–$205; doubles, $190–$230; mini-suites, $230–$255; suites, $340–$770. Waldorf Towers: $260–$300; suites, $350–$3,000.**

When the Waldorf-Astoria opened in 1931, it was the largest hotel in the world. It had 1,600 rooms and no 2 of them were alike. Today, after a $150 million renovation, not only are they still not alike, but they've been given the world's most expensive facelift. Come to the Waldorf and you'll see that every penny was well spent.

Even the most jaded of travelers gets a big kick out of pulling up to the entrance of the Waldorf and seeing all those overhead flags dancing in the wind. Suddenly, you feel like the most important person in the world. Inside, the lobby glows like a dazzling Deco dream. Part Egyptian temple and part interplanetary way station, it seems as though everybody on the planet passes below the repainted bas-relief ceiling, around the elegant black-marble columns, and winds up on the luxurious furniture. This unique setting is like a big, friendly St. Bernard that allows the kids to crawl all over it and pull its tail without getting grumpy. The lobby never loses its dignity.

The Waldorf is such an institution that, for the moment, you tend to forget there are rooms upstairs just for sleeping. Well, there are—and they are comfortable and bright and quiet. Try to reserve on the Park Ave. side for a city view that can put you into the picture postcard business. The Waldorf Towers is a super-plush hotel within the hotel, with its own entrance and staff accustomed to catering to the whims of such diverse guests as Albert Einstein, Queen Elizabeth, and Frank Sinatra. (Separate rooms, please!)

Hotel Westbury   UPPER EAST SIDE, p. 5, D10
15 East 69th St. (at Madison Ave.), 10021; (212) 535-2000, 1-800-223-5672, Telex: 125388, Fax: 212-535-5058. **Singles, $210–$250; doubles, $230–$270; suites, $325–$1,000.**

While all eyes have focused on the British invasion of Broadway, there's been a backstage takeover at some of the city's best hotels. That accounts for the Devonshire cream that appears regularly at tea in this Trusthouse Forte property. As elegant as the avenue on which it is located, the Westbury has just enough stiff upper lip to make you check your Filofax to be certain you're in New York and not London.

You certainly can't tell from the lobby. It's all creamy and beige with tapestries on the wall and Queen Anne chairs to set the tone. The beautifully carved oval ceiling and the balcony that discreetly overhangs the room give you a good idea why the hotel was landmarked recently.

Upstairs, three hundred rooms and suites are fitted in chintz, florals, and Ralph Lauren plaids. Some may have canopy beds while others are distinguished by fabric on the walls: All are supremely comfortable. They each have their own lush, dramatic cachet—no two are the same. Just like the clientele.

Wyndham Hotel   MIDTOWN WEST, p. 6, C11
42 West 58th St. (between Fifth & Sixth aves.), 10019; (212) 753-3500. **Singles, $95–$105; doubles, $110–$120; suites, $155–$185.**

Every once in a while you come upon something that has no relation to its time and place. It belongs frozen in the *deja-vu* of a wonderful past experience. That's probably the feeling most people have after they've stayed here. It doesn't conform to the present, to its snitzy location, or to the usual New York hotel experience. The Wyndham is as personable and theatrical as its guest list: Peter Ustinov, James Clavell, Harold Pinter, Eva Marie Saint, Carol Burnett, the Cronins, the Oliviers, and dozens of other show-biz show-stoppers passing through town.

John and Suzanne Mados, who own, run, and keep the lamplight burning at the Wyndham, have an office filled with more memorabilia than Sotheby's could auction in a week: Ginger Rogers's favorite pineapple juice, Roger Mudd's toaster oven, and Peter O'Toole's sketches—all waiting for their owners return. The astonishing thing about the Wyndham, aside from whom you see in the elevator, is the room rates. Here you are, in one of the most expensive neighborhoods in town, around the corner from Central Park South, a stone's throw from Fifth, and a luxuriously furnished suite with a kitchenette costs less than a single room at one of the biggies.

Wait until you see these rooms. Some of them are the size of small tennis courts. Mrs. Mados has whipped them into looka-likes for Scarlett O'Hara's boudoir. The fabric on the walls matches the dramatically draped drapes. Beds are king-size. Parlors (and they are parlors here) often have sectional sofas sweeping across the room, fireplaces, Impressionist art on the walls, plants, and all the personal touches that transform a room into an inviting apartment. The Wyndham is a wonderful hotel because John and Suzanne Mados make it wonderful. Book as far in advance as possible to get one of the two hundred rooms.

BED AND BREAKFASTS

B&Bs started in England years ago and are still a welcome fix-ture on the travel agenda. The theory is that people with extra rooms in their apartments offer visitors bed and breakfast at a price well under the going rate in hotels. Aside from the econom-ics, many people like the idea of staying with a New York family. It's a great way to meet the locals, and there's almost always a spare umbrella in the closet or a little advice on how to navi-gate the city. The hosts say they enjoy the challenge of meeting people from all over the world and helping them to feel at home.

You find B&Bs through the agencies we've listed. Here are some of the ground rules: There is usually a minimum stay of two nights required as well as a deposit. You are given your own key and may come and go at will. There is no maid service, but a continental breakfast is provided. Most rooms have private baths, but be sure to inquire. All B&Bs have been visited by the agencies and the hosts have been screened. Aside from single and double accommodations, you can rent studio, or one- and two-bedroom apartments from the agencies.

City Lights Bed & Breakfast Ltd.
Box 20355, Cherokee Station
New York, N.Y. 10028
(212) 737-7049
Singles, $40–$60; doubles, $55–$75; apartments, $85–$150.

New World Bed & Breakfast
150 Fifth Ave., Suite 711
New York, N.Y. 10011
(212) 675-5600, or 1-800-443-3800
Singles, $40–$80; doubles, $50–$100; apartments, $80–$200.

All agencies urge you to reserve as far in advance as possible. If you cancel with notice, your deposit is refunded less a service charge. If you cancel without notice, one night's fee is charged.

4

PRIORITIES

A visit to New York is like being invited to an extravagant banquet prepared by the world's greatest chef. You pick up a plate and head eagerly for the buffet table. The question is how to sample all those goodies without having to make a second trip? The answer is simple. You can't.

But that doesn't mean you have to go away hungry, just be selective. That requires a turn or two around the table before you know what you really want. At the feast known as Manhattan, the best way to take those turns is via a triple-treat of land, air, and water.

The Story Is in the Skyline

You don't rate your financial portfolio on the performance of a single stock. Similarly, you need to see New York in its proper perspective. That means seeing the skyline for all it's worth—ASAP. Our favorite sites for viewing are:

LOOKING UP
1. The deck of the Staten Island Ferry
2. The promenade in Brooklyn Heights

LOOKING DOWN
3. A window table in the Hors d'Oeuvrerie lounge at Windows on the World
4. Observation deck atop the World Trade Center
5. Observation deck atop the Empire State Building

What to Do on the First Day of Your First Trip to New York

Corny as it sounds, if you're a stranger in a strange land, a half-day bus tour (see Tours) is strongly recommended as the most painless form of orientation. Sure, nobody wants to look like a hick, especially in New York, but put on some casual clothes, abolish the word "elitist" from your vocabulary, at least for the morning, and book yourself onto a bus tour.

It's worth every penny to ensure that your first view of the city is hassle free.

Plan to have an informal lunch at the South Street Seaport or Chinatown or Little Italy and then head for the open sea. Take a boat ride. The Circle Line has a three-hour sightseeing cruise around Manhattan (see Touring). Or, if time is a problem, a twenty five-minute ride on the Staten Island Ferry offers a postcard-perfect view of the skyline as well as of the Statue of Liberty.

It's probably dusk by now. Time to head for either the observation deck atop the World Trade Center or the 102nd floor of the Empire State Building for equally thrilling views of New York as it takes on a rosy glow. You can, of course, put this plan in reverse and head for the hills after lunch, saving your view of the skyline at night for the deck of the Staten Island Ferry.

Okay. Now it's time to pamper yourself. Hop into a cab and go back to your hotel. Dress for dinner. You'll already have made a reservation and this is the night to zero in on the best restaurant you can afford. You've driven through the streets, you've sailed across the harbor, you've climbed every mountain. While your eyes are still popping, go for the glitz! Give yourself one truly posh nosh before you become cranky about the dirty streets and the deafening traffic. Tomorrow is another day, time enough to reevaluate your priorities (and your bankroll). Whatever you do, don't save this $1,001 night as your farewell to the city. First, we don't believe in long goodbyes and, second, by the time you're ready to leave, you'll most likely have found some funky little joint in Soho where you're on a first-name basis with the owner's cat.

But wait a minute. The night is still young! After dinner, head over to 59th and Fifth and take a carriage ride through the park. Stop in for a nightcap at the Plaza and then you'll have completed all the requirements for Elementary New York.

What to Do
on Your Fiftieth Trip to New York

Make certain you've done everything you should have done the first day of your first trip. If you still haven't seen the skyline from the water, now's your chance. If you've been to New York dozens of times on business and have purposely avoided "being a tourist" and haven't gone to the top of the World Trade Center, for heaven's sake, go!

There's so little in travel that's predictable, it's a crime not to take advantage of the tried and true. The only comforting thing about clichés is that they usually are dependable. The cityscape at night is everything they say it is. And unless you've seen it from both ends, looking up *and* looking down, you just haven't seen it.

Setting Priorities

No matter how sophisticated a traveler you are, it's easy to become overwhelmed by the abundance of "must-see" activities in New York. Part of the problem is that the city keeps changing. There's always something new to do. Just when you think you've covered all the bases, they go and slip in Soho. Then, watch out! Here comes Noho!

Don't expect to be able to cover everything on this list during any one trip. But be assured that by the time you're ready to go home, you'll probably outrank most New Yorkers. For all their street smarts, the locals are notoriously naïve about counting their own blessings.

Make a game plan by selecting your most important priorities and noting the locations. Then read about the neighborhoods in which they're located. See if there are other things of interest to you nearby and estimate how much time you want to spend at each. The goal is to group priorities by neighborhood in order to avoid zigzagging your way back and forth across the city.

Like hotels, priorities are keyed into the color maps at the back of the book: the page number of the color insert and the appropriate map coordinates are noted.

THE TOP THREE SIGHTS

The Statue of Liberty
LOWER MANHATTAN, p. 8, C20

Every bit as corny as Kansas in August and as stirring as Kate Smith singing "God Bless America." If you had to symbolize the entire United States as well as New York, it would have to be Eiffel's other tower. There's a reason they didn't put Lady Liberty in Cleveland: New York was the official port of entry through which millions of immigrants came seeking personal freedom. Restored for its centennial in 1986, the structure engineered by Gustave Eiffel and designed by sculptor Frederic Bartholdi makes for a once-in-a-lifetime experience. If you can, climb the steps to the crown for a quintessential view of New York's skyline.

Take the number 1, N, or R train to South Ferry. The Circle Line Statue of Liberty ferry leaves at 9:15 A.M. and every half-hour between 10 A.M. and 4 P.M. $3.25 round trip; $1.50 under 12 (269-5755).
Nearby: The Staten Island Ferry, the New York Stock Exchange, the World Trade Center, South Street Seaport.

The Empire State Building
FIFTH AVENUE, p. 6, C13

For some of us true New Yorkers this will always be the world's tallest building—at least in spirit. The World Trade

Center's twin towers have all the warmth of an iceberg, and who cares about the Sears Tower in Chicago, anyway? The Empire State Building is merely 204 feet shorter than the Sears thing and a barely noticeable 127 feet less than those boring Siamese monoliths. There's an open platform on the 86th floor (50-mile view on a clear day) and a closed observatory on the 102nd (up to 80-mile visibility). Open until midnight, this place gives heightened meaning to the term "nightcap."

34th Street and Fifth Avenue. Take a bus heading down Fifth Avenue. Open 9:30 A.M. to midnight (last ticket sold 11:30 P.M.) $3.25; $1.75 under 12 (736-3100). But before you go in, stand across the street and look up.

Nearby: You're close to some of New York's major department stores: Macy's, B. Altman's, Lord and Taylor. The Morgan Library is closeby, too, at Madison and 36th.

Rockefeller Center   FIFTH AVENUE, p. 6, C12

Okay. We all know that the name "Rockefeller" is magical enough to make oysters and primitive art respectable. But give credit to the Center for the statue of Atlas, the statue of Prometheus (above which the nation's most famous Christmas tree is placed), Radio City Music Hall, the RCA Building, the Rainbow Room, the Channel Gardens, and the skating rink. The ultimate city-within-a-city, the birthplace of (nobody's perfect) the mall, Rockefeller Center is a unique urban spectacle that has never lost its 20/20 vision. Everything about it works and has worked since the last building in the complex opened in 1940.

49th to 51st streets and Fifth Avenue. The B, D, and F trains stop here. You can wander through the public spaces on your own or take tours of both the Radio City Music Hall or the National Broadcasting Company (NBC). NBC tours are given Monday through Saturday, 9:30 A.M. to 4:30 P.M. $6 (664-7174). Radio City Music Hall tours last one hour; call before you go—if the theater is in use no tours are given; 10 A.M. to 4:45 P.M. $5 (246-4600).

Nearby: MOMA and the rest of Fifth Avenue.

THE TWENTY NEXT BEST

The Brooklyn Bridge   LOWER MANHATTAN,
p. 9, D19

A work of kinetic art that masquerades as a bridge. It was, for twenty years, the world's longest suspension bridge, a darkly beautiful Gothic stone and steel symbol that opened the era of giant skyscrapers. It was finished in 1883 at a cost of $25 million and twenty lives. Kenneth Clark, British historian, said, "All modern New York, heroic New York, started with the Brooklyn Bridge." If the weather is good and your shoes are comfortable, head down to City Hall and take a taxi across the bridge to Cadman Plaza East near Prospect Street in Brooklyn. Enter the pedestrian promenade and walk back to Manhattan, as dazzling a mixed media event as you're likely to find, what with the water below, cars whizzing by, the spectacle of the huge overhead cables crisscrossing the sky, and (if you time your walk for near sunset), the drama of the city lighting up for the night.

The 4, 5, and 6 trains stop near the bridge.

Nearby: Lower East Side Shopping, Chinatown, Little Italy.

Chinatown

There is something uniquely New York about Chinatown, despite everything the locals have done to retain their Chineseness. The streets are impossible to navigate, the shops daunting to enter, the restaurants overwhelming in number. You undoubtedly can find some of New York's best food down here if you know where you're going and what you're ordering. Mulberry, Mott, and Pell are the major streets.

Canal Street is the subway stop; take the B, D, N, R, Q, or 6 train.

Nearby: Stroll over to Little Italy for an espresso and pastry. The bargains on the Lower East Side are all within walking distance.

The Chrysler Building   MIDTOWN EAST, p. 7, D12

An Art Deco masterpiece, its distinctive spire has graced the skyline since 1930. For one brief shining moment, until completion of the Empire State, it was the tallest building in the world. Many consider it the female counterpart to the Empire State Building. A combination of geometric patterns, mirror-like stainless steel, gargoyles, and auto icons (after all, it was built by Walter Chrysler) makes it a dazzling and unforgettable piece of New Yorkiana. Be sure to go inside and see the richly veined African marble lobby.

405 Lexington Avenue, between 42nd and 43rd streets. Trains 4, 5, 6, 7, and S (shuttle from Times Square) stop at Grand Central Station, right across the street.

East Village

This is the perfect time to visit the most neurotic zip code in the book. The area has gone through shock waves from its growing pains and has established itself as a force to be reckoned with—but you'd better get there before everyone becomes gentrified and discovers catalog shopping and shirts with alligators.

The number 6 train stops at Astor Place.

Fifth Avenue

Because it's there.

Greenwich Village

Once upon a time, a hotbed for ideas. A magical kingdom where everyone had visions and translated them into books and paintings and plays. It can still be exhilarating to return to the scene of the shrine—if you avoid the weekend and the thundering hordes of pragmatic, humorless adolescents.

The West 4th Street/Washington Square subway stop is in the heart of the Village. The A, C, E, and F trains all stop there.

Guggenheim Museum FIFTH AVENUE, p. 5, D8

The Frank Lloyd Wright building is a glorious incongruity smack bang on sedate Fifth Avenue. The truth is, it would be incongruous anywhere on this planet. A crafty swirl of modernism still poses the question, does this form follows function? Does the building compete with the art for your attention? Or does the design of the building help you to better appreciate the art? (Because of the ramps inside, works can be viewed from the opposite side of the museum.)

1071 Fifth Avenue (88 to 89th streets). Buses travel up Madison and crosstown, to and from the West Side, at 86th Street. Wednesday through Sunday, 11 A.M. to 4:45 P.M.; Tuesday 11 A.M. to 7:45 P.M.; closed Monday. $4 admission; $2 for seniors; wheelchair access (360-3513).

Nearby: The Guggenheim is across the street from Central Park and in the heart of Museum Mile: up the street from the Metropolitan and the Frick, down the street from the Cooper-Hewitt.

Lincoln Center UPPER WEST SIDE, p. 4, B10

Between you, me, and Avery Fisher Hall, we don't consider this a sight to see, just a place to be. Why in the world would anyone go to Lincoln Center unless she or he had tickets to a performance or were headed for a stroll on the Upper West Side? We are not talking great architecture, splendid plazas, or lovely cafés. But, apparently, there are enough people interested in early-morning lobbies and empty theaters to support a tour program (877-1800) that charges $6.25, which would be better spent toward the price of a ticket to the Metropolitan Opera House, the New York State Theater, Avery Fisher Hall, or the Vivian Beaumont Theater (see Entertainment).

Broadway and 65th Street. The number 1 train stops at 66th Street.

Nearby: The restaurants, bars, and trendy stores of Columbus Avenue stretch uptown from here.

Lower East Side

Save this one for Sunday morning when it's jammed with bargain hunters. (Most store owners close on Saturdays anyway for the Jewish Sabbath.) The press of humanity sometimes offers a thrilling reminder of a vibrant street life long gone.

The F train stops at East Broadway.

Nearby: Break for sustenance in Chinatown or Little Italy.

Madison Avenue   MIDTOWN EAST/UPPER EAST SIDE
Once known primarily as the business address of the man in the gray flannel suit, upper Madison has become so continental, you don't expect to hear English spoken.

The Metropolitan Museum of Art   FIFTH AVENUE, p. 4, C8
Still the champ, the Met is bigger and better than ever. Its four-block sprawling façade is a major sight in itself. On weekends, the area is transformed into the Big Apple version of a medieval square: there are musicians, jugglers, and mimes at the foot of the massive staircase that leads up to the entrance and the Great Hall, one of the city's few interior landmarked spaces. The largest art museum in the Western Hemisphere, the Met houses more than paintings—it revives entire environments: the Temple of Dendur is one of the most stirring sights. But there's also the Great Armor Hall with mounted knights, a labyrinth of reconstructed Egyptian tombs, the astonishing Rockefeller collection of primitive art, and on and on. Plan to spend as much time here as possible. There's nothing stuffy about the Met.

Fifth Avenue and 82nd Street. Buses run up Madison and cross the park at 79th and 86th streets. Wednesday through Sunday, 9:30 A.M. to 5:15 P.M.; Tuesday, 9:30 A.M. to 8:45 P.M.; closed Mondays. $5 suggested admission; $2.50 for seniors and children; wheelchair access (535-7710).
Nearby: All the museums of Museum Mile are relatively close—but the Met will probably fill your museum quotient for one day. After the museum, consider strolling in Central Park or browsing through Madison Avenue's shops and galleries.

The Museum of Modern Art   MIDTOWN WEST, p. 6, C11
Only in New York could you sell your air rights, make a fortune, renovate, and reopen to complaints that it's not like it used to be. MOMA is one of the great city experiences; its collection of modern art, daily film programs, and sculpture garden have been discussed as heatedly as back-fence gossip. While sometimes suspiciously less daring than with its original collection, MOMA has courageously embraced industrial objects and even kitchenware as well as Dali, Degas, and Duchamp. Don't make the mistake of thinking once you've seen one museum, you've seen them all and so why not take a tour of Lincoln Center, Ethel? MOMA and the Met are as different as MGM and 20th Century Fox.

11 West 53rd Street. The E and F trains stop at Fifth Avenue and 53rd Street; buses travel down Fifth. Friday through Tuesday, 11 A.M. to 6 P.M.; Thursday, 11 A.M. to 9 P.M.;

closed Wednesday; $6 admission; $3 for seniors; Thursday 5 to 9 P.M.; pay what you wish; wheelchair access (708-9500). **Nearby:** Rockefeller Center is only steps away—as are other major Fifth Avenue sights—St. Patrick's Cathedral, Trump Tower, Tiffany's, the Plaza Hotel.

New York Stock Exchange

LOWER MANHATTAN, p. 8, C19

At last! A chance to visit your money. Still going strong despite an occasional "correction," some arrests, and a mean-spirited movie. The Exchange was founded in 1792 by 24 brokers who no longer wished to conduct business on street corners and in coffeehouses. After helping to finance the War of 1812 and the Erie Canal, the Exchange began to be taken seriously. As a vivid view of our system at work, it's a sight not to be missed.

20 Broad Street (off Wall Street). The 2, 3, 4, and 5 trains stop at Wall Street. Third-floor visitors gallery, 9 A.M. to 3 P.M., Monday through Friday. There are exhibits and a short film for the Gordon Gekko in all of us (656-5168).
Nearby: The World Trade Center is just east of the Stock Exchange.

SoHo

Nowadays, no more daring than a Julie Andrews movie, SoHo is SoWholesome and user-friendly that even accountants can have a good time among the loft dwellers.

Take the E train to Spring Street; the N or R to Prince Street; the 1 to Houston.

South Street Seaport

LOWER MANHATTAN, p. 9, D19

Proof positive that New Yorkers are no less susceptible to being malled to death if it's done with style. One of the city's most beautiful locations.

Take the 2, 3, 4, or 5 train to Fulton Street.
Nearby: If you spend half a day at the Seaport, consider capping the day with a view from the World Trade Center or the Staten Island ferry.

Staten Island Ferry

LOWER MANHATTAN, p. 8, C20

Ocean-going kitsch that's not to be missed. It's the best five-mile, 25-minute, 25-cent ride in the world. Although it is rumored that people actually live on Staten Island, all you have to do is turn around and come right back to Manhattan, surrendering your gripes about the city to the majestic skyline in front of you. The ferry is located at the tip of Battery Park and runs every hour between 6 A.M. and 4 P.M., more frequently between 4 P.M. and midnight.

The 1, N, and R trains to South Ferry.
Nearby: The Stock Exchange, World Trade Center, South Street Seaport.

Times Square
MIDTOWN WEST, p. 6, C12

Ugh! You want to talk urban blight? Still, no self-respecting visitor should miss this bit of Americana. Grit your teeth. Go at night when the signs are all lit up, hopefully on your way to the theater. Stand on 42nd Street and Broadway and look uptown. That's where they stand to take the picture-postcard views. Hold onto your purse or wallet while you're looking and then head north (uptown). Do not walk along 42nd Street unless you happen to be with Charles Bronson and Chuck Norris. What used to be naughty is nowadays seedy and very sad. There are no more thrills left on 42nd Street.

If you take our advice and go at night, take a cab—the subway station here is particularly squalid, nor do you want to hang around on street corners waiting for the bus.

Trump Tower
FIFTH AVENUE, p. 7, D11

New York's most elegant monument to the city's *nouveau riche*. A terraced glass tower that's no place like home, unless the name on your bank book is Andrew Lloyd Webber. A truly luxurious residential-office building, Trump's civic triumph is in offering public spaces that are worth every penny he spent on them. The atrium is a fantasy of polished pink marble, gleaming brass, steep waterfalls, and shops chock-a-block with goodies for those terminally afflicted with conspicuous consumption. There's a café on the lower level and if you're lucky, the pianist will be playing right in the middle of everything.

Fifth Avenue, between 56th and 57th streets. Take a bus down Fifth. Open from 9 A.M. to 10 P.M. daily.
Nearby: MOMA and all of scenic Fifth Avenue.

United Nations
MIDTOWN EAST, p. 7, E12

There is a melancholy today about the U.N.: it has become more newsworthy as a locale for demonstrations than as a battlefield for human rights. Like the League of Nations and the Pillsbury Bake-Off, it somehow seemed more important at the time. Instead of its political impact, people nowadays talk mostly about the U.N.'s Gift Center in the basement—it sells NYC-tax-free exotic items from around the world (daily from 11 A.M. to 5:45 P.M., 963-1234)—or the Delegates Dining Room with its splendid view of the East River (lunch Monday through Friday, 963-7625 for reservations). Designed by an international team of architects, most notably Le Corbusier and Oscar Niemeyer, the U.N. complex is purposely situated counter to the grid pattern of New York's streets. It is very much international territory, a forum for delegates from over 150 countries. Forty-five-minute tours are given daily every half-hour, $4.50 (963-7713).

United Nations Plaza, 42nd to 48th Streets and First Avenue. Take buses on First Avenue (uptown) or Second Avenue (downtown).

World Trade Center

LOWER MANHATTAN,
p. 8, C19

Very big. The twin towers look like a big number 11. 110 floors. 1,200 offices. 50,000 people working. 80,000 visitors daily. You don't come here for the view of the World Trade Center, but the view from it. Absolutely not to be missed: number 2 World Trade Center Observation Deck.

The E and number 1 trains stop under the complex. Daily from 9:30 A.M. to 9:30 P.M. $2.95; $1.50 for seniors and children (Observation Deck: 466-7377).

Nearby: The New York Stock Exchange, the Staten Island ferry, the ferry to the Statue of Liberty, South Street Seaport.

What to Do If You Have Only One Day in New York and You've Never Been Here Before and (Even If) You're All Alone

7 A.M. Start off with a "power breakfast" in the Edwardian Room at the Plaza Hotel. It costs a fortune but the room is gorgeous, the people are gorgeous, the view is gorgeous, and even the corn flakes look better than they do in your Little Orphan Annie bowl back home. It's a hotel dining room and no one will think that you don't have a friend in the world because you came down to eat breakfast alone.

8 A.M. Sprint across the street, take a deep breath, and inhale the elegance of Grand Army Plaza before you dash down into the subway. Take the R train downtown to Whitehall/South Ferry, get off and ask to be pointed in the direction of Battery Park. Be early for the first ferry to the Statue of Liberty. You can be out and back in about two hours.

11 A.M. Grab a cab and go to the South Street Seaport for a whiff of Old New York. You're early enough to beat the Wall Street lunch crowd. Have something light and fresh for lunch, preferably "walking" food, while you stroll along Pier 17 for the best view possible of what's been called the most beautiful bridge in the world, the Brooklyn Bridge.

1 P.M. Another cab, this time tell him you want to go along the Bowery, up Third Avenue to the Gramercy Park area. Ask him to turn up on 19th Street—the block between Third Avenue and Irving Place is one of the most charming in the city. Then, up Madison Avenue and over to the Empire State Building.

2 P.M. After a quick look at the city, it's time for a stroll up Fifth Avenue, or if you're out of breath from the view, walk one block to Madison and take a bus up to 50th Street, passing the Morgan Library on 36th Street. While the best part of Fifth is farther uptown, your walk will give you a feel for the pace of the city, and bring you cheek to cheek with the literary lions in front of the New York Public Library on 42nd Street. Now for a bit of fast footwork. Turn right on 42nd Street and walk east to one of the Beaux-Artsiest buildings in the city, Grand Central Terminal. As you reach Lexington Avenue, look up at the Art Deco pizzazz of the Chrysler Building. Go in through the Lexington Avenue entrance and let the sight of the lobby soothe your sore eyes. You can take the Lexington or Madison Avenue bus uptown to 50th Street and walk over to Fifth. However, if you'd like to work both sides of the street, in perfect safety, hop onto the number 104 bus heading west on 42nd. Ask for a transfer when you get on. The bus takes you along the most notorious street in the city— the block between Seventh and Eighth avenues is where all the X-rated action is—before turning up Eighth Avenue. Stay on the bus until 50th Street and take the 50th Street crosstown bus over to Fifth Avenue and Rockefeller Center.

3 P.M. to 4 P.M. By this time you should be standing on Fifth Avenue, between 49th and 50th streets, facing the Channel Gardens and the spectacular RCA Building, which has been hailed as the greatest urban complex of the 20th century. Walk down to the sunken plaza for a good look at Prometheus and then perhaps a bit of refreshment at the Sea Grill or American Festival Café or even the coffeeshop that sneaks you a peek of plaza activity. Go into the lobby of the RCA Building to see the glorious murals, and then, at the very least, hurry down the street for a glance into Radio City Music Hall. Once back on Fifth, you're directly across the street from the original Saks Fifth Avenue and St. Patrick's Cathedral. And then, for heaven's sake, go into one of the Fifth Avenue stores between 50th and 59th streets and buy yourself a present.

6 P.M. After a pit stop back at your hotel to pick up the ticket your concierge got you for a Broadway show, you're now ready for a night on the town. Dress casually, i.e., a comfortable dress, or jacket and tie—a sports jacket is fine. You're going back downtown now and will have to decide between a cab and the subway. Don't even consider the bus; it will take too long. Head for the World Trade Center and wet your whistle at the Hors d'Oeuvrerie on the 107th floor of number 1 World Trade Center (938-1111) where the view, and the hors d'oeuvres (pricey), are equally delicious. Don't be afraid of spoiling your appetite: that *is* dinner. You're going to "graze" instead of dine.

10:30 P.M. By the time the curtain comes down, you're ready to put your money where your mouth is. Here is the city at its most seductive. You can choose The Four Seasons for an after-theater supper, the Carnegie Deli (remember *Broadway Danny Rose?*) for after-theater heartburn, or go to Greenwich Village and hang out at the Village Gate or Sweet Basil. There are comedy clubs, dance clubs, and bars listed under Entertainment. Be prepared, however, that whatever you choose will be tinged with a touch of the bittersweet. You will always wonder, as you review the glories of the evening, "Well, maybe I should have gone to XXX instead?" But isn't that why they invented "next times"?

5

TRANSPORTATION

From Kennedy

The trip from J.F.K. (John F. Kennedy International Airport) into midtown is the longest, most aggravating, and most expensive 15 miles you're likely to travel outside of a Malaysian jungle. No matter how you do it, or what you pay, it's going to take you about an hour.

Welcome (?) to New York City

The minute you arrive in any city, sad to say, is the moment you're most vulnerable to pickpockets and thieves. Before getting off the plane, train, or bus, check that your wallet is in a safe place. Do not let go of hand luggage while still in the terminal. Be especially cautious when making phone calls, using rest rooms, or arranging for ground transportation. Those in the light-fingered trades know you are tired and distracted after a journey. There is probably no other time during your trip that you will be as easy a mark.

TAXI

There is usually a line of people waiting for taxis, and usually uniformed taxi dispatchers to help you, although they often supply more heat than light. The important things to remember are that drivers are required by law to take you any place you want to go within the city limits; one fare pays for all passengers (although at times there may be a line set up just for people who want to share cabs; the price is specified per person when the dispatcher fills up the cab—tipping is extra); be sure the meter is operating when the cab is in motion; and you are required to pay tolls and a $.50 surcharge between 8 P.M. and 6 A.M. The officially quoted fare from J.F.K. to midtown is $28, but chances are you'll find yourself paying something close to $35 depending upon the traffic. Tip about 20 percent of the fare.

EXPRESS BUS

Carey Airport Express, $8, (718) 632-0500, leaves for East and West 42nd St. every thirty minutes. You can pick up the bus in Manhattan at various locations for the trip to the airport; call for details.

SUBWAY

J.F.K. Express, $6.50; (718) 858-7272—this one is a real puzzle. Why bother getting onto a bus and then a train for such a modest saving over the Express Bus? However, it's popular. Buses depart each J.F.K. terminal every twenty minutes for Howard Beach subway stop where special trains take you to Manhattan and Brooklyn.

MINIBUS

You'll find these vans at all J.F.K. terminals. Make arrangements at the Ground Transportation Counter.

Abbey's Transportation, $11; (718) 361-9092. Approximately sixty minutes to major midtown hotels.

Giraldo Limousine Service, $11–$15; (212) 757-6840. Drop-off anywhere between 14th and 90th sts.

HELICOPTER

New York Helicopter, $58; (800) 645-3494—do it for the view. Departs from TWA Terminal to East 34th St. Heliport. Travel time is 15–20 minutes, not counting the time it takes to get to the TWA Terminal.

PUBLIC TRANSPORTATION

The best way to save money. Take the Q10 bus (Green Bus Lines; 718-995-4700) or the Q3 bus (N.Y.C. Transit Authority; 718-330-1234) to connect with the N.Y.C. subway system. Bus fare is $1 (exact change only; they don't take dollar bills). Subway fare is an additional $1. Takes forever—1½–2 hours.

LIMOUSINE

Make arrangements at Ground Transportation Counter or in advance from

Airlimo; (516) 872-4754
Giraldo Limousine; (212) 757-6840
Transport/Classic Limousine; (800) 645-1164

From La Guardia

If you can possibly book yourself into L.G.A. (La Guardia Airport), do so. It's the most convenient, easiest to negotiate, airport in the city. If you grit your teeth, you can hop into a cab and be in midtown in 25 minutes. Meter should run about $15 plus toll and tip. (See taxi notes under J.F.K.)

EXPRESS BUS

Carey Airport Express, $6, (718) 632-0500, leaves for East and West 42nd St. every twenty–thirty minutes. Travel time is approximately forty minutes. For information on buses from Manhattan to L.G.A., telephone.

MINIBUS

These depart from all L.G.A. terminals. Make arrangements at Ground Transportation Counter.

Abbey's Transportation, $8; (718) 361-9092. Approximately 45 minutes to major midtown hotels.
Giraldo Limousine, $8–$15; (212) 757-6840. Drop-off anywhere between 14th and 90th sts.

FERRY

Pan Am Water Shuttle $20; (800) 54-FERRY. Operates mornings and late afternoons Mon.–Fri. from L.G.A. to Wall St. or East 34th St. and the East River.

PUBLIC TRANSPORTATION

Bargain basement. Take the Q33 bus (Triboro Coach; 718-335-1000) to connect with N.Y.C. subway system. Bus fare is $1 (exact change only; no dollar bills; subway tokens accepted). Subway fare is an additional $1. ETA: under an hour with good connections.

LIMOUSINE

Make arrangements at Ground Transportation Counter or in advance from

Airlimo; (718) 995-5592
Giraldo Limousine; (212) 757-6840
Transport/Classic Limousine; (800) 645-1164

From Newark

Okay. So, N.I.A. (Newark International Airport) is in New Jersey. It's not as convenient as L.G.A. but it's better than J.F.K. Red alert to dedicated budgeteers: there is no public transportation into Manhattan. If you can afford to think about a taxi, which will run about $30 plus tolls and tip, you might as well have a cleaner, more comfortable ride in a limo. Traveling *to* Newark, taxi fare is calculated on the meter, plus $10 and tolls. And tip. (Also see taxi notes under J.F.K.)

EXPRESS BUS

N.J. Transit Express, $7, (201) 460-8444, leaves for Port Authority Bus Terminal every 15–30 minutes. Travel time is approximately 30–45 minutes.
Olympia Trails Express Bus, $7, (212) 964-6233, leaves every twenty minutes for World Trade Center and Grand Central Station. Travel time same as above.

MINIBUS AND SHARED RIDE

Make arrangements at Ground Transportation Counter. Travel time is approximately 55 minutes.

N.I.A./N.Y.C. Minibus, $12; (201) 961-2535. Departs all N.I.A. terminals to major midtown hotels.
Giraldo Limousine, $13–$18; (212) 757-6840. Drop-off anywhere between 32nd and 90th sts.
Newark Airport Limo, $35; (201) 242-5012. Drop-off anywhere between Battery Park and 59th St.

LIMOUSINE
Make arrangements at Ground Transportation Counter or in advance from

Airport Limousine Express; (201) 621-7300
Airport Jet Express; (201) 961-2501
Newark Airport Limousine and Car Service; (201) 242-5012
Carter's Executive Limousine; (201) 316-5651
VIP Limousine; (201) 289-3600

From Grand Central Station
42nd St. between Madison and Lexington aves. (212-532-4900)
If your luggage is heavy, get a porter. It's a hefty walk from the
train platform to the street. Then, you're on your own unless you
hire someone to get you a cab. This is not as silly as it sounds
because you don't want to leave your luggage unattended on
the street while signaling for a cab to stop. A dollar for your new
"press agent" will do the trick. (But, feel free to ignore these
guys and hail a cab for yourself.) If you're determined to take
public transportation, check the maps in the back of this book.
   Note: Don't depart the premises without looking up, inside
and out. It's a fabulous building.

From Pennsylvania Station
33rd St. between Seventh and Eighth aves. (212-736-4545).
Same rules apply as Grand Central. There's nothing worth noticing about Penn Station except its proximity to the glorious General Post Office (across from the Eighth Ave. entrance).

From the Port Authority Bus Terminal
41st St. between Eighth and Ninth aves. (212-564-8484). This
is rough turf. Hold onto your belongings tightly and get into a
cab as quickly as possible. Do not linger here. There is a cab
line at the Eighth Ave. entrance; waits for a cab may be longer
than you'd like, but you won't have to tip anyone—just queue
up and wait your turn.

A word about car rental: Don't.

GETTING AROUND TOWN
You know the old joke.
                Q: How do you get to Carnegie Hall?
                A: Practice! Practice! Practice!
It says a lot more about New York than most people realize.
   Look at any bus or subway map and you'll find that getting
to Carnegie Hall is a cinch. The real joke is that no self-
respecting New Yorker equates the phrase "getting somewhere" in terms of transportation.
   Getting around New York has one major prerequisite: forget
about driving. Although there are numerous expensive and inconvenient West Side parking lots for the New Jersey and Connecticut Saturday night theater trade, those facilities are useless

to all but dedicated suburbanites. Once you've set foot in New York City, middle-class concepts such as "valet parking" are pure fantasy.

The best way to get around the city is to be outrageously wealthy and have a chauffeur-driven limousine. Otherwise, the choice is simple. Walk.

The numbered streets that run north to south are relatively short. Even without seven-league boots, you'll be able to cover ten blocks in about 15 minutes. The east to west avenue blocks are often significantly longer and it takes almost triple the time to get from Fifth to Sixth Ave. than it does from 59th to 60th Street. Here's what you'll need for hassle-free transportation:

1. A plan
2. Comfortable shoes
3. A collapsible umbrella

Midtown Traffic Golden Rules

During the morning rush hour, it is more difficult going downtown. During the evening rush hour, it is more difficult going uptown. It is *always* more difficult going across town (east/west) than going uptown or downtown.

The plan is an easy one to make. All you have to do is group activities by neighborhood so that you can walk from A to B to C. Use a map to be certain that A to B to C goes in the same direction as the traffic and you'll have the option of hopping onto a bus or into a taxi. Look at your map to locate a hotel or some major landmark near your final destination. That's the best way to find a taxi. As a last resort, head for the nearest subway stop. Nothing beats the subway for speed.

New York has more bus and subway stops than Hamelin had rats. Back in the days when city commissioners spent time doing things other than being indicted, somebody put together a real neat package to get people from here to there with breathtaking efficiency. Buses and subways are still conveniently situated and form a logical routing system.

However, as a visitor to the city, your priorities—and your sensibilities—are likely to be considerably different from those of hard-core New Yorkers. For some strange reason, out-of-towners sometimes cringe at the thought of stepping into a hole in the ground and being jammed into an airless, graffiti-scarred, sadistic-killer-filled subway car doomed to catch fire in a dark tunnel. *The New York Attitude:* Everybody's a prima donna!

Let's face it, even though a few of those horror stories about the subways are true, almost everybody believes the old adage about safety in numbers and burrows in during rush hour. Simply, there's no faster or easier way to get around the city.

How to Take the Subway

With caution.

Subways run 24 hours. The peak rush periods are 7:30–9:30 A.M. and 4:30–6:30 P.M., and should be avoided if possible. It's a good idea to stand in the designated "off-hours waiting areas." These are generally in sight of the token booth where someone is on duty. Travel in a middle car near the conductor, or in the first car near the driver. Do not ride in the last car or in an empty car. Do not stand at the edge of the platform.

You can usually change train lines without paying an additional fare. Check with the agent on duty in the token booth. You'll find subway stations are well marked, making line changes relatively easy. As a rule of thumb, subways run uptown and downtown rather than across town.

Be certain your valuables are not easy pickings. A favorite trick is to grab a purse or wallet in that split second before the door closes, leaving the victim on the train, while the thief exits safely along the platform. In all fairness, many New Yorkers ride the subways at all hours and experience no problems. And the aforementioned tips would apply to subway travel in any city in the world. But don't tempt fate. If you plan to travel after midnight, grit your teeth and take a cab.

SUBWAY FARE: $1. Buy a token at the token booth. But booths are not always open. If you plan to travel by subway and bus (the same token is accepted), it's advisable to buy a few extras. Don't expect to be able to cash in your extras, however.

How to Take the Bus

As often as possible.

In addition to being safer, cleaner, and generally more convenient than subways, buses allow you to see the city as you travel. Not all bus lines run 24 hours, so be sure to check if you're planning to use the bus after midnight. Rush-hour periods are the same as the subway.

Buses are pure Chekhovian modes of transportation. They are slow enough to allow for introspection, offer lots of characterization, and a surprising amount of humor while the rest of the world just rolls by.

Use some street smarts waiting for a bus during off hours. If you're alone, and it's dark, wait near an open store. While buses are relatively free from the kind of violence that stalks the subways, thieves will grab a purse when the bus pulls into a stop and then exit down the street.

Buses allow you to transfer from one bus route to another without paying an extra fare, letting you go from uptown or downtown to east or west. Simply ask the driver for a transfer when you get on. However, if you already handed him a transfer as your fare, you cannot get another one.

BUS FARE: $1. Drivers do not make change nor do they accept bills. You must have $1 in exact change or else a subway token.

How to Take a Taxi

With a grain of salt.

Once upon a time, the cliché Manhattan cabbie was a lovable, garrulous Brooklynish kind of lug with a heart of gold who was just waiting for you to step in and shout, "Follow that car!" Forget it. The typical eighties cabbie can sometimes be short-tempered and rude, or a recent arrival to this country who barely speaks English, who knows New York about as well as you know

Timbuktu. Occasionally, you'll come across one who smiles and says, "Thank you," but as a group, they should be approached with the same caution as a pool of snapping turtles.

By law, the driver is required to take you to any destination within the five boroughs. If you have a problem, though, simply note down the driver's identification number and ask for help at your hotel.)

Somehow, it always seems to cost either $5 or $10 to take a taxi, regardless of where you're going. (Obviously, it can cost more than $10 to go from South Street Seaport to the Upper West Side.) Remember: meters are keyed into waiting time as well as distance traveled (so you're paying for the time that passes as you're stuck in traffic). If you only have something larger than a $10 bill, ask the driver if he or she has change before you get in.

Adding a 15–20 percent tip to the fare on the meter is the norm. Do not calculate your tip to include any tolls or the highway robberish $.50 surcharge that is legally added by most cabs after 8 P.M. For extra service in handling bags or being almost human, make it 20 percent. If the driver doesn't say thank you, or has been rude in any way, don't lose your cool: Simply open the door, get out, and conveniently forget to shut it.

Then there are gypsy cabs, thousands of unlicensed, uninsured cabs that roam the streets like a mobile East Germany—officially unrecognized but in full view. These are the guys with the foam rubber dominoes, baby shoes, or plastic saints hanging on the rear view mirror, who may or may not have meters and who charge whatever the traffic will bear. These caballeros have no visible identification and are likely to vanish into thin air should there be any trouble. While we don't hesitate riding the gypsies around town, they are definitely not recommended for long hauls.

In other words, walk. Walk as much as possible.

How to Write Manhattan

When writing addresses, there are two simple rules to remember.

1. Use numerals for streets (59th Street).
2. Spell out names of avenues (Fifth Avenue).

Curiously, this practice does not apply to the other boroughs.

N.Y.C. Midtown Street Guide

STREET NUMBERS
Here's how to tell between which avenues a midtown address is located:

East Side
>   1–49 / Fifth and Madison
>   50–99 / Madison and Park
>   100–149 / Park and Lexington
>   150–199 / Lexington and Third
>   200–299 / Third and Second
>   300–399 / Second and First
>   400–499 / First and York

West Side
>   1–99 / Fifth and Sixth
>   100–199 / Sixth and Seventh
>   200–299 / Seventh and Eighth
>   300–399 / Eighth and Ninth
>   400–499 / Ninth and Tenth
>   500–599 / Tenth and Eleventh
>   600–   / Eleventh and Twelfth

Even-numbered addresses are on the downtown (south) side of the street; odd-numbered addresses are on the uptown (north) side of the street.

AVENUE NUMBERS
Here's how to find (within a block or so) the nearest cross-street for a midtown avenue address:

Cancel the last number of the address (666 Fifth Ave. = 66)
Divide by two (66 ÷ 2 = 33)
Add or subtract the key number given below (33 + 20 = 53 = 53rd St)

First Ave.:	add 3
Second Ave.:	add 3
Third Ave.:	add 10
Lexington Ave.:	add 22
Park Ave.:	add 34
Madison Ave.:	add 26
Fifth Ave.	
up to no. 200:	add 13
up to no. 400:	add 16
up to no. 600:	add 18
up to no. 775:	add 20
Sixth Ave.:	subtract 12
Seventh Ave:	
up to no. 1800:	add 12
above no. 1800:	add 20
Eighth Ave.:	add 9
Ninth Ave.:	add 13
Tenth Ave.:	add 14
Eleventh Ave.:	add 15
Broadway:	subtract 30

6

NEIGHBORHOODS

Fifth Avenue

There is probably no one street in the world that stirs up images of an entire city the way Fifth Avenue does. Not even the Champs-Élysées, for all its splendor as the world's grandest boulevard, epitomizes Paris more than Fifth Avenue symbolizes New York.

From its beginnings in Washington Square Park, Fifth Avenue was built heading north. Uptown. It was the address for America's best known millionaires from Astor to Vanderbilt; an avenue of mansions that symbolized the great American dream. For the millions of immigrants who fled persecution and lack of opportunity, Fifth Avenue was the mythic street paved with gold. By the end of the Civil War, there were nearly four hundred townhouses built on the avenue.

The Famous "400"

The phrase denoting the "in" group came about when Mrs. Astor, in 1892, sent out precisely four hundred invitations to a ball she was giving in her Fifth Avenue mansion. It is reported that four hundred represented the number of people who could be accommodated.

It was in the 1920s and 1930s, first with department stores like Saks Fifth Avenue and then with Rockefeller Center, that Fifth shifted from being known for the most expensive residences in the world to being known for the most expensive shopping. Again, the millionaires moved north. Like the Valley of the Kings, midtown Fifth was flanked by great monuments filled with worldly possessions. But these were for sale. Instead of ogling residences of the rich and infamous, even the poorest of New Yorkers could indulge in window

46

shopping, the first symptom of a galloping consumerism that swept the nation after World War II.

During the fifties, airlines and foreign tourist boards began "shop-lifting." They were willing to pay exorbitant rents to have a Fifth Avenue address from which to launch a booming travel industry. Simultaneously, many merchants took off and started branching out into suburban malls. Once this shift began, Fifth was never the same. The "going out of business today" rug merchants appeared, along with the discounters and the fast food mafia. Incredibly, Fifth's powerful image has survived them all—at least for ten blocks or so from 59th Street on down.

Today, there are three separate "Fifth Avenues": midtown Fifth, lower Fifth, and upper Fifth. The fact that they are sufficiently unrelated and might as well be in three different cities is part of what makes New York so frustrating. And exciting. It's what makes New York, New York.

MIDTOWN FIFTH

This stretch of the avenue is worth some kind of build-up. It is, after all, 24-carat New York. Try starting at 63rd or 64th and Fifth and walk down from there. If you're into the wonderful world of incongruities, think about scheduling a stop at the newly refurbished **Central Park Zoo** at Fifth Avenue between 63rd and 64th streets. Indisputably the world's best address for an animal refuge, the original zoo was more reminiscent of a rich man's indulgence than a wildlife environment and was long overdue for a major overhaul. $35 million later, the monkeys are in full swing in one of three "environments" that make all the animals feel much more at home. See Central Park.

The quintessential Fifth Avenue begins at **Grand Army Plaza** and 59th Street, where a statue of Pomona, the goddess of abundance, graces the tiered pools of the Pulitzer Memorial Fountain. There's hardly a movie shot in New York that hasn't included this spot, from *Arthur* to *The Way We Were.* One of the reasons is the faux French Renaissance grandeur of the legendary **Plaza Hotel.** The Plaza, built in 1907 for the then incredible sum of $12.5 million, is still making headlines. Recently, it was bought by Donald Trump for $390 million. If you're not staying here, put the Plaza on your sightseeing list.

Right on the northeast corner of 59th Street is one of New York's most splendid delights, **À la Vieille Russie,** a shop of impeccable taste and credentials, offering rare jewelry treasures from Czarist Russia, including the masterworks of Fabergé. You won't find a more spectacular gift in the city.

One of the grandest dames among New York shops is the landmark **Bergdorf Goodman,** between 57th and 58th

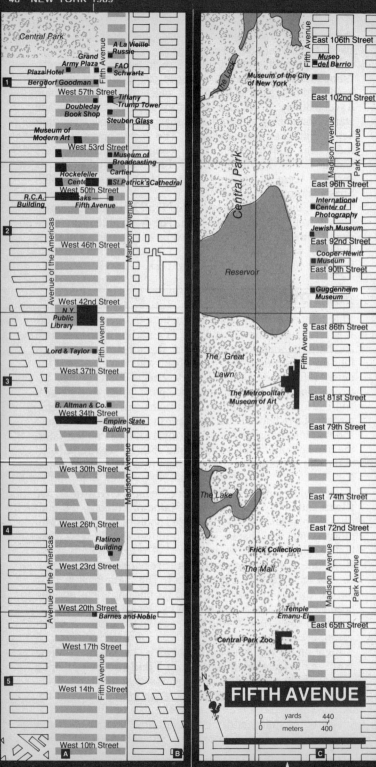

Central Park

A La Vieille
Russie

Grand
Army Plaza

FAO
Schwartz

Plaza Hotel

Bergdorf Goodman

1

Fifth Avenue

West 57th Street

Tiffany

Trump Tower

Doubleday
Book Shop

Steuben Glass

Museum of
Modern Art

West 53rd Street

Museum of
Broadcasting

Cartier

Rockefeller
Center

St.Patrick's Cathedral

West 50th Street

R.C.A.
Building

Saks
Fifth Avenue

2

Avenue of the Americas

Madison Avenue

West 46th Street

West 42nd Street

N.Y.
Public
Library

Fifth Avenue

Lord & Taylor

3

West 37th Street

B. Altman & Co.

West 34th Street

Empire State
Building

West 30th Street

Madison Avenue

West 26th Street

4

Flatiron
Building

Avenue of the Americas

West 23rd Street

West 20th Street

Barnes and Noble

West 17th Street

Fifth Avenue

5

West 14th Street

West 10th Street

A

B

East 106th Street

Fifth Avenue

The Lock

Museo
del Barrio

Museum of the City
of New York

East 102nd Street

Madison Avenue

Park Avenue

Central Park

East 96th Street

International
Center of
Photography

Jewish Museum

East 92nd Street

Cooper-Hewitt
Museum

East 90th Street

Reservoir

Guggenheim
Museum

East 86th Street

The Great

Lawn

Fifth Avenue

The Metropolitan
Museum of Art

East 81st Street

East 79th Street

The Lake

East 74th Street

East 72nd Street

Frick Collection

The Mall

Madison Avenue

Park Avenue

Temple
Emanu-El

East 65th Street

Central Park Zoo

N

FIFTH AVENUE

| 0 | yards | 440 |
| 0 | meters | 400 |

C

streets. Mr. Bergdorf, a tailor who specialized in recutting men's suits to fit women (talk about being ahead of the times!), was bought out by Mr. Goodman in 1901. It took 27 years before the store moved to its present location, site of the old Cornelius Vanderbilt mansion. Today, the Bergdorf name is still synonymous with being on the cutting edge of fashion. Very European in design, Bergdorf's buzzes with a cluster of tiny boutiques: Turnbull & Asser, Chanel, Fendi, Angela Cummings, and others—along with nooks and crannies jam-packed with the store's signature items. Bergdorf's knows their customers aren't afraid to take risks, so you're likely to come upon one-of-a-kind items here.

Note: Bergdorf's has the best department store ladies room in town—with a great view of Central Park.

If you have children, grandchildren, godchildren, or even just a Peter Pan complex, don't leave 58th Street without a stop at **F.A.O. Schwarz,** which is to toys what Bergdorf's is to debutantes' gowns. A bona-fide branch of Santa's workshop—if you can't find it here, it probably doesn't exist.

Heading toward **57th Street,** it becomes clear why you're not in Kansas anymore, Toto. If Fifth is the avenue that epitomizes New York City, then 57th is the only street with enough panache to dare cross it. Broader in both size and scope than Fifth, 57th is the art gallery capital of the Western Hemisphere, the home of Carnegie Hall, the Hard Rock Café, and Hermès. (See the 57th Street section, below.) Smack on the corner of 57th and Fifth is the store whose name has become as synonymous with luxury and quality as it has with breakfast: **Tiffany's.** There's more good taste within this building than the entire chocolate factory in Hershey, Pennsylvania. Not surprisingly, you will find that even relatively inexpensive items (key chains, pens, stationery) become instant treasures because of their provenance. Abraham Lincoln, Diamond Jim Brady, and Sarah Bernhardt all shopped here. Shoppers are treated with courtesy and respect. Don't be afraid to browse.

It's only a few steps from ritzy Tiffany's to glitzy **Trump Tower,** but they're light years apart in the same way old money is from new. There's an inbred, cultivated style to Tiffany that money can't buy. Trump Tower, on the other hand, is everything that money can buy—if you know how to buy well.

 You can have a snack at the foot of the waterfall to fortify yourself during a boutique break. Or, there's a very snappy little bistro on the 5th floor called the **Terrace on Five.** It has a sprinkling of tables overlooking Fifth Avenue and a menu that doesn't appear to overlook anything: from walnut pâté to mozzarella with roasted peppers, and even a macrobiotic menu.

Among the smart shops on 5 are the Tony Papp Gallery, with a dazzling display of contemporary silver jewelry; Saity, with an impressive collection of American Indian crafts; and Beauty & the Beast, which is cheek to jowl with unbearably wonderful teddys, plush puppies, and more stuffed animals than a happy-hour buffet. Down on 4, you'll find an outpost of Abercrombie & Fitch right next to a branch of Martha's, the Grande Dame of designer originals. La Petite Étoile has some of the most lavish kid's clothes in town. Definitely not sand-box attire. On the 3rd level is a branch of Fred Leighton with more of the extraordinary antique jewelry for which the shop has been known for years. Circle Gallery of Soho offers a quick peek at today's art scene for those who know what they like. Krystalos is a favorite browse. A museum-like store, it sells crystal formations of heroic proportions. Price tags to match. Aspreys has the most expensive bundles from Britain, Harry Winston is the perfect place in which to get stoned, and Charles Jourdan will give you a boot on the main floor.

🐾 **The Bistro** is a smart Italian café on the lower level. Also **DDL Foodshow** (as in *D*ino *D*e *L*aurentiis) to cater on-the-spot snacks while watching the waterfall fall. If part of your rest stop includes a freshen up, you can thank Donald Trump for providing some of the classiest bathrooms in town.

One of the things that makes New York so civilized is the **Doubleday Book Shop** directly across the avenue. It has four floors of books stocked by a buyer who really appreciates the printed word, one of the city's best record and tape departments for really hard-to-find items that are fun for grownups to listen to, and, as if that weren't enough, it stays open until midnight.

If you're in the mood for foreign intrigue, step over to **Ferragamo** on 56th Street for leather smart enough to get elected to the Roman Senate. Once you go into **Steuben Glass** (glass slippers by order only), you'll understand why you hated drinking out of jelly jars. The brilliantly creative fusion of elements that results in blown glass, cut glass, and cut crystal is no better produced than at Steuben. This stuff is expensive, but worth every penny; however, butterfingers beware.

Given our druthers, we'd pass right by **Gucci.** But there are legions of out-of-work Hollywood producers who swear by Gucci loafers. Your choice. If you've got money to burn, split your net worth between Ferragamo and the really classy (read: no designer initials) leather goodies at **Bottega Veneta** on Madison Avenue (see Upper East Side).

The prime reason you'll be interested in 53rd Street is because it's the gateway to the **Museum of Modern Art.** For devotees of 20th-century art, MOMA is a must—despite recent renovations intended to make the museum more accessi-

Diamond Mining on Fifth

For those who believe diamonds are a girl's best friend, Fifth Avenue begins at **Van Cleef & Arpels,** crosses over to **Buccellati,** heads speedily toward **Harry Winston,** allows for as much time as you want at **Cartier,** but only a minute to peek in and turn up your nose at **Fortunoff's** before careening down to 47th Street and the diamond district. Take a deep breath and turn right on 47th, where movie buffs will recall Laurence Olivier was identified as a Nazi doctor in *Marathon Man.* There are more diamond dealers here than in any maximum-security prison in the country. If truth be told, they should award a doctorate in diamonds to anyone who can make it all the way from Fifth to Sixth on this monomaniacal block. There is likely to be no danger to your self-esteem or net worth if you know what you're doing.

ble but which, in fact, take away much of its former intimacy. MOMA may have lost some muscle with the transfer of Picasso's *Guernica* to the Prado in Spain, but its collection of Picasso paintings and sculpture is the best to be seen this side of the Atlantic. In addition, MOMA is home to some of Matisse's most exquisite interiors; some of the most exciting Gauguins, Vuillards, Toulouse-Lautrecs, Chagalls, Mirós, and Giacomettis to be found anywhere. There is an extensive display of the constructivist movement led by Mondrian and Malevitch and a collection of surrealistic masterpieces that includes some of Magritte's eeriest paintings. Not to be missed is the "meditation corner" with Monet's fabulous triptych *Water Lilies.*

You'll find American masterpieces that are bigger than life and, on a smaller scale, a treasure trove of drawings and prints by Johns, Rauschenberg, Stella, and the elders Picasso, Munch, and Toulouse-Lautrec. The photography gallery paints its own picture of 20th-century America, as does an extraordinary film library (there are free showings daily).

A voracious collector, MOMA also keeps track of modern furniture, utensils, and architecture, and even has some of the craziest cars ever designed. The cafeteria is unpretentious and a light lunch overlooking the sculpture garden with works by Rodin, Matisse, and Newman is the best buy in midtown. Even the bookstore is great, with its selection of books, cards, and souvenirs. But the real shopper's delight is the gift shop.

The museum (11 West 53rd Street, 708-9480) is open Thursday, 11 A.M. to 9 P.M.; Friday to Tuesday, 11 A.M. to 6 P.M. Closed Wednesday. For film listings, call 708-9490. Admission is $6; seniors, $3. On Thursday from 5 to 9 P.M., pay what you wish.

The **Museum of Broadcasting,** on the east side of Fifth, has a collection of seven thousand radio and ten thousand television broadcasts spanning a sixty-year period. These tapes are available to the public via broadcast consoles at which you can enjoy anything from your favorite episode of *I Love Lucy* to one of FDR's fireside chats. Located at 1 East 53rd Street (752-7684), the museum is open Tuesday, noon to 8 P.M.; Wednesday to Saturday, noon to 5 P.M. Suggested contribution is $4; children and seniors, $2.

A pair of 1905 mansions on the corner of 52nd Street serves as home base for one of the world's great jewelers. Like Tiffany's, **Cartier** is a gem of many facets. And that's despite the ho-hum "Les Musts" line developed to serve those whose trust funds are temporarily in limbo. The real Cartier's is as first-class as you can get, and its good taste suits every palate if not every pocketbook. The store itself is a sightseeing event.

When **St. Patrick's Roman Catholic Cathedral** opened in 1879, New Yorkers complained because it was too far out of town for them. The ground on which it stands was purchased originally as a cemetery—at the time the city did not extend above 42nd Street. It is today in the very heart of the metropolis, just opposite Rockefeller Center and Saks. Patterned after the cathedrals in Cologne and Rheims, it ranked eleventh among the world's largest churches.

Rockefeller Center (see Priorities) is the unchallenged hub of the city and is to be seen as part of the Fifth Avenue experience or on its own. Be sure to tour the area, either as part of a group or on your own. Head for the lobby of the RCA Building, known to locals as "30 Rock" (the address is 30 Rockefeller Plaza) for tour tickets as well as information on do-it-yourself sightseeing. Under no circumstances miss a chance to get inside Radio City Music Hall—either buy a ticket to a scheduled event or take a tour. It's the largest indoor theater in the world.

Rockefeller Center: The Inside Story

There are:

388 elevators
48,758 office windows
65,000 people working
97,500 locks
100,000 telephones
175,000 daily visitors
240,000 daily population
(only 60 U.S. cities exceed this total)

Saks Fifth Avenue, taking the entire blockfront on Fifth between 50th and 49th streets, is the only thing to rival Rockefeller Center in its monumental salute to capitalism. Saks isn't glitzy or trendy or particularly young at heart, but like an aging beauty it is still devoted to glamour. Okay, the glamour of yesteryear. This was the place the boss's wife always shopped. A New York version of Harrods, where quality still counts. Chances are you are already familiar with Saks, but the main store, unlike its spinoffs in malls across the country, retains an aura of sophistication that would be difficult to duplicate elsewhere. Perhaps it's the setting: St. Patrick's on one side and Rockefeller Center across the street, but the store has worn well through the years and continues to attract millions of shoppers. Savvy New Yorkers know that when Saks has a sale, the markdowns are major.

The stretch of Fifth down to 42nd Street is only mildly interesting and certainly not worth the trek unless you haven't seen Patience and Fortitude, the marble lions in front of the **New York Public Library** on 42nd Street. One of the world's leading research institutions, the main branch of the New York Public Library is the country's third largest library (after the Library of Congress and Harvard's Widener Library) and is housed in one of the city's architectural gems. Within its restrained Beaux Arts façade are some 63 miles of shelves and such rare items as a letter by Columbus and a draft of the Declaration of Independence in Jefferson's own handwriting. On a nice day, you're likely to find the steps filled with office workers eating lunch and street performers taking advantage of a captive audience. Open Monday through Wednesday, 10 A.M. to 9 P.M., Thursday through Saturday, 10 A.M. to 6 P.M. (221-7676).

That portion of Fifth between 42nd and 34th streets is distinguished mainly for two department stores, **Lord & Taylor,** and **Altman's.** It is because of the **Empire State Building** (see Priorities) that this otherwise uninteresting area is on everyone's agenda. The primary feature of the New York skyline since it was completed in 1931, the Empire State Building rises 1,250 feet. Before the tower's completion, the general public was concerned about its stability, but—except for the dirigible mooring that proved a bad idea—there can be no doubt that this building is successful (some suicides and a plane crash around the 78th floor notwithstanding). Somehow architects Shreve, Lamb, and Harmon managed to design a suitably imposing structure that doesn't oppress the street.

There are two observation decks, one open on the 86th floor, one glass-enclosed on the 102nd. Hours for both are 9:30 A.M. to midnight daily (736-3100).

While staring up at the Empire State Building, think about this: It was right on 34th Street that Mrs. Astor had her huge brownstone. (Remember, this was in the 1880s when no one ever went above 42nd Street except to picnic.) Mrs. Astor's nephew, William *Waldorf* Astor, after unsuccessfully wrestling for society leadership with his aunt, tore down his mansion next door and built, horror of horrors, a hotel. How better to devalue her property than to have the estimable Mrs. Astor reside next door to a motley crew of transients. (In those days, anybody who was anybody stayed with a relative rather than at a hotel.) Mrs. Astor, finding herself next door to the Waldorf Hotel, decided to go to her nephew one better. First, she moved all the way up to 65th and Fifth. Then, her son built the fiercely competitive Astoria Hotel right next to the Waldorf Hotel. (Can you guess what's coming next?) Eventually, both hotels were run under the same management, until 1929 when they were demolished in order to make way for the Empire State Building. (See Hotels, Waldorf-Astoria.)

The Real Genuine Authentic Waldorf Salad Recipe

Created by the legendary maître d', Oscar Tschirky, otherwise known as Oscar of the Waldorf, for the first charity ball held in America.

> 4 apples (peeled, cored, and diced)
> Juice from half a lemon
> ¾ cup diced celery
> ¾ cup mayonnaise
> ¼ cup chopped walnuts
> Lettuce

Place diced apples in a bowl and squeeze lemon over them. Add diced celery and mayonnaise to apples and mix all ingredients thoroughly. Chill mixture and serve on any type of lettuce. Sprinkle with walnuts. Serves six.

LOWER FIFTH AVENUE

Once you leave the Empire State Building, Fifth becomes impossibly boring for quite a stretch. The avenue has narrowed, both physically and mentally. There are blocks that are downright tacky and you have better things to do with your time. The one exception is the **Flatiron Building** on the corner of 23rd and Fifth. Originally the Fuller Building, its distinctive triangular design reminded people of a flatiron and the nickname stuck. Only six feet wide at one end, the building is a major architectural treat: an Italian Renaissance *palazzo* façade over the wackiest layout since the pyramids.

"23 Skiddoo!"

Rumor has it that the phrase originated with policemen trying to keep traffic moving at the base of the Flatiron Building on 23rd Street. Men stood there to watch women's skirts being blown by the wind current created by the building's design. "23 Skiddoo!" the police would shout.

This is not a particularly fertile stretch on Fifth. Things don't improve dramatically until you've reached 14th Street. However, given the slim pickings, you might wish to drop into **Barnes & Noble** (105 Fifth Avenue at 18th Street; 807-0099) where they stock more textbooks than you can remember carrying to school. Right across the street is their huge sale annex. Dedicated booklovers can spend an entire day between the two stores. **Folklorica** (89 Fifth Avenue between 16th and 17th streets; 255-2525) may not have the best bargains in town but the variety is staggering. You'll find crafts and clothing from South America, Africa, and the Orient. **B. Shackman & Co.** (85 Fifth Avenue between 16th and 17th streets; 989-5162) is the ideal place for stocking stuffers. Since 1898, they've been selling favors and novelties that are wonderful for the child in all of us.

The lower end of Fifth, below 14th Street, belongs more properly to Greenwich Village. Unless you're planning to visit the village, stop where you are.

UPPER FIFTH AVENUE

It's above 59th Street that Fifth makes the transition from commercial concourse to residential boulevard. You could drop down out of the air on almost any block between 59th and 96th to find your basic blue-chip doorman standing beneath your basic blue-chip canopied entrance. With rare exception, the large apartment houses on Fifth are understated to the point of monotony.

What makes this section of Fifth a must for visitors is the liberal sprinkling of museums that's resulted in Museum Mile, a grouping of cultural institutions between 82nd and 104th streets. The upper end of Fifth is reached easily via Madison Avenue buses and taxis that are one block east of Fifth.

El Museo del Barrio is devoted to the art and culture of Puerto Rico and South America. Barrio is a term for the Hispanic ghetto that shares space in what was once exclusively black Harlem. The museum is for many Hispanic New Yorkers, a major cultural bond with their heritage. For others, it is an opportunity to expand their appreciation of these cultures via lectures, films, concerts, and exhibits.

The museum's address is 1230 Fifth Avenue (at 104th Street); 831-7272. Open Wednesday through Sunday, 11 A.M. to 5 P.M. Suggested contribution: $2; $1, students and seniors.

Museum of the City of New York was originally located in Gracie Mansion, but was moved in 1930 because the mansion wasn't fireproof. It says something about New York's regard for politicians that the mansion was declared fit as a fiddle for use as the official residence of the mayor. So it has remained ever since. Meanwhile, back at the museum you'll find as loving a collection of New York memorabilia as anyone has ever gathered. There are models and dioramas chronicling the city's growth from its beginnings as a Dutch outpost in the New World. Laced with theatrical mementos, taped city sounds, historical paintings, and period rooms, it's the perfect place to wander before setting forth. Check with the desk about their walking tours. The museum's address is Fifth Avenue at 103rd Street; 534-1672. Open Tuesday through Saturday, 10 A.M. to 5 P.M.; Sunday 1 P.M. to 5 P.M. $3 suggested contribution.

While on your way to the **International Center of Photography,** take a peek down the block on 97th Street at the Russian Orthodox Cathedral of St. Nicholas, with its gorgeously anachronistic onion domes. The Center, a must for shutterbugs, changes exhibits to focus either on a photographer or a type of photograph. You'll find programs and workshops on everything you've always wanted to know from aesthetics to technique, from the 19th century to now, and from masters like Cartier-Bresson to emerging talents. The gift shop has posters, books, and catalogs.

The center is at 1130 Fifth Avenue (at 94th Street); 860-1777. Open Tuesday, noon to 8 P.M.; Wednesday through Friday, noon to 5 P.M.; Saturday through Sunday, 11 A.M. to 6 P.M. $2.50 admission; $1, students and seniors. Free admission on Tuesday from 5 P.M. to 8 P.M.

The Jewish Museum, under the aegis of the Jewish Theological Seminary of America, houses the most extensive collection of Judaica in the world, ranging from coins and medals to books, manuscripts, ceremonial objects, folk art, and a permanent exhibit focusing on Biblical archaeology. Both contemporary and historical themes are highlighted in a variety of educational programs. Modern artists such as Jasper Johns, Louise Nevelson, Modigliani, Chagall, and Lipchitz have all been represented here. Special exhibits cover the range of Jewish experience.

1109 Fifth Avenue (at 92nd Street); 860-1888. Open Monday, Wednesday, Thursday, noon to 5 P.M.; Tuesday, noon to 8 P.M.; Sunday, 11 A.M. to 6 P.M. $4 admission; $2, students and seniors. Free admission on Tuesday from 5 P.M. to 8 P.M.

The **Cooper-Hewitt Museum** is the Smithsonian Institution's National Museum of Design, located since 1976 in Andrew Carnegie's landmark mansion. Philanthropist Peter Cooper's granddaughters, the Hewitt girls, founded the collection that today spans three thousand years of design history and includes drawings, prints, textiles, furniture, metal- and woodworks, ceramics, glass, and wallpaper. One of the world's preeminent design archives, the museum has permanent holdings of some 170,000 objects, displayed on a rotating basis. The library contains more than fifty thousand books and a large picture collection.

The address: 2 East 91st Street; 860-6868. Open Tuesday, 10 A.M. to 9 P.M.; Wednesday through Saturday, 10 A.M. to 5 P.M.; Sunday, noon to 5 P.M. $3 admission, $1.50, students and seniors. Free admission on Tuesday from 5 P.M. to 9 P.M.

The **Guggenheim Museum,** designed by Frank Lloyd Wright, has been controversial since the day it opened in 1959. Architects are still arguing over whether it is, as described by masterbuilder Philip Johnson, "the most beautiful building in New York," or a bun, or a snail, or an upside-down beehive, or an insult to art. The only thing most people do seem to agree on is that the interior of the building is more successful as a work of art in itself than as a gallery for paintings. An elitist dilemma if ever we heard one. Europeans consider the Guggie one of the most beautiful buildings in the city, a truly successful piece of environmental sculpture. Put your preconceptions on hold and go. Take the elevator to the top and curl your way down. Between the art and the architecture, you'll have an unforgettable experience.

The collection includes some five thousand paintings, sculptures, and drawings that date from the Impressionists to the present. Exhibits change frequently but you're bound to find one of your favorite superstars represented: Van Gogh, Kandinsky, Klee, Léger, Chagall, Degas, Renoir, et al.

1071 Fifth Avenue (88th to 89th Street); 360-3513. Open Tuesday, 11 A.M. to 7:45 P.M.; Wednesday through Sunday, 11 A.M. to 4:45 P.M. $4 admission; $2, students and seniors.

The Metropolitan Museum of Art provides a dynamic finale to Museum Mile. It is, as one critic put it rather prosaically, "the supermarket of American museums." No matter. You can find almost anything you want here from primitives to Picasso, from a Chinese garden to an Egyptian tomb to a Viennese palace to a Manhattan mansion. The Met is the largest museum in the country—fourth in the world after the British Museum, the Hermitage, and the Louvre. It is impossible, due to its size, to see it all in a day, or even a week.

Here's what to do. Stand across the street on Fifth Avenue. Enjoy the neo-Renaissance or Ruskinian Gothic or Beaux-Arts façade (depending what you read) with its fountains, pillars, and flocks of nouveau culture vultures hanging out on the Met's steps as their first commitment to art for art's sake. Walk around them carefully as you enter the museum and surrender all your aesthetics to the expansive grandeur of the Great Hall with its domed ceilings and circular skylights. Before you lose your senses, this is where to check the latest information on current exhibits and perhaps even find a lecture of interest scheduled.

The Met's gift shops are more fun than the Horchow and L.L. Bean catalogs combined. You can do all your Christmas shopping here, or at the very least, find a treasure chest of "only in New York" gifts to take back home.

The museum is at Fifth Avenue and 82nd Street; 535-7710. Open Tuesday 9:30 A.M. to 8:45 P.M.; Wednesday through Sunday 9:30 A.M. to 5:15 P.M. Closed Monday. $5, suggested admission; $2.50, students and seniors.

In the Met, Be Sure Not to Miss

- **Rockefeller Collection of Primitive Art**—the collection as well as the display is unlike that in any other museum.
- **Rembrandts and Goyas** for the country's quintessential collections of these artists.
- **Impressionist collection,** especially the series of Van Goghs, including paintings valued at over $50 million each.
- **Lila Acheson Wallace Wing,** with one of the best Paul Klee collections in the country—important contemporary art that is as majestic in size as it is in scope. Included is Andy Warhol's last self-portrait, a Marisol life-size wood sculpture of The Last Supper, and some super superrealists. You'll also find here a collection of modern furniture that offers a history of the genre.
- **The Lehman Pavilion,** a transplant of rooms from the Lehman Mansion that includes the smallest of details from woodwork, doorknobs, and fireplaces to the extraordinary collection of art and *objets d'art* ranging from medieval to modern times.
- **The Japanese Collection,** housed around an inner court with a garden which includes woodblock prints, screens, kimonos, and an audio-visual experience in a contemporary Japanese crafted environment.
- **The Temple of Dendur**— a three-dimensional environmental experience.
- **The Chinese Collection,** boasting one of the world's major holdings of porcelain, screens, and scrolls.

Everyone loves **The Frick Collection** because the Frick does its best not to let you know it's a museum. The block-long mansion is in the style of Louis the Something-or-Other, a château you might expect to come upon in the French countryside rather than on Fifth. The charade here is that you're simply wandering through the Frick Mansion in which Henry Clay Frick, steel magnate, robber baron, partner of Andrew Carnegie, sequestered his Duveen-selected art collection rather than expose them to the pollution of Pittsburgh.

The Frick, then, is a double-whammy treat. Not only do you get to see how the mega-rich lived, but what they lived with: Mrs. Frick's living room is fully outfitted with eye-popping furniture as well as an El Greco here and a couple of Titians there. The Frick, probably the only show in town that's manageable in a single visit, is an art lesson and a history lesson all wrapped up in one gorgeous, not-to-be missed package.

The address is 1 East 70th Street; 288-0700. Open Tuesday through Saturday, 10 A.M. to 6 P.M.; Sunday 1 P.M. to 6 P.M. $2 admission; $.50, students and seniors; $3 on Sunday.

57TH STREET

The Street That Dares to Cross Fifth Avenue

If we had to select one street (not avenue) that best exemplified New York, it would be 57th. From its grungy west end to posh Sutton Place, it highlights all the intellectual, sometimes pretentious, occasionally ugly, and highly creative aspects of the city. After a walk on 57th you feel as though you've really been someplace. And you have.

On the presumption that everything west of Broadway is best left to the locals, our irreverent tour (including selected art galleries) begins at

Coliseum Books, 1771 Broadway (757-8381), has a large selection of discount and remaindered books as well as one of the best paperback sections in town.

Hard Rock Café, 221 West 57th (489-6565), most likely has the wittiest canopy in town: half a Cadillac over the entrance. You'll also find the Hard Rock Store next store selling T-shirts and other instantly forgettable memorabilia (see Restaurants).

Carnegie Hall, 881 Seventh Avenue (247-7800), is still the grandest concert hall in New York, especially after undergoing its recent facelift. The acoustics here are the closest you can get to Mt. Olympus. Tchaikovsky was guest conductor during opening week ceremonies.

Uncle Sam's Umbrella Shop, 161 West 57th (247-7163), will keep you singin' in the rain. They're all handmade from small folding jobs to huge doorman-sized varieties. Also canes and walking sticks.

The Russian Tea Room, 150 West 57th (265-0947), is neither Russian nor a tea room but is as much a part of the New York environment as the Empire State Building (see Restaurants).

Stack's Rare Coins, 123 West 57th (582-2580), is one place where they may take a wooden nickel. Numismatists throughout the world have been flipping over Stack's since 1858.

Sidney Janis Gallery, 110 West 57th (586-0110), features European and American modern art.

Allan Frumkin, 50 West 57th (757-6655), is a gallery with an emphasis on east and west coast figurative artists.

Kennedy Gallery, 40 West 57th (541-9600), displays work by American artists.

Marlborough Gallery, 40 West 57th (541-4900)—mixed styles, various media, 19th- and 20th-century artists.

Rizzoli, 31 West 57th (759-2424), is as close as you'll get to Italian elegance without crossing a border. Perhaps the most sumptuous digs for a bookstore that you're likely to find.

Fischbach Gallery, 29 West 57th (759-2345)—modern American painters.

Tibor de Nagy, 41 West 57th (421-3780)—sculpture and nonobjective art.

Associated American Artists, 20 West 57th (399-5510)—etchings, lithographs, serigraphs by new and established American artists.

Blum/Helman Galleries, 20 West 57th (245-2888)—American and European contemporary painting and sculpture.

Charivari Ltd., 16–18 West 57th (333-4040), is the sleekest, most downtown (in many ways) shop in this 14K gold chain.

Henri Bendel, 10 West 57th (247-1100), has super styles for the super-thin and super-rich. If you've decided to redo yourself from stem to stern, this is the place to come. (Bear in mind, however, that most people have pretty good stems even before they set foot in the store.) The premises are totally New York, ever-changing, and despite being a tad less distinctive and avant-garde since it was taken over by The Limited, it still sets trends for the needy trendy. Good ladies' rooms, too.

The Sharper Image, 4 West 57th (265-2550), is the catalog store to end all catalog stores. Everything is right there for instant gratification.

The Corner of 57th Street and Fifth Avenue is well worth a few moments. Stand in front of **Bergdorf's** and then cross over to **Tiffany's.** Look up and down the avenue. It doesn't get much more New York than this, except perhaps at night when the buildings are lit up.

Bonwit Teller, 4 East 57th (593-3333), used to be where Trump Tower is today. Always an elegant specialty shop in the guise of a department store, it has reappeared in an abbreviated but no less stylish version. Not to be missed for great designer costume jewelry and evening clothes.

Chanel, 5 East 57th (355-5050), serves hot Coco all year round. Karl Lagerfeld, having taken over helm and hem, serves up a dollop of drama along with the drop-dead chic of the little wool suit.

David Webb, 7 East 57th (421-3030), designed treasures for the Duchess of Windsor, and his namesake store is still turning out fabled jewels for fabled people.

Burberry's, 9 East 57th (371-5010), has the most beautiful bundles from Britain. In addition to the famous raincoat that defies the London fog, there are four floors of Burberry plaid for him and her. Luggage to match.

Hermès, 11 East 57th (751-3181), is yet another French connection, this time with some of the most expensive (and wonderful) leathers and perfumes in the world. (All those H's are for the hundreds and hundreds you can spend here.)

James Robinson, 15 East 57th (752-6166), has English antique silver, bone china, and jewelry for the fastidious collector accustomed to one-of-a-kind price tags. *The* place to go if you're determined to find that silver lining.

Wally Findlay Galleries, 17 East 57th (421-5390), spotlights European and American artists.

Laura Ashley, 21 East 57th (752-7300), offers little-girl styles for little girls of all ages. All the romance of Victorian England is sewn up in a classic Laura Ashley dress. There are fabrics, linens, and perfumes to complete the picture.

Pace Gallery, 32 East 57th (421-3292)—modern and contemporary artists' works. Adjoining galleries have prints and primitive art.

Victoria's Secret, 34 East 57th (758-5592), is out of the bag for anyone who loves giving or wearing luxurious lingerie and lounge clothes. The store itself is equally sumptuous and filled with good scents. Some designer undies for men as well.

André Emmerich Gallery, 41 East 57th (752-0124)—contemporary and pre-Columbian.

Marisa del Re Gallery, 41 East 57th (688-1843)—shows European and American painting, abstract art.

Pierre Matisse Gallery, 41 East 57th (355-6269)—for modern European art.

Robert Miller Gallery, 41 East 57th (980-5454)—has contemporary art.

Hammer Galleries, 33 East 57th (644-4400)—19th- and 20th-century European and American artists.

Louis Vuitton, 51 East 57th (371-6111), is the place to go for a double dose of LV's on everything from key chains to steamer trunks, although why anyone would want to use a perfect stranger's initials is beyond us.

Mitsukoshi, 461 Park Avenue (935-6444)—upstairs is a shop for Japanese pottery, and downstairs is a sushi bar and restaurant. Reserve a place at the small bar but be prepared for a good-size tab.

S.J. Shrubsole, 104 East 57th (753-8920), has marvelous antique British silver that would leave even Henry Higgins at a loss for words.

The Galleria, 119 East 57th (751-7474), is a seven-story public "galleria" above which are luxury apartments. You can walk through the arcade and exit on 58th Street. There's a café for dining, too.

Place des Antiquaires, 125 East 57th (758-2900), is a collection of—dare we call them—"shops" that are so highbrow the landlord offers free lectures on fine and decorative arts. Descending into this place is like going down into King Tut's tomb. The merchandise on display is priceless enough that you almost expect to be charged admission.

Hammacher Schlemmer, 147 East 57th (421-9000), is basically an entire department store for gadgets priced anywhere from a few dollars to a few thousand. Electric shoe-shiners, exercycles, ice-cream machines—everything that's sold is tested by the Hammacher Schlemmer Institute so you can be sure your cuckoo clock is perfectly sane.

Lillian Nassau, 220 East 57th (759-6062), has the other big Tiffany collection on 57th Street, but this is Tiffany art glass from the past. Even if you're not a collector, it's worth a trip to see this Technicolor wonderland.

Midtown

Ever since Hollywood first used those opening shots of Manhattan skyscrapers and bustling crowds to set the scene for a movie in New York, everyone's image of the city has been midtown. Can you hear "Rhapsody in Blue" on the sound track? You remember the scene: well-dressed people, all hurrying off to make a big deal or meet the most important person in the world.

Midtown Manhattan. Pure magic. The East Side shops are filled with fantasies that money can buy, and the West Side theaters with priceless dreams. The streets in-between form the grid for a board game named "Power." This is where some people come to work and others come to play and the really big winners (those for whom there's no difference between work and play) come to live. What gives midtown its incredible energy is that everyone you see is actively pursuing a success story.

MIDTOWN EAST

East of Fifth Avenue, from 59th Street down to 34th, is where you'll find some of the city's most exclusive residences (see Sutton Place, Beekman Place, Murray Hill, and Good Old Turtle Bay) as well as the great commercial buildings in which New Yorkers earn the fortunes they need to pay the rent. The streets are not ripe with chic shops or little bistros. They are, instead, bursting with high hopes. No visit to New York would be complete without a brief walk along Madison or Third avenues just to keep in step with the high kickers. It should be noted that the pulse you feel on Fifth Avenue is New York

East 60th Street
Bloomingdales
East 59th Street
Roosevelt Island Tram

General Motors Building

Chanel Burberry's
Louis Vuitton

Trump Tower
Bonwit Teller
AT&T Building

East 57th Street

East 55th Street

Fifth Avenue
Madison Avenue
Park Avenue
Second Avenue
First Avenue

Citicorp Building
East 53rd Street

Franklin D. Roosevelt Drive

St. Bartholomew's Church

St. Patrick's Cathedral

East 50th Street

Waldorf-Astoria

Lexington Avenue
Third Avenue
Second Avenue

East 46th Street

United Nations

Brooks Brothers

Helmsley Building
Pan Am Building

East 44th Street

First Avenue

Chrysler Building

East 42nd Street

Daily News Building

East River

Grand Central Station
Manhattan Air Terminal

Madison Avenue

East 40th Street

Lexington Avenue
Third Avenue
Second Avenue

East 37th Street

Park Avenue South

Pierpont Morgan Library

Franklin D. Roosevelt Drive

Fifth Avenue

B. Altman & Co.

East 34th Street

East 33rd Street

N

MIDTOWN EAST

0 yards 440
0 meters 400

Plus: the plus is all the visitors and shoppers. For a whiff of pure New York, go east, young man. Go east.

Madison Avenue

Most famous for being the business address of *The Man in the Gray Flannel Suit,* midtown Madison is no longer inhabited solely by ad agency Type-A pre-cardiac patients. More pragmatic communicators, like IBM and AT&T, have settled in where CBS (now on Sixth Avenue), Random House (now near Third Avenue), and *Look* magazine (now a memory) once held court.

One of the most hotly discussed buildings in New York is **AT&T Headquarters** (550 Madison Avenue), between 55th and 56th streets, which people either love or hate. A daring structure brilliantly designed by Philip Johnson and John Burgee, it has aroused passions with its Chippendale top and the open Romanesque colonnade at its base, houses one of the city's most unusual public spaces. The famous statue of Golden Boy was taken from the top of AT&T's old downtown building, regilded, and set in place right inside the lobby.

The **AT&T Infoquest Center** (605-5555) is adjacent and offers a free exhibit that explores Information Age technologies (lightwave communications, microelectronics, and computer software). Open Tuesday through Sunday.

In the event you're a dedicated foodie, the highly praised and highly expensive restaurant, **The Quilted Giraffe** (593-1221), is in an arcade behind the public space. Right next store is **The Quilted Giraffe Take-Out.**

The **Villard Houses** between 50th and 51st streets were built in 1885 for Henry Villard, founder of the Northern Pacific Railroad, and were later shared by Random House and the Archdiocese of New York (St. Patrick's Cathedral is right across the street). Then, in one of the strangest bedfellow deals in recent memory, they were sold to Harry Helmsley and "incorporated" into his Helmsley Palace Hotel (455 Madison), which rises like a Phoenix (strictly Arizona) behind the graceful Florentine Renaissance *palazzo* styling of the original façades.

Crouch and Fitzgerald (400 Madison) has all the fine old luggage names and an excellent collection of women's handbags and accessories. **F.R. Tripler** (366 Madison) was established in 1886 and is still selling fine men's clothing. The measure of the Madison Avenue man, however, is still **Brooks Brothers** (346 Madison), which has been in style since 1818. Synonymous with the "Ivy" look and button-down shirts, it is probably least well known for the fact that Abraham Lincoln was wearing a Brooks Brothers suit the night he was shot.

Once past 42nd Street Madison dissolves into Murray Hill.

Park Avenue

59th and Park is one of our favorite corners. At 502 Park, you'll find two legends headquartered side-by-side. First, there's **Regine's** (826-0990), the chic French disco that's recently added a delicious bonus in the person of superchef Michel Fitoussi who makes his own music in the kitchen. Then, there's **Christie's** (546-1000), the fine-arts auction house that has been making headlines for over two hundred years. Be sure to check the papers for pre-sale exhibits: there's no more New Yorkish way to spend an afternoon than browsing and perhaps bidding on some of those goodies you see in museums but aren't ever up for grabs.

On the same block as the Japanese restaurant **Mitsukoshi** (461 Park Avenue, 935-6444), is one of the city's true finds, the **Akbar** (475 Park Avenue, 838-1717), a first-rate Indian restaurant with prices that would be low even in the Bronx (there's a prix-fixe lunch for under $15).

The **Mercedes-Benz showroom** at 430 Park is more notable as being the first New York work by Frank Lloyd Wright. Park continues downtown attracting business headquarters because of the cachet attached to its name. You'll find more lawyers here than at a twenty-car pile-up on the highway.

St. Bartholomew's Church, between 50th and 51st streets, is located on a piece of land that formerly housed the Schaefer Brewing Company back in the late 1800s when this part of Park Avenue was nearly on the outskirts of the city. Back then it had railroad tracks and was a desirable location only for brewers and manufacturers. Tunneling the trains didn't happen until the early 1900s, when people began taking Park seriously. St. Bart's is one of the avenue's oldest structures and certainly its most Byzantine. The salmon-colored exterior bricks were handmade and the ornate portico is by Stanford White.

If you've heard of New York, you've heard of the Waldorf. The **Waldorf-Astoria Hotel** (see Hotels) takes up the entire city block from 49th to 50th streets and from Park to Lexington avenues. It also takes up a whole lot of New York's social history. From the day it opened, October 1, 1931, in the midst of the Great Depression, the Waldorf has been making news right along with some of the most notable tenants in its lofty towers: Herbert Hoover, Frank Sinatra, the Duke and Duchess of Windsor, and Cole Porter. Despite an Edwardian renovation that removed some of the Art Deco chic, the public rooms are a sight for anyone's sore eyes.

The former New York Central Building on 46th Street was built in 1929 as a coda to the avenue (it stands behind Grand

Central Station and faces uptown) and has become **The Helmsley Building** without any loss to its former self. It is a lovely structure, daunted only by the monolithic, ugly, and intrusive **Pan Am Building** (200 Park Avenue), that squeezed itself in behind the New York Central Building.

This version of Park Avenue effectively ceases at the entrance to The Helmsley Building. The Park Avenue that continues on the other side of Grand Central Station is legally Park Avenue but is more identifiable with its Murray Hill location than its uptown provenance. Of note, however, is **Philip Morris Headquarters** (120 Park Avenue; 880-5000), the gray granite building across from Grand Central, because it houses **Whitney Midtown,** a branch of the Whitney Museum (see Upper East Side) that features a sculpture court with 20th-century American sculpture and an adjacent gallery for rotating exhibits. Open Monday through Saturday from 11 A.M. to 6 P.M.; admission is free.

Lexington Avenue

If you need us to tell you that **Bloomingdale's** is on the corner of 59th Street and Lexington, where have you been? The most important retail establishment since the souvenir counter at Lourdes, Bloomie's is the classic example of being in the right place at the right time. The scoop here is that Lyman Bloomingdale worked at a store in New Jersey with Benjamin *Altman* and Abraham *Abraham* (who overcame his parents' practical joke and finally tied up with Mr. *Straus*). Lyman teamed up with his brother Joseph and after a couple of moves, found themselves on 59th and Third in the shadow of the Third Avenue El (the New York train system was *ele*-vated before it went underground and became a subway—you can still ride els in Brooklyn, the Bronx, and Queens).

When the Third Avenue El came down in 1954, the East Side suddenly became a "hot" location. Bloomingdale's, which had been a very lower middle-class store, changed its image more rapidly than a chameleon on a rainbow. Quite literally, people thronged to Bloomingdale's on a weekly basis just to keep up with the latest in fashion and house furnishings. It was, in the late fifties and into the sixties, a happening. You met everyone you ever knew at Bloomie's, you ate at Bloomie's, and the store even had its own jail for shoplifters.

Alas, the tail began to wag the dog. The boutique concept coupled with the designer-label craze turned a truly distinctive department store into little shops of horrors. Bloomingdale's is still tops, but it has become the "anti-Christ" of department stores: It is more fashionable these days to complain about Bloomingdale's than to adore it. No matter, its publicity people are brilliant at making eagerly awaited events out of each new store promotion. They could make the Black Plague seem trendy. By all means go.

The stretch down Lexington from 59th to the Citicorp Center between 53rd and 54th is six blocks in search of a character. There's nothing of major import here, lots of small stores selling indifferent merchandise and grab-a-bite snack shops that ought to be passed as quickly as possible. Things literally look up at 54th with the white aluminum **Citicorp Center** that tops off with a slanted 45-degree roof that can't be missed as part of the cityscape.

Since 1977, **The Market at Citicorp Center** (559-9992) has offered New Yorkers a midtown shopping mall complete with some better-than-usual food possibilities plus some offbeat shopping. However, you don't have to do either to enjoy the multi-storied atrium space for its free concerts, movies, and exhibits. And good public bathrooms.

There are tables and chairs for brown-baggers or those, like us, who stop in at the Scandinavian deli, **Nyborg and Nelson,** for some herring, super fresh salad, and black bread to munch in the atrium during a concert.

Among the most notable shops in the Citicorp Center is a branch of **Conran's** for impeccable housewares, and **Pan American Phoenix** for Mexican pottery, glassware, jewelry, and clothes.

Caswell-Massey at 48th Street (755-2254) is understandably proud of being the oldest pharmacy in the United States and is the only drugstore we've ever been to that has crystal chandeliers and carved-wood paneling. They sell their own line of products, including the cologne favored by George Washington, as well as imported soaps and toiletries. You can get your prescriptions filled here, too, which is sure to make you feel better.

With the very notable exception of the fabulous **Chrysler Building** (see Priorities), which was the world's tallest building for one year and is still an outstanding example of 1930s Art Deco architecture, Lexington loses its cachet the closer it gets to Grand Central Station. You will find some discount camera stores that often have excellent buys—if you really know what you're buying.

Grand Central Terminal at 42nd Street is outstanding as a work of engineering, as well as for its Renaissance-style architecture. There are two levels of tracks to accommodate more than five hundred trains daily. Its main concourse is one of the largest rooms in the world.

By the time Lexington reaches the lower forties, it's passionately into its Murray Hill mode (see below), almost as a last-ditch effort to avoid the low thirties and upper twenties where it becomes (dare we say it?) ethnic: lots of quiet little Indian restaurants and neighborhood shops.

Third Avenue

Third, like Sixth Avenue on the West Side, is an urban Cinderella story. Most people who haven't been to New York recently still retain the "toidy-toid and toid" image of an avenue made infamous in the alcoholic nightmares of the movie *The Lost Weekend*. By the mid-fifties, with all traces of the El gone, Third Avenue turned around faster than a pickpocket in a crowd. Once the domain of derelicts and pawnbrokers, the creepy crawly caterpillar sprouted wings. Purely commercial wings, to be sure. The tenements are long gone and in their place, barely distinguishable from one another, are the generic office buildings that finally made the area respectable.

Opposite the Third Avenue entrance to Bloomie's is **Papaya King** (1545 Third Ave.), one of the best fast-food chains in town. (There's another one at 86th and Third.) A fresh juice bar (our favorite is the coconut "champagne") that's well-known also for top-quality frankfurters.

This part of Third is movie heaven (or, on a Saturday night, with the lines of movie fans—movie hell). There are four theaters alone between 59th and 60th, with others tucked away in the downtown cross-streets. You wouldn't be the first person to have a terrific New York day by wandering through Bloomies, stopping at Papaya King for a hot dog and fruit drink, and then recuperating at an early movie.

If you're the type who judges a meal on the basis of how much you couldn't finish, **Dine-O-Mat** on Third and 57th St. is a trendy eatery for the Pump Boys and Dinette set. Run by Horn & Hardart, it's a combination diner and luncheonette with booths, old schoolroom lamps, neon, and artifacts from the 1950s. The portions are huge, the prices are very reasonable, and although the food doesn't live up to its claims of recapturing the beloved Automat cuisine of our youth, it's worth a visit just to watch the entire staff and gather to do a musical number.

P.J. Clarke's (see Restaurants) should be approached from the other side of Third Ave. It's on 55th St. and is perhaps most notable for being the bar used in *The Lost Weekend*.

As you head down Third, the architecture becomes somewhat nervous, as though everyone decided to rebel against the glass-and-metal skyscrapers by diverting your attention. There are funky ground-level plazas and yet another atrium and even a building by Philip Johnson that's been nicknamed the "lipstick" building. You won't have any trouble finding it.

If you're a serious kitchen person, and find it hard to believe anything could begin to compete with the Williams-Sonoma catalog, head for **Bridge Kitchenware** (214 East 52nd Street; 688-4220) for the ne plus ultra in cooking equipment. This is where the pros go and once you open the door, you'll know why. The staff doesn't hesitate to give opinions and even if you walk out empty-handed, you won't leave empty-headed.

🐎 We admit it: we're suckers for popcorn. **Jack's Corn Crib** (700 Third Ave.; 370-4480) is a tiny store popping with customers who can't decide which of the whacky varieties to order—jalapeño popcorn, or strawberry or cheese or butterscotch.

The **Horn & Hardart Automat** (200 East 42nd St.; 599-1665) is the last gasp for a chain of cafeterias that raised a generation of kids. When dinosaurs roamed the earth and there were no Burger Kings, there was an Automat that made going out a family event. The deal was that a cashier (in a marble booth) changed your dollar into nickels and for twenty nickels you could eat like a king. Even if you weren't a king, you could sit all day over a five-cent cup of coffee. And if times were really bad, you could help yourself to some hot water in a cup, add some ketchup, and *voilà!*—H&H tomato soup.

The fun of the Automat was to put your nickels in a slot next to the sandwich or danish or casserole of your dreams and watch the little glass window pop open. Okay, so they won't take nickels anymore (it costs $.75 for each token) and your dreams are more upscale than a young broker. But there's still a wall of little glass windows and they still have dolphin head spiggots that spit out coffee heavily flavored with déjà-vu.

Large generic office buildings continue for a few blocks down Third, after which the avenue becomes a proper residential area that isn't particularly exciting for visitors.

Second Avenue

The major sight at 59th and Second is traffic, traffic, traffic, as cars pile onto and off of the Queensboro Bridge totally unaware of passing over Sutton Place while en route to Long Island City (Queens). However, if you take a ride on the overhead bright red **Roosevelt Island tram** (think cable car), the traffic actually looks good.

Roosevelt (formerly Welfare) Island was reconceived as a "new town" way back in the 1970s, an urban utopia with no cars. A people-place to live in the middle of the East River with smashing views of the East Side skyline. We'll stick to a tram ride at night on the Rube Goldberg-esque tinkertoy. Located between 59th and 60th streets on Second Avenue, it does not run all night (Monday through Friday, 6 A.M. to 2 A.M.; Saturday through Sunday 6 A.M. to 3 A.M.). Leaves every 15 minutes. You'll need a subway token each way.

❦ **Le Steak** (1089 Second; 421-9072) is an old standby for those who adore French-style steak with frites just like Mama used to make. The thin-cut beef is served with a light mustard sauce, a top-drawer salad, and lots of crisp *pommes frites*. Dessert (try *la surprise de Monique,* made with chestnuts and walnuts) is included in the $19.95 prix-fixe dinner.

Fossner-Timepieces (1059 Second; 980-1099) will not only repair golden-oldies, but they'll make Grandpa's pocketwatch into a trendy wristwatch. What really makes this place tick is its huge vintage watch collection. While you're feeling nostalgic, head for the **Manhattan Art & Antiques Center** (1050 Second; 355-4400), which is open Monday through Saturday from 10:30 A.M. to 6:30 P.M., and Sundays from noon to 6 P.M. You could spend the entire week here. There are three levels of shops. The main floor is heavy on jewelry and silver with the two lower levels covering everything from china to furniture to glass and beyond. A favorite beyond is on the second concourse, the Hemingway African Gallery.

❦ If you like David's Cookies (need we ask?), then imagine what food pro David Liederman would do with his own French restaurant. The answer is found at **Chez Louis** (1016 Second Ave.; 752-1400), an affectionate *hommage* to Paris's famed L'ami Louis restaurant. Pure bistro cuisine (every critic has raved about the roast chicken and potatoes).

Still in the fifties, **Winston House** (997 Second Avenue; 752-2665) has an unusual collection of primitive art and antiques from all over the world. Museum quality with prices to match. Most of Second Avenue is wall-to-wall restaurants and apartment buildings and unless you're heading for a real New York steak at The Palm (see Restaurants), you might as well take the bus down to 42nd Street.

Movie buffs will recognize the **Daily News Building** (220 East 42nd Street), a milestone of Art Deco architecture, as the model for the "Daily Planet" headquarters in the *Superman* series. Recessed and revolving in the lobby is the world's largest indoor globe.

❦ There's a really snazzy little restaurant in the building called **"Extra! Extra!"** (767 Second Ave.; 490-2900) that's a hot place for news hounds from the *Daily News,* as well as anyone with printer's ink in their blood. The scoop here is the super-crisp fried calamari, the pizzas, and (if you must) carrot fettuccine with veal. Prices run from $5.95 to $16.75. You get the headlines on the walls and the ink blots on the floor for free.

Don't bother venturing any farther down Second because it quickly turns into an access route for the Queens Midtown Tunnel, which is a rotten thing to do to any avenue.

First Avenue

Tack First Avenue onto your trek down Second Avenue. Turn the corner on Second Avenue and 42nd Street and head east. The **Ford Foundation Building** between First and Second avenues has a 12-story cool, leafy green atrium. This is the atrium against which all others are measured. It's also the most elegant, with one-third of an acre, well over a dozen trees that would be at home in any self-respecting forest.

United Nations Headquarters is located on an 18-acre parcel of land donated by John D. Rockefeller, Jr., now international territory. The U.N.'s signature structure is the Secretariat building. Purposely constructed counter to the city's grid, the 39-story building was New York's first all-glass tower (slabs of white Vermont marble keep the glass in place). The General Assembly building, with its carved roof and central dome, is an integral part of the U.N. profile.

An international team of architects worked on the design, but the most dramatic aspects are credited generally to Le Corbusier, even though he later withdrew from the project. Works of art from all major nations are on display, most notably British sculptor Barbara Hepworth's abstraction dedicated to U.N. secretary-general Dag Hammarskjöld who was killed in a 1961 air crash while on a peace mission in Africa.

Visitors enter on the north side of the General Assembly building (45th Street) through one of seven nickel-bronze doors donated by Canada. Inside the lobby you'll see the Tamayo mural titled "Brotherhood" which was a gift from Mexico, and above you is a Soviet gift—a replica of their 1957 Sputnik. Take note of the Chagall windows in the lobby. Stop at the information desk: There are a limited number of free tickets to open sessions of the General Assembly, which are usually held at 10:30 A.M. and 3:30 P.M.; call 963-1234 in advance. Tours are given every half hour from 9:15 A.M. to 4:45 P.M. ($4.50 for adults; $2.50 for students) and they cover not only the history of the U.N. but also the art collections. Check at the tour desk in the lobby or call 963-7713.

The **U.N. Gift Center** is a place that savvy New Yorkers have been patronizing ever since it opened and not merely because there's no city sales tax. You'll find jewelry, art objects, and handicrafts from member nations sold at very favorable prices. The selection is terrific and if you can't at least find enough to fill a Christmas stocking, surrender your credit cards at the door. Open seven days from 9:15 A.M. to 5:15 P.M.; 963-7700.

🌿 The **Delegates' Dining Room,** with its terrific view of the East River and the U.N. gardens, is open to the public for lunch between 11:30 A.M. and 2:30 P.M. Aside from not knowing who's likely to be powwowing at the next table, the menu keeps changing with a list of international specials from member nations. Buffet

lunches are $15.75; entreés are priced from $11.50 to $17.50.
Reservations (963-7625) are a must.

SUTTON PLACE, BEEKMAN PLACE, MURRAY HILL, AND GOOD OLD TURTLE BAY

A quartet of marginally interesting East Side locales, most notable, these days, for their famous residents: Auntie Mame,
J.P. Morgan, Greta Garbo, and Katharine Hepburn. Be forewarned. You are no more likely to come upon the latter two
than the former.

Sutton Place

Sutton Place, for dedicated pragmatists, is merely the southern end of York Avenue, from 59th down to 53rd Street. For
the rest of us, it's the ultimate arrival area. Built in 1875 it
went relatively unnoticed until J. P. Morgan's daughter set
down stakes at Number 1 Sutton Place nearly fifty years later.
Sutton Place is most posh as it gets closer it gets to the Queensborough Bridge (Simon and Garfunkel's "59th Street
Bridge"). We are talking real wealth here: The folks on Park
Avenue still work for a living. Not so on Sutton where the
co-op board decided a while back that Gloria Vanderbilt was
unsuitable to buy into the building. Must be due to her reces-
sive jeans.

Some of Hollywood's favorite views of New York are from
the cul-de-sacs at the eastern ends of the streets here, notably
the mini-park at the eastern end of 57th Street. The small park
at the river end of 58th Street provides a glorious view of the
bridge overhead, as well as a glance into Riverview Terrace
which may well be the most monied charm in town: a cluster
of brownstones in a uniquely private setting.

Beekman Place

Beekman Place is perhaps the city's pre-eminent residential
boutique. It runs for two blocks, from 49th to 51st streets between First Avenue and the East River. Although officially no
more than a street address, Beekman Place is second only
to the Bowery for instantly identifying the social status of its
tenants. There are some well-manicured town houses here;
otherwise there is nothing to see, since all the rich people
are out spending the interest on their money.

 The **Beekman Tower Bar,** 49th and First, is a good place for
a quiet drink and a view of the city. The voyeur can have some
fun peeking into fabulous apartments across the way.

River House (433 East 52nd Street) is one of New York's most exclusive residences, built in otherwise depressed 1931 with tennis courts, a swimming pool, and even a dock for yachts. Reportedly, this is where the Kissingers live.

Turtle Bay

Turtle Bay (an area from the mid-to upper forties, east of Third Avenue) began coming into its own at the end of the first World War. But it wasn't until the United Nations appeared on the scene in 1947 that the area became its upscale self. The prettiest spot here is the **Turtle Bay Gardens Historic District** (226 to 246 East 49th Street and 227 to 247 East 48th Street), ten houses on each street that are back-to-back with common gardens.

Murray Hill

Murray Hill is located in the general area between 34th to 42nd streets and Madison to Third avenues. It stakes its claim to prominence on a historic incident during the Revolutionary War when Mrs. Murray kept General Howe and the British troops at bay (Kips Bay, specifically) while serving tea slowly enough to allow American troops time to escape uptown. The area became fashionable in the late 1800s by virtue of its rubbing elbows with the Belmonts, Rhinelanders, and the Tiffanys who built along Fifth, Madison, and Park avenues. Not to be left out, J. P. Morgan made his home in the freestanding Italianate brownstone at 231 Madison Avenue (at 37th Street) that was built in 1852. It is currently owned by the Lutheran Church of America. Around the corner is the pink Tennessee marble **Pierpont Morgan Library** (29 East 36th Street, 685-0008; open Tuesday through Saturday, from 10:30 A.M. to 4:45 P.M.; Sunday from 1 P.M. to 4:45 P.M., $3 suggested contribution), where you'll finally have a chance to see a Gutenberg Bible amid what was, in its time, the finest private collection of books in the country. There are drawings, manuscripts, prints, and book bindings on display in rooms that are themselves worth seeing. Don't miss the museum shop.

The area is currently one of the city's low-profile neighborhoods mainly because there isn't much of interest going on here. However, as with a fading floral bouquet, one can still inhale the past. While the "four hundred" kept eyes front to Park and Madison avenues, their drivers were turned toward Third. There still remain today a number of carriage houses in the area, most notably the enclave at 152 East 36th Street called **Sniffen Court.**

A favorite shop in the area is **Astro Minerals** (155 East 34th Street, 889-9000) where you can find everything from gorgeous geodes to African masks, Indonesian carvings, Russian lacquer boxes, and enough jewelry to fill Ali Baba's cave.

Something is always on sale, and especially in the African collection, a bit of discreet bargaining is always tolerated.

While on the hoof, you might want to check out 31st and 32nd streets between Second and Third avenues if you're passionate about lovely old town houses.

 For an inexpensive meal, try the area's Indian restaurants, which appear on Lexington and side streets in the low thirties and upper twenties. **Shalimar** (39 East 29th St.; (889-1977) is one of the best.

MIDTOWN WEST

West of Fifth Avenue, 59th Street down to 34th, brings more of a change in attitude than direction. Within a three-block radius you'll find Petrossian (the people who gave caviar a brand name), the Hard Rock Café, and the Carnegie Deli (see Restaurants for all three). Midtown West is Broadway. Carnegie Hall. Times Square. Radio City. The garment district. Porno movie houses. Opening nights. Drug raids. Chic and sleaze mingle like salt and pepper on a sunnyside-up egg.

As for the West Side, everything is a matter of life and death. (On the East Side, one is concerned with the *quality* of life.) There is a sense of danger in Midtown West (even if it's only fear of 47st. photo) that gives the area more ups and downs than a roller coaster. Your spirits will soar and your sensibilities despair. Do not cross Fifth Avenue without being prepared to view the human condition in all its guises. One thing is certain: you will not leave untouched.

Avenue of the Americas

The Avenue of the Americas is most famous for really being Sixth Avenue. Otherwise beloved Mayor La Guardia committed the urban sin (however well-motivated) of changing the name. As a result, whether you call it Sixth, as the locals do, or that other name, is how New Yorkers separate the men from the boys. (To make you feel more at ease, the powers that be have put up bi-lingual street signs: they say Sixth and the other thing.) Frankly, unless you say Sixth Avenue, you might as well walk down the street carrying a milk pail.

The star attraction on Sixth is still **Radio City Music Hall,** the only theater worth going to even if there's no show. It is a masterpiece of Art Deco styling and people have been writing about every aspect of it since it opened in 1932, including the rest rooms (a mural from the men's room was relocated to the Museum of Modern Art). At the time, Radio City was the largest theater in the world, and it's still America's biggest indoor auditorium. But the success story here is not mere size, it is the attention to detail lavished by Donald Deskey: the carpeting, murals, lighting, and trim are sheer per-

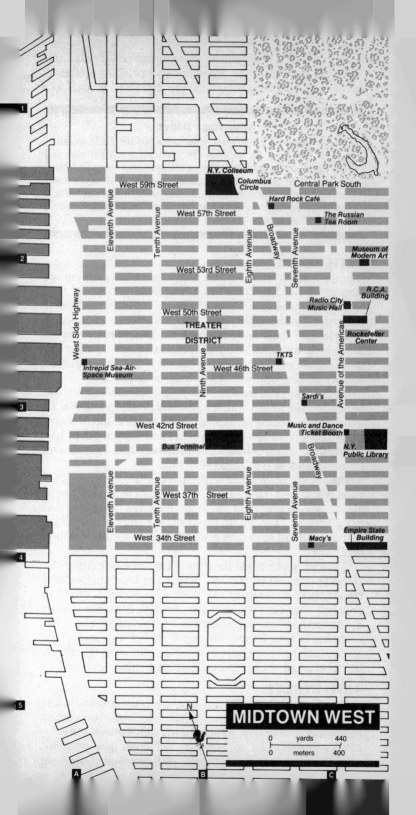

fection. Even if you attend a performance—ideally, the Christmas show with the precision tap-dancing Rockettes—the one-hour backstage tour ($5; call 246-4600) is fun.

Weather Alert

If you're caught in a sudden downpour, or it's too chilly or hot, consider riding out the elements by spending a few minutes in the Rockefeller Center Concourse, a below-ground two-mile labyrinth lined with shops that connects all buildings in the complex. You can browse your way from 49th and Sixth to 51st and Fifth, even stopping for a subterranean snack en route. Save this tip for your "Desperation" file.

47TH STREET

Despite Sixth Avenue making every effort to create an art form out of bland, it couldn't do a thing about 47th Street. One of the most boisterous blocks in the city, this is the kind of place that could happen only in New York. The **Diamond District** (the shops on 47th between Fifth and Sixth avenues) is credited with conducting 80 percent of all U.S. diamond deals and almost all those deals are made on a handshake by somber-looking bearded men in long black coats.

(At one time, the Irish were cops and the Chinese had the best laundries. That's where ethnic began and ended. Not so today. Without being prejudicial, simply as the result of observation, New York has lots of Korean fruit stores, Greek luncheonettes, [East] Indian newsstands, and, of course, Hassidic Jews in the Diamond District.)

The big question about 47th Street is whether you get a good buy or not. That's up to you. If you know what you're buying and can recognize the goods, it is often possible to find a real bargain. Even if it isn't, you will see more of a selection here than almost anywhere else and the prices will be competitive.

If you're in the mood for a bit of culture shock, leave the Hassidic diamond enterprises behind and head for **Gotham Book Mart & Gallery** (41 West 47th Street; 719-4448). Founded over sixty years ago by Frances Steloff, a woman as passionate about her authors as her customers, this is the bookshop of your literary dreams: It's filled with poetry, obscure journals, books that don't sell beyond family members, but most of all—respect for the printed page.

45TH STREET

On our first trip to Hong Kong, we brought with us ads from New York's most famous electronics and photographic equipment discounters, **47st. photo,** with its main store, located—surprise—on 45th Street. We knew just what we wanted to buy and couldn't wait. Well, we waited. And we waited and we waited. Not one shop had prices as low as 47-st. photo, (115 West 45th Street; 260-4410). Not in Hong Kong, Singapore, Taipei or Tokyo. However, if you watch the ads closely in the Sunday *New York Times*, at the back of Section 1, you will find a few beavers eager to shave 47st.'s prices.

The good thing about 47st. photo is their impeccable dependability. Not their charm, mind you. This is not a place to shop, it is a place in which to buy. Most items are not on display. If you want to browse, go somewhere else first and then come here. You line up. You tell them what you want. You pay. You leave. Nobody smiles. But the prices and selection are tops. Closed on Saturdays.

BACK TO SIXTH

There's not enough worth seeing to make continuing down Sixth a good option for anyone with limited time. More big buildings. A nearly fatal brush with 42nd Street. **Bryant Park** (in back of the gorgeous public library building), still valiantly trying to reclaim itself, was a pauper's graveyard in 1822 when the area was on the northernmost edge of the city. Currently, there's a $14 million plan to revitalize (i.e., get rid of the druggies and build a couple of restaurants) in the park. Located near the corner of 42nd Street is the **Music and Dance Ticket Booth** for half-price tickets to that day's performances (382-2323).

MACY'S

Note to purists: yes, Macy's is on 34th Street between Broadway and Seventh Avenue. It takes up the whole block. You can't miss it. We know it isn't on Sixth Avenue. But if you look at the map, Sixth and Broadway criss-cross on 34th Street, just south of Macy's. Besides, you just can't talk about this part of 34th Street and ignore Macy's.

Billed as the biggest department store in the world, Macy's (131 West 34th Street; 695-4400) is at least a contender for your sightseeing list if not for your shopping list—although, they have made a highly successful effort to pull themselves up by their boutique-straps in order to narrow the gap between themselves and Bloomingdale's. No longer the province of upper-lower and lower-middle class shoppers, Macy's now sells things nearly as expensive as Bloomie's and Saks, albeit without the panache. Still, the range of products is astonishing, and in their antique jewelry a best-kept secret.

Seventh Avenue

Talk about hard luck. Seventh is stuck between the Sixth Avenue renaissance (from a former el route to boulevard of corporate headquarters) and the glitz of Broadway. No one gives their regards to Seventh Avenue. There aren't broken hearts for every bulb on Seventh. The first thing that comes to mind when you think of Seventh Avenue is the Garment Center between 40th and 26th streets. Then when you finally get down there, to make matters worse, they've added a new name to the signposts: Fashion Avenue.

The best part of Seventh begins at 59th and Central Park South after flexing its muscles at the New York Athletic Club, and ends abruptly one block later on the corner of 58th Street at the **Alwyn Court Apartments** (180 West 58th Street), which also happens to be the home of the Dr. Feelgood of restaurants, Petrossian (see Restaurants). The Alwyn is worth a special trip. It is the minimalist's nightmare: every inch of exterior is covered in terra-cotta doo-dads like a brilliantly woven tapestry.

The two **Carnegies** (Hall and Deli) are on 57th and 55th streets, respectively. And all hail the new **Equitable Center** between 51st and 52nd streets (757 Seventh Avenue), an office building with a heart. Not only does it house Le Bernardin and Palio (see Restaurants), but a branch of the **Whitney Museum** (554-1113) with changing exhibits of 20th-century American art; open Monday through Friday, 11 A.M. to 6 P.M. (to 7:30 P.M. on Thursday); noon to 5 P.M. on Saturday. Admission is free.

As for the rest of Seventh, the most positive thing to be said for this dowdy thoroughfare is that it gets you to Pennsylvania Station, Macy's and the Garment Center. There are no simple joys en route except for a brief flurry of activity when Broadway and Seventh intersect in Times Square (see Priorities). The **Visitor Information Center** on 42nd Street between Broadway and Seventh Avenue is open every day (Monday through Friday, 9 A.M. to 6 P.M.; Saturdays, Sundays, and holidays from 10 A.M. to 6 P.M.).

The most outstanding feature of the Garment Center is that it has the world's largest collection of brothers-in-law. Never mind that one-third of America's clothes are manufactured here or that this is where designer-oracles foretell the future of your closet. The only thing most visitors get to see are brothers-in-law. They congregate on corners, stand in front of buildings, sip diet sodas, ogle the receptionist-models, and tell one another dirty jokes.

If you're headed for the Garment Center because you're a compulsive shopper who is beyond reason and beyond retail, think twice before you go. Don't get us wrong; there's lots of cheap merchandise in this area, if cheap is all you want. But don't waste time looking for that third-floor factory on the cutting edge of *haute couture* where they're "giving things away" if you just say Izzy sent you.

However, once determined to shop on Seventh, there are a few places tucked away for those afflicted with discountitis. Try **Ben Farber** (462 Seventh, 3rd floor, 736-0557) for women's clothing; **Better Made Coats** (270 West 38th Street, 12th floor; 944-0748) for designer labels; and **S&W** (165 West 26th Street; 924-6656), four stores on the block offering big savings on designer goods. A word of advice: don't go at lunch time. The streets, already clogged with racks of clothes being pushed by hopelessly myopic young men who have all the directional discretion of a tidal wave, are further congested by workers (all 300,000 at once) eager for a breath of fresh air.

Assuming you're so pleased with your new image that you want to take a picture, the area below 34th is filled with **discount camera shops** all competing with one another. Check the back pages of Section 1 of the Sunday *New York Times* for prices. Some of the more dependable places you'll find are Willoughby Camera (110 West 32nd Street; 564-1600), Camera Barn (1272 Broadway; 947-3510), Executive Photo (120 West 31st Street; 564-3592), Olden (1265 Broadway; 725-1234), and Brothers (130 West 34th Street; 695-4158). Call for hours, some are open on Sunday. Most carry electronic equipment.

Broadway

There are so many Broadways it's almost impossible to keep track of them all. While streets are known to change character from one end to the other, Broadway has a long-running, sold-out, standing-room-only identity crisis. It is the amazing technicolor dreamcoat of multiple personalities.

In midtown, Broadway means the theater district. So much so that from 59th Street down, until you see the *Les Miz* logo, and the *Cats* marquee, Broadway might as well be the Indian path it once was.

The Great White Way, the wonderfully naïve Broadway that celebrated the end of World War II in Times Square, the Broadway of the ball dropping on New Year's Eve, of an opening night for another Rodgers & Hammerstein hit—that Broadway is long gone. The crowds in Times Square are often unruly, the area is rife with druggies, and these days there are wags on TV who shoot down shows before the opening night party ever begins.

But Broadway, "the fabulous invalid," isn't ruled by logic or reality. (Thank heavens!) It is a kingdom of the heart where what you see is most assuredly not what you get: It is merely what you see. The street named Broadway is, at best, tacky. There is nothing to recommend your presence other than to get half-price tickets at **TKTS** at 47th Street (see Entertainment) or have one brief nightime look at the lights. Open your eyes, take a good look, and get out of there.

But if you must live in the past, there's **Roseland** on 52nd Street where well-mannered couples actually dance with their arms around one another, and **Sardi's** on 44th Street between Broadway and Eighth Avenue where the only famous people you're likely to see these days are the caricatures on the wall. As of this writing, Broadway from 49th Street to 45th Street is almost totally under construction as part of the program to revitalize the area.

Below 42nd Street, Broadway is strictly garment center until it pauses to catch its breath at Macy's.

Eighth Avenue

Do not plan to spend any time on Eighth Avenue. If you have to get somewhere on foot, use Ninth or Seventh. No visitor to the city needs to explore Eighth. It's dirty, sleazy, and unsafe. If you have to go in or out of the Port Authority Bus Terminal, use the Ninth Avenue side.

Ninth Avenue

Ninth is much better mannered than Eighth. There's even a sense of family, a feeling that real people are alive and well on Ninth Avenue.

The neighborhood west of Ninth Avenue from 57th down to the thirties is properly called Clinton, a name favored by the realtors. It is, however, best known as Hell's Kitchen, which was once one of the city's worst slums and most dangerous locales. Not so today. You can still see the tenements, but many of them are being reclaimed and there are numerous housing projects in the area.

Today, Ninth Avenue is synonymous with food. It began around the turn of the century, when the informal alliance of Jewish and Italian peddlers who gathered under the shadow of the el (yes, there was one here, too) became known as Paddy's Market. When the approaches to the Lincoln Tunnel were built off Ninth Avenue, it signaled the end of street life and the shops on Ninth were the only markets.

The annual **Ninth Avenue Food Festival** held in May is the town's biggest open-air pigout: nearly a million hungry New Yorkers storm the avenue from 37th to 57th to sample a cornucopia of goodies at street stalls that represent nearly every ethnic food combination possible. The rest of the year, Ninth is predominantly Italian. The rule of thumb is that everything above 40th Street is for taking home: There are butchers, bakers, and ravioli makers.

Once you get down to the **Supreme Macaroni Company** (511 Ninth Ave.; 502-4842) you're into hands-on eating. The Supreme is a shop filled with pasta and a back room with a restaurant (Guido's) left over from your fantasies of *Moonstruck* Italian restaurants with red-checked tablecloths.

Very well-known to New Yorkers is **Manganaro's** (492 Ninth Ave.; 947-7325) where the motto states that heroes are made, not born. Maybe because Manganaro's is the hero-maker who invented the six-foot-hero sandwich that even shows up at Sutton Place parties.

Tenth Avenue

There is nothing on Tenth for most visitors. Not even bona-fide sleaze.

 However, we should mention that even here, yuppies show signs of settling in: **Mike's American Bar and Grill** (46th and Tenth; 246-4115) is a popular local place for Tex-Mex style food and beer (don't let the outside deter you; "unpretentious exterior" is an understatement!).

Eleventh Avenue

Nothing much here either. Except for the new **Jacob K. Javits Convention Center,** a glass, post-modern Crystal Palace-ish place. The largest convention center in the western hemisphere, it occupies a five-block, 22-acre strip between 34th and 39th streets.

Twelfth Avenue

Even worse. New York is one of the world's few cities to treat its riverbanks so shabbily. Once the site of the raised West Side Highway (demolished because it was an unsafe structure), the piers and riverside are areas of decay. With the exception of the glitz piers where you may catch a glimpse of fabulous ocean liners in port, Twelfth Avenue is a highway.

As always, there's an exception—notably the ***Intrepid Museum*** housed in a World War II aircraft carrier that served in the Pacific. "Sea, air, space" is the motto of this museum with planes parked on deck and items from our history in space on display. If ever there were a kid's dream come true, this is it. Pier 86, West 46th Street and Twelfth Avenue; 245-0072. Open Wednesday through Sunday, 10 A.M. to 5 P.M. Admission is $4.75; $2.50 for kids.

Central Park

There is a theory that New York could not exist without Central Park. It has nothing to do with the ozone layer or environmental science: it is strictly a matter of emotional ecology. Kerplunk in the middle of more concrete, asphalt, and desperate dreams than the Road to Hell, Central Park is a living work of art in which to rebalance the psyche and refresh the senses.

People tend to think of the park as a "preserve," a naturally wooded area that was always there. Wrong. The original site was scruffy, a garbage dump, the location for a bone-boiling works. There were mosquito-infested swamps, pigs and goats ran untended, and squatters lived in makeshift shanties. "A pestilential spot where miasmic odors taint every breath of air," was one description. That was in 1844, when Washington Square Park in Greenwich Village was considered uptown, and the city ended at 42nd Street. Poet William Cullen Bryant and author Washington Irving campaigned vigorously for a large public area. It was decided in 1857 to hold an open competition for the design of a park.

Frederick Law Olmsted and Calvert Vaux were chosen from among 33 entrants. They called their winning plan "Greensward" and to implement it required 3,000 workers, 400 horses, and 20 years. More than 1,400 species of trees, flowers, and shrubs were planted as ten million cartloads of earth and stones were brought in or out of the park. Driveways were purposely curved to prevent them from being used for horse racing.

Central Park is an artist's creation in which every tree was put in place like a brush stroke. It was, and remains, perhaps even more dramatically, a brilliant example of the democratic concept that defined America. The park was a place for all the people: from the children of immigrant workers to Lillian Russell who pedaled through on her monogrammed, gold-plated bicycle.

The park, today, is home to Joseph Papp's *free* summer **"Shakespeare in the Park"** (861-7277), *free* performances by the **Metropolitan Opera** (362-6000) in June and the **New York Philharmonic** (580-8700) in August. There are also marathons, ice-skating, bicycling, baseball, children's playgrounds, a zoo, a carousel, horseback riding (call **Claremont Riding Academy,** 724-5100), an obelisk, and boating. Also drug dealers, muggers, and rapists. During the day, and especially on weekends, the park is reasonably safe, if you know where your wallet is at all times. At night, when attending performances, some additional caution is required, as common sense would dictate.

One cardinal rule: *Do not ever go into the park alone at night.* **In this context, our definition of alone is fewer than two hundred people.**

Jogger Alert

Central Park has been called the most heavily run 6-mile course in the United States. It is separated into four jogging areas: a 6-mile loop, a 4-mile loop, a 1.7 mile loop, and the most famous of all—the reservoir path (1.6 miles) that circles (you guessed it) the reservoir between 85th and 96th streets. Visitors staying in midtown can enter the park from 59th Street (Central Park South). The south loop of 1.7 miles is perhaps the most trafficked run and therefore is considered the safest. Joggers should use the inside left lane of all roadways in the park and must go in one direction with the traffic flow (north on the East Drive, south on the West Drive).

One of the most user-friendly approaches to Central Park is from 59th Street and Fifth Avenue, across from Grand Army Plaza. (See color map of Central Park.) To your left is a pond and, farther into the park, the **Wollman Rink** for ice skating (517-4800). The path leads to the newly renovated **Central Park Zoo.** A $35 million three-year transformation has replaced all the prison-like cages with an environment more comfortable for animals and humans alike. Visitors will not find elephants and tigers, but only those animals that can be cared for properly in the limited space available. However, there is a greater variety and number of animals than in the old zoo. Open Monday through Friday from 10 A.M. to 5 P.M., and until 8 P.M. on Tuesdays. Weekends and holidays, the zoo is open until 5:30 P.M., and from November through March until 4:30 P.M. Admission is $1; $.25 for children. Formal entry to the zoo is from Fifth Avenue and 64th Street.

What's New at the Zoo

Three major ecological areas are featured:

Tropic Zone. A re-creation of a tropical rain forest, with river-bank, cave, treetop, close-up, and other habitat galleries. Monkeys, crocodiles, snakes, bats, insects, free-flying birds, and many other tropical species are to be found.

Temperate Territory. Outdoor habitats for Asian and North American mammals from climates like our own. Includes Japanese snow monkeys, waterfowl, red pandas, river otters, etc.

Polar Circle. Animals from the Arctic and Antarctic. Multiple above-water and underwater views of polar bears, harbor seals, and Arctic foxes living side by side. There is a special "Edge of the Icepack" area for penguins and puffins.

The **Sea Lion Pool** in the Central Garden simulates the rocky California coast and is surrounded by a garden with year-round plantings. There is a **Zoo Café,** an indoor-outdoor cafeteria for snacks and refreshments; a **Zoo Gallery,** with changing exhibitions of art, photography, and other objects on animal-related themes; and a **Zoo Shop** for souvenirs, books, stuffed animals, and so on. Call the **Zoo School** (439-6538) for information on special lectures.

Near 65th Street in mid-park, is the delightful **Carousel** (879-0244) with its handcarved wooden horses. Another of the local landmarks is **The Dairy** (mid-park at 64th Street; 397-3156), an 1870 Gothic Revival building built as a refreshment stand for mothers and children that now serves as the park's official **information center.**

Weather and time permitting, one of the best park walks is to continue north, passing the **Sheep Meadow,** on your left, where sheep continued to graze until 1934. The sheep went to sleep counting people at night in what has become Tavern-on-the-Green (see Restaurants). Today, the Sheep Meadow is one of the loveliest areas in the park, a haven for sunbathers and romantics—the city is kept at bay by a hedge of trees pressed up against the buildings to the east, west, and south. **Roller skates** may be rented at the Mineral Springs Pavilion (861-1818).

The Mall, heading north again, is a tree-lined formal promenade area. There's a bandshell for concerts, bronze statues, a pretty pergola, and a slice of park life that includes everything from musicians to drug dealers. Continue heading north to our favorite spot in the park, the **Terrace** and **Bethesda Fountain** (72nd Street). Designed to link the Mall and the lake, a graceful double staircase reaches down to the Terrace and the Fountain. You can continue to walk around the lake to Bow Bridge, an elegant cast-iron span across the lake to the heavily wooded (read: dangerous if you're alone) area known as the **Ramble.**

Back at the Bethesda Fountain end of the lake, rowboats can be rented for $6 per hour at the **Loeb Boathouse** (517-2233), or if you're strictly a landlubber, you can **rent a bicycle** at the Boathouse (861-4137). Refreshments are available here as well as restrooms.

The star attraction is the **Loeb Boathouse Café** (517-2233), which serves outdoor and indoor Northern Italian dinners 7–10 P.M., daily. No reservations accepted, but a Boathouse "trolley" picks up diners at Fifth Ave. and 72nd St., 79th St., 86th St., and 90th St. periodically between 7–10 P.M. and brings them back after dinner. Entrees are priced $10.50–$17.95.

Continuing farther north will bring you to **Belvedere Castle,** which was designed as a scenic element and purposely built small to make it appear farther away. The **Delacorte Theatre** is where free Shakespeare is held during the summer. Lines form early in the afternoon for free tickets, so plan to arrive in plenty of time—preferably with a picnic basket. In back of the Metropolitan Museum of Art is the 71-foot tall obelisk built in 1600 B.C. and nicknamed **Cleopatra's Needle** because the Romans had it located near a temple built by Cleopatra. Farther north is the **Great Lawn,** another venue for concert performances in the park.

Visitors often stop at a restored knoll near the West 72nd Street entrance to the park. Called **Strawberry Fields,** it is dedicated to the memory of ex-Beatle John Lennon.

If you're pressed for time, or incurably romantic, bite the bullet and head for 59th Street (Central Park South) between Fifth and Sixth avenues and hire a **horsedrawn carriage.** You'll be charged $17 for the first half-hour, and $5 for each quarter-hour thereafter. Plus tip. (Stop grumbling.) It will be a memorable half-hour.

Upper East Side

Think rich. Then think very rich. Double it. Double that. You're getting there. The Upper East Side is the capital of Rich. You won't find it on any map even though it borders on Sinfully Rich. Close to Excessive. In the heart of It Should Only Happen To Me! But remember, gentle reader, we told you way back when that N.Y.C. was the most democratic of cities. Here's the proof. It doesn't matter whether you've just shelled out the last *pfennig* in your Fendi wallet or are flush with this month's paycheck, annuity, or dividend. As long as you keep spending, no one cares whether you're rich. This is what democracy-in-action boils down to.

If you want to be an instant New Yorker, come to the Upper East Side. One reason that New York is such a great place to visit is the city's obsession with the best. Nowhere is the best more apparent or accessible than on the Upper East Side.

Madison Avenue

Imagine Bond Street, the rue St. Honoré, and the Via Veneto all wrapped up in one package. That's Madison Avenue. Once you've crossed the border (59th Street) and have left midtown mania behind, Madison eases into America's biggest, most expensive shopping spree. With the exception of the Whitney Museum (see below), Madison has absolutely nothing of redeeming social value to distract you from counting your change, tearing up your carbons, and wondering how in the world you're going to schlepp all you bought back home.

 Our favorite dining experiences on Madison center around the coffeeshops and burger joints. Just a little something to keep body and soul together while on the battle line. Some of the swells from the Hotel Pierre sneak over to the **Viand Coffee Shop** (673 Madison, at 61st St.) for bacon and eggs or tuna fish sandwiches that are more nostalgic than delicious. Still, they have a certain retro charm. There's another **Viand** up at 1011 Madison and a small, cozy coffeeshop, **Nectar,** at 1022 Madison.

MARCHING UP MADISON
(A Selective, Follow-the-Numbers Shop-Till-You-Drop Guide)

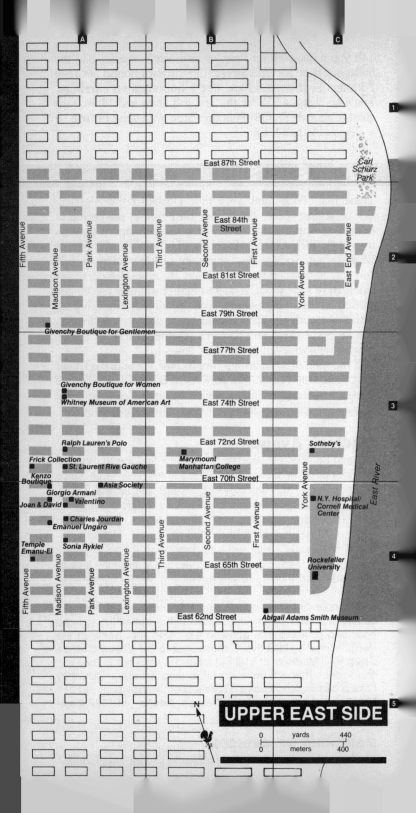

A
B
C

1

East 87th Street

Carl
Schurz
Park

Fifth Avenue
Madison Avenue
Park Avenue
Lexington Avenue
Third Avenue

East 84th
Street

2

Second Avenue
First Avenue

East 81st Street

York Avenue
East End Avenue

East 79th Street

Givenchy Boutique for Gentlemen

East 77th Street

Givenchy Boutique for Women

Whitney Museum of American Art   East 74th Street

3

Ralph Lauren's Polo   East 72nd Street

Sotheby's

Frick Collection
St. Laurent Rive Gauche
Marymount
Manhattan College

Kenzo
Boutique   Asia Society   East 70th Street

Giorgio Armani

Joan & David   Valentino

York Avenue

N.Y. Hospital/
Cornell Medical
Center

East River

Charles Jourdan
Emanuel Ungaro

Temple
Emanu-El   Sonia Rykiel

Second Avenue
First Avenue

4

East 65th Street

Rockefeller
University

Fifth Avenue
Madison Avenue
Park Avenue
Lexington Avenue
Third Avenue

East 62nd Street   Abigail Adams Smith Museum

N

5

UPPER EAST SIDE

| 0 | yards | 440 |
| 0 | meters | 400 |

635 / Bottega Veneta
Italian leathers so beautiful and so expensive they could be put on a shelf at home for exhibit.

660 / Gazebo
Huge collection of patchwork quilts from around the country. More Americana here than a Fourth of July parade.

679 / Sherry-Lehmann
The Andrew Lloyd Webber musical of wine shops. A must for oenophiles, the selection is dazzling and beautifully displayed. At the very least, bring your wine-lover back home a Sherry's catalog.

680 / Perry Ellis
There's no business like shoe business.

683 / Georg Jensen
Superb Scandinavian silver, china, and pottery. Everything you buy here carries a warranty for elegance. Worth every kroner.

690 / Lancel
Luggage and leather goods. Pricey but nearly indestructable, brilliantly tasteful. Just like the French.

699 / Jolie Gabor
Yes, she's the mother of you-know-who and you-know-who and you-know-who. An extraordinary collection of fabulous fakes. (The jewelry.)

710 / Coach Store
If you're a coach collector, this is the place. Large selection of bags, luggage, and accessories.

711 / Loewe
Viva Espana! A rainbow of colors on some of the softest leather since Sancho Panza's saddle. Drop-dead chic collections of leather clothing, handbags, and luggage.

716 / M.J. Knoud
Everything you need for your next fox hunt. Saddles, jodhpurs, boots, and even polo accessories.

717 / Erica Wilson
For those who believe in a stitch in time. Needlework buffs from all over the planet come to Erica Wilson's.

725 / Charles Jourdan
For boulevardiers and femmes fatale.

727 / La Bagagerie
French handbags from a shop with branches in Lyons and Tokyo.

746 / Betsey Bunky Nini
Boutique clothes that are trendy to the nth.

773 / Fred Leighton
Extraordinary collection of antique jewelry. The Czarina and Lillian Russell would be equally at home. Prices for these once-in-a-lifetime pieces match the quality. Almost more a museum than shop.

792 / Sonia Rykiel
French designer boutique.

OOPS! We Forgot to Tell You Something

For heaven's sake, keep your eyes open as you cross the street. There are all sorts of hidden treasures tucked into the blocks between Madison and Fifth, and Madison and Park. Be sure not to miss gems such as **Tender Buttons** (143 East 62nd Street) for what may well be the country's most complete collection of buttons for every occasion; **ffolio** (33 East 68th Street) for a smashing stock of stationery and desk accessories. Custom binding and printing. We dare you to leave this place empty-handed. And **Sointu** (20 East 69th Street), where they take design for living seriously. Gift items, desk necessities, jewelry, and glassware for those who lead sleek and functional lives.

---

803 / Emmanuel Ungaro
Of the same name.

807 / Cerutti
Some of the snazziest clothes in town for bambini and grandbambini too young to shop in Italy.

812 / Billy Martin
What the well-dressed cowpoke will wear. Gorgeous handmade silver belt buckles, extravagant boots. Must be well-heeled to shop here.

815 / Giorgio Armani
The original sweet smell of success. Gets better every day.

816 / Joan & David
Top of the line shoe designs from the people who tiptoe through department stores all over the country.

823 / Valentino
More Italian designs for your *dolce vita.*

824 / Kenzo Boutique
Kicky young fashions from cutting-edge Japanese designer.

829 / Pratesi
Sheet-maker to the stars. Barbra won't sleep on anything else. Sinatra's linen closet is filled with them. Liz buys sheets and lingerie.

831 / Lanvin of Paris
The answer to what's in a name.

836 / Missoni
New York home of the Italian family who put the boutique sweater on the map.

841 / Piaffe
Tiny shop with tiny clothes for tiny women. Named after tiny French singer by someone who couldn't spell.

844 / Mina Rosenblatt
A woman who can spell Tiffany. The glass lamps are dazzling. Has fabled collector's items at prices to match.

849 / Mabel's

A store devoted to feline fantasies. Categorically unique, it's filled with sweaters, toys, jewelry, furniture, and primitive art all celebrating Mabel and Mabel's descendants. Mabel was an elegant black-and-white cat. The shop is *purrr*fectly enchanting.

854 / Matsuda

Direct from Tokyo, imperial goodies for men and women.

855 / St. Laurent Rive Gauche (Boutique Femme)

859 / St. Laurent Rive Gauche (Boutique Homme)

867 / Ralph Lauren's Polo

Housed in one of New York's most beautiful mansions, this is the flagship store that carries everything Lauren designs from clothes to home furnishings. Magnificent interior.

870 / Jean La Porte

The best-smelling store in town. Jewel box of a boutique to showcase highly individual scents brought from France.

870 / Pierre Deux

French fabrics, china, glassware, personal and home accessories. Fabrics are translated into bags, luggage, table linen, wallets, and lots more.

886 / Portantina

Devoted to Italian brocades for upholstering you or your furniture. Some of the most luxurious fabric in the world.

924 / Poster Originals

Irresistible for browsing, one of the largest collections of posters in the city. Framed or un.

930 / Le Petite Bateau

Famous French label for kids' clothes.

931 / Fraser-Morris

Gourmet goodies displayed as in a food museum. Each strawberry is a work of art. Delicious for all tastes.

939 / Books & Co.

More than just books, this is where you'll find people who eat, drink, and sleep books. Judy Krantz and Jackie Collins take back seats here to literary movers and shakers.

950 / D. Leonard & Gerry Trent

Will knock your eyes out with its one-of-a-kind collection of fabulous antique jewelry from Van Cleef to David Webb.

954 / Givenchy Boutique for Women

Le plus grand even if you're not Audrey Hepburn.

962 / Time Will Tell

The entire store is devoted to antique and contemporary watches for people with time on their hands.

974 / Villeroy & Boch

Most of the world's elegant restaurants have you eating off this china. A full selection of all patterns.

995 / Women's Haberdashers

A landmark on Madison for women's tailored clothes. Known for creating coat and dress ensembles.

1015 / Linda Horn Antiques
Chock full of terrific treasures that Linda Horn couldn't find room for at home. Has the look of an Italian palazzo: anything that doesn't have a burnished glow, twinkles.

1020 / Givenchy for Gentlemen
Even if you're not one when you go in, you will be when you come out. Be sure to sample the colognes.

1070 / Éspiritu
African, Indian, and South American artifacts: carvings, jewelry, and ritualistic pieces.

1089 / San Francisco Model Ship Gallery
For those who are all at sea over miniature ships. Exquisite models of schooners and yachts, and others.

1100 / Neil Isman
Vintage watches from the twenties and thirties for men. Antique and modern jewelry.

1122 / Malvina Solomon
Antique jewelry and art pottery. Fabulous marcasite collection.

The **Whitney Museum of American Art** (945 Madison Avenue, at 75th Street; 570-3676), like the Guggenheim, is housed in a building that competes for attention with the art on display. Designed by Marcel Breuer of Bauhaus (and Breuer chair) fame, the Whitney looks, at first glance, upside down. Its three tiers of concrete seem to defy gravity as they cantilever out over the street.

Founded by Gertrude Vanderbilt Whitney in 1931 (her personal collection serves as the museum's core), the Whitney moved into its new home in 1966, by which time it was established as the preeminent address for 20th-century American art: Hopper, Nevelson, Johns, Rauschenberg, Calder, Warhol, et al. The focus and exhibit spaces here are quite unique, not to be confused with MOMA. A café looks out onto the sculpture garden, and the lobby shop sells prints and books. Open Wednesday through Saturday, 11 A.M. to 5 P.M.; Tuesday 1 P.M. to 8 P.M. (admission free from 5 to 8 P.M.); Sunday, noon to 6 P.M. $4.50 admission; $2.50 for seniors.

Despite the move of Sotheby's auction house to York Avenue, and the predicted loss of some galleries, Madison still remains, along with 57th Street and now Soho, a prime venue for movers and shakers in the art world. Some of the most famous (or our most favorite) **galleries** are:

Acquavella Gallery, 18 East 79 Street
Alaska Shop, 31 East 74 Street
David Findlay Gallery, 984 Madison Avenue
Graham Gallery, 1014 Madison Avenue

Hirschl/Adler Modern, 851 Madison Avenue
James Goodman Gallery, 1020 Madison Avenue
Jaro Art Gallery, 955 Madison Avenue
Knoedler, 19 East 70 Street
La Boetie Gallery, 9 East 82 Street
Marvin Kagan Gallery, 991 Madison Avenue
Paul Rosenberg, 20 East 79 Street
Perls, 1016 Madison Avenue
Robert Schoelkopf, 825 Madison Avenue
Saidenberg, 1018 Madison Avenue
Sindin Galleries, 1035 Madison Avenue
Weintraub Gallery, 989 Madison Avenue
Wildenstein Gallery, 19 East 64 Street

As Madison heads past 86th Street, it makes a dramatic shift into a residential area. Barely a boutique in sight as the high-rise apartments spawn a real live-in neighborhood. Grocers, bakeries, services. But just to keep a hand in, there's the irrestible **Soldier Shop** (1222 Madison) with thousands of tiny toy soldiers, military miniatures, campaign prints, and regimental memorabilia.

One of our favorite lunch places is **Sarabeth's Kitchen** (1295 Madison), a branch of the West Side restaurant that keeps everyone happy with fresh, wholesome G-rated food. Burger-lovers should mosey on down to **Jackson Hole** (1270 Madison) for really big burgers to fill all those wide open spaces.

Park Avenue

It's sometimes difficult to believe that Park is right around the corner from Madison. While on Madison Avenue, it's always Saturday; on Park Avenue, it's always Sunday. But that's New York: Cross the street and you're on another planet.

Once past 60th Street, there are no shops to speak of and after the Regency Hotel and the Mayfair Regent (see Hotels), Park Avenue, like any self-respecting ghetto, pretty much keeps to itself. As though not wishing to provoke attention, the buildings on Park are, for the most part, boring. Undistinguished for anything other than solidity. Still, in a disposable world, permanence may be the ultimate elitism.

Unless you're checking out the neighborhood before buying in, Park Avenue—shrewdly—has no attractions to draw anyone but the have-lots who live here.

But, if you've got the yen, head for **The Asia Society** on 70th and Park (725 Park Avenue; 288-6400). You'll find exhibits here including a core collection given by John D. Rockefeller III, photographic essays on Asian life, art from Aboriginal Australia, and Japanese arts. A highly manageable gallery, it is open Tuesday through Saturday from 10 A.M. to 5 P.M.

(Thursday until 8:30 P.M.); Sunday from 1 P.M. to 5 P.M. $2 admission. The bookstore is excellent.

Lexington Avenue

Years ago, Lexington was a really interesting avenue. It was upscale enough to provide services for Park, and middle-class enough to do the same for the families who lived between Lexington and Third. But as the middle-class left the side streets and Third became gentrified after the El was torn down, Lexington started getting snooty. Not that it's anything like Madison, but there are no bargains left on "Lex" (as it's called by the locals). Everything is expensive.

The decision about whether to spend time heading up Lex from Bloomie's will depend upon how shopped-out you are. There is no reason to spend time on Lex unless you're open to a little commerce.

Lex is nowhere as chic as Madison, or even Third, but it has a number of shops that most likely couldn't exist elsewhere and are well worth looking into. The **New York Doll Hospital** (787 Lex) has been a landmark on the avenue since 1900, when they opened for repair work. Today, not only will they make Raggedy Ann well again, but they can sell you her ancestors.

The **Elder Craftsman** (846 Lex) is a wonderful store that's stocked with the creations of senior citizens. You'll find toys, children's clothes, knitwear, and accessories for the home, just like your grandparents might have made. Two shops that feature larger-size clothes for women are **Ashanti Bazaar** (872 Lex) and **The Forgotten Woman** (888 Lex). Ashanti has a select, more unique collection while The Forgotten Woman is the flagship store for a nationwide chain.

Il Papiro (1021 Lex) sells exquisite paper and stationery. All those elegant marbelized patterns you've seen inside leatherbound books are used to cover desk accessories. Perfect for all your paper tigers. **La Terrine** (1024 Lex) is filled with French country pottery. No self-respecting pâté would come to the table in anything but.

If you're not worried about having to shop at The Forgotten Woman (now or in the near future) head for **Succès La Côte Basque** (1032 Lex) for gorgeous pastries. Primarily a bakery, you can stop in for coffee and a few million calories or have a light lunch while watching the passing parade.

William Poll (1051 Lex) feeds East Siders' appetite for gourmet treasures with wonderful baked goods and fantastic chocolates. **Mortimer's** (1057 Lex) feeds—in the guise of being a restaurant—the New York passion to "do" lunch. This is one of those everyone-knows-everyone places that attracts all the big names in fashion and society (the two not being redundant terms in the least). People like to knock Mortimer's for the very reason it's successful. Not fair. Especially when there's so much else to knock.

Sylvia Pines (1102 Lex) is known for her extraordinary collection of antique beaded bags. Some of the frames are silver, some are jeweled, all are one of a kind. She also has antique jewelry with an emphasis on fine marcasite pieces dating from the twenties and thirties. **Go Fly A Kite** (1201 Lex) really means it. Their collection of kites makes you itch to experience Central Park at the end of a string. **Japan Gallery** (1210 Lex) is heaven for collectors of Japanese woodblock prints. **Himalayan Crafts** (1219 Lex) is a tiny shop with enough Tibetan treasures to make the Dalai Lama happy. Fabrics, clothes, and jewelry from Nepal, China, and the rest of Asia—and if that isn't enough, they'll even arrange a tour.

Third Avenue

Wow! Did you catch that? Look over there! Trends speed by on Third faster than New York cabs through a red light. Unlike most East Side avenues, Third has little (if any) of its original character left. When the El came down and Bloomingdale's came up, Third not only mellowed out—it disappeared. What remains today is, for the most part, without character or grace. A graveyard for passing fancies. Still, an occasional wildflower keeps hope alive amid the generic highrise apartment houses that march up the avenue.

🐾 Right on the corner of 60th St., opposite Bloomie's, is a doubledecker of restaurants, the venerable **Yellowfingers** (on street level) and **Contrapunto** (above), that have been souped up by the Santo family who owns them both, plus **Arizona 206** next door (see Restaurants) and the gorgeous Sign of the Dove (again see Restaurants, and below). Three cheers for nepotism! Yellowfingers has been updated and Contrapunto fine-tuned with a pasta menu that's truly al dente. Perfect for restoring your equilibrium on an out-patient basis.

Zoe Coste (1034 Third) is Art Deco-cum-L.A. with some of the kickiest costume jewelry around. With branches all along the French Riviera, who's to argue?

🐾 A good spot to get lost in conversation is the bar at **Sign of the Dove** (1110 Third). Even if you're not having dinner (see Restaurants), you can take your pause in the day's occupations while someone tickles the ivories with sophistication appropriate to the décor. Right across the street is **David K's** (1115 Third) run by David Keh and his wife who have fought an uphill battle raising Chinese restaurants above the red-flocked-wallpaper idiom.

Grace's Marketplace (1237 Third) is to this neighborhood what Balducci's is to the Village. Small wonder: Grace is a member of the Balducci dynasty who wandered north to open a big, beautiful store loaded with gourmet goodies and great take-out delicacies. **J.G. Melon** on 74th and Third has been called by one restaurateur we trust, a truly quintessential New York eatery. Featuring burgers, fries, and lots to drink.

Gordon Foster (1322 Third) has a very personal collection of Japanese pottery (modern and antique), Chinese porcelains, baskets, and African art that reside harmoniously in this charming shop. **Stiegler & Co.** (1332 Third) is the closest you'll find to an old-fashioned Third Avenue antique shop. They have a mix of knickknacks, glass, and furniture at prices that won't take your breath away. Best of all, it's run by friendly people who will answer your questions without making you feel as though you were brought up by wolves. **Rogers Tropea** (1357 Third) is an extraordinary-looking shop that matches the merchandise. The décor is as designy as the crafts on sale: striking tableware, china, pottery, and furniture.

Martell's (1469 Third) is a long-time resident on 83rd St., responsible for serving beers and good burgers to generations of East Siders. (There are outdoor tables in warm weather, too.) But we must admit to being real suckers for a hot-dog and coconut "champagne" at the 86th St. branch of **Papaya King.**

Second Avenue

Second Avenue is the kitchen of the East Side. There are more restaurants here than in many emerging nations. Sometimes it seems as though Second Avenue has more Italian eateries than Rome. Restaurants to the right, restaurants to the left . . . If you look above street level on Second, you may just catch a glimpse of what life was like before restaurants would sooner close than put a red sauce on the menu. The blocks between Third and Second are long stretches, which may account for the increased population that must be fed. Second still has a neighborhoodish feel.

Once past the brouhaha surrounding the Queensborough Bridge and the Roosevelt Island Tram, Second Avenue allows itself to be more than an express lane for exiting Manhattan. **Cachet** (1159 Second Avenue) is the place for anyone who's crazy about the Il Bisonte leather creations from Florence—at discount prices, yet.

Swensen's Ice Cream Factory between 65th and 66th sts. is one of the few real-live ice-cream parlors left in New York. Not that Swensen's is leftover—it's new, big, and bursting with sodas, sundaes, and a food menu as well.

Oaksmith Antiques (1321 Second) is jam-packed with oak furniture, and a charming collection of turn-of-the-century prints.

Pamir (1437 Second) is where to go when you're in the mood for chick peas and yoghurt. The Afghan cooking at this restaurant has won kudos from critics and locals alike, none of whom have overlooked the very moderate prices for a very exotic cuisine. (What did you think? We were going to list every Italian restaurant?) **Pig Heaven** (1540 Second) is a really good-natured place where David Keh's porcine preferences translate into some of the best Chinese pork you're going to get in the city. Ribs, suckling pig, and the scallion-and-turnip pancakes are enough to make you smile when you say "th-th-th-that's all, folks!"

Part of what keeps Second smiling is the fact that it still retains an ethnic identity more meaningful than alligators on sport shirts. There are German, Hungarian, and Czech populations that give Second Avenue in the upper seventies and eighties (and part of First Avenue as well) a gentle reminder that there was life before the Me Decade. One of the most unique shops in town is **Paprikas Weiss** (1546 Second), which not only stocks all the staples you need for the goulash of your dreams, but Hungarian handicrafts as well. There are spices, dried fruits, nuts, and 17 varieties of coffee. Even if your suitcase is jammed with Bloomie's boxes, save a centimeter for a small feather wand used to spread butter over strudel dough without tearing it.

Mocca (1588 Second) is a true Hungarian rhapsody for budget gourmets: breaded mushrooms, herring, stuffed cabbage, duckling, chestnut purée, and palacsinta. The most expensive entrée on the menu is $13, and if that's more than you care to spend, consider their three-course $5.45 lunch.

Oldies, Goldies, and Moldies (1609 Second) is not—with a name like that—a restaurant. It's antique kitsch heaven: fiesta-ware dishes, neon signs, and neon clocks from extinct diners.

There isn't much left to Yorkville (the German section of the Upper East Side) these days. Way back when, 86th Street was a Bavarian Broadway *mit schlag*. The blocks between First and Third avenues pulsed with the sound of oompah bands from beer gardens that served everything from the best to the wurst of German specialties. Alas, the discount stores and sushi bars have moved in.

However, if you hurry (walk on the south side of 86th from Third to Second aves.), there are still a few "konditorei" for gorgeous pastries and coffee (**Café Geiger** and **Kleine Konditorei** also serve meals). **Ideal** (238 East 86th St.) is a no-nonsense counter restaurant where the food is so hearty that nouvelle cuisine means no second helpings. We are talking bare-bones eating for about $8. The **Elk Candy Company** (240 East 86th

St.) often has lines into the street before Christmas and Easter. The all-shapes, all-designs marzipan candies draw a standing-room-only crowd to this tiny shop. Around the corner on Second is **Schaller & Weber** (1654 Second), an old-country butcher shop and deli where more German is spoken than at the embassy.

Everyone has heard about the legendary **Elaine's** (1703 Second) where the literati meet the linguine. On any given evening (after 10 P.M.) you'll find the room filled with more scribes than ancient Egypt. Because Elaine's virtually (re)invented the power-restaurant concept, it's taken the rap for bad manners and bad food from precisely those people who should never be here. Elaine's is not Sardi's. No one comes to be seen except by their enemies at the next table. If all you want is a glimpse of Woody Allen, try the movies instead. Our advice to visitors: don't go unless you're with someone who knows Elaine.

First Avenue

Former capital of the swinging singles scene, the one-time boulevard of bars is beginning to show its age. (You know there's a midlife crisis the moment you see the **Chippendale's** male strip joint on 61st Street). Which is not to say that First isn't still out for a good time—even if the natives are searching for higher ground.

Miss Grimble, at 65th and First, is still turning out some of the best cheesecakes and brownies in town. Now, you can dine from a limited menu as well.

There's a section once called the Czech Quarter that runs along First Ave. from the mid-sixties up for about ten blocks or so. There are a few specialty shops in the area, but most notably there's the **Vasata Restaurant** (339 East 75th St.), which is the closest you can get to old Prague without a passport. The roast duck and the goulash may well have collaborated on inventing the word "hearty." Definitely not spa cuisine. Very reasonably priced.

Spanky's (1454 First) is currently the "hot"/"in"/"action" bar for the young set. Beer, beer, and more beer. Jam-packed on weekends, this is one place you can still find real New Yorkers. **Albuquerque Eats** (1470 First) offers Tex-New-Mex at reasonable prices (entrées from $8.95 to $11.95). A big Southwestern room complete with cacti and bleached cow skulls on the wall.

Panama City (1572 First) is Caribbean kitsch all the way. Downing food called "Cajun-Caribbean," and drinks that may be life-threatening (Dr. Voodoo, Pink Flamingo, etc.), the kids who come here are understandably animated. **Primavera** (1578 First) is a whole other story. We are talking serious food here. Northern Italian (that is, no sauce to stain your tie) dishes such as roasted kid, lamb, and, naturally, pasta primavera. A grown-up, dress-up place that is not only "in," it's good! Alas, pricey.

Speaking of Italian restaurants, there's no way to leave the area without at least mentioning the Lattanzi family who run **Erminia** (250 East 83rd St.), **Trastevere** (309 East 83rd St.), and **Trastevere II** (155 East 84th St.). Erminia serves Tuscan food, while the Trastevere twins have a much more southern accent.

York Avenue

No doubt about it, unless you're heading for New York Hospital (and we hope you aren't), the star of York Avenue is **Sotheby's** at 72nd Street (1334 York). As a fine-arts auction house, Sotheby's has been operating since 1744 in England and in New York, after merging with Parke Bernet in 1964. By all means, do not leave the city without attending an auction: It's high drama, gambling, and art all rolled into one. Sotheby's Arcade Auctions held approximately every other week have items within the reach of mere mortals. Even if there isn't a sale, it's worth going to one of the exhibitions. Unlike a museum, you can touch things at an auction house—and learn a great deal as you watch dealers appraise the goods.

If you're desperate for redeeming social value, there's the **Abigail Adams Smith Museum** (421 East 61st Street; 838-6878). This is the house in which President John Adams's daughter lived and is presently maintained as a museum with fully furnished Federal rooms. Open 10 A.M. to 4 P.M., Monday through Friday; $2 admission. But trust us: Be sure you like Federal furniture before you go.

Another sight we personally might not take time for in a tight schedule is **Gracie Mansion,** since 1942 the home of the Mayor. On the other hand, if you find yourself in **Carl Schurz Park** on 90th Street and East End Avenue, you might take a peek. Diehards can call for tour information (570-4747).

Upper West Side

If Pinkerton had married Madame Butterfly, or if things had worked out differently for Anna Karenina and Count Vronsky, chances are they would have wound up on the Upper West Side. This is not the side of town for marriages of convenience. Everything on the West Side is inconvenient, or at least West Siders make it seem that way. Nothing is cool or pragmatic. Everything is passionate, a fight to the finish: be it for the love of your life or being next on the lox line at Zabar's. The West Side is the East Side with a short fuse. Always wearing its heart on its sleeve.

Geographically, the Upper West Side may be narrower than the Upper East Side, but socially, it spans an ethnic and economic mix that is a demographic nightmare. There are falling-down drunks on the street in front of trendy new boutiques. The homeless line-up each morning at soup kitchens in local churches as Wall Street daddies drop their kids off at private schools. Now, you must understand that this suits most West Siders just fine: They are, typically, liberals who feel guilty for having it better than others. The dudes who live "Way Out West on West End Avenue" (a Gershwin song title) don't mind a little raunchy reality. Not in their pricey, high-ceilinged three- and four-bedroom pre-war co-ops, mind you, but a couple of blocks away is fine. Keeps things in perspective for the kids. Good for the soul.

The West Side jealously guards its position as the Left Bank of New York. It imposes no dress or behavior codes. It accepts the homeless and the beggars as it does the "first amendment" peddlers who narrow the sidewalks by lining them with elaborate displays of unwanted magazines and dog-eared books. Too liberal or too guilty to protest, the West Side has grown fat devouring yuppies. (The area has been dubbed the "Yupper West Side.") Now deeply rooted in middle age, the former vie de bohème translates into laissez-faire. The saving grace is that, unlike the Upper East Side, the West Side has never lost its sense of humor. Although, after all it's gone through, it could have.

During the 1960s and into the 1970s, the West Side was a hornet's nest of drug dealers, boarding houses, and underprivileged minorities. The avenues (Central Park West, West End, and Riverside Drive) were enclaves of great wealth from which it was dangerous to venture out except by car. Muggings and robberies were common topics of conversation when neighbors walked their dogs (in groups). Those West Siders who hung in have today reaped a bonanza. Cooperative apartments purchased for under $50,000 now bring $750,000 and more. Not surprisingly, however, most people didn't turn a quick buck. They stayed.

The official point of entry to the Upper West Side is **Columbus Circle** where Central Park South (59th Street), Broadway, and Eighth Avenue meet in a head-on traffic collision beneath the statute of Columbus erected in 1894. Since then, the area has had more ups and downs than the *Santa Maria.* The ill-fated Gallery of Modern Art (built by Edward Durell Stone for Huntington Hartford) appeared in 1965 amid heckles that its Middle Eastern white marble façade was in conflict with everything else in sight. The Gallery soon closed and the building limped along for a while in the guise of the New York Cultural Center. When that didn't work out, it became the New York Convention and Visitors Bureau where the **Visitors Information Center** (2 Columbus Circle; 397-8222) dispenses brochures, TV tickets, half-priced theater tickets, and information.

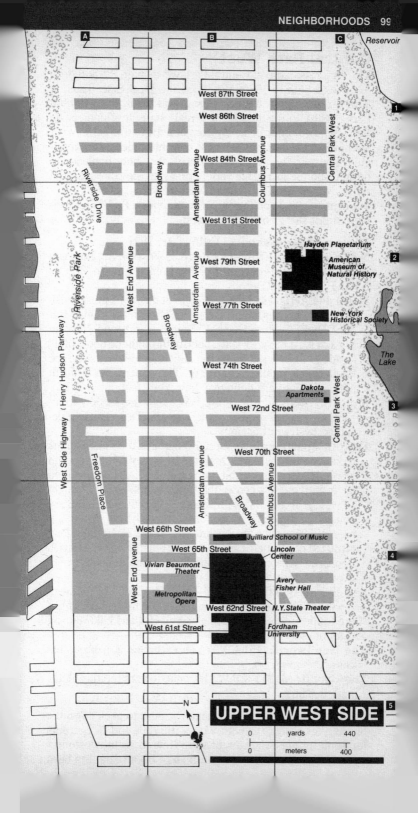

Reservoir

West 87th Street

West 86th Street

West 84th Street

West 81st Street

Broadway

Amsterdam Avenue

Columbus Avenue

Central Park West

Riverside Park

West End Avenue

Hayden Planetarium

American Museum of Natural History

West 79th Street

West 77th Street

New-York Historical Society

The Lake

West 74th Street

Dakota Apartments

West 72nd Street

West Side Highway (Henry Hudson Parkway)

West 70th Street

Broadway

Freedom Place

Amsterdam Avenue

Broadway

Columbus Avenue

Central Park West

West 66th Street

Juilliard School of Music

West End Avenue

West 65th Street

Lincoln Center

Vivian Beaumont Theater

Avery Fisher Hall

Metropolitan Opera

West 62nd Street

N.Y. State Theater

West 61st Street

Fordham University

N

UPPER WEST SIDE

| 0 | yards | 440 |
| 0 | meters | 400 |

Central Park West

The commissioners of Central Park were given the authority to develop 55th to 155th streets on the West Side. Thus, at 59th Street, Eighth Avenue's name was changed to Central Park West in order to stimulate real-estate development on the western border of newly completed Central Park. What we have today is the city's most elegant boulevard of apartment houses. The attention to detail, the sheer opulence of design, and the incredible variety of styles are not duplicated on any other single stretch in New York.

Begin your walk on the park side of Central Park West, taking note of the following buildings:

Century Apartments, 25 C.P.W.; Art Deco
N.Y. Society for Ethical Culture, 2 West 64; Art Nouveau
Prasada Apartments, 50 C.P.W.; French Empire
55 C.P.W.; more Deco
Hotel des Artistes, 1 West 67; one of the city's most lavish apartment houses where the roster of tenants included Isadora Duncan, Noel Coward, Fannie Hurst, and Norman Rockwell. At the very least, peek in through the neo-Gothic façade at the devastatingly romantic Café des Artistes (see Restaurants) on the ground floor. This entire block is worth noting for its very definitive New York feel.
Majestic Apartments, 115 C.P.W.; note the window treatment that wraps around corners on this Deco building designed by Irwin Chanin
Dakota Apartments, 1 West 72; perhaps the most famous residence in New York. Designed by Henry J. Hardenbergh who was also responsible for the Plaza Hotel on a site so far from the city's center that wags in 1884 said "it might as well be in the Dakota territory." The ultimate in luxury living, the Dakota's apartments originally ran to twenty rooms. The setting for the film *Rosemary's Baby,* it has long attracted celebrities from the arts as tenants: Lauren Bacall, Leonard Bernstein, Boris Karloff, etc. John Lennon, a resident, was shot as he was about to enter.
San Remo Apartments, 145–146 C.P.W.; one of the twin-towered buildings that's a familiar part of the skyline. These are topped with Roman temples yet. Hot and cold running celebrities.
The Kenilworth, 151 C.P.W.; an excercise in glorious excess.
The Beresford, 211 C.P.W.; Baroque towers top this block-long building.

While strolling along the avenue, be sure to peek down the blocks, especially 67th, 68th, 71st, 74th, 75th, and 76th streets for some prime examples of the "New York brownstone." Central Park West, between 75th and 77th streets, has been designated as a Historic District that includes 76th Street down to Numbers 51 and 56, as well as 44 West 77th Street.

New York Brownstone Recipe

Get lots of Triassic sandstone (iron ore is responsible for the coloration). Build a one-family house that's four or five stories high and two or three windows wide. Put in a big doorway, lots of front steps. Then subdivide the interior into small apartments, being sure to remove all features of architectural interest. Season with kids and neighbors to sit on the steps during hot summer nights.

The New-York Historical Society (170 Central Park West; 873-3400) has the oldest museum in the city, as well as the dubious distinction of being the only organization to hyphenate New-York as it was done in 1804, the year the Society was founded. The Society Library has over 600,000 books, over one million manuscripts (including the first printing of the Declaration of Independence), and thousands of photographs that document New York's origins. Check for special (as well as continuing) exhibitions scheduled along with concerts, lectures, and walking tours. Holdings here include all 433 known Audubon watercolors, collections of American silver, Tiffany lamps, paintings, and decorative arts. The society is open Tuesday through Saturday, 10 A.M. to 5 P.M.; closed Sunday and Monday; $2 admission; discretionary admission on Tuesdays.

The **American Museum of Natural History** (79th Street and Central Park West; 769-5100) actually occupies the entire area from 77th to 81st streets and Central Park West to Columbus Avenue. The *Guinness Book of World Records* cites it as the world's largest museum: "It comprises 19 interconnected buildings with 23 acres of floor space." It has also been described as a "colossus" and "an architectural hodgepodge." Whichever, it cannot be overlooked.

From the life-size display of a herd of wild elephants to a 94-foot-long diving whale to an actual 34-ton meteorite to the fossilized skeletons of reconstructed dinosaurs to the fabulous Star of India 563-carat sapphire, the museum offers a dazzling kaleidoscopic view of the peoples of Asia, Mexico, and pre-colonial America. You can peek into a tepee, hear songs of Africa, and go island hopping in the Pacific.

Often called a museum for kids, the Museum of Natural History is, if anything, an adult view of what kids should like. Prior to our entry into a visual society dominated by television and movies, the scenes portrayed in the museum's dioramas of animal and human life were pure theater. Today, a kid waits for the figures to move: Where is Disney when you need him? But for adults who can go beyond the impact of the display to the art of making the display, this is a wondrous theme park devoted to animal and human life.

The **Naturemax Theater** (769-5000), inside the museum, has the city's largest indoor movie screen: four stories high and 66 feet wide. Programs take you on journeys around the world. Admission (in addition to museum admission) is $3.25. Shows are held Monday through Sunday from 10:30 A.M. to 4:30 P.M., every hour on the half-hour.

The main entrance is on Central Park West, although the "carriage" entrance on 77th Street allows entry without walking up steps. Hours are Monday through Sunday, 10 A.M. to 5:45 P.M., except Wednesday, Friday, and Saturday to 9 P.M. $3.50 is the suggested admission for adults; $1.50 for children. Friday and Saturday evenings (5 to 9 P.M.) free. The gift shop often has interesting jewelry and artifacts.

Long before there were men on the moon, there were kids in outer space at the **Hayden Planetarium** (81st Street near Central Park West; 769-5920), the Astronomy Department of the Museum. Happily, the Planetarium, with its distinctive copper dome, has lost none of its magic despite our newly acquired sophistication. While the Guggenheim Space Theater has a 40-foot model of the solar system on its ceiling, the real show is in the Sky Theater where a projector illuminates the inside of the dome with the night sky to show everything from the birth of the planets to cosmic illusions. If you're looking for a close encounter of a psychedelic kind, the Planetarium hosts a laser show on Friday and Saturday evenings that is coupled to a dynamite sound system. Be sure to see the items on display at the gift shop if you need something for the kids back home. Admission is $3.75; $2.75 for students and seniors. Sky Show performances are Monday through Friday, 1:30 and 3:30 P.M.; Saturday through Sunday, each hour from 1 to 4 P.M. (additional shows from October through June). Admission to the laser show is $6. Performances are Friday through Saturday at 7:30, 9, and 10:30 P.M.

Columbus Avenue

It's at 59th Street that Ninth Avenue loses control and becomes Columbus. Although renamed in 1890 to enhance the value of its real estate, it wasn't until the 1970s (a decade after the arrival of neighboring Lincoln Center) that Columbus began to get its sea legs. An avenue of tenements and stores offering support systems for the well-to-do on Central Park West, the avenue's upgrading saw many mom and pop businesses shut down due to increased rents by social-climbing landlords. For a while, there were lots of empty storefronts. Then it seemed as though every shopkeeper in Paris, Milan, and Tokyo rushed to open a boutique on Columbus. Now, sadly, many of them have closed and we are back to seeing empty storefronts for the first time in years.

The growth spurt on Columbus was more of a shock than the first sight of your teen-ager after a summer away at camp. It seemed as though everything had changed overnight. Despite all the grumblings from diehard West Siders, the perking up of Columbus has been a major contribution to the area's maturation.

To say nothing of its appetite. Bars were transformed into pubs, and restaurants popped up like hives after a strawberry festival. While there are probably as many restaurants per block here as on First and Second avenues, there are not as many good ones. You have to be highly selective.

Sometimes, that's very easy as in the case of **Shun Lee West,** (43 West 65th St.; 769-3888), the hands-down winner as the best-designed Chinese restaurant in town, as well as the West Side's best Chinese restaurant. Period. A huge white dragon made of plaster and wire mesh wraps itself benevolently around the all-black, mirrored, and tiered room that's usually filled with an upscale crowd (prices are upscale for Chinese food, but so are the surroundings). As overseen by the inscrutible Michael Tong, Shun Lee has a kitchen staff of 22 to keep up with Michael's conviction that variety is the essence of Chinese food: His menu has some ninety different selections and he tries to change at least 15 percent of the dishes annually, though we can guarantee he won't take away Woody Allen's favorite shrimp dumplings or dishes that put stars in the eyes of Lauren Bacall, Madonna, or Paul Newman. Favorites include Szechuan wonton, honey baby ribs, crispy see bass Hunan style, vegetable duck pie (a mock Peking duck presentation), and a truly spicy orange beef. Shun Lee Café, a separate room, has a dim sum menu ($3.50 per dish), perfect for pre- or post-Lincoln Center light dining.

Columbus (the restaurant), on 69th St., is the latest celeb hangout on the West Side. Owned by Baryshnikov and his comrades, there's an active bar scene as well as a large glassed-in room in which to see and be seen. Cuisine doesn't rise above burger level, but that's perfect before or after an event at Lincoln Center. (Speaking of burgers, probably the best-tasting and best-priced ones are to be found at **Diane's,** just below 72nd St.)

Lenge (202 Columbus) and **Rikyu** (210 Columbus) are two very popular Japanese restaurants with the former a tad more formal in atmosphere. **Victor's Cuban Café** on West 71st St. is a landmark: the first Cuban restaurant to hit the big time. Once considered adventurous (in the era before people began eating recently deceased uncooked fish), Victor's has settled in as a friendly place to restore your faith in arroz con pollo.

Dallas BBQ (27 West 72nd St.) is strictly for those suffering rib withdrawal and in need of an inexpensive fix. **Sidewalker's** (12 West 72nd St.) tends to another craving: crab at prices that won't make you crabby. For $17.95 (Sun. and Mon.) you can "crab-bash," with all the crab, onion rings, fries, and slaw you can eat.

Memphis (329 Columbus) serves American regional food (read: Cajun and Southern) in a plush setting. Ribs, catfish, crawfish, jambalaya, Southern fried chicken, and black bottom pie. Priced toward the high end of moderate. There's no sign on Memphis; but you'll see it right next door to the **Cherry Restaurant**—a simple, coffeeshop-style place. **Fujiyama Mama** (467 Columbus) is where to come for 21st-century sushi in a high-tech, futuristic setting. There's a big menu and a D.J. playing rock-and-roll so that you don't notice the prices. This place is fun! **Panarella's** (513 Columbus) is a romantic hideaway that looks as though it were transplanted from the via Veneto. It's got a charming Old World look with its carved-oak bar and large Italian menu. Moderate to expensive. **Bazzini's** (520 Columbus) is small, homey, Italian, and comfortably old-fashioned. No surprises here except the inexpensive prices.

DISCOVERING COLUMBUS

(Dancing Shop to Shop Up the Avenue)

222 / Oliver Grant
Perhaps *the* men's store on Columbus right now. Very expensive. Dynamite sweaters.

232 / Dapy
Very trendy toys for the Peter Pan crowd as well as the latest in eighties gadgets, knickknacks sure to please your favorite yuppie.

250A / Kenneth Jay Lane
Costume jewelry boutique with the master's own designs. Fabulous fakes at knockout prices.

256 / To Boot
Men's custom-made boots and designer shoes. Exotic leathers make this a shoe-in for original craftsmanship.

274 / Artesenia
Brightly colored sweaters and other handmade clothing from Ecuador and Guatemala. Some leather as well.

274 / The Silver Palate
Famous for its cookbooks and scrumptious take-out.

290 / The Last Wound-Up
A treasure of mechanical toys. Some antique.

313 / Think Big
A branch of the Soho shop in which everyday items are transformed into larger-than-life collectibles. There's a social comment in here somewhere, but mainly lots of fun.

339 / Putumayo
South American boutique with an accent on great colors. Especially good for blouses and skirts.

370 / Mythology Unlimited
A very sophisticated shop that realizes just because you want to have fun, that doesn't make you a kid. There's always a wind-up toy or antique game to buy, as well as some

wonderful books and crafts. Leave the kids home: What do they know about flights of fancy?

380 / Alice Underground

Head down this rabbit hole if you're after antique clothing or retro-chic threads. A maze of rooms with racks of men's and women's clothes, antique linens, and even bomber jackets. All at terrific prices.

398 / Laura Ashley

Offers a complete selection of her very individual look in clothing, fabrics, sheets, and bath accessories.

410 / Mishon, Mishon

A seriously smashing collection of costume jewelry. Next door, they've opened a branch for fine jewels. Definitely "today" designs.

441 / Charivari

H.Q. for yupperwear parties: designer clothes for all known sexes. Elegant, sophisticated, and has branches all over the west side.

448 / Penny Whistle Toys

A must stop if you have kids, know kids, or ever were one yourself.

450 / Endicott Booksellers

One of New York's most handsome bookstores. Oak tables with paisley cloths display new titles. Wonderful nooks and crannies to relax in while you browse through their superb collection of titles.

453 / Maxilla & Mandible

If you want to pick a bone with someone, this is the place to come. Bleached cattle skulls, human bones, vertebrae from reptiles, and other anatomical kitsch.

487 / Handblock

Indian fabrics made by woodblock printing onto various weaves. Magnificent prints of all descriptions made into linens, quilts, tablecloths, clothing, etc.

495 / Screaming Mimi's

Looks like the kind of shop in which Madonna buys her dress-up outfits. Choice used duds for the younger unisex crowd.

503 / Mouse Dynasty

Cartoon clothing and accessories. All the Disney characters, and some other comic book favorites, in kids and adult sizes.

518 / Down Quilt Shop

A great selection of down comforters and pillows, plus handmade patchwork quilts (some antique).

Amsterdam Avenue

Before the Upper West Side put on its top hat, white tie, and tails, Amsterdam was the ugly duckling of the three "service" avenues—Columbus, Broadway, and Amsterdam. It still is. But the West Side's frame of reference has changed so drastically that it's like a reviewer calling Pavarotti someone who can carry a tune.

Once the domain of Hispanic groceries and fix-it shops, Amsterdam has gone from being bilingual to bicoastal. But not entirely. It still suffers from urban schizophrenia: There are probably few avenues in the entire country that have boutiques, a gas station, a funeral home, trendy new restaurants, a public school, bodegas where English is barely spoken, and a hot new preppy piano bar—all within a few blocks. The mix is as dazzling as its ingredients. It's at 72nd Street that Amsterdam crisscrosses Broadway and begins to hit its stride.

Savvy West Siders line up outside **Genoa** (271 Amsterdam), a tiny, family restaurant that, despite its name serves Sicilian specialties. Prices are like old Sicily, too.

Star Magic on the corner of 73rd Street is a heavenly store that covers all the stars except those in Hollywood. This is where astronomy meets astrology meets space nuts with a little psychedelic froufrou thrown in for good measure. It's a treat just to walk into this place even though the really good stuff costs the moon.

Coastal on 74th St. serves great fish in a bare-bones setting best enjoyed by the hearing impaired. Prices are better modulated than the noise level.

J.G. Melon (340 Amsterdam) is one of those places you go to almost as much for the atmosphere as the food. Very old-time bar with a middle-of-the-joint kitchen that turns out great burgers, omelets, and everything you could possibly want for brunch.

Accents Unlimited (360 Amsterdam) is a tiny boutique with antiques and giftware displayed as though they were museum treasures. Sometimes they are. **Aris Mixon & Co.** (381 Amsterdam) has an extraordinary collection of bibelots—everything from antiques to new glass, pottery, carvings, and jewelry. We've found wonderful things here. **Charivari** (201 West 79th Street) is the expensive clothing boutique that seems to be all over the place. Newest location is right on the corner of Amsterdam.

For the next few blocks, Amsterdam goes nuts. Nothing but restaurants. A new one every day. Yesterday it was a shoe repair shop, today it's a trattoria. One opens, one closes. It is a paean to the human spirit that a single species can devise so many different places to eat—and get so many people into such small spaces—and then make them pay for it.

The Ultimate, Inside, Uncensored Guide to Grazing and Drinking on Amsterdam Between 79th and 83rd Streets

407 / Broadway Baby

Born a piano bar at which to hear show tunes while having a drink. Has matured into cabaret acts and a light menu.

410 / Pasta Vicci

Serves pasta of all nations. So they say. Well, maybe you should put your credibility on hold while sampling hot and spicy penne à la vodka (Russia). Ultimate reach is fettuccine with sautéed shrimp in Provençal sauce (Swiss). But you have to love them for trying.

412 / Baci

Yuppie Italian. Minimal setting but homemade sauces to the max. Designer carbo-cals that could have inspired Michelangelo to paint faster. Always crowded.

423 / Sarabeth's Kitchen

THE place for brunch. Terrifically wholesome and expensive but worth it. Good place to lose the bends from being trendy.

424 / Good Enough to Eat

Small cheery place for down-home cooking that runs the gamut from comfort to Cajun. The lines form at breakfast for homemade scones, continue into lunch for bowls of thick, rich soup, and through dinners that finish with a flourish of dynamite desserts.

428 / Amsterdam's

Calm spot for lunch, but packed in the evening. Yuppie stronghold known for its reasonably priced grilled meats and chicken.

430 / ?

We don't understand "no-name" bars, but this is one of them. Except, it actually does have a name: Below the dim lighting but above the black-and-white tile floor, there's a clock with the inscription **K.C.O.U. Radio.** It's a quiet place for a drink until late in the evening—when a crowd just this side of the drinking age takes over.

448 / Piccolino

A very, very piccolino place with just enough room to twirl your pasta. An annex next door for those who order broader noodles.

450 / Yellow Rose Café

Tex-Mex, great ribs, plates heaped high. Run by a real Texan who is there to welcome lovers of chicken-fried steak and lumpy mashed potatoes like they used to make on the chuckwagon. Good margaritas, too.

477 / Forest & Sea International

Think luncheonette with a French-Thai connection and you have it. Mussels in Thai sauce, Bangkok chicken, and omelets all at pre-yuppie prices.

Broadway

Although Broadway is the only West Side avenue that doesn't change its name after crossing 59th Street, it undergoes no less a transformation. The downtown razzmatazz comes to an abrupt halt. Honky-tonk is put on hold as it metamorphoses into a gracious boulevard one might find in Europe. Indeed, city planners in 1866 designed Broadway to follow the path of the old Bloomingdale Road, anticipating it would be lined with posh private homes. Like Park Avenue, there are "islands" of greenery to separate the north- and southbound traffic. But on Broadway, both sides of the street are filled with shops, shoppers, window shoppers, and street vendors selling things you don't even want to know about.

The Upper West Side concept of Broadway has nothing to do with make-believe, but it is still pure theater. Broadway is the "street life" capital of the West Side. While Amsterdam and Columbus are busy reflecting only themselves, Broadway is an open stage on which thousands of highly individual dramas are performed daily.

Everyone who lives on the Upper West Side has a special part of Broadway that belongs to them. Every three or four blocks is its own small town. Even the beggars and crazies define their turf according to this most organic of thoroughfares. Practically umbilical, Broadway is the support system that leads from bakery to bookstore to florist. People are constantly bumping into people they know, checking out those they don't, updating their perceptions with every step. Sidewalk space is at a premium on weekends because everyone has an urgent, chic, or indulgent reason for being there, and Broadway becomes Calcutta, Paris, or Baghdad.

LINCOLN CENTER

The one part of Broadway that belongs to everyone, including West Siders, is a few blocks north of Columbus Circle at the Lincoln Center for the Performing Arts, a 14-acre complex of six buildings devoted to theater, music, and dance. Here's where you'll find the Metropolitan Opera, the New York Philharmonic, the New York City Ballet, the New York City Opera, Lincoln Center Theater, and the Chamber Music Society of Lincoln Center. Lincoln Center became a hit despite urban planners objecting to the traffic congestion, sociologists who felt that a working-class neighborhood had been sacrificed for the cultural pleasure of the affluent, and architecture critics who panned the project for its lack of proper aesthetics.

The genesis of Lincoln Center began in 1955 when the Lincoln Square area was slated for a healthy dose of urban renewal. Everyone knew that many of the tenements lining Amsterdam Avenue in the mid-sixties were slated to be torn down. Coincidentally, the Metropolitan Opera was looking for a new home, and to add a little *pizzicato,* the New York Philharmonic had been told that Carnegie Hall was about to be demolished. Clearly, there was nothing to do but relocate nearly 1,700 families and plan for a fountain.

To be fair, Lincoln Center's taken it on the chin for years, and rather unfairly. We've often been there when all four theaters break, and it's quite manageable—if somewhat difficult to get a taxi. (So what else is new?) The families would have been relocated no matter what. The most outstanding debit seems to be the lack of imagination in building the three major properties that form a U around the black marble fountain in the plaza: Avery Fisher Hall (formerly Philharmonic Hall), the Metropolitan Opera, and the New York State Theater.

Not that the architects, headed by Wallace K. Harrison, weren't thorough. The scoop is that these guys even measured tushes to be sure the seats would be comfortable. The overall effect outside and in is rather stultifying.

Lincoln Center Tours: A Totally Objective View

According to the *Lyons Guide to Empty Theaters,* (a very short book, indeed), one-hour tours of the Met, Avery Fisher Hall, and the N.Y. State Theater are given with alarming frequency and are incomprehensibly popular. Call 877-1800, extension 512, if you can't figure out what else to do with $6.25.

For dedicated bookworms only: there are free tours of the **New York Public Library at Lincoln Center.** Arrive with your bottle of No-Doze at 11 A.M. on Thursdays and you'll be shown (they promise!) ways to use the library. Seriously, folks, they do have a superb performing arts collection here. Call 870-1670, if you must.

The best vantage point from which to experience Lincoln Center au naturel is standing in the center of the plaza near the fountain. As you face the ten-story-high façade of the **Metropolitan Opera House,** at the curve of the U, the focal point shifts to the two Chagall murals. The one to your left, as you face the Met, is *Le Triomphe de la Musique;* to your right is *Les Sources de la Musique.* The latter has a King David–like figure, a Tree of Life in the Hudson River, while the former updates the sources into a montage of performers against the New York City skyline. If you walk into the lobby, on your right is an attractive shop with operatic memorabilia.

Avery Fisher Hall is the home of the New York Philharmonic. The most arresting piece of art here is in the main foyer (partially visible from the plaza): a two-part hanging metal sculpture by Richard Lippold—*Orpheus* and *Apollo*. The lobby has a gift shop as well as a bar and two restaurants.

The **New York State Theater** has some brilliant pieces of art on display, most notably two enormous marble statues by Elie Nadelman: *Two Nudes* and *Two Circus Women*.

Between Avery Fisher and the Met is the entrance to the Library and the Eero Saarinen-designed **Vivian Beaumont Theater,** surely the best-looking structure of the lot. But the real star is the **reflecting pool** with its two-piece bronze by Henry Moore, aptly titled *Lincoln Center Reclining Figure*. Also, don't miss the **Calder black steel mobile** near the entrance to the Library, which, all previous jokes aside, has mounted some compelling exhibits.

Walk from north to south in front of the Met and you'll find yourself in **Damrosch Park,** a mini bit of green with a wonderful bandshell for outdoor concerts. Voila! You've done it! Now buy yourself a ticket for some wonderful event and see the inside the way it should be seen: in performance.

WHERE TO EAT AT LINCOLN CENTER

Unless it's raining and you've just twisted your ankle, the restaurants at Avery Fisher Hall and the Met are, at best, generic. You'll fare better within a block or two, or if the night is young and you're in the mood for a walk, do a little sightseeing up Columbus while you search for nourishment.

The Ginger Man. Run by Michael O'Neal (in partnership with actor brother, Patrick), this is still the quintessential Lincoln Center bistro. Years back, you'd find Bernstein holding court in one corner, while two-by-two actors filled the front tables. But the real stars here have always been simple and down to earth: burgers, omelets, grilled meat, and salads (51 West 64th St.).

The Saloon. Get here early. It will take you an hour just to read the menu. Surely, one of (if not *the*) most extensive cartes du jour in town. And it goes every which way: Tex to Mex to Cajun to Slavic and back to Asian. If you can't find at least six major choices, you're hopeless. Be careful of the waiters: Some of them are on roller skates. Great for people watching: The Saloon is one of the few places in the city where a sidewalk café really works (1920 Broadway).

Poccino. A newcomer to the scene, very Italian, lots of small tables for something terribly chic (from carpaccio to gnocchi to cappuccino) in a smart little café that could be right off the Via Veneto (1889 Broadway).

Opera Espresso. Perfect for a dish of gelato, an ice cream soda, or a sandwich. Maybe even a little tea and symphony (1928 Broadway).

Lincoln Square Coffee Shop. A sprawling coffeeshop with an extensive salad bar. Sheer heaven for bargain hunters (2 Lincoln Sq., between 65th and 66th sts.).

Shun Lee West. See Columbus Avenue.

And, for a really special evening, **Café des Artistes** (see Restaurants).

To add to the melee at Lincoln Center, there'a a terrific branch of **Tower Records** (1965 Broadway), which has become hang out heaven for the under-legal-drinking-age set. Don't let that deter you. It's a wonderful shop for browsing and is open until midnight 365 days a year! A few steps north on Broadway is **Tower Video** where VCR hounds gather.

At 73rd and Broadway is the **Ansonia,** a Beaux-Arts fantasy with a high mansard roof, rounded corners, iron balconies, and terra-cotta ornamentation. It was built in 1904 as one of the largest apartment hotels in the world, fronting all of Broadway from 73rd to 74th streets. Toscanini, Caruso, and Stravinsky all lived here. So did the great Ziegfeld, Theodore Dreiser, and (!) Babe Ruth. It was at a now-defunct gay bathhouse in the basement of the Ansonia that Bette Midler performed early in her career.

Upper Broadway comes into its own as a major artery right in front of the Ansonia. Although Columbus and Amsterdam have developed into fatal attractions for people from all over the city, Broadway is still the underbelly of the West Side.

A popular neighborhood hangout is **Ernie's** (between 75th and 76th sts.), an airplane-hangar-size (and sounding) Italian/yuppie restaurant that has a variety of designer pizzas at moderate prices, as well as a hearty repertoire of pastas and grills. It is the performances being given by everyone in the room except you that's the most memorable thing, however.

The **Apthorp Apartments** take the entire block between 78th and 79th streets and Broadway and West End Avenue. Small wonder. If you've ever been inside an Apthorp apartment, you know why it takes up an entire block. They are grand in the great tradition of luxury living. Peek in through the gates to the large interior court. Some movie studio or other is forever filming at the Apthorp.

There are lots of new apartment houses along this stretch of Broadway, starting with The Broadway, between 80th and 81st streets, right opposite Zabar's. Of note is the **Conran's** branch on the ground floor, and on the corner of 81st, a wonderful bookstore, **Shakespeare & Company,** where regulars stop in on their way home after a night on the town. Best browsing on the West Side. *Mmmmm.* Did we mention Zabar's?

How to Zabar

Zabar's began as a small kosher deli in the 1930s and has developed into the M-G-M of gourmet markets. This place has taken on the cachet of a national monument, as though it were The Tomb of the Unknown Herring. Better than the Polo Lounge for bumping into celebs. Partner Murray Klein says that if you can still see floor between the feet of the mobs that line up here, he's not doing enough business. You'll see overachieving West Siders hot on the trail of a perfect piece of brie, harried housewives lugging out imported pasta machines and ice-cream makers bought at Zabar's discount prices, blue-haired Riverside Drive matrons picking up their weekly five pounds of smoked salmon for the family's Sunday brunch, and (hold on to your hats!) a busload of Japanese businessmen taking pictures in front of the salamis.

Even if you're not planning a snack in your penthouse suite at the Pierre, it's worth taking a turn around Zabar's to see what all the excitement is about. The sheer variety of products on display is staggering. Especially when you realize that nothing, absolutely nothing, they sell is required for the continuation of life as we know it on this planet. It is all excess. Frivolity. Froufrou. Sure, the elitists and gourmets claim they would sooner die than be without their favorite brand of extra virgin olive oil or imported strawberry preserves, but let's face facts: Zabar's is an entire industry based upon the icing on the cake.

The things to remember are:

- You need a number for purchases at the cheese, deli, and smoked fish counters and the wait on weekends can be as long as an hour.
- Generally speaking, you are entitled to a taste of anything that is being cut for you—and if you don't know the difference between the Eastern salmon and the Western salmon, ask for a taste of each. Everyone does.
- They will ship for you—what better way to take home a bite of the Big Apple?
- Don't let the low-hanging New York "attitude" of the crowd and staff put you off—it's nothing personal.

There are lots of restaurants along this stretch of Broadway, but our personal favorite is **Teachers Too** between 81st and 82nd sts. The "Too" is because there was an original Teachers next to Zabar's that got swallowed up in The Great Deli Expansion. Teachers wisely decided to clone itself even before the original closed and re-created the entire restaurant one block away. First, the food here is consistently good and has a terrific Thai accent. Great for burgers, chicken *sate* with peanut sauce, and lots of daily specials. It's always jammed with local celebs and civilians. Prices are astonishingly low.

Murder Ink (271 West 87th Street, between Broadway and West End; 362-8905) is sheer heaven for those who care about the ah! sweet mysteries of life. We've never met anyone more knowledgeable than owner Carol Brener about the entire genre of murder/mystery/intrigue.

Dock's (2427 Broadway; 724-5588) is the West Side's answer to *Jaws*. A terrific seafood restaurant in a smart tiled demi-Deco style, the only fault we can find is that it's always jammed. Prices are at the high end of moderate but the quality is top of the line. Lots of "catch of the day" specials, but we keep surfacing for the fried oysters. If you just want to stick your toe in the water, there are some small tables perfect for a plate of denizens on the half shell and a sip of champagne.

West End Avenue

The blocks behind Lincoln Center are taken by one of the West Side's most ambitious projects, Lincoln Towers, which has recently been co-oped. Once north of 72nd Street, West End is not zoned for commerce. Strictly a residential avenue in the European tradition, this is where you find family living at its peak. The old West End Avenue apartments were built generously for a well-to-do clientele, and although West End has none of the cachet of Park Avenue, it is a stronghold for old money. For visitors, it has little excitement. Especially with the competition one block west.

Riverside Drive

Riverside, like Central Park West and Fifth Avenue, fronts a park and has the added benefit of the Hudson River. For sheer drama, nothing in the city beats Riverside Drive. It is open, airy, offers river views, and a landscape that includes the skyline or the George Washington Bridge. The blocks along the Drive are dotted with some superb architecture, notably along 75th, 77th, 80th, and 81st streets.

Riverside Park itself is a sliver of green, window dressing at times to obscure the West Side Highway, but a cherished part of the neighborhood. Designed by Olmsted and Vaux of Central Park fame, it (unlike Central Park) doesn't have to be shared with the East Side and is guarded jealously by all those who live west of Broadway. Mommies and nannies head for the park as do joggers, cyclists, dog walkers, and singles out for a little sun. A special feature is the **79th Street Boat Basin,** where some hardy New Yorkers live year-round on their boats while others use the dock seasonally.

Gramercy Park

New York's only private residential park was the brainchild of 19th-century real-estate dabbler, Samuel Ruggles, who bought a twenty-acre farm and squared off 66 lots with the elitist extra that buyers alone would have access to the park.

The park was later donated to the city by the Ruggles family, along with another piece of choice real estate—Washington Square Park. The proviso was that if the gates to Gramercy Park were ever thrown open to New York City's flotsam and jetsam, the family would reclaim Washington Square Park.

Poor Mayor LaGuardia tried calling the family's bluff, declaring that city spaces must be open to one and all. Uh uh. An army of lawyers stood in front of the gates, warning the "Little Flower" that more than Washington Square Park was at stake: There is a major confluence of subway lines beneath Washington Square Park that would suddenly become privately owned. So much for public access to Gramercy.

The park itself is most exclusive. A pocket of green for those with green in their pockets. It is locked. No dogs allowed. No frisbees either. Pretty magnolia trees, very tame squirrels, and a statue of Edwin Booth as Hamlet. Benches have brass plaques with the names of donors. Very fancy names, too. Which may account for the fact there is even a dress code for those in the park. (Give us a break!)

The only way aliens may enter is by staying at the Gramercy Park Hotel: Guests are given access, but not keys.

The Gramercy Park area is a triumph for realtors, and they speak about it in the same hushed reverent tones usually reserved for the Queen Mother. To be sure, there are gorgeous blocks here, especially 19th Street between Third Avenue and Irving Place, and those on the perimeter of the park; some of these houses have been designated national landmarks. (The **Players Club** at 16 Gramercy Park South is a Gothic Revival townhouse remodeled by Stanford White after actor Edwin Booth donated it as a club for his cohorts in the theater.)

Pete's Tavern (129 East 18th St.; 473-7676) is where supposedly O. Henry wrote "The Gift of the Magi." Booth no. 1, please. Pete's is a comfortable place for burgers, omelets, and other forms of yuppie cuisine downed by the stockbrokers who come to trade tips.

Stubbs Books & Prints (28 East 18th Street) is a real find for architectural books, old and new, rare and inexpensive. A country library setting with Oriental rugs, big oak tables, bowls of potpourri, and two peppy Chinese pugs dashing around to greet visitors. There's an uptown branch at 835 Madison Avenue (69th to 70th streets).

Jimson's Novelties (30 East 18th Street) is a temple to the tasteless things that make some people double over with laughter: rubber chickens, rude bumper stickers, whoopee cushions, and well, you get the idea.

❦ You can drop into the **Old Town Bar** (45 East 18th St.) to recharge yourself. Tin ceilings, battered wooden booths, and lots of old pictures on the dark brown walls. This is, by the way, the bar photographed for the opening credits of the David Letterman TV show. Regulars here are middle-class neighborhood types, models, and photographers from nearby studios and ad agencies.

Everyone makes excuses for going to **America** at 9 East 18th St. (505-2110), as though *haute cuisine* were the only reason for going to a restaurant. Hey, what about a deafening noise level? Or moderate prices? Or some of the best people-watching?

"Perfume Row" is the name given to 17th Street between Broadway and Fifth Avenue. It's lined with shops selling brand-name perfumes and toiletries at a discount of 10 to 20 percent off department store prices. Although these are rough-and-tumble establishments, the goods are real—except for some knock-off fragrances clearly marked as Fake Opium, Fake Giorgio, and so forth. Sniff a whiff at Jay's Perfume Bar (28 East 17th Street), Perfume Encounter (25 East 17th Street), or M&P Perfumes (24 East 17th Street). Before you leave, check Lower Fifth Avenue.

Fourteenth Street, which forms the border with Greenwich Village, was once a very classy boulevard: It was "uptown" New York, the center of the theatrical district, site of the legendary Luchöw's restaurant. Not so today. While in the midst of what is claimed to be a renaissance, **Union Square Park,** once the heart of 14th Street, is a street urchin. The park was a hotbed of radical outrage in the early 1900s—the place you could always find anarchist Emma Goldman clenching her fists.

The most radical thing to be found in Union Square these days is the farmers' Greenmarket on Wednesdays, Fridays, and Saturdays.

❦ **Metropolis Café,** at 31 Union Square West at 16th St. (675-2300), is located in a restored building lobby. All white marble with potted palms and, in the evening, a piano. A few steps away is the **Union Square Café** (see Restaurants).

And while you're in the area, why not stop into **Revolution Books** (13 East 16th Street) for a look at Third World publications and posters in a friendly but earnest atmosphere.

Chelsea

The nice thing about Chelsea is that it's a place where people live rather than reside. It is the Minnesota of New York, an endangered habitat for the last of the middle class. An urban battleground on which locals have suffered the attack of the gourmets and near devastation at the hands of decorators, Chelsea is still grungy enough, ethnic enough, and genteel enough not to have lost the war. Yet.

The problem with gentrification is that it takes no prisoners. Today, a fix-it shop; tomorrow, Benetton. Nothing works but it looks good. If you're planning to visit Chelsea, do it fast while there are still dry cleaners, hardware stores, a *bodega* here, a *carniceria* there. Uh oh. Another boutique. Junk shop to junque shoppe. Men's chic apparel on Eighth Avenue, where, in the old days, chic was a new flannel workshirt.

The land acquired by Thomas Clarke in 1750 was a tract that went from what is now Eighth Avenue to the Hudson and from 14th to 24th streets. Reportedly, he named the estate Chelsea after London's Chelsea Hospital. A century later, grandson Clement Clarke Moore thought it "'twas a good area to develop into a residential district." (Yes, the very same C. C. Moore who wrote "'Twas the Night Before Christmas.") Hence, the catalog of Gothic and Greek Revival and Italianate townhouses that make it such a joy to walk up and down 20th and 21st streets between Ninth and Tenth avenues.

A richly ethnic area, Chelsea was the New World outpost for a Spanish-speaking community that emigrated from Spain long before people became hyphenates such as Hispanic-Americans. You'll find Spanish markets and restaurants on 14th Street that attract gringos and even Hispanics eager to wander amid the mantillas and saffron of Iberia. But the demographics change more rapidly than the taxi fares. The draw here is the dynamic quality of a quiet area in which you can still hear yourself think and one in which rents have not yet gone through the roof. Hence, Greenwich Village refugees arrive daily, fighting for air space with Wall Streeters who've discovered the area after coming to shop at Barney's.

To characterize **Barney's New York** (106 Seventh Avenue at 17th Street; 929-9000) as a clothing store is tantamount to calling the Eiffel Tower a radio antenna. Simply, this former frog of a discount men's store has been transformed into the city's most expensive and avant-garde designer shop for men and women of all sexes. Valentino, Armani, Cerutti, Versace & Company—you'll find them hanging out here. The Co-Op is a slightly less expensive women's shop within the store, which is good news if you're an 18-year old willowy model saving every penny for a new Porsche. For the rest of us, it's a treat just to rub elbows while browsing.

Chelsea's other landmark is the description-defying **Hotel Chelsea** (222 West 23rd Street, between Seventh and Eighth avenues; 212-243-3700), where Thomas Wolfe, Brendan Behan, Arthur C. Clarke, Arthur Miller, and William Burroughs wrote, Virgil Thompson and Bob Dylan composed, and Sid Vicious and Dylan Thomas died. Far too eccentric to be included as one of our hotel selections, the Chelsea is, on its own terms (and that's the only way the Chelsea can be taken—on its own terms), a real treasure. Walking into the lobby is comparable to stepping onstage in the midst of *Once in a Lifetime,* the play about a nuttier-than-a-fruitcake family with a heart of gold. The pink brick and iron grillwork Victorian-Gothic exterior of the first building in the city to be designated a New York Landmark both for architectural and historical interest in no way prepares you for the near chaos of a gallery-lobby filled with enormous and sometimes quite wonderful canvases, sculptures, and more characters than a Fellini movie. Still, the Chelsea has to be seen to be believed—or at least seen before you decide to make a reservation. The people who stay here love it, the ones who don't are mystified by it all.

Meriken (162 West 21st St. at Seventh Ave.; 620-9684) is a nouvelle Japanese restaurant whose name mimics the Japanese pronunciation of "American." Very trendy, lo-cal cuisine.

Wooden Indian (60 West 15th Street; 243-8590) is a hideaway for discounted glassware, the perfect place to stock up on old Cola-style glasses, swizzle sticks, and laboratory bottles for use as cannisters.

Jam Envelope and Paper Discount Outlet (621 Avenue of the Americas at 19th Street; 255-4593) is for dedicated paper hounds only. If you're tickled pink at the thought of shocking pink computer paper and chrome-yellow interoffice envelopes, the prices are right.

Tobacco Products Co. (137 Eighth Avenue at 17th Street; 989-3900) is an old-fashioned place where they huff and puff from making cigars and reading the Surgeon General's report. It's the kind of shop you hardly ever find anymore and might be the end of your search for what to bring Uncle Sylvester.

Miss Ruby's Café (135 Eighth Ave. at 16th St.; 620-4055) bills itself as serving "American Eclectic Cooking" and they won't have any problem with the "truth in advertising" folks. The menu changes every two weeks or so from Tex Mex to Cajun to Midwestern No Nonsense. Basically, it's Texas Discovers America and how can you not love a place that serves chicken livers with lime, scallions, bourbon, and pecans; wild boar sausage with spicy corn relish; and corn-meal-fried catfish with onion hush puppies, spicy tartar sauce, and tomato-scallion salad with orange zest? Prices are moderate.

Other drop-ins are **Man Ray** (169 Eighth Ave. at 19th St.; 627-4220), a French bistro like the French never had. Trés chic thirties décor and abuzz with fashion-biz people who wouldn't be caught dead anyplace touristy or above 39th St.

Mary Ann's (116 Eighth Ave. at 16th St.; 633-0877) is a local paradise: brick walls, wooden floors, and what just might be the most reasonably priced Tex Mex food outside of the Ponderosa.

Two old standbys in Chelsea that share, with Barney's, credit
for bringing trendsetters west are the Pottery Barn and the
Empire Diner. **Pottery Barn** (231 Tenth Avenue at 24th
Street; 206-8118) is where everyone who needed inexpensive
but well-designed glassware and dishes for their cold-water
flats went twenty years ago and they now go back to outfit
their houses in the Hamptons. It's always filled with the best
kinds of bargains: those that don't sacrifice taste for price.

As for the **Empire Diner** (210 Tenth Ave. at 22nd St.; 243-
2736), this is where people who wouldn't be caught dead in a
diner go. It's open 24 hours a day for insomniac models and
guilt-ridden stockbrokers who kid themselves into thinking that
life is a cabaret. While there are a few tasty goodies on the
menu, the clientele comes to feast their eyes. On themselves.

Greenwich Village

When we were growing up in Manhattan, it seemed to us that
anything exciting in New York—with the exception of Ethel
Merman—was in the Village. There was, in those days, only
one Village. Of course, everyone said (even way back then)
that the Village wasn't what it used to be.

In that respect, nothing has changed: Greenwich Village
still isn't what it used to be. The problem with this former
Camelot of creativity is that it's trapped in the nostalgia of
everyone's memories and hasn't redefined itself. There are
still coffeehouses and jewelers and off-Broadway theaters and
Italian restaurants. But the only parts of the Village in which
one is likely to succumb to déjà vu is along Bleecker Street,
and south of Washington Square Park along MacDougal, Sullivan, and Thompson streets. Dear old 8th Street has been van-
dalized by fast foodies and discounters. While we were all
watching the East Village and Soho and Chelsea and the
Upper West Side, someone came and stole Greenwich Village.

But that's been going on for years, as far back as the Dutch
who came and stole the settlement named Sapokanican from
the Indians. Granted, the area that became Washington
Square was only marshland surrounding old Minetta Brook,
but it was soon subdivided into farms and its value increased
so that by the time the British arrived in the early 1700s, it
was renamed Greenwich (Green Village). Later in the century, downtown residents headed north to the healthy country
air of Greenwich Village to avoid the raging yellow fever and
smallpox epidemics. Wall Street banks that checked out of the
seaport area for the duration of the scourge relocated on what
became known as Bank Street.

By the late 1800s, the population increased significantly
with the arrival of Irish and Italian immigrants. Local landlords

converted houses into tenements, hotels into sweatshops. On the heels of oppression came activists, radicals, and freethinkers who, by this time, even had a middle-class American culture against which to rebel. Attracted to this hotbed of anarchists and suffragettes were artists and writers who lingered long after the battles moved on.

However cranky one is with the village for not realizing its potential as the "Left Bank" of New York, it did, at the very least, attract a more prominent and diverse list of creative talent than anywhere else in the city. It was here that Eugene O'Neill got his first break at the Provincetown Playhouse (133 MacDougal Street), and Ruth McKenney lived with her sister Eileen (14 Gay Street). Artists from Winslow Homer to Diego Rivera, most of the jazz greats, almost all the social comedians, and even latter-day folk heroes such as Bob Dylan, strutted their stuff in the Village.

Today's major strutters are members of the gay community who fought long and hard for their rights in private and then in public. The Village, with a history of nurturing artistic and social passions, supported vigorously the "gay pride" movement that gained momentum in its backyard.

Eat Your Zip Code Out
A List of the Artsiest Addresses in the Village

85 West 3rd Street / Edgar Allan Poe.

18 West 11th Street / The original town house here was destroyed by the Weathermen in 1969 while using the premises as their bomb factory. Dustin Hoffman, who lived next door, moved uptown.

75 ½ Bedford Street / Edna St. Vincent Millay, and later John Barrymore.

309 Bleecker Street / Thomas Paine.

145 Bleecker Street / James Fenimore Cooper.

21 Washington Place / Henry James was born here.

11 Fifth Avenue / Henry James lived here.

57 West 14th Street / Ditto.

19 Washington Square North / Henry James's grandmother lived here. This is where H.J. soaked up atmosphere for you-know-what book, which they say developed from an anecdote actress Fanny Kemble told him.

16 Washington Square North / This is where Henry J. set his novel, *Washington Square,* no doubt figuring his crafty change of venue would fool everyone.

21 East 11th Street / Home of Minnie Jones, a friend of Henry James's, who married Edith Wharton's brother.

7 Washington Square North / Edith Wharton.

487 Hudson Street / Bret Harte.

14 West 10th Street / Samuel Clemens (a.k.a. Mark Twain).

61 Washington Square / Known as Mme. Katharine Branchard's "House of Genius" because it was rumored that Crane, Dreiser, O. Henry, O'Neill, Willa Cather, Lincoln Steffens, and

Dos Passos all lived here. If it's true, there must have been quite a line-up for the bathroom in the morning.

5 Bank Street / Willa Cather.

42 Washington Square South / John (*Ten Days that Shook the World*) Reed. Also Lincoln Steffens who lived in the room below Reed's.

Patchin Place / John Reed and Louise Bryant (Warren Beatty and Diane Keaton in *Reds*).

38 Washington Square / Eugene O'Neill (Jack Nicholson in the same movie).

24 West 16th Street / William Cullen Bryant.

165 West 10th Street / Theodore Dreiser.

14 St. Luke's Place / Marianne Moore.

139 Waverly Place / Edna St. Vincent Millay.

54 West 10th Street / Hart Crane.

4 Patchin Place / e. e. cummings, visited here by (uppercase) T. S. Eliot and Dylan Thomas.

3 Washington Square North / Edmund Wilson.

263 West 11th Street / Thomas Wolfe.

37 West 10th Street / Sinclair Lewis.

393 Bleecker Street / Mark Van Doren.

54 Washington Mews / Sherwood Anderson stayed here.

172 Bleecker Street / James Agee.

215 West 13th Street / Anais Nin.

82 Washington Place / Richard Wright.

18 Gay Street / Mary McCarthy.

45 Greenwich Avenue / William Styron.

3 Washington Square / John Dos Passos.

38 Washington Square South / Eugene O'Neill.

50 West 10th Street / Edward Albee.

49 Grove Street / Vance Bourjaily.

and just for good measure:

35 East 12th Street / Mikhail Baryshnikov.

451 Washington Street / Bette Midler.

14 Washington Place / Mayor Ed Koch.

The Village, at first glance, seems somewhat daunting. Its geography is as nonconformist as its residents. You want to talk alternative lifestyles? This is a neighborhood that straddles both sides of Fifth Avenue—the only area in the city with that particular distinction! How you see the Village (literally and figuratively) depends as much upon time as perspective.

The best way to psych things out is a walk along Bleecker Street, named for 19th-century scholar Anthony Bleecker who gave the land for the street to the city. Start at the Abingdon Square end and go east. En route, take a few steps into the cross streets (among the most interesting in the Village) and by the time you're through, you'll have experienced enough to know how much exploring you want to do.

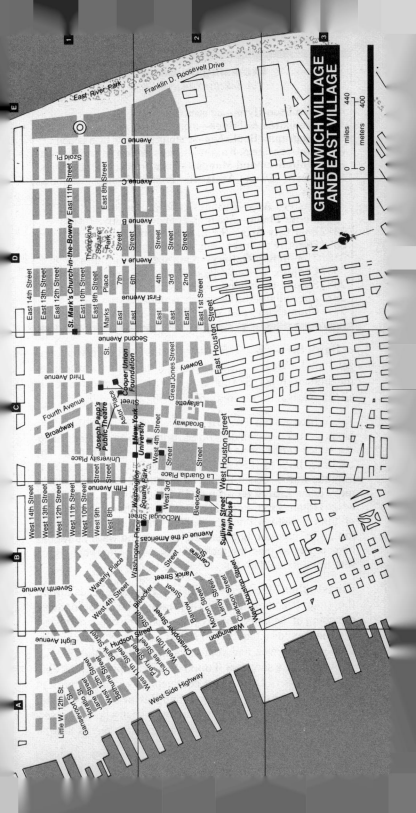

GREENWICH VILLAGE AND EAST VILLAGE

0 — miles — 440
0 — meters — 400

N

East River Park

Franklin D. Roosevelt Drive

East River Park

Szold Pl.

St. Mark's Church-in-the-Bowery

East 14th Street
East 13th Street
East 12th Street
East 11th Street
East 10th Street
East 9th Street
St. Marks Place

Tompkins Square Park

Avenue D
Avenue C
Avenue B
Avenue A

7th Street
6th Street
4th Street
3rd Street
2nd Street

First Avenue
Second Avenue

East 8th Street
East 7th Street
East 6th Street
East 5th Street
East 4th Street
East 2nd Street
East 1st Street

Third Avenue
Fourth Avenue
Broadway

Cooper Union Foundation
Astor Place
Joseph Papp's Public Theatre
New York University

Great Jones Street
Bowery
Lafayette Street
Broadway

West 4th Street
West 3rd Street

Fifth Avenue
University Place
Washington Place
Washington Square Park
McDougal Street

La Guardia Place

East Houston Street
West Houston Street

Bleecker Street

Sullivan Street Playhouse

West 14th Street
West 13th Street
West 12th Street
West 11th Street
West 10th Street
West 9th Street
West 8th Street

Seventh Avenue

Waverly Place
West 4th Street
Bleecker Street
Barrow Street
Morton Street
Leroy Street
Clarkson Street

Carmine Street
Varick Street

Washington Street
West Houston Street

Eight Avenue

Little W. 12th St.
Gansevoort St.
Horatio Street
Jane Street
West 12th Street
West 11th Street
Bethune Street
Bank Street
Perry Street
Charles Street
West 10th Street
Christopher Street
Hudson Street

West Side Highway

West Side Highway

1
2
3

A
B
C
D
E

Browsing on Bleecker
A Selective Guide to Shops

413 / **Hamilton-Hyre**—antiques
409 / **Treasures & Trifles**—more antiques
400 / **Biography Bookshop**—truth is stranger than fiction
383 / **Constantine & Knight**—serious clothes for serious men
375 / **Whitehead and Mangan**—great selection of rare prints
369 / **Pierre Deux Antiques**—French country furniture, fabrics
365 / **Eastern Arts**—paintings, carvings, and jewelry
361 / **Kelter Malce**—American primitive, country artifacts
341 / **Lost City Arts**—N.Y.C. architectural antiques
335 / **Dorothy's Closet**—hot, sexy antique clothing
318 / **Tim McKoy Gallery**—repro statues, sculptures
306 / **Chapitre 3**—most elegant duffles and totes in town
283 / **Second Childhood**—kid's toys for adults
282 / **Aphrodisia**—herbs, spices, perfume oils
270 / **Chameleon**—post-World War II-ish nostalgia clothes

Bank Street is the first intersection and here you'll find some of the Village's nicest homes, 19th-century row houses: numbers 16 to 34, 37 (noted as one of the best examples of Greek Revival in the area), 55, 57, 68, 74, 76, 128, and 130.

The **White Horse Tavern** (567 Hudson St.; 243-9260), one block west of Bleecker on 11th St., is famous as a writer's hangout, which translates as inexpensive for a burger and brew. The bar dates back to 1880 but is really a landmark because Dylan Thomas was a regular there in the early 1950s. A few blocks away is the **Lion's Head** bar (59 Christopher St.; 929-0670), which is literary with a capital L. This is an author's hangout rather than a writer's (though "writers" have been seen here, too . . .). There are book jackets all over the walls as well as hamburgers all over the tables. Expectedly, somewhat pricier, with more formal fare than the White Horse.

Christopher Street crosses Bleecker and as it heads toward the river becomes the official parade ground for baroque members of the homosexual community. The order of the day is to be flamboyant and so no matter your level of sophistication, you may well find your eyes widening a bit.

Two favorite shops are **Topeo** (94 Christopher Street; 255-4523) for lots of Deco, great contemporary crafts, American pottery, and tons of gift goodies; and **Bellardo** (100 Christopher Street; 675-2668) for even more Deco in a sprawling setting that includes contemporary and costume pieces as well as gorgeous repros of Tiffany lamps.

The Pink Teacup (42 Grove St.; 807-6755) has nothing to do with New York except that it attracts hungry New Yorkers who scarf down huge platters of grits and eggs, fried pork chops, or barbecue chicken. Southern comfort that's inexpensive, homey, and hearty. If your tastes run in another direction, stay on Bleecker until it intersects with Seventh Avenue South, a major traffic artery with numerous restaurants including **John Clancy's Restaurant** (181 West 10th St.; 242-7350) for elegant fish; **One If By Land, Two If By Sea** (17 Barrow St.; 228-0822) for a romantic, if expensive, continental dinner in Aaron Burr's coach house; and the **Manhattan Chili Company** (302 Bleecker St.; 206-7163) for its dynamite Texas Chain Gang Chili.

While in the area, you might consider—if you can find it— **Chumley's** (86 Bedford St.; 675-4449), a bar between Barrow and Grove sts. Look for an unmarked door with a grill on it. If it opens into a former speakeasy that's filled with uptown yuppies, you're in the right place. Good for a burger.

The part of Bleecker that runs between Seventh Avenue South and Sixth Avenue is the last remaining block of ethnic Bleecker Street. You'll find Italian bakeries and butchers and grocers that will make you wish they delivered back home.

One place that delivers on the spot is **John's Pizzeria** (278 Bleecker St.; 243-1680), a counter-chic venue for close encounters of the crispy kind. Deliciously old-fashioned, always crowded, this is the place for pre-gourmet Italian pizza.

MacDougal Street is filled with coffeehouses and students. Still a mecca for kids who've just discovered Beethoven and Kierkegaard, and grown-ups who've just discovered they want to be kids again.

On the corner of Bleecker is **Café Le Figaro** (184 Bleecker; 677-1100), which became famous as a "beat" hangout during the fifties and is still going strong. **The Caffè Reggio,** (119 MacDougal; 475-9557) dates from 1927 and loyal followers claim you get the best cappuccino here. The **Caffè Dante** (79-81 MacDougal; 982-5275), on the other hand, has been cited for having the best espresso.

Follow MacDougal down to Houston, make a left, and come back up on Sullivan Street. You'll find the **Sullivan Street Playhouse** (181 Sullivan; 674-3838) home of the world's longest-running musical, *The Fantasticks*. Make a right on Bleecker, follow Thompson Street (where you may wish to defect to **Little Bucharest** at 170 Thompson; 529-2933, for a plate of cornmeal mush with feta cheese and sour cream like Mama used to make) and then come back to Bleecker via La Guardia Place, which is alive with street vendors, crafts people, and students from neighboring N.Y.U.

To complete the day's excursion, head north on La Guardia to **Washington Square Park** which is recognized generally as the heart (if not the soul) of the Village. This is the park in which Robert Redford was *Barefoot in . . .* and the center of street life on weekends. You'll find mimes and thieves, artists and drug dealers, an almost medieval mix of professions seeking voluntary and involuntary compensation. A far cry from the original concept for the area when a wooden Memorial Arch designed by Stanford White was erected in 1876 for the nation's centennial. The arch created a sensation. Paderewski, not merely a great pianist but also a well-known arch supporter, held a benefit performance and donated the proceeds to the fund for a permanent structure. The arch, completed in 1892, was significant also as being the standard-bearer for a City Beautiful Movement staged by architects who fought the concept that big is beautiful. They argued that American cities should offer more than size: Scale and neo-classical ideals were cited in this first push toward an American Renaissance.

As much as we'd like to ignore it, a word is in order concerning the architectural blight caused by N.Y.U.'s presence in the area. One must question what this educational institution expects us to learn from its total disregard for the cultural environment.

If you have more time and are interested in antiques, head east of Fifth Avenue. The blocks between 8th Street and 13th Street, bordered by University Place and Broadway, are filled with some of the most wonderful **antique shops** to be found this side of the Seine. While many are "to the trade only," there are enough to keep you busy for weeks. See East Village, for two V.I.P. Broadway bookshops, **Strand,** and **Forbidden Planet.**

For Dedicated Foodies Only: put on a blindfold, walk down ugly old 8th St. to Sixth Ave., turn right and head for **Balducci's** (424 Avenue of the Americas; 673-2600), between 9th and 10th sts. Almost everything is available for tasting, the selection is miraculous, and the quality simply can't be beat.

A Greenwich Village Advisory. Shops and restaurants open and close more frequently here than Third World nations. But it doesn't matter. The Bleecker Street routing, however limited, offers the full range of experiences and attitudes that are distinctly "the Village."

East Village

If ever a neighborhood wore its heart on its sleeve, that's the East Village. Situated geographically, and emotionally, between the Lower East Side and Greenwich Village, the area is as ethnic as Zorba the Greek and every bit as passionate. Life-support systems are fueled by a finely adjusted blend of oxygen, rebellion, and *sturm und drang*.

The creative spirits who live east of Broadway are not successful enough yet to move away. The citizens of Alphabet City (the avenues east of First Avenue are avenues A, B, and C) cannot afford the West (Greenwich) Village or Soho—and it is unthinkable to them that anything worthwhile in life could ever happen north of 14th Street. There's enough excitement down here to keep them, and you, hopping.

Let's face it: This is not a pretty place. The traffic on the streets can be daunting—not vehicular but drug traffic. The terrain is dominated by tenements, many of which are as burned out as the men who sleep nearby in doorways on the Bowery. On abandonded buildings, there are garish Third Worldish murals that shout incoherent messages. Still, the odds are that whatever is to be New York's next avant-garde sensibility, it will rise out of the urban rubble and ego drive east of Broadway.

The East Village is a war zone. The battle is against conformity, and outrageousness is the weapon of choice. The reasons for coming here are to people watch, gallery hop, shop, attend performances (this is where *Off*-Off Broadway began) and to discover inexpensive, delicious, and sometimes frightening-looking ethnic food. There are no dazzling historic landmarks, lush gardens, or darling shoppes. No one makes the trip down here to see the **Renwick Triangle** (a series of Italianate townhouses between Stuyvesant and East 10th streets), or **St. Mark's Church in the Bowery** (Second Avenue at 10th Street), even if it is the oldest continuously used church in town. They don't even come to see the building at **206 East 7th Street** where "Beat Generation" poet Allen Ginsberg lived, Jack Kerouac hung out, and where William Burroughs finally moved in.

The official point of entry into the East Village is **St. Mark's Place,** which is, in reality, East 8th Street. This was a fashionable place to promenade in the 19th century (townhouses are set back from the street giving the block a boulevardish appearance), when the area was part of the Lower East Side ethnic stew and the accents were heavily German. Then Polish, Ukrainian, and Russian. None of which prepared the area for discovery by the social backlash of the sixties: the hippies, runaways, druggies, and even members of Andy Warhol's Velvet Underground. While everyone else has metamorphosed, one loyal group remains: Hell's Angels. You'll find their headquarters on East 3rd Street, between First and Second avenues. It's hard to miss. Lots of bikes out front. Lots of guys you just know never eat quiche.

Second Avenue was once the great white way for New York's Yiddish Theater and then home to the equally legendary Filmore East, where every group worth its groupies rocked the rafters. What remains today is a creative anarchy of paintings, clothes, jewelry, and theater. But the East Village offers more than a feast for the eyes.

You won't go home hungry from the **Second Avenue Deli** (156 Second Ave., near 10th St.; 677-0606), the "Elaine's" of New York's kosher mafia; or the **B&H Dairy Restaurant** (127 Second Ave. near 8th St.; 777-1930), a narrow, crowded Formica joint famous for the borscht, blintzes, and an entire catalog of doughy/eggy things; the **Kiev Coffee Shop** (117 Second Ave. near 7th St.), for short-order vaguely Russian dishes that don't cost a Czar's ransom—i.e., there's a $1.50 minimum at the tables; **Sugar Reef** (93 Second Ave. between 5th and 6th sts.; 477-8427), a hip Caribbean festival mini-extravaganza sporting leopardskin barstools and tutti-frutti milkshakes with palm-tree swizzle sticks; and almost all of East 6th St., the jewel in the crown of the East Village for lovers of cheap Indian food. **Mitali** (334 East 6th St.; 533-2508), serving Northern Indian dishes and deliciously low prices, is a favorite.

And that's just for starters. The **Ukrainian East Village Restaurant** (140 Second Ave. at 8th St.; 529-5024) has 1940s prices (most main courses are below $5) and 19th-century portions. Sip a $1.60 bowl of (what else?) Ukrainian borscht and go on to splurge with a (what else?) Ukrainian Combination Platter ($6.30) of stuffed cabbage, four varieties of pierogi, cabbage, and kielbasa.

Thirsty? **McSorley's Old Ale House** (15 East 7th St.; 473-9148) first opened in 1854 and only let women in after a 1970 court battle. Lincoln, Roosevelt, and Kennedy are said to have quaffed here. Draft ale, sandwiches. Heavy on the atmosphere. **Gem Spa** (131 Second Ave. at St. Mark's Place) is where you'll find one of the great staples of Manhattan life: the egg cream. This beverage is to New York City dwellers what mint juleps were to Scarlett O'Hara, brandy to Churchill, nectar to the gods. Made with neither egg nor cream, the Official N.Y.C. Egg Cream is a chocolate soda with milk that has more controversy surrounding ingredients and techniques than any dry martini.

The Official N.Y.C. Egg Cream Recipe

Fox's U-Bet Chocolate Syrup
One cylindrical 8-ounce glass
Whole milk
Seltzer in a pressurized cylinder (no bottles, please)
One spoon

All ingredients must be very cold. Put one inch of syrup into the glass. Add one inch of milk. Tilt the glass as you aim seltzer onto the spoon. You should get a big chocolatey head. Stir, shake your head approvingly, and drink. Then shake your head again.

Many of the shops and galleries in the East Village are so avant-garde you don't expect them to survive their leases. Often they can't. Among the galleries to try are **Bridgewater** (208 East 7th; 505-9977), **Gracie Mansion** (167 Avenue A; 477-7331), **Pat Hearn** (735 East 9th; 598-4282), **La Galleria Second Classe** (6 East 1st; 505-2476), **PACA Gallery** (131 East 7th; 505-1713), **Postmasters** (66 Avenue A; 477-5630), and **Sragow** (436 East 11th; 477-6284). The *Gallery Guide,* which many galleries distribute free, lists who's exhibiting what where.

Kiehl's Pharmacy (109 Third Avenue at 13th Street; 475-3400) is headquarters for herbal remedies. Filled with homeopathic goodies, they've been selling natural substances since 1851—fragrances, tonics, and creams to soothe the savage beast in all of us. **Civilisation** (78 Second Avenue at 4th Street; 254-3788) is one of the best-known trendsetters in the city. Lots of punk ceramics, cutting edge jewelry, and all the postmodern gifts and housewares you need. Prices are steep but dig a bit to find things that mere mortals can afford: faux marble switchplates for $10. The owners describe their buying practices saying they look for artists creating things with an edge. Bring Band-Aids. They may still have those huge ceramic platters with snarling dogs painted on them: $250.

If you have the time, walk down East 1st Street toward Avenue A: past the offices of *The Catholic Worker,* St. Joseph House, where the homeless are fed, some brand-new 1950s housewares and furniture emporia, and some boutiques selling the same clothes you'll find up on 57th Street at Charivari. The mix on this block pretty much sums up the contradictions that make the East Village tick.

More shops. **Alphabets** (115 Avenue A; 475-7250) has the best selection in town of clever greeting cards, lots of paper goods, novelty toys. **Clodagh Ross Williams** (122 St. Mark's Place; 505-1774) has the ultimate in chic, expensive gift items. Come here for everything from TVs built of stone to jewelry made of rare metals. **Einstein's** (96 East 7th Street; 598-9748) has nothing to do with relativity. The stock is off the wall. Ditz to the *n*th degree. Novelty hats, dresses for men, jewelry made from discards. Give your barrel of monkeys the day off. **Finyl Vinyl** (89 Second Avenue; 533-8007) specializes in rock records from the fifties and sixties. This is the place to find that missing album in your Temptations collection. **Gabay's** (225 First Avenue; 254-3180) sells overstocked, damaged, or returned merchandise from some of New York City's best stores. You can find shoes, shirts, gowns, flatware, and dresses, albeit sometimes distressed but not yet dead. True believers say there are often items in perfect condition.

On the fringe of the East Village mentality is Astor Place and Lafayette Street, once the most elegant and wealthiest residential area in the city. This is where the Astors, the Delanos, and the Vanderbilts lived. The Astor Library is now the home of **Joseph Papp's Public Theatre** where *Hair* and *A Chorus Line* were first mounted.

Across the street is the trendy **Indochine** (430 Lafayette St.; 505-5111), where blue-plate specials are Vietnamese but the reason people come is to watch who else eats here.

Broadway from 12th Street down is more Greenwich than East Village. **Strand Bookstore** (828 Broadway; 473-1452) is the big apple for bookworms. With over two million books in stock, Strand boasts an incredible selection of reviewer's copies of brand new tomes that sell at 50 percent off list price. Science fiction buffs will "beam up" at **Forbidden Planet** (821 Broadway; 473-1576), where they have enough games and books to keep you occupied until you reach Mars. Eight blocks down is the original New York **Tower Records** (692 Broadway; 505-1500), where the selection is so good that at times you almost don't care about the show in the aisles. While tuning up, compulsive shoppers can check out the **Unique Clothing Warehouse** at 718 and 726 Broadway (674-1767).

Soho

Soho is a theme park for rich kids in their thirties and forties. The theme in this magic kingdom is that you don't have to be poor to be creative, and that there is life after divorce. (She keeps the co-op, he sacks out at the Harvard Club and has a brief but meaningless fling with the real-estate agent from whom he winds up buying a loft in Soho.) *Voila!* A neighborhood is born.

All right, reborn. During the mid-1700s, Soho was Indian territory: home of the self-same Indians against whom settlers built the wall for which Wall Street was named. By the 1850s, Soho was the hub of the city. Its very elegant residential area spun off restaurants, theaters, shops, and hotels. As the city center continued its move north, Soho was no longer fashionable. The drop in real-estate prices attracted manufacturers who filled their sweatshops with immigrant workers. In the 1950s, by which time Soho had been zoned exclusively as a light manufacturing (and not residential) area, artists fleeing the rising rents in Greenwich Village began moving in illegally, renting substandard housing in return for unusually large studio space. In the sixties, Soho went legit and was rezoned. Artists, realizing how much their space was now worth, didn't have to starve anymore. They sold and moved to Brooklyn or Hoboken. Suddenly, the community became a haven for the terminally trendy.

What the Names Mean

Soho	*S*outh *o*f *Ho*uston Street (pronounced *How*ston not *Hew*ston)
Tribeca	*Tri* angle *be*low *Ca*nal Street
Soso	*S*outh *o*f *So*ho—Tribeca
Noho	*No*rth *o*f *Ho*uston Street
Dumbo	*D*own *U*nder the *M*anhattan *B*ridge *O*verpass

Note: No real New Yorker has heard of any places other than Soho and Tribeca. Maybe Noho.

Soho is one of the city's best attractions. It rivals 57th Street as the art capital of New York. It is an area filled with shops that sell the kind of classy goodies once associated with upper Madison Avenue before it smothered itself in chic Eurotrash. Soho has restaurants for every taste and a weekend street life that is the talk of the town.

As a visitor, your best day for Soho is Saturday. (Most galleries are closed on Sunday; everything is closed on Monday. The next best times—Tuesday through Friday—tend to be quiet.) Nothing much is open before noon.

The most important architectural feature of the area is its concentration of cast-iron façades, the largest in the world. If you really want to test your mettle, head for Greene Street, the bull's-eye in Soho's Cast-Iron Historic District. There's more than a quarter mile of the late 19th-century Italianate-ish structures that presaged modern steel-frame buildings. Devotees can indulge themselves on bold Tuscan columns, delicate Corinthian pilasters, and even a Second Empire roof or two. Specifically, see numbers **28 to 30,** and numbers **72 to 76.**

At first glance, Soho seems eminently manageable. The main drag is West Broadway, with Sullivan, Thompson, Wooster, Greene, and Mercer running parallel. Prince, Spring, Broome, and Grand cut across in perpendicular lines. Simple. Uh uh. With some of the city's best shops and most appealing restaurants, Soho can be as demanding for those with limited time as it can for those with limited budgets.

Our ideal itinerary begins at about noon with lunch at **Food** (127 Prince St.; 473-8790, no credit cards), a large cheerful self-serve restaurant (don't even think cafeteria) with diabolically healthful portions built-for-two. Sharing is something everyone does. Soups are meals in themselves, the prices are low, the company very eclectic—paint-stained artists next to minked matrons.

Another popular stop is the **Cupping Room Café** (359 West Broadway; 925-2898), which starts with breakfast at 7:30 A.M., serves brunch every day, and features Australian food and wine

SOHO, LOWER EAST SIDE, TRIBECA, BOWERY, CANAL, LITTLE ITALY

East River Park
Franklin D. Roosevelt Drive

Corlears Hook Park

East River

Williamsburg Bridge

Lewis St.

Jackson St.

Columbia Street

Pitt Street

Ridge Street

Clinton Street

Attorney Street

Suffolk Street

Norfolk Street

East Houston Street

Stanton Street

Rivington Street

Delancey Street

LOWER
EAST SIDE

Broome Street

Grand Street

Ludlow Street

Willet St.

Park

Broadway

Gouverneur St.

Montgomery St.

Clinton Street

Jefferson

Rutgers St.

Pike St.

Manhattan Bridge

East

South St.

Market Street

Water Street

Cherry St.

Henry Street

Catherine St.

Governor Smith
Houses

Brooklyn Bridge

Frankfort St.

Forsythe St.

Eldridge St.

Canal Street

Chrystie Street

Bowery St.

Hester Street

Elizabeth St.

Mott Street

Mulberry Street

LITTLE
ITALY

CHINATOWN

Park Row

Baxter St.

Madison Street

Prince Street

Spring Street

Dean & DeLuca

Tootsi
Plohound

Agnes B.

Harriet
Love

Dapy

Think Big

SOHO

Mercer St.

Greene St.

Wooster Street

West Broadway

Broome Street

Grand Street

Lafayette Street

Museum of
Holography

Canal Street

Lispenard St.

Walker St.

White St.

Franklin St.

Leonard St.

Worth St.

Thomas St.

Duane St.

Reade St.

Broadway

West Broadway

Chambers Street

Civic Center

City Hall

West Houston Street

McDougal Street

Thompson Street

Avenue of the Americas

Varick Street

Fire
Department
Museum

Houston St.

King St.

Charlton St.

Greenwich Vandam St.

Greenwich Street

Dominick St.

Watts St.

Debrosses St.

Vestry St.

Laight St.

Hubert St.

N. Moore St.

Harrison

Greenwich Street

Hudson Street

Holland
Tunnel

West Side Highway

Pier 40

Pier 25

Hudson River

N

yards   0   440
meters 0   400

at dinner. However, if you're into truly serious dining, at truly serious prices, do not overlook **Chanterelle** (6 Harrison St.; 966-6960), which has been gathering kudos from foodies all around town. David Waltuck's version of classic French cooking keeps the tables booked well in advance.

Recognizing that there isn't enough time to do Soho in one visit, check out the galleries first. Use the Friday or Sunday *New York Times* or *New York* magazine or *The New Yorker* to find shows that are of interest. If you're not a gallery person, then build your schedule around the shops, bearing in mind that it's nearly impossible to stick to any kind of timetable in Soho: These stores were made for browsing. You can window shop on Madison and Fifth more easily than you can on West Broadway.

HOW TO SPEND THE REST OF YOUR LIFE
(And All Your Money)
ON WEST BROADWAY

383 / **O.K. Harris**
Lively exhibits at one of the pioneer Soho galleries.

386 / **D.F. Sanders**
High-tech housewares often of museum quality.

390 / **Think Big**
Everyday items (paper clips, pads, pencils, aspirin) re-created in huge sizes for grown-up kids.

393 / **DIA Art Foundation**
A nonprofit organization that features work by new artists.

410 / **Ad Hoc Softwares**
Everything soft and smooth for bed and bath.

410 / **American High**
A sweats shop for the fashionable. As corny as Kansas in August. Not to be missed.

412 / **Harriet Love**
Old clothes never had it so good.

414 / **Paracelso**
What the well-dressed female activist would wear if she cared what she wore.

417 / **Mary Boone Gallery**
One of the leaders in contemporary art.

420 / **Leo Castelli**
One of the country's most famous dealers, the quality (and prices) here are always top.

420 / **Sonnabend**
Well-known gallery for photography as well as paintings.

431 / **Dapy**
Funny plastic thingamajigs for stocking stuffers. Toys for the world weary.

436 / **Joovay**
Well-behaved women's lingerie that knows it is meant to be seen and not heard.

451 / **Victoria Falls**
Antique wedding gowns. Even the new clothes have the feeling of yesteryear. Wonderful hats and accessories. Prices are reasonable, considering the quality and unique design.

454 / **Rizzoli Bookstore**
The latest in art books.

456B / **Artwear**
Very Left-Bankish. High-tech one of a kind jewelry in a gorgeous setting.

457 / **Jordan Volpe Gallery**
Paintings.

457 / **Martin Lawrence Galleries**
Limited editions and original works by leading contemporary artists. Has an installment purchase plan.

468 / **Circle Gallery**
Aside from their collection of contemporary artists, they feature limited edition jewelry called "Art to Wear." All signed and numbered, pieces are by Erté, Agam, Braque, and others.

474 / **IF**
Drop-dead chic designer clothes for every sex.

New York had 102 breweries in 1879. By 1976, there were none. Three cheers for the recently opened **Manhattan Brewing Company** (40 Thompson St.), which not only makes "Manhattan Royal Amber" beer but five ales—and has the good sense to serve them on premises. Start your Thompson St. tour with a fresh brew or two in the Tap Room with its four giant-size copper brewing kettles. Hearty pub food is served.

On Greene, Spring, and Prince streets you can while away the hours and learn the true meaning of cash flow:

Luna D'Oro / 66 Greene—South American folk art.

Zona / 97 Greene—Southwestern and Mexican furnishings.

Greene Street Café / 101 Greene—two-tiered nightclub and restaurant in a very palmy setting.

Soho Kitchen and Bar / 103 Greene—informal, eclectic and spirited: crispy, designer pizza and dozens of wines by the glass (via Cruvinet).

Agnes B. / 116 Prince—French duds for the entire family.

Tootsi Plohound / 110 Prince—what else with a name like that? Shoes!

Mood Indigo / 181 Prince—Bakelite, Fiestaware, chrome jewelry. Depressionware gone happy.

Elephant & Castle / 183 Prince—where the locals go for burgers and brunch.

Omo Norma Kamali / 113 Spring—a branch of the uptown shop should you need a shoulder-pad fix.

Grass Roots Gallery / 131 Spring—folk art from Latin America, Haiti, and other Caribbean isles.

Bon Jour France / 155 Spring—a fantasy shop filled with dolls (for grown-ups) that are true works of art.

With all the galleries in Soho, a museum would be redundant—except for the **Museum of Holography** (11 Mercer Street. Open Tuesday through Sunday from noon to 6 P.M.; 925-0526) which is as avant-garde as the local environment. What you get here is the latest in 3-D images made by combining laser beams and photography. As though that weren't enough, you could go broke in the gift shop, which is crammed with the latest in visual images.

Dean & DeLuca (560 Broadway) is the Louvre of gourmet food shops. Their new location is a stunner. Bring a camera *and* a checkbook.

Tribeca

The *Tri*angle *Be*low *Ca*nal Street is a triangle no more. This "son of Soho" has outgrown its original boundaries to become, along with Battery Park, one of the city's most rapidly changing areas. Tribeca is about a decade behind Soho: People from New Jersey wonder who would be crazy enough to live in a desolated area like this. Who else? A New Yorker.

There is still a sense of frontier in Tribeca. All the streets and shops have not been conquered by the Army of the Chic. Hallelujah! There is ugliness to be seen! There are still grungy little coffeeshops that would sooner die than serve red lettuce. On the other hand, you don't need a crystal ball to know what's going to happen down here.

Like Soho, Tribeca is filled with warehouses, and ex-sweat shops that operated euphemistically as "light manufacturing." Unlike Soho, many of them are still in operation. This is not an area rife with street life. If truth be told, this always was an interesting area for its oddball discount shopping. The reason to see Tribeca today is that those stores will doubtless be replaced by the three B's: boutiques, Benettons, and brunch.

Hudson Street best represents the area and is a peek back in time to what Soho once was.

One Hudson Café (1 Hudson St.; 608-5835) offers wine by the glass and, at night, jazz to sip it by.

Check out **Artists Space** (223 West Broadway) for performance as well as wall art; and the **Alternative Museum** (17 White Street) for music as atonal as its art; and **Franklin**

Furnace (112 Franklin Street) for its collection of published art.

If you're hungry, you might opt for a burger at **Hamburger Harry's** (157 Chambers St.; 267-4446) where the mesquite-grilled critters are topped with almost everything from aardvarks to zinnias. In the event you're into dining with a capital D: there's **Montrachet** (239 West Broadway; 219-2777). Carved out of an industrial space in the middle of downtown nowhere. Drew Nieporent's restaurant serves some of the most elegant food in town amid an equally imaginative Adam Tihany setting. **Bouley** (165 Duane Street; 608-3852) is where chef David Bouley dishes out his special blend of Provençal cuisine to enthusiastic diners. **Arquà,** (281 Church Street; 334-1888) is simply glorious—it's a big, bright pink room that fills up with people as new wave as the variations on homemade pasta. Venetian in concept, the food is both adventurous and successful.

But if you have time for only one meal in Tribeca, go to the **Odeon** (145 West Broadway; 233-0507) not because the food is better than Montrachet, but history was made here: It was the first of the Tribeca hangouts and, like Sardi's, it has a cachet that transcends cuisine. The Odeon, a former cafeteria, is at its best after midnight. Grilled chicken with mashed potatoes and spinach, steak fries, roast duck are all under $20.

The good news for all you fans of *Architectural Digest* is the **Woolworth Building** (233 Broadway), which in 1913 was the world's tallest. Today, although three U.S. cities have taller structures, none are more steeped in history. Woodrow Wilson, by remote control from the White House, pressed the button that illuminated all 80,000 light bulbs in the building, while a band on the 27th floor played the national anthem. "The Cathedral of Commerce" built by the five-and-dime king is anything but penny pinching. The lobby in this American Gothic version of London's Houses of Parliament is one of New York's most elaborate, with Greek marble, vaulted mosaic ceilings, murals representing "Commerce" and "Labor," and a sumptuous marble staircase. There's a small caricature of Woolworth counting his nickels and dimes and one of the architect, Cass Gilbert, clutching a model of his building. Woolworth, who they say was fond of overripe bananas, personally picked out the mailboxes and bathroom fixtures.

Pure guilt at never having wanted to be a fireman makes us take note of the **Fire Department Museum** (278 Spring Street; 691-1303) with its antique fire engines, etc. Pure heaven, even if you don't wear red suspenders. It's open Tuesday through Saturday, 10 A.M. to 4 P.M.

Lower East Side

Think pickles. Sweet. Sour. Kosher. Pickle barrels, pushcarts, and immigrant dreams. Comedians, gangsters, intellectuals, activists, businessmen, songwriters—they all came out of the ghetto. The Jewish heritage of the Lower East Side has become part of New York's cultural heritage and belongs to every New Yorker. More than just morning bagels, it is the sarcasm, the shrug, the laughter, and the determination in the face of urban adversity, whether trying to find a parking space or a better job.

At eye level, the area seems as hurly-burly and rundown as ever, except now Hispanics have begun moving into the old tenements above the discount handbag shops and the "appetizing" stores that put lox (smoked salmon) on the map. Many Jews, like the Italians in Little Italy, have moved on while Puerto Ricans and Chinese, the next generation immigrants, have moved in. Still, visitors flock here from all over the country. The Lower East Side is a state of mind; it represents a universal struggle.

Although the streets are easier to navigate during the week, almost everyone comes on Sunday (shops are closed for the Jewish Sabbath from Friday afternoon through Saturday night). Simply, you can't have a ghetto without a crowd and the ghetto, albeit one of affluent expatriates, is what many people come for. And the shopping. And the eating.

Oh, the eating. It begins the moment you cross the border (Houston St.) and are within sight of **Yonah Schimmel's Bakery** (137 East Houston St.) where we suspect Olympic weightlifters could workout selling the potato, spinach, and kasha knishes. For those just arriving from Mars, knishes are large, stuffed, single-portion pastries, any one of which is filling enough to support life as we know it for some time to come. Continue down to **Ben's Cheese Store** (181 East Houston St.) for a piece of baked strawberry farmer cheese or some fresh cream cheese, and then next door to **Moishe's** for bagels, and then next door to **Russ and Daughters** for lox.

There are two major delicatessens in the area: **Katz's** (205 East Houston St.) is one of those places everyone has been saying "used to be better" since the day it opened. But somehow, they still come. Maybe to complain. Katz's is a barn of a place, with about as much heart as a movie usher. You can order your corned beef cafeteria style, thereby avoiding the wrath of the waiters, or sit down in the service section and avoid the wrath of the countermen. Not anywhere as good as the Carnegie Deli (see Restaurants), Katz's endures because it's been at the right place for a long time.

Bernstein-on-Essex (135 Essex St.) is another story. This deli is Kosher as though Kosher were going out of style. Not content to slice up mountains of pastrami, Bernstein's has superimposed the fine art of "glatt Kosher" upon the unsuspecting

cuisine of ancient China to produce a hybrid even more unset-
tling than the nectarine. Unless you're kosher and can't head
for Chinatown, stay with the deli meats: They don't get any better in this part of town. Nor do the pickles. No matter that the
barrels at **Guss' Pickles** (35 Essex St.) aren't antique, the
pickles and peppers and sour tomatoes are positively Olympian.

However, the ultimate in Lower East Side eating (notice we
didn't say "dining") is at **Sammy's Roumanian** (sic) **Steak
House** (157 Chrystie St., 673-0330). Never mind that they call
this a "steak house," Sammy's is sitcom Jewish. The tables are
set with syrup pitchers filled with chicken fat (schmaltz), bottles
of seltzer, containers of milk, and jars of Fox's U-Bet chocolate
syrup (for do-it-yourself egg creams). Under appetizers, there's
kishka, patcha, kreplach, and karnatzlack (is this an old Danny
Kaye tongue-twister or what?). Meanwhile, there's bar mitzvah
style ear-shattering you-call-this-music? music, and tables filled
with people wolfing down Roumanian (again, sic) tenderloins
and side dishes of mashed potatoes with schmaltz and "gre-
evens" (crispy bits of chicken skin) as though cholesterol were
on sale. Sammy's is nothing if not raucous, good-natured, delicious, expensive (you call $60 a couple cheap?), and someplace
no one should tell the Surgeon General about or else he'll close
it down.

It's time to flex your muscles as a shopper. But however facile
you may be in the aisles at Saks, unless you've majored in
Marrakesh Markets, a few words are in order. Everyone
knows that the only reason to shop down here is to get a bargain. Therefore, savvy shopkeepers would sooner die than
ruin their images by providing elegant uptown extras such as
sufficient light, space to breathe, or a smile. While looking at
the goods, keep your ears open to hear whether prices are
negotiable. If they are, communicate that you are interested.
Whatever price you're quoted, say no. Reconfirm that you're
prepared to buy, but need a better price. If he still says no,
tell him you're prepared to pay cash. If he still says no, and
you still want it, smile and buy it. The rule of thumb is that
prices are 20 percent to 60 percent under what you'd pay elsewhere.

Orchard Street is the main artery for shoppers and it turns
into a pedestrian mall on Sunday to give street vendors lots
of street on which to peddle their wares. This is where you'll
find most of the men's and women's clothing shops. Grand
Street is known for bridal gowns, linens, and fabrics. Allen
Street is the authority on men's ties and shirts, as well as antiques. Essex Street is for foodies and electronics mavens.

 Hungry again? The dairy restaurant (where no meat products
are served) is where you'll find the rest of the Lower East Side's
signature cuisine: blintzes, potato pancakes, potato pudding,
French toast made from traditional challah bread, gefilte fish,
borscht, herrings in all sizes and shapes, and enough sour

Orchard Street At A Glance
A Selective Guide to Help You Shop Till You Drop

Number	Name of Shop	Specialty
37	Arnie's Place	Designer jeans
50	Pan Am Men's Wear	Men's clothing
54	Goldman & Cohen	Lingerie
55	R.C. Sultan	Hosiery
58	Penn Garden Grand Shirt Co.	Men's shirts
62	G&G Projections	Men's clothing
73	A.W. Kaufman	Lingerie
75	Orchard Bootery	Shoes
79	Ber-Sel	Handbags
91	Maximum	Shoes
93	Sam's Knitwear	Women's clothing
96	Victory Shirt Co.	Men's shirts
105	Klein's of Monticello	Children's wear
106	Antony	Men's clothing
110	Lace Up Shoe Shop	Shoes
117	Cohen's Optical	Eyeglasses
119	Fine & Klein	Handbags
125	Breakaway	Women's clothing
125	Sam Beckenstein	Men's fabrics
130	Sam Beckenstein	Women's fabrics
131	H&J	Sneakers
132	Jules Harvey	Sneakers
163	Peck & Chase Shoes	Shoes

cream to make the Surgeon General very nervous. **The Grand Dairy Restaurant** (341 Grand St.) has terrific food, but it's hard to resist **Ratner's** (138 Delancey St.) for the cultural experience: The crowds are hungrier, the waiters are ruder, the décor kitschier, and the heartburn deadlier.

THE BOWERY

Peter Stuyvesant, the last Dutch governor of New Amsterdam (1647 to 1664), looking for the shortest distance to his *bouwerie* (Dutch for farm) built the straight road that became known as the Bowery. In the mid-19th century, the area was a thriving, if boisterous, theatrical center. But the good times didn't last. People began hearing stories about the "Bowery Boys," a gang of thieves who preyed on those coming to the area for a night out. The street never recovered its loss of reputation and lost heart. If every town has a Skid Row, then like almost everything else in N.Y.C., ours is one of the best or worst: a place of shadows and whispers, a street peopled by those even more bereft than the homeless—the hopeless.

Enter the speculators. It's apparently a given in the N.Y.C. Real Estate Game that as soon as an area is as low down as it's likely to get, people come in and buy property. There are happy yuppie couples living in gorgeously renovated lofts all along the Bowery just waiting for their investment to zoom upward. But don't let the realtors fool you: The Bowery is nowhere near being gentrified.

Other hardy New Yorkers trudge down to the Bowery for **professional kitchen equipment** (Empire Food Service Equipment, 114 Bowery; 226-4447, and AAA Restaurant Equipment, 280 Bowery; 966-1891) as well as to squint their way through some of the most eye-popping truly inexpensive, **lighting fixture stores** in town (Bowery Lighting, 132 Bowery; 966-4034) and at least one that's a real pacesetter in design—Thunder 'N Light, 171 Bowery; 219-0180).

CANAL STREET

Canal Street runs farther east than the Bowery (it goes under the Manhattan Bridge, with its wonderfully out-of-place Beaux-Arts colonnade entrance, and into the Lower East Side). And it goes farther west than Sixth Avenue (it is a major artery for Holland Tunnel traffic to New Jersey and continues along to West Street). The stretch we've selected is where Canal Street really comes into its own.

Canal Street was so named because it had been proposed as a canal in the early 1800s to siphon off waters from the freshwater pond that covered Foley Square in what is now the civic center. Only a few years later plans were shelved. Decades followed during which runaway slaves and immigrants were housed in sub-standard units as the city's focus, and wealth, moved north.

Echoing the bargain basement economics of its inhabitants, Canal Street became the end of the pushcart for many who dealt in reclaimed debris, broken or used parts, the things no one else in an increasingly affluent city wanted to sell. Surprisingly, however, there were lots of people who wanted to buy. Unlike the street peddlers on the Lower East Side end of Canal who were offering diamonds at glass prices, the vendors on this part of Canal sold only glass.

What remains today, mainly between Broadway and Sixth Avenue, is a cornucopia of electronic parts, audio supplies, stationery, automotive goods, and wearables that have reached the end of the line. Buyers and sellers know that final sales are the order of business down here. And that's part of what makes these few blocks so exciting. Everything is unpredictable. Come back in a few weeks and all the merchandise has changed.

One of our favorite places is **Pearl Paint** (308 Canal Street; 431-7932), a bona-fide extravaganza for people who paint or draw or have been carrying on love affairs with papers and pens and lovely envelopes. Everything is priced low enough to satisfy dedicated skinflints. As though there weren't enough stores, flea markets appear during good weather in almost every available space. One of the best is on the corner of Canal and Greene.

We dare not reveal our opinion of anyone who would even consider eating on Canal Street, when one block north to Little Italy or south to Chinatown are some of the city's finest restaurants. Walk along Canal, buy, browse, and build up an appetite to be sated elsewhere.

Chinatown

One of the reasons there are so many restaurants in Chinatown has to do with an old immigration law that allowed only Chinese *men* to enter the country. Restaurants and laundries (offering services usually provided by wives) were the two businesses that Chinese immigrants were allowed to run, since they were considered noncompetitive with jobs wanted by Caucasian workers.

The arriving Chinese settled in the city's worst slum area, known then as Five Points. Even today, much of Chinatown's housing is substandard. However, visitors come here not for the sociology but for the cuisine. There's very little of historic interest, no visual treats except for some pagoda phone booths and a bit of kitsch architecture on Chatham Square. The reason Chinatown is on everyone's itinerary is that you can eat better and less expensive Chinese food here than almost anywhere else in the country.

Be forewarned: Do not collect two-thousand-year-old eggs. This is, first and foremost, a Chinatown for the Chinese.

Important things to bear in mind are:

(1) Chinese chefs come and go faster than a speeding egg roll. The restaurant that was great last week may have lost its edge while trying to find a replacement chef. There truly is a ratio between the number of Chinese families in a restaurant and the quality of the food.

(2) Chinatown Chinese is not uptown Chinese. We're not talking L.A.-style "Chinois" or designer chic. Think Formica, paper napkins, and cans of soda. Once in a while, a liquor license.

(3) Many Chinese waiters belong to a school of service that begins and ends with carrying food from the kitchen. Be prepared: There is rarely any logical sequence to the appearance of food on your table. This is not bad service. This is good service. Bad service is never getting your food.

Oddly enough, the best restaurants in Chinatown are still Cantonese (most of the early Chinese immigrants were from Canton). If your tastes run to the spicier dishes of Hunan or Szechuan, go to the uptown Chinese restaurants.

Here are some favorites to get you started:

20 Mott Street, 20 Mott St.; 964-0380. Crabs in a rich black bean sauce, egg foo yung that's as feathery as the finest French omelet, and a lunch dim sum service that's one of the best.

Canton, 45 Division St.; 226-4441. Fish is the order of the day. Carp, sea bass, flounder are prepared with a light touch. One of the few restaurants in which you can ask questions and it's safe to stick with specials. For starters, try lettuce leaves that you stuff with beef, chicken, or vegetables and fold.

Phoenix Garden, 46 Bowery (in the arcade); 962-8934. Order the pepper and salty shrimp, and the lemon chicken, and gaze lovingly across the table at whomever you're with—this place is not a pretty sight, but the food is.

Silver Palace Restaurant, 52 Bowery; 964-1204. An enormous restaurant that's perfect for beginners. Service is easy, the menu is extensive, and we're not ashamed to admit that the sweet-and-sour pork is terrific.

Peking Duck House, 22 Mott St.; 227-1810. If you've never had Peking duck, or if you don't want to go through the circus some restaurants make about ordering it in advance, this is the place for you. Good naturedly rough and tumble. Don't let them talk you into appetizers or side dishes unless you're descended from Henry VIII.

Tai Hong Lau, 70 Mott St.; 219-1431. Hong Kong kitsch cuisine that begins with good old lettuce leaves stuffed with minced pork, clams, and cashews, and then zaps into beef, ginger, water chestnuts, and crispy-fat-noodley things. Shrimp with black sesame seeds and slivers of red cabbage. Which way to the Star Ferry?

If you're feeling even more adventurous, there are lots of noodle houses (read: Chinese luncheonettes) for big bowls of sloppy slurpy noodles in broth with a toss of chicken or pork. **Hong Fat** (63 Mott St.) is open 24 hours a day and has been around forever. More interesting, though, are the shops that sell steamed buns filled with pork (*char siu* buns) and dumplings stuffed with shrimp or beef. This is strictly street food, visible as you pass by. Just point to what you want. The same body language holds true when passing Chinese bakeries on Mott St. Try **Lung Fong** (41 Mott).

The souvenir shops in Chinatown are, by and large, disappointing. Try your luck instead at one of the Chinese "department stores" such as **Pearl River** (277 Canal St.), where you'll find everything from woks to kids' p.j.'s to stocking stuffers. Don't hesitate going into a Chinese grocery store such as **Kam Man Food Products** (200 Canal St.)—you might find just the thing for that gourmet on your list. The best walking in Chinatown is along Canal to the Bowery, down to Mott, and back along Mott to Canal.

Little Italy

Once upon a time, when people were still discovering something magical called "tomato pie," and pasta was known as spaghetti, Little Italy was a wondrous place to which New Yorkers flocked for Italian home cooking. But the Italians aren't home anymore. Not too many of them, anyway. The younger generation has integrated itself into more up-market sections of the city, leaving behind an aging community rapidly being replaced by the expansion northward of Chinatown.

Still, in late September during the Feast of San Gennaro, when canopies of lights sparkle on Mulberry Street, there is no clock ticking. Outdoor stalls seduce your senses with the aroma of sausage and onions, and the sound of Italian conviviality. The *paisanos* are back and the street life is rich and festive. Which is not to say that you can't head for Mulberry Street on a Tuesday in April. There are legions of New Yorkers who just don't believe they're eating real Italian food anywhere else. For them, food is the music of love and the melody lingers on in Little Italy.

On a short walk along Mott, Mulberry, or Grand streets, you'll find Italian groceries, butchers, and bake shops that are as wonderful as ever. Bursting with exotic salamis and cheeses and freshly made pastas, cans of imported oils and tomatoes, breads studded with chunks of prosciutto, and pastries stuffed with ricotta—there is an authenticity in these local Italian markets that can't be matched by any gourmet shop in the city.

By now you're hungry. The only problem is making a choice. Many people have heard of **Umberto's Clam House** (129 Mulberry St.; 431-7545) for reasons other than the cuisine: It was here that mobster Joey Gallo was gunned down in 1972. But that hasn't stopped it from attracting an uptown celebrity clientele—Umberto's is open until 6 A.M. Less dramatic but still known for good food and lots of atmosphere at very reasonable prices are **Puglia** (189 Hester St.; 966-6006), where singing and seating take place at communal trestle tables, and **Luna's** (112 Mulberry St.; 226-8657), a sliver of a room that's always filled. **Il Cortile** (125 Mulberry St.; 226-6060) is chic, with a garden room that allows for conversation, Northern Italian selections on the menu, and, blessedly, a real martini-making bar.

Grotta Azzurra (387 Broome St.; 925-8775) is retro-dining at its most nostalgic. This basement room is everybody's idea of a 1950s raucous Italian restaurant with an open kitchen, garrulous waiters, and barely enough breathing space between tables. Big pitchers of wine with fruit, plates piled high with garlic bread that will keep you vampire-free for life, and red sauce, red sauce, red sauce.

Vincent's Clam Bar (119 Mott St.; 226-8133) has been around since 1904 with a recipe for hot sauce that would blow the stack off any diehard Tex-Mex fan. There's a bar up front and a dining room in the rear that serves seafood and pasta, but the specials are clams or shrimp doused in red lightning that they say comes in three strengths: mild, medium, or hot. Unless you're a fireman, proceed with caution. Prices are modest.

Then, if life weren't complicated enough, there are the two Benitos: **Benito I** and **Benito II** just across the street from one another; under separate management, but both offering Sicilian-style cooking. We'd stay with Benito I (174 Mulberry St.; 226-9171) for the house scaloppine, and for the waiters. But no matter where you eat, don't have dessert.

The dessert story in Little Italy is a competition more fierce than the one between the two Benitos. People swear by **Ferrara's** (195 Grand St.; 226-6150) for Italian pastries and espresso. Enjoy.

Lower Manhattan

Lower Manhattan is not only the birthplace of New York City, but of modern America. From Bowling Green where the Dutch bought the island from the Indians, to the Statue of Liberty welcoming "your tired, your poor," to the first boom on Wall Street that promised to make everyone rich—the skyline of Lower Manhattan silhouettes the American Dream.

If you have time to cover only one area in addition to Midtown, it should be Lower Manhattan. Not for its history, but for its perspective. The dissonance of architectural styles, the zigzag of time frames, and the panoply of hopes they represent are staggering: Trinity Church, the World Trade Center, Federal Hall (where Washington took his oath as first President of the United States), the New York Stock Exchange, the Fulton Fish Market, City Hall, Battery Park City, and Ellis Island (which will not be open to visitors until 1990).

Unlike other New York neighborhoods, this part of town was open only during business hours. No one lived down here. By six o'clock in the evening, the streets were deserted. On weekends, the place was a ghost town. Not anymore.

The change began with the building of the World Trade Center by the Port Authority of New York and New Jersey to establish a downtown locus for international business. By the time the twin towers opened in 1973, 1.2 million cubic yards of earth had been excavated and put into the Hudson River as landfill to create 23.5 acres for Battery Park City, a brilliant new residential complex. At about the same time, interest peaked in restoring the South Street Seaport area. In 1981, the Vista International (the only hotel in Lower Manhattan) had opened and, by 1986, the centennial celebration of the Statue of Liberty brought millions of people who were welcomed to a spiffy, hospitable Lower Manhattan.

Although it doesn't much matter where you start out, plan on winding up at the South Street Seaport for a little R&R before heading back uptown. Most people tend to start at the **World Trade Center** (see Priorities) and the view from the Observation Deck (get your tickets on the mezzanine of number 2 World Trade Center). Then, as you ride up to the 107th floor, you might think about this: You're traveling at a speed of up to 1,600 feet per minute; over 1,200 international businesses are headquartered here; some 50,000 people work in the Center and nearly 500,000 visit daily; the floors are column-free and each covers about one acre; the underground garage has space for 2,000 cars; there are 43,600 windows in the Twin Towers, accounting for over 600,000 square feet of glass.

Next, take a stroll along the esplanade at **Battery Park City,** just across the street. Look up at the tops of the buildings in this complex: each one is finished off with a different geometric shape. Be sure to peek in at the glorious **Winter Garden,** a glass and steel fantasy that has even been supported by the architecture critics. The view from the Esplanade is particularly stirring: Miss Liberty; Ellis Island (where immigrants first touched American soil); Governor's Island with its historic fortification; the port of New York; and to tell the truth, even New Jersey, right across the Hudson River, doesn't look so bad from this vantage point.

Keep walking downtown to Battery Park. You'll see **Castle Clinton,** a 19th-century fort that, prior to landfills, was two hundred feet offshore. Now restored and manicured, it's about as fierce as a paper tiger. But let's not blame it all on the National Park Service: In 1850, Castle Clinton became Castle Garden, a venue for serious theatrical fare. How serious? Would you believe that P.T. Barnum selected it for the American debut of Jenny Lind? Open Monday through Friday, 9 A.M. to 5 P.M.; from June to September, open Wednesday through Sunday; closed late December to mid-March. Admission is free.

Follow the promenade along the river's edge and you'll reach one of our favorite structures, Pier A (West Street and Battery Place)—the 1885 **fireboat station.** Jubilantly painted as though it were a set for a Disney film, it is a riotous anachronism of color and style.

The Battery was so named for the cannons that lined the shore to protect the Dutch settlers—the self-same group of Type-A overachievers who, in 1653, built a wooden wall "uptown" (Wall Street) to protect their tushes from the Indians. Unlike the promissory notes on Wall Street, **Battery Park** offers a gracious expanse of green from which to view the harbor. The Circle Line ferry (269-5755) to the **Statue of**

Reade Street
Chambers Street
Greenwich Street
West Broadway
Warren St.
Murray St
Park Pl.
Barclay St.
Woolworth Building
Vesey Street

Civic Center
City Hall
Broadway
Park Row

Governor Smith Houses
Robert Wagner Sr. Pl.
Brooklyn Bridge
Frankfort St.
Spruce Street

Church Street
World Trade Center
Liberty St.

Ann Street
Fulton Street
John St.
Williams St.
Gold Street
Cliff Street
Beekman Street
Pearl St.
South Street Seaport

Trinity Church
Albany St.
Carlisle St.
Broadway
Rector St.
Nassau Street
Liberty St.
Pine St.
Fletcher La.

N.Y. Stock Exchange
Wall Street
Exchange Pl.
Water Street
Front Street
Elevated Highway

Brooklyn-Battery Tunnel
Approach
Old Slip

Battery Park City
Beaver St.
Whitehall Street
Stone St.
Bowling Green
Battery Pl.
Fraunces Tavern
South Street

Moore St.
State Street

East River

Castle Clinton
Battery Park

Staten Island Ferry Terminal

Ferry to Statue of Liberty
Brooklyn-Battery Tunnel

N

LOWER MANHATTAN

| 0 | yards | 440 |
| 0 | meters | 400 |

A
B
C

Liberty leaves from here every day except Christmas, 9:15 A.M., then every half-hour from 10 A.M. to 4 P.M. Round trip fare is $3.25; children under 11, $1.50. (See Priorities.)

The **Staten Island Ferry** (at the foot of Whitehall Street) is one of those things you simply have to do. For the paltry sum of $.25, you will be treated to a mini-cruise that is second only in sensory thrill to being launched into outer space. Trust us. Even if you'd sooner die than miss an hour of shopping to go to the Statue of Liberty, you're not too sophisticated for the Staten Island Ferry—that is, unless you're on the guest list for Malcolm Forbes's yacht. (It's named the *Highlander* and you'll recognize it by the *Forbes* magazine helicopter parked on the top deck.) For the rest of us mortals, the ferry leaves every hour from 6 A.M. to 4 P.M., more frequently between 4 P.M. and midnight. Figure about half an hour each way. If time is a problem, take the ferry and you might decide to pass on the Statue of Liberty ride.

Bowling Green, at the foot of Broadway, is where Peter Minuit supposedly consummated the $24 deal that won him the Good Shopper Award of 1626. After years as a cattle market, and then a parade ground, it was leased to the city as a spot for public bowling. The fence that surrounds the area was built in 1771 and is a city landmark. The **U.S. Custom House** (1907) on Bowling Green is one of New York's most opulent buildings. It shares a Beaux-Arts heritage with the Metropolitan Museum of Art and is considered by some to be an even grander structure. Cass Gilbert was the architect, and Daniel Chester French (who did the Lincoln Memorial in Washington) designed four powerful sculptures out front symbolizing Asia, North America, Europe, and Africa. Inside, you'll find a superb rotunda with scenes of early New York's harbor as painted by Reginald Marsh. Alas, the Custom Service has opted for trendier digs in the World Trade Center.

Fraunces Tavern (54 Pearl St.; 269-0144) is billed as a "conjectural" restoration that was made in 1907 using structural elements of the De Lancey House built there in 1719, which later became the property of Samuel Fraunces, a West Indian of black and French heritage. Fraunces opened the Queen's Head Tavern in 1763 and it was here that George Washington said farewell to his troops at the end of the Revolutionary War in 1783. The Tavern is now a restaurant open Mon.–Fri. for breakfast, lunch, and dinner with a very extensive, and moderately priced menu.

Upstairs, and in four adjacent 19th-century buildings, is the **Fraunces Tavern Museum** with its collection of prints, paintings, decorative arts, and artifacts relating to American and New York City history. A ten-minute audiovisual presentation chronicles the city's early days. Open Monday through

Friday, 10 A.M. to 4 P.M., and selected Sundays from noon to 5 P.M. Admission is $2.50. (425-1778).

Fraunces Tavern is on the corner of Pearl and Broad streets. Broad Street was a canal during the Dutch period, which explains its unusual width and hence its name. Pearl Street, once the shore line of the East River, was so named because of the pearl-like shells found there. (All right, so they weren't too imaginative about place names: i.e., Wall Street, Stone Street—the first to be cobbled.) Walk up Broad Street to number 8 and hold your breath: it's the **New York Stock Exchange.** A must-see (see Priorities), only if you've graduated from the peanut gallery to the visitors' gallery (entrance at 20 Broad Street; open Monday through Friday, 9 A.M. to 3 P.M.). By all means go and eat your heart out. It is a guaranteed out-of-body experience for those of the right persuasion. Our favorite insider-trading story is the one about disguising sheet metal to replace the disintegrating stone on the original mythological figures that decorate the Stock Exchange. It was all done very hush-hush, lest the great unwashed suddenly get the idea that the "institution" was in any way vulnerable.

No matter what flavor portfolio you have, the original Custom House, which was later the Subtreasury Building and is now **Federal Hall National Memorial** (28 Wall Street), is a mini-Parthenon on the Acropolis of High Finance. This particular temple, outfitted with Doric columns carved out of Westchester County marble, is where Washington took the oath as first president in 1789. The statue that's been marking the spot since 1883 is the one you see in all the pictures (he was actually sworn in on a second-floor balcony). There's a free historic exhibition inside (open Monday through Friday, 9 A.M. to 5 P.M.; 264-8711).

The best way to approach **Trinity Church** is from Wall Street. The church sits on Broadway at the head of Wall Street almost as a conscience reminding the brokers to take stock. There's been a Trinity Church here since 1699, in one form or another. The first church was destroyed in the Great Fire of 1776, the 1839 version was demolished for fear it would collapse due to poor construction, and the current model appeared in 1846 with optional extras in 1876, 1913, and 1965. This is the city's oldest Episcopal parish (Trinity received a generous land grant from Queen Anne in 1705) and was, for a time, its tallest structure. The doors to the church were modeled after the Ghiberti doors on the Baptistry in Florence (the south doors offer scenes of Manhattan's history). Sharing the church's fame is its **cemetery,** which must be one of the world's most visited. The oldest gravestone dates back to 1681, and the most famous are those for Alexander Hamilton and Robert Fulton. There's a small **museum** attached, with displays of communion silver and other items of historical interest to the parish. Hours are 9 A.M. to 3:45 P.M. Admission is free (285-0872).

South Street is where New York became the nation's pre-eminent port in the 1800s. Having grown from its origins as a Dutch trading post in the 1600s, it was here that you'd find clipper ships from the China trade, as well as ships arriving from Europe. As the result of numerous landfills, the original shoreline of Pearl Street stretched out to the present-day South Street. At the time, it was lined with warehouses and counting houses. Not until the Fulton Ferry (to Brooklyn) began in 1816 did retail shopkeepers open up here to serve those who traveled by ferry. The Fulton Market was initially a produce center for Brooklyn and Long Island farmers, and, later, a fish market.

At the end of the Civil War, the emergence of steamships made it necessary to use the deepwater piers on the Hudson River. South Street began a decline that continued until the mid-1960s when plans emerged for a restoration of the area that resulted in the 1983 opening of an 11-block landmarked setting called the **South Street Seaport Museum.**

But first, forget all previous concepts of a museum. Think instead of Quincy Market in Boston, Ghirardelli Square in San Francisco, the new Covent Garden in London. The Seaport is a museum without walls, where historic buildings on cobblestone streets are lined with elegant shops; where you can eat pizza by the slice, oysters by the half-dozen, and pickles by the barrel; where you can board the second-largest sailing ship in existence, watch someone build a big ship in a small bottle, have stationery made in a 19th-century print shop.

Let's face it: The reason New Yorkers flock to the Seaport is that it's so *unlike* New York. (Except for its provenance and vistas.) Imagine this: a cobblestone pedestrian mall filled with nothing but creature comforts! Simply put, this is one of the most gracious spots in town and experienced New Yorkers don't count a lot on gracious with their daily rations. For example, the new Pier 17 with its wraparound, water's edge, multitiered deck: You've got the river right there, the tall-masted schooners tied up at Piers 15 and 16, the Wall Street skyline, the Brooklyn Bridge, and—if the wind is right, an occasional whiff of the Fulton Fish Market. Okay, okay, it does get a little crowded on weekends but you're a visitor, you don't have to go on a weekend unless you're a dedicated people-watcher, in which event you should bring eye drops. There are rockers and yuppies and Brazilian sailors and old ladies with walkers and up-tight suburbanites worried about whether the guy in the parking lot dented the Audi and little kids who don't want to go home and even bigger kids who don't want to go home either.

The fun of the Seaport is that it's a little bit Colonial Williamsburg, a little bit Olde Mystic, and a little bit 42nd Street (in the best sense). The several-block area has buildings that date from the early 19th century and which housed merchants, sailmakers, riggers, printers, and grocers. They've also got a great collection of ships moored at the piers: schooners, tugboats, ferries, and so on. There are walking tours, excursion boats, craft demonstrations, educational programs, and films. Stop at the Visitors Center (207 Front Street; 669-9424) for complete information.

Start out (as most people do) near the Titanic Memorial Tower at Fulton and Water streets—close to the Visitors Center. Among our favorite shops here are **The Nature Company** (8 Fulton Street; 422-8510) for adult toys, nature posters, crystals, semi-precious jewelry, animal carvings, etc. (They serve complimentary herbal tea. Does that sound like New York to you?) Next, there's **Captain Hook's** (10 Fulton Street; 344-2262) for sea memorabilia: shells, mirrored portholes, and even decorative diving helmets. There's a **Laura Ashley,** for clothes with a Victorian cut; **Brookstone,** with its assortment of ultimate gadgets; **Abercrombie & Fitch,** with everything imaginable for the sporting family; and even a branch of **Caswell Massey** for the most historic toiletries in town.

Our favorite part of the seaport is **Pier 17,** a renovated pleasure pier filled with shops and restaurants and surrounded by the aforementioned deck with views of the East River traffic, the Brooklyn Bridge, and the Statue of Liberty that make everything taste even better. One of our most memorable meals was a shared order of shopping-mall-generic chow mein (don't laugh: Haven't you ever explored the wonderful world of gastronomic nostalgia?), savored while staring at the skyline of Wall Street against the elegant rigging of ships.

Caroline's at the Seaport (89 South St., Pier 17; 233-4900) is a yuppie clam bar with tropical colors, modern art on the walls, and comedy performers at night. Also outside seating for those interested in the passing parade. While talking about food, there's **Pedro O'Hara's** (19 Fulton St., Pier 17; 267-7634), a very 20th-century Mexican restaurant with rich red walls, neon trim, and sleek tiles. They have a huge bar that faces the view, with margaritas and nachos to pass the time. **Fluties** right next door (693-0777) has the look of an old fish house: tile floors, wooden tables, tin ceiling, and Deco lights. The menu here goes from top to bottom of the deep. Oyster stews, pan roasts, chowders, wine by the glass. **Jade Sea** (Pier 17, second level; 285-0505) is a Chinese restaurant (not where we ate our generic chow mein) with beautiful puffy clouds painted on the glass doors. For Cantonese cuisine. **Harbor Lights** (Pier 17, second level; 227-2800) adds sailing murals to the walls and wood paneling—none of which disturbs the wonderful view.

Our hot tip is to arrive early—perhaps for a late breakfast or brunch. Find yourself a nice table, or go outside on the deck. You'll be able to have the views all to yourself.

But food is only half the story in this yuppie palace. The shops are geared for the young in heart: **Banana Republic** (ready to supply the right clothes for a safari through the Seaport), **The Sharper Image** (for catalog buying), **Hats in the Belfry** (every possible type of chapeau), and **Express** (trendy women's trendy clothes).

On the second level is **Pavo Real** (233-3721), one of our favorite shops for its works by Buitamante, an artist who works in papier mâché, copper, and brass. His designs are animals, fish, and birds of such brilliant extravagance it nearly takes your breath away. The **Last Wound Up** (Pier 17; 393-1128) is crammed with every variety of mechanized toy around. **Mariposa** (Pier 17; 233-3221) is a gallery of mounted butterflies. **A to Z** (Pier 17; 233-4640) is for gadgets.

Best of all, there are two-or three-hour **cruises** on the *Pioneer,* an 1885 schooner that will take you along lower Manhattan and past the Statue of Liberty. (Bring along your own picnic.) Or you might elect an hour-and-a-half ride on the *De Witt Clinton,* a replica of a turn-of-the-century steamboat. Call 669-9424 for hours and prices.

Although most shops close by 8 or 9 P.M., the Seaport goes on into the night with evening cruises, jazz performances at Harbor Lights, Flutie's, and the Ocean Reef Grille. And the comedy performances at Caroline's keep the kids laughing well past midnight.

P.S.: **City Hall** is located in City Hall Park (Broadway and Murray Street). It has been called "an outstanding example of Federal period architecture . . . among the most beautiful buildings in America." Call 566-8681 and ask for Ed.

Upper Manhattan

Defining Upper Manhattan isn't easy. (For the people who live in Soho, it's defined as any place above Houston Street.) But since this is a book for visitors, we've leaped zip codes and civic sensibilities in a single bound, alienating some dear chums who, due to our myopic VisitorVision, now find themselves relocated from the Upper East and West sides to Upper Manhattan. The truth is, with the exceptions of forays to Lincoln Center and Museum Mile, visitors spend most of their time below 59th Street.

A funny thing happens to Manhattan on the way to 125th Street: it starts getting real skinny. Also, the East River turns right as Manhattan turns left. Enter the Harlem River. And, of course, Harlem. What most people don't realize, however, is that just as there are many Manhattans, there are many

Harlems: Black, Spanish, and Italian. The other misconception is that Harlem comprises all of Upper Manhattan.

East Side

The Upper East Side, above 96th Street, develops a distinctly Latin beat that minds its manners around the Mt. Sinai Hospital complex on 100th Street and Fifth Avenue but once liberated from Museum Mile and the medicos, bursts into Spanish Harlem. "El Barrio," unlike Madison Avenue in the seventies, is not a casual browser's delight. While there have been some improvements, East Harlem is an overcrowded area where people are often housed in tenements sorely lacking basic services. When traveling in this area, know exactly where you are going, and do not rely upon public transportation. Spring for a cab (if the driver balks at taking you up there, remember that he's legally bound to take you anywhere within city limits). Travel during peak hours, and recycle the witty Lorenz Hart lyric about not going to Harlem in ermine and pearls into a little friendly advice concerning your dress code.

In addition to **El Museo del Barrio** on 104th Street and Fifth Avenue (see Upper Fifth Avenue), our favorite place for the intrepid traveler is **La Marqueta.** With Spanish Harlem the "Puerto Rican capital" of New York, this covered five-block market (enter *and exit* from 116th Street and Park Avenue) offers a dazzling tour of tropical fruits and vegetables as well as African goods and the makings for soul food. The Marqueta experience is that of an exuberant Caribbean bazaar where you are as much on display as the *batatas* and sugar cane. Be sure to stop at one of the *botanicas,* stalls that sell herbs and potions mixed to cure problems both imaginary and real. The 116th Street entrance fronts a very busy area where you are likely to find transportation easily.

Part of East Harlem's ethnicity belongs to the Italians who hang on tight from about 114th to 120th streets and between Second Avenue and the East River. You'll find an enclave of diehards here whose determination shows: The streets are in apple pie order, the *paisanos* live in well-tended brownstones that radiate a sense of pride.

If you're still on 116th St., you might stop in at **Morrone & Sons Bakery** (324 East 116th; open Tues.–Sun., 7 A.M.–6 P.M.; 722-2972) for some of the best Italian bread in the city.

Imagine, if you will, a little Italian restaurant on East 114th St. (How little? Eight tables!) that's as hot a ticket as any of the midtown glamour spots. There isn't a Hollywood producer worth his Rolex who hasn't limoed up to **Rao's** and come out smiling. You mention Rao's to any editor or agent in NY and they shriek, "The seafood salad! The lemon chicken!" to let you know they're members in good standing. Frankly, it's a major schlepp to get to Rao's, assuming you've cleared the incredible hurdle of snaring a reservation before the leaves change color (you'll have to arrange this well before you leave home). However, we know lots of savvy eaters who find the brouhaha part of the fun: After all, isn't that what being a New Yorker is all about? Our only problem is we're not sure that's what being *a visitor* to New York is all about. Rao's is open for dinner, Mon.–Fri. (455 East 114th St.; 534-9625; no credit cards).

West Side

Meanwhile, back on the Upper West Side, the buzz continues—although once past 90th Street, Broadway takes a seventh-inning stretch. There's a distinctly Hispanic flavor that's in conflict with the "Manhattan Valley" image realtors are pushing (where do they get these names from?) to make the area appear to be the pot of gold at the end of the yuppie rainbow—although Riverside Drive and West End Avenue have no identity crisis. Not even this far north.

The best news about Broadway from 90th to 110th sts. is that while short on culinary breakthroughs, there are enough way stations to calm even the most demanding palate. **Empire Szechuan Gourmet** (2574 Broadway; 663-6004) is one of many Chinese restaurants that have stir-fried themselves into the Upper West Side repertoire. This one is a standout for chili sauce fans: There's not a dry eye in the house. **Bahama Mama** (2628 Broadway; 866-7760) is Caribe bright enough to make island food such as curried goat almost taste chic. **Border Café West** (2637 Broadway; 749-8888) is a branch of the East 79th St. restaurant that's owned by baseball player Dave Winfield. The Tex-Mex here is translated into a very sleek setting. **Lucy's Surfeteria** (2756 Broadway; 222-4453) is one of your typical West Side wacky, tropical, neonish bar and grills that serves burgers and fancy drinks to busy Broadway surfers. **107 West** (2787 Broadway; 864-1555) dishes out Southern cooking that features gumbo and jambalaya from a Cajun kitchen.

The dividing line between West Side Broadway and Columbia University Broadway is 110th Street, which also likes to be known as Cathedral Parkway. The area between Cathedral Parkway (or 110th Street) and 125th Street is known as Morningside Heights—once a very pastoral area ideal for the Leake & Watts Orphan Asylum, and the Bloomingdale Insane Asylum (which, as we all know, moved to 59th and Lex).

New York becomes a college town past 110th Street: depressed undergrads and repressed faculty wives, beer-bellied frat members, and studious Kansans wander from Chinese restaurant to burger joint—not ever struck by the anomaly that they are on (for heaven's sake!) Broadway. Small wonder. This stretch is so "college town" it boggles the mind: we are talking Saturday night photocopying!

And, happily, we are also talking Riverside Church, the Cathedral Church of St. John the Divine, Grant's Tomb, and the

Columbia University campus. To get our priorities in order: **St. John's** is, at present, the largest Gothic church in the world. Second only in floor space to St. Peter's in Rome, it will be, upon completion, the largest church of any kind in the world. Begun in 1892, the church is only about two-thirds complete—which means you may not want to hire the contractor, but by all means, go. It is splendid. Located at 112th Street and Amsterdam Avenue (316-7400), open daily from 7:15 A.M. to 5 P.M.

Equally memorable, but on a totally different scale, is **Riverside Church** at 122nd Street and Riverside Drive. Here (amid the so-who's-going-to-know? steel frame carefully covered with Indiana limestone and decorated with stained glass and stone carving to resemble the Cathedral at Chartres) is the world's largest carillon with 74 bells, including the largest bell ever cast. You can hear it played (by the carillonneur, who else?) on Sundays before and after services, again at 3 P.M., and on Saturday at noon. Visit the Observation Deck in the tower for a glorious view of the Hudson. Open Monday through Saturday, 11 A.M. to 3 P.M.; Sunday, 12:30 to 4 P.M. (222–5900). Admission $.25.

Q: Who's buried in Grant's Tomb? A: General *and* Mrs. Grant. The **General Grant National Memorial** (Riverside Drive at 122nd Street; 666-1640) is open Wednesday through Sunday, 9 A.M. to 4:30 P.M. Admission is free to the open crypt (inspired by Napoleon's tomb) where the Grants lie inside matching black marble sarcophagi.

While Barnard College, Union Theological Seminary, and the Jewish Theological Seminary are all located here, **Columbia University** is the best known of the area's academic institutions. As long as you're in the neighborhood, by all means go in through Columbia's 116th Street and Broadway entrance for a look at the Low Memorial Library around which the campus was built. If you're old enough to remember the student riots in the late sixties, this is where they took place. Columbia was chartered in the 18th century by King George II as King's College and has matured into one of the wealthiest (they own real estate in Rockefeller Center which turns a pretty tuppence or two) and most respected of American universities.

Harlem

Harlem is defined geographically as the area from 110th to 155th streets and from river to river (skirting around Morningside Heights). But Harlem also borders on the Pacific Ocean, Canada, and Mexico. It is the spiritual and cultural capital of Black America. It is from Harlem that signals are sent across the nation. Black pride. Black frustration. Black successes and setbacks.

There is no denying that bitterness and anger are among the most lethal narcotics trafficked on the streets of Harlem. The community's reputation has been widely reported and not always exaggerated. This is one of the areas in the city to be best seen via an organized tour. You'll get the whole spectrum of the Harlem experience: from slums to shining achievements—without having to worry about wandering off in the wrong direction.

Nieuw Haarlem was established by the Dutch in 1658 to take advantage of a fertile farm area. And so it remained for nearly two hundred years, even attracting wealthy merchants who built summer homes far from the downtown heart of the city. In the 1830s, with the coming of the Harlem Railroad, the area grew rapidly as a fashionable suburb. By the late 19th century, the streets were lined with aristocratic apartment houses and brownstones. There were Germans, Irish, Jews, and Italians. Everyone anticipated the arrival of the middle-class from downtown.

But the boom never came. Blacks, who lived mainly in the west thirties, had to move due to the construction of Pennsylvania Station. The only place apartments stood empty, and landlords cared only about the color of your money, was Harlem. Blacks moved into apartments built for the white middle-class. They were charged exorbitant rents because they were black and ripe to be exploited: They had no place else to go. The ghetto that Harlem became, then, is unique because unlike similar communities across the country, blacks did not inherit a slum. The lack of education and opportunity turned the broad boulevards of Harlem into a reflection of its citizens' inner turmoil.

It was in the 1920s that scores of black writers, artists, and entertainers emerged. But future generations of blacks had to wait until the 1960s for civil rights issues to hit the front pages, and until today for the renaissance of the area to finally begin. There are still ugly sights and blind anger in Harlem, but there is something more.

Among the places to be covered on a Harlem tour is **Strivers' Row,** a string of handsome townhouses (some designed by Stanford White) between 138th and 139th streets between Seventh and Eighth avenues. The houses were intended for the upper white middle-class that never came. But the black upper middle-class was every bit as ambitous. W.C. Handy, Eubie Blake, and many black civic and professional leaders lived here. The houses are still among the city's finest.

"Sugar Hill" is the name given to the area from 143rd to 155th streets, between St. Nicholas and Edgecombe avenues. The high-income section of Harlem, this is where Duke Ellington, Cab Calloway, and Bill Robinson lived. All of which is not to make it sound as though Harlem was, or is, a simply dandy place to be living. You will see the abandoned buildings and empty lots featured on the six o'clock news as well as the troubled youths and hopeless elderly. No one needs a guide book or a tour to point them out. But in a headline-oriented world, some of the good news is never reported.

The **Schomburg Center for Research in Black Culture** (515 Lenox Avenue, between 135th and 136th streets; 862-4000) is a branch of the N.Y. Public Library with the world's largest collection of books, photographs, prints, personal papers, etc., documenting the history and literature of black people. Open Monday through Wednesday, noon to 8 P.M.; Thursday through Saturday, 10 A.M. to 6 P.M. The **Abyssinian Baptist Church** (132 West 138th Street, 862-7474) was built in 1808 and became the city's most important black church under the leadership of the mercurial Adam Clayton Powell, Jr. A room with memorabilia from Powell's career is open to the public.

There's probably no single street that signifies the "real" Harlem more than 125th Street. It is one of the strongest mental images we carry, and perhaps the most misleading. Back in the days when New York's café society trekked uptown to the Cotton Club, and the shows at the now-closed Apollo Theater featured the likes of Bessie Smith, Billie Holiday, and Count Basie, 125th Street lit up Harlem. While still the area's main commercial strip, head for the **Studio Museum in Harlem** (144 West 125th Street; 865-2450) to see the works of black artists, **Mart 125** (260 West 125th Street), a publicly financed peddler's market that includes aspects of black culture (African clothing, handcrafted jewelry) as well as T-shirts and buttons, or to the **Black Fashion Museum** (155 West 126th Street; 666-1320) for its collection of the history of black design, fashion information, and memorabilia. **Aunt Len's Doll Museum** (6 Hamilton Terrace, near 141st Street; 281-4143) has one of the world's leading doll and toy collections. Open by appointment.

Hope you're hungry by this time. **Sylvia's** (328 Lenox Ave., near 127th St.; 996-0660) has been hailed as the Lutèce of soul food. Just as the limos line up at Rao's and Sammy's Roumanian, the radical chic have boomeranged their way to Sylvia's. Go for the "smothered" chicken or ribs. Open Mon.–Sat., 7:30 A.M.–10:30 P.M.; Sun., 1 P.M.–7 P.M. No credit cards, but you'll probably be able to get out for around $10 per person.

Harlem meets Washington Heights at **Trinity Cemetery** (entrance on 153rd Street and Riverside Drive; 368-1600), where the Astors share eternity with the Van Burens, John James Audubon, and the author of the immortal, " 'Twas the Night before Christmas," Clement Clarke Moore. Even more impressive is the complex of small museums on Audubon Terrace (Broadway between 155th and 156th streets) that are clustered around a neo-classical, Beaux-Artsish plaza built on land once owned by John James Audubon. You'll find the **Museum of the American Indian** (283-2420), with the largest collection of Native American art in the world (including shrunken bodies). Open Tuesday through Saturday, 10 A.M. to 5 P.M., Sunday, 1 P.M. to 5 P.M. Admission $3. The **Hispanic Society of America** (926-2234) focuses on Iberian rather than Latin American culture. Open Tuesday through Saturday, 10 A.M. to 4:30 P.M., Sunday, 1 P.M. to 4 P.M. The **American Numismatic Society** (234-3130) has America's most complete numismatic library, as well as displays of coins, medals, and paper money. Open Tuesday through Saturday, 9 A.M. to 4:30 P.M.; Sunday, 1 to 4 P.M.

The **Morris-Jumel Mansion** (160th Street and Edgecombe Avenue; 923–8008) was built in 1765 and was George Washington's headquarters during the Revolutionary War. The oldest private residence remaining in Manhattan, it was originally a summer villa, 12 miles from what was then New York City. Open Tuesday through Sunday, 10 A.M. to 4 P.M.

If you're into bridges, the **George Washington Bridge** (179th Street and Broadway leads onto the walkway) was, for a while, the longest bridge in the world, but is still one of the most impressive.

The real attraction at this end of Manhattan is the **Cloisters,** a reconstruction of French and Spanish monastic cloisters located in Fort Tryon Park, property donated to the city by John D. Rockefeller, Jr. One of the loveliest spots in the entire country (the Hudson River views are as glorious as the relics collected in Europe), the Cloisters houses the medieval holdings of the Metropolitan Museum of Art. The chapels were brought from Europe and rebuilt stone by stone in as idyllic a setting as one could find. Among the highlights here are the famous Bury St. Edmunds Cross made of walrus-tusk ivory and carved with biblical figures, the Merode Altarpiece in which a 15th-century Belgian artist daringly portrayed the Virgin in a contemporary living room, and the Unicorn Tapestries—a series of seven tapestries that are stunningly realistic. Open Tuesday through Sunday, 10 A.M. to 4 P.M. Admission $5. Tours are given Tuesday and Thursday at 3 P.M. (923-3700).

A shuttle bus to the Cloisters leaves the Metropolitan Museum every hour from 10 A.M. to 2 P.M. on Fri. and Sat. only. Two hours later, the bus returns to the Met. Cost is $4; call 879-5500.

Otherwise, you can take the number 4 bus up Madison Ave. to the last stop, or the A train to 190th St. and Overlook Terr. and then walk through Fort Tryon Park.

Boroughs

Unless you're in town to visit relatives, New York means Manhattan. The Bronx, Brooklyn, Queens, and Staten Island are not bursting at the seams with tourist attractions (despite every New Yorker having a favorite restaurant or bakery or park or museum in one of the boroughs). Locals travel back and forth across rivers and bridges to visit family, or sample the ethnic delights of ebulliently Italian Arthur Avenue in the Bronx, or because they've succumbed to a Grecian yearning to be in Astoria, Queens. The so-called "outer" boroughs are culturally rich outposts that offer nourishment to one and all.

In addition to sporting events (see Entertainment) that will lure you out of Manhattan, we've compiled a highly selective list of places to go. But before attempting to cross any body of water larger than the fountain at the Plaza, be advised that while the law requires cabs to take you to any destination within the five boroughs, you're likely to hear some mighty fast talking when you dash out of your hotel and tell the driver you want to go to the Jamaica Bay Wildlife Refuge—and step on it! Advice from the front lines: plan on public transportation.

THE BRONX

The Bronx Zoo. Fordham Road and Bronx River Parkway; 367-1010. Rates vary between winter and summer. Open daily, 10 A.M. to 4:30 P.M., until 5:30 P.M. on Sunday and holidays. Admission at presstime: $2.50; children, $.75; by donation on Tuesday and Thursday. IRT No. 2 train to Pelham Pkwy station. Also Liberty Lines express bus from Madison Ave. Call 881-1000.

One of the most spectacular zoos in the world. Over 3,000 animals and birds can be seen in simulated natural habitats. Jungle World is the newest indoor home for tropical Asian wildlife. Other exhibits include the World of Darkness (for nocturnal animals); Wild Asia, where an elevated monorail takes you through elephant, rhinoceros, and tiger country; the African Plains, where only moats separate you from the wild ones. All this plus one of the most original children's zoos in the country (an entrance fee is requested).

New York Botanical Garden. Southern Boulevard, north of Fordham Road; 220-8700. Open daily, dawn to dusk. Admission free. Enid Haupt Conservatory is open 10 A.M. to 4 P.M., Tuesday through Sunday. Admission $2.50. IND No. 4, C, or D trains to Bedford Park station, then No. 17 bus to Webster Avenue.

A gorgeous 250 acres of azaleas, roses, herb gardens, pine and hemlock forests, and the Bronx River waterfall. The star attraction is the Enid Haupt Conservatory—a Victorian crystal fantasy that has been landmarked.

Poe Cottage. East Kingsbridge Road and the Grand Concourse; 881-8900. Open Wednesday through Friday, 9 A.M. to 5 P.M.; Saturday, 10 A.M. to 4 P.M.; Sunday, 1 P.M. to 5 P.M. Admission: $1. IND C or D train to Kingsbridge Road station.

A real treat for Edgar Allan Poe fans. Our early-American Stephen King lived here from 1846 to 1849 during which time he wrote *Annabel Lee* and *The Bells*. The house has been preserved as a museum, and guides lead visitors through the rooms.

Van Cortlandt Park (and Van Cortlandt Mansion). 246th Street and Broadway; 543-3344.

Two square miles of park that was part of a Dutch land grant dating back to 1646. Van Cortlandt has facilities for swimming, tennis, horseback riding, and picnicking. It's also the site of the Van Cortlandt Mansion (open Tuesday through Saturday, 10 A.M. to 4 P.M.; Sunday noon to 5 P.M. Admission: $1), which served as headquarters for British and American troops during the Revolution. Washington *really* slept here many times.

Wave Hill. 249th Street and Independence Avenue, Riverdale; 549-2055. Open daily from 10 A.M. to 4:30 P.M. Admission is free on weekdays; Saturday, Sunday, and holidays, $2. Liberty Lines express bus from Third Ave. Call 881-1000.

A fabulous estate on 280 acres of beautiful grounds overlooking the Hudson. Wave Hill consists of two manor houses, plus sculpture and flower gardens. Theodore Roosevelt, Mark Twain, and Toscanini were former owners of the estate. The music collection includes all of Toscanini's work.

BROOKLYN

Aquarium. West 8th Street and Surf Avenue; (718) 265-3474. Open daily 10 A.M. to 4:45 P.M. Admission: $3.75. IND F train to West 8th Street station.

Whales, sea turtles, and eels swim fin to fin. A pretty scary shark tank and, in summer, an outdoor dolphin show are featured. Special exhibits at the Children's Cove allow the kids to see and touch (but not the sharks).

Brighton Beach. IND D or Q to Brighton Beach station.

It's only a short walk south from Coney Island to Brighton Beach, which today has become known as "Little Odessa." The area, home to over 20,000 Russian immigrants, is crowded with people shopping at imported food stores or eating at exotic restaurants. You're always only a pirogi's throw from a big bowl of borscht. If all you want is a snack, there's Mrs. Stahl's knishes at the corner of Brighton Beach and Coney Island Avenue.

Brooklyn Botanic Gardens. 1000 Washington Avenue; (718) 622-4433. Admission free (on weekends $.25 to see the greenhouses.) Hours change with the season, so call ahead. Closed Mondays. IRT No. 2 or 3 train to Eastern Parkway/Brooklyn Museum station.

Fifty acres of gardens, flowers, trees, and new glass conservatories costing more than $25 million. The cherry blossoms that bloom in May are said to rival those in Washington, D.C. If you're going to be here in the spring, call ahead for the exact dates of bloom. Among the rest of the showstopping exhibits are the Cranford Rose Garden (with 90 varieties of roses), the Shakespeare Garden, the Fragrance Garden for the Blind (with Braille markings), and the exquisite Japanese Garden. Continuing in an Oriental vein, the gardens also offer the country's largest collection of bonsai trees.

Brooklyn Children's Museum. 145 Brooklyn Avenue; (718) 735-4432. Open Monday, Wednesday, Friday, 2 P.M. to 5 P.M.; Saturday and Sunday 10 A.M. to 5 P.M. Suggested admission: $2. IRT No. 3 train to Kingston Ave. Walk 6 blocks north to St. Marks Avenue. Turn left and go down the block to the museum.

This was the world's first museum designed exclusively for children. Fossils, mounted mammals, prehistoric exhibits, as well as technological and environmental displays.

Brooklyn Heights. IRT No. 2 or 3 train to Clark Street.

One of the loveliest and most peaceful neighborhoods in all the city. Originally, "The Heights" was an area for merchants to build their homes. Most of the brownstones and carriage houses are still as beautiful and elegant today as they were when they were put up in the early 1800s. Clark Street leads down to The Esplanade (called "The Promenade" by residents) for a spectacular view of the Manhattan skyline across the East River. Other streets with magnificent houses are Pierrepont Street, Cranberry Street, Pineapple Street, and Joralemon Street. Montague Street is the place for shops and restaurants.

Brooklyn Museum. 200 Eastern Parkway; (718) 638-5000. Open Wednesday to Monday, 10 A.M. to 5 P.M. Suggested contribution: $3. IRT No. 2 or 3 train to Eastern Pkwy/ Brooklyn Museum stop.

It's the seventh largest art museum in the U.S., with an Egyptian collection that's considered to be one of the best in the world. Also known for its Japanese, Korean, and Primitive African art. There are rooms from a typical 17th-century Brooklyn house that have been reconstructed, and the sculpture garden has artifacts and relics from "lost New York." And the museum's gift shop, chock full of crafts from around the world, is a great source of inexpensive gifts to take home.

Coney Island. IND F, B, D, N, and Q trains to Stillwell Avenue station.

Back in the 1880s, when Coney Island was a chic resort, there were elegant hotels, miles of immaculate beaches, a race track, a choice of amusement parks, and a fine boardwalk. Today all that remains is the boardwalk and the beach. But even though it's a tacky shadow of its former self, Coney Island still attracts those eager to catch the ocean breezes, take a stroll on the boardwalk, or visit the Aquarium. There's only one amusement park left in Coney—Astroland, which has the king of roller coasters, "The Cyclone." There are other amusements, not to mention hot dogs at Nathan's Famous, cotton candy, and corn on the cob. For safety's sake, don't plan on being at Coney Island alone, or, no matter who you're with, at night. Definitely not for the faint-of-heart, a visit to Coney Island is best paid on a sunny—and crowded—summer afternoon.

Prospect Park. Grand Army Plaza. (718) 788-0055. Call for hours; they change seasonally. IRT No. 2 or 3 train to Grand Army Plaza.

A 526-acre expanse of lush meadows, lakes, and ponds with a boathouse, a zoo, and a skating rink that was designed by that great team, Olmsted and Vaux, who gave us Central Park. The main entrance at Grand Army Plaza is dominated by the Soldier's and Sailor's Memorial Arch, completed in 1892 to commemorate the Civil War. The newest eye catcher at the park is a completely refurbished boathouse where you can get information about special events or arrange to join one of the tours. Unfortunately, Prospect Park suffers from the safety problems of most N.Y.C. parks—don't go at night, and it's probably best not to go alone.

QUEENS

The American Museum of the Moving Image. 35th Avenue at 36th Street, Astoria; (718) 784-0077. Open Monday through Thursday, 1 P.M. to 5 P.M.; Friday 1 to 8 P.M.; Saturday 10 A.M. to 8 P.M.; Sunday, 10 A.M. to 5 P.M. Admission: $4. IND R train to Steinway Street. Walk to 35th Avenue and turn right.

Fascinating exhibits that take you from the very beginning of film up to the present. There are two floors of costumes and memorabilia that predate the forties, a projection imaging machine so that you appear to be wearing a costume from a classic such as *Gone With The Wind,* and most offbeat of all, tapes that allow you to listen in as famous directors coached actors in their films.

Jamaica Bay Wildlife Refuge. Broadchannel West; (718) 474-0613. Open daily from 8:30 A.M. to 5 P.M. Admission free. IND A train to Broadchannel station. Ask directions from there.

Some 2,800 acres of land and 9,000 acres of water are reserved for nature walks, bird watching, and relaxation. More than 300 species of shore birds, water fowl, and small mammals are featured. There are also guided tours on the weekends.

STATEN ISLAND

Jacques Marchais Center of Tibetan Art. 338 Lighthouse Avenue; (718) 987-3478. Open April, October, November: Friday to Sunday, 1 P.M. to 5 P.M.; May to September: Thursday to Sunday, 1 P.M. to 5 P.M.; closed December through March. Admission: $2.50. From Staten Island Ferry station, take bus number 113 to Lighthouse Avenue.

Two stone buildings designed to look like a Tibetan monastery house the largest collection of Tibetan art in the Western Hemisphere. The center also features art from Japan, China, India, and Southeast Asia. There are gardens and a lotus pond for peaceful meditation.

Richmondtown Restoration. 441 Clarke Avenue; (718) 351-1611. Open Monday to Friday, 10 A.M. to 5 P.M.; Saturday, Sunday, holidays, 1 P.M. to 5 P.M. Admission: $4. From Staten Island Ferry station, take bus number 113 to St. Patrick's Place.

Remarkably, this is an entire 96-acre historic village right in New York City. The restoration comprises 26 buildings dating from the 17th through the 19th century. Visitors can see demonstrations of early American leatherworking, tinsmithing, carpentry, printing, spinning, weaving, and cooking. There is also an historical museum with exhibits on regional history.

7

SHOPPING

Shopping in New York is as idiosyncratic as New Yorkers themselves. If you're a bargain hunter, you can find better quality at better prices than anywhere else. If you're out to snare something totally unique, goodies that wouldn't be caught dead on the pages of a mail-order catalog, you will find them in New York. And if you're a card-carrying Sybarite, you'll see more luxury goods here than in Marie Antoinette's closet. Sometimes a pleasure and sometimes an adventure, shopping in New York has as many nuances as the glance you're given in the rearview mirror after asking a cabbie if he has change of twenty dollars.

For example: Let's say you've fallen in love with a designer dress from the newest sew-and-sew in town, Yves St. Shapiro. You can: (1) head for his boutique and feel the earth move as you posh-out; (2) grab a cab to a department store where they're selling an "original copy" of the same design at a fraction of the cost; or (3) take the subway down to the Lower East Side to Frieda's Friendly Frocks where the St. Shapiro line is more deeply discounted than a starlet's cleavage.

Thanks to the sheer number of shoppers in New York, and a no-holds-barred discount policy, you can buy everything from Japanese cameras at prices that are cheaper than Tokyo, to clothes on sale at prices that hover close to cost. The name of the game here is "motion"—the merchandise has to move. Everything in this town, including shirts and shampoo, is governed by real estate.

With shops reflecting the neighborhoods in which they're located, you'll find upscale goods on Fifth and Madison Avenues, and on 57th Street; bargains on the Lower East Side; avant-garde in Soho and Greenwich Village; rock culture kitsch in the East Village, etc., but there are also museum shops, flea markets, auction houses, and street vendors. (No, of course, you shouldn't buy watches on the street. But you might find a dynamite pair of earrings or gloves.) Also beware of places that have "lost our lease" and are "going out of business." What most of them have lost is the second hundred years on their lease and are going out of business in the year 2085.

Tours of all of the neighborhoods above give numerous shopping suggestions. We discuss some of our specific favorites below in the section that follows. If you have some special interests not covered, check the New York Yellow Pages. Also, the old standbys: the *New York Times, The New Yorker,* and *New York* magazine list street fairs, flea markets, and special sales. Be aware that the smaller the business, the more unpredictable the hours. If there's someplace you're determined to go to, call before you leave. And check on method of payment so that you're not faced with a dilemma immediately after tracking down the pickle fork of your dreams.

Note: if you have items shipped back home, you can avoid the 8.75 percent NYC sales tax.

Antiques

As the savvy dealers say, they're not making antiques like they used to. They're not selling them like they used to either. Once upon a time, you could wander along Third Avenue or through the Village and really discover treasures. But now the "everything old is new again" nostalgia has priced them out of sight. The good news is that New York offers an incredible selection of quality antiques that rival those found in London and Paris.

Largely due to the rise of major auction houses such as **Sotheby's** (1334 York Avenue at 72nd Street; 606-7000) and **Christie's** (502 Park Avenue at 59th Street; 546-1000) and the knowledgeable buyers attracted to record-breaking sales, New York dealers find themselves selling to a more international and sophisticated clientele. All you have to do is walk through **Place des Antiquaires,** 125 East 57th Street, or the **Manhattan Art & Antiques Center** (see below) to know that quality is at an all-time high.

The only area in which New York can't begin to compete with the capitals of Europe is that of flea markets. The spectacle of Portobello Road or the Marché aux Puces is simply not to be found on the city streets. Still, check the weekly and daily publications for announcements of street fairs and flea markets. It's still possible to pick up some memorabilia we guarantee you'd never find back home. Also, be sure not to overlook the auction houses for some of the finest browsing and buying in town.

While the city has hundreds of antique shops, the **Manhattan Arts & Antiques Center** 1050 Second Avenue at 55th Street, is a good place to start. A terrific antiques market in the European sense, everything is under one roof: a flock of dealers who carry everything from tiger teeth to Van Cleef tiaras. Further uptown, **Linda Horn Antiques,** 1015 Madison Avenue, is one of those stores that's chock full of brilliant bibelots and collector's items. **À la Vieille Russie,** 781 Fifth Avenue at 59th Street, is possibly the most unusual antique jewelery shop in town with the ultimate in gorgeous glasnost: treasures from Mother Russia, including works by Fabergé that are worth a czar's ransom. There are still some shops on Amsterdam and Columbus avenues where prices haven't yet gone through the roof. Be sure to check out the antiques corners at department stores: we're particularly fond of the one at Bloomingdale's (see Department Stores, below). If you're not adverse to reproductions, the shop at the Metropolitan Museum of Art has some lovely jewelry and glassware.

Books and Records

As the center of publishing in America, it's understandable why New York has the country's best selection of bookstores. From specialty shops such as the **Biography Bookshop** (400 Bleecker Street) to sci-fi adventures at **Forbidden Planet** (821 Broadway at 12th Street) to the Eurochic of the **Rizzoli** stores (454 West Broadway and 31 West 57th Street between Fifth and Sixth avenues), it's easy to find something for every taste—even for those with no taste who haunt the X-rated bookstores on 42nd Street.

A real bonus for visitors is the **Strand Bookstore** (828 Broadway at 12th Street), where you can pick up "reviewer's copies" of new bestsellers at half the list price. Even more interesting for dedicated bookworms is the dazzling variety of used and out-of-print books shelved at Strand. (Be sure to go downstairs for the oversize books, art books, and more reviewer's copies.) **Endicott** (450 Columbus at 81st Street) and **Shakespeare & Co.** (2259 Broadway at 81st Street) are favorites for intelligent stock, and **Books and Co.** (939 Madison at 74th Street) takes the literati prize. **Gotham** (41 West 47th Street) for poetry and letters, and **Doubleday** (724 Fifth Avenue at 57th Street) for late-night browsing and hard-to-find tapes. While en route to Bloomingdale's, stop in at **Argosy** (116 East 69th Street)—if not for the books, at least to browse through the prints and maps. While most shops have extensive travel book collections, you'll find lots of special treats at the **Complete Traveller Bookstore** (119 Madison at 35th Street) and the **Traveller's Bookstore** (22 West 52nd Street). **Barnes & Noble** discounts all books in their sale annex (105 Fifth Avenue).

J&R Music World (23 Park Row, downtown) is not just for what's hot today, but also for back issue and out-of-stock records and tapes. Prices are rock bottom. **Tower Records,**

which also sells at a discount, is a happening in itself. Acres of records and tapes and people. Open 365 days from 9 A.M. to midnight, locations are 692 Broadway near Astor Place and 1965 Broadway (at 66th Street). You'll find post-adolescent pre-yuppies hanging out here on Saturday nights. Great prices and people watching.

Cameras and Electronics

Someday we're going to write a book on the joys of buying at list price. Discounting may have become a national obsession but it has to be approached with lots of backup information. Buyers must be especially beware when dealing with the camera and electronics discounters. Even more than being beware, you should have made a few comparisons before settling on the shop of your choice. One of the main things to consider is whether saving is worth having to deal long distance with some of those rough and tumble characters you're likely to find behind the counters.

Prices are alluring, often unbeatable, but unless you're really expert in the field, be very wary when the salesman tries to sell you another brand or model. It might work out wonderfully, but then again the name of the game at a discount shop is turnover and not service.

That said, you'll find better bargains than in Hong Kong.

Brothers
130 West 34 St.; 695-4158

Brothers
466 Lexington Ave. at 45 St.; 986-3323

Camera Barn
1272 Broadway; 947-3510

Executive Photo
120 West 31 St.; 564-3592

47st. photo
115 West 45 between 6th and Broadway; 260-4410

Grand Central Camera
485 Madison Ave.; 986-2270

Olden
1265 Broadway at 32 St.; 725-1234

Willoughby Camera Store
110 West 32 St between 6th and 7th aves.; 564-1600

Clothing

Even more than its restaurants, New York's clothing stores reflect the neighborhoods in which they're located. For the ultimate in drop-dead chic (at drop-dead prices) there's a nest of activity that swarms from 59th to 57th streets (including **Bendel,** 10 West 57th, **Bergdorf,** Fifth Avenue and 57th, and **Bonwit,** 4 East 57th) and then over to Madison where you can charge up the avenue declaring war on your closet. Quality men's stores (which usually have women's departments, as well) can be found on Madison in the 40s: **Brooks Brothers,** 346 Madison; **F.R. Tripler** 366 Madison; and **Paul Stuart,** Madison at 45th. You may want to leave the neighborhood and head to **Barney's,** 106 Seventh Avenue at 17th Street; known as one of New York's finest men's stores, it sells women's wear, too.

If you're into "funk," head down to the East Village. Soho offers an easy off-beat elegance, and the Upper West Side is a leader in expensive casual threads starting with **Charivari** (numerous outlets, with stores at 441 Columbus and 201 West 79th Street selling for both men and women) and then onto the Columbus Avenue shops. Be advised that they are known to open and close faster than a Rockefeller's checkbook. Columbus and Madison are also good places to outfit rich kids.

And then there's the Lower East Side where the selection is not as lavish as on the avenues but where the discounts are designed to take your breath away. Not missing a trick, New York is filled with shops selling "antique" clothes, military surplus, and previously-owned (read: used) clothes. Try **Alice Underground,** 380 Columbus; **Gaby's,** 225 Fifth Avenue; **Dorothy's Closet,** 335 Bleecker.

If all of this sounds too exhausting, or your time is limited, you can always head for Bloomingdale's, Saks, Lord & Taylor, or Macy's where you'll find designer boutiques as well as "house labels" (plus snack shops and bathrooms) that reflect New York style at its best.

Department Stores

New York's department stores have set a standard throughout the country. No matter which out-of-state branch you've been to, the flagship stores are different because being different and taking chances is what keeps them from being malled to death. It's no accident that Sears hasn't opened on Fifth Avenue.

Of all the department stores, **Alexander's** is the only one that offers "discount" prices. (As of this writing, Alexander's future is up in the air. Owned by Donald Trump, the store isn't telling if and when it will be shut to make way for a multiuse facility.) As long as it remains open, Alexander's, 731 Lexington, is somewhere between Bloomingdale's (right across the street) and the Lower East Side: alas, without the panache or style of either, but you're likely to find a bargain or three to make up for the lack of culture shock. There's also a branch of Alexander's at 4 World Trade Center.

Despite all our complaints, if you have time for only one department store, make it **Bloomie's,** 1000 Third Avenue. The sheer vitality and range of goods available almost elevates it to the category of a "sight." **Macy's,** 131 West 34th Street, **Saks Fifth Avenue,** 611 Fifth at 50th Street, **Lord & Taylor,** 424 Fifth Avenue at 39th Street, and **Altman's,** 361 Fifth at 34th Street, are all solid and traditional. And then, there are the three B's: **Bendel,** 10 West 57th Street, **Berg-dorf,** 754 Fifth Avenue between 57th and 58th, and **Bonwit,** 4 East 57th Street, who sell to a different (and usually wealthier) drummer.

Remember that if you send your package home, you won't have to pay NYC sales tax.

Jewelry

In New York, a girl's best friend can be million-dollar diamonds or dollar rings. As with everything else here, the variety in jewelry is staggering. From faux to Fabergé is sold in settings as grungy or gorgeous as the jewelry itself: you'll find "would-you-buy-a-used-car-from-this-man?" street vendors practically right outside of posh diamond mines such as **Harry Winston,** 718 Fifth Avenue at 56th Street. And then the "have-I-got-a-bargain-for-you!" dealers in the "diamond district" (47th Street between Fifth and Sixth avenues).

Cartier, 653 Fifth Avenue at 52nd Street, and **Tiffany,** 727 Fifth at 57th Street, speak for themselves, but **David Webb,** 7 East 57th Street, designed for the Duchess of Windsor and the shop is still turning out fabled jewelry for fabled people. **Fortunoff,** 681 Fifth Avenue, is at the end of the price tag, but its selection and design of fine jewelry is tops. **Fred Leighton,** 773 Madison at 66th, has been a favorite for years. The shop has a truly extraordinary collection of antique jewelry—alas with prices to match the quality.

No matter where you buy, the key is knowing what to buy. If you don't, play it safe and stay with designer boutique costume jewelry where you're clearly paying for what's in a name. All department stores have reputable jewelry collections in price ranges to fit most budgets. As long as you're not empty headed, there's no reason to go home empty handed.

Scents and Cosmetics

If you're planning a super-splurge night on the town, the **Make-up Center,** 150 West 55th Street, does evening (or day) faces and gives you a lesson en route. Believers in the sweet smell of success should head for **Jean La Porte,** 870 Madison, where you can blend herbs, flowers, and flavors to create a signature scent all your own. (Vanilla is a hot number here.) For revolutionary (American Revolutionary) colognes and perfumes, **Caswell Massey,** 518 Lex at 48th, and 21 Fulton Street, South Street Seaport, has house brands that reek of deja vu. Since this is the town for discounts on everything, the **Perfume Encounter,** 25 East 17th Street, will give you 10 to 20 percent off on most of your favorites. A good place to sniff out a bargain.

Food Shops

New York will give you a chance to sample some of the most
extraordinary take-out goodies in the world. Places like **The
Silver Palate,** 274 Columbus, **Dean & DeLuca,** 560
Broadway, and **Balducci's,** 424 Sixth Avenue at 9th St.,
excel in preparing mini-meals to be enjoyed on those nights
you just want to say to hell with it, soak in a tub, and rest
your feet.

Another thing to consider is the golden oldie that food is
love: you might want to bring someone back home a tasty re-
membrance of your trip. One of our favorite ways of easing
re-entry to the real world is to bring ourselves back a special
treat over which to savor the last details of our adventure.
Zabar's, 2245 Broadway at 80th, is particularly helpful in
packing things to be taken back home.

Women's Shoes

In New York, the "step on it" philosophy of life applies as
much to shoes as speed. A few heart and sole choices are
Maud Frizon (49 East 57th Street), for Parisian high kicks,
Joan & David (various locations: 1293 Broadway, 816 Madi-
son, 805 Third Avenue, 3 East 57th, and 25 Fulton Street)
for elegant understatement and urban chic, **Perry Ellis** (680
Madison) for a finely tailored look, and **Ferragamo** (717 Fifth
Avenue) for the dolciest vita this side of Rome (there's also
a Ferragamo men's store at 730 Fifth). For realists, **Orchard
Bootery** (75 Orchard Street) offers the best for the least.

For the Home

In a city where everyone is always eager for a new look,
housewares and home furnishings are almost as important as
plastic surgeons. Among our favorite shops are **Wolfman
Gold & Good** (484 Broome) for some of the most unique
tableware and crystal. The store itself smells of spices and
potpourri, a feeling of cozy elegance. Prices go in so many
directions, there's always a goodie to be found. **Sointu** (20
East 69th Street at Madison) is sleek, sophisticated, and continental: browsing there is like crossing the border into the
Kingdom of Good Taste. **Ad Hoc Softwares** (410 West
Broadway near Spring Street) is part housewares and part
hardware. Very eighties, this is the place for techie gadgets.
D.F. Sanders (386 West Broadway near Broome Street) is
a *Whole Earth Catalog* shop for yuppies—as well as for those
who may have succumbed to fiftysomething but still haven't
lost every shred of good taste. **Pottery Barn** (various locations throughout the city, including 231 Tenth Avenue, 1292
Lexington, and 250 West 57th) is where most New Yorkers
bought their first wine glasses and fondue sets. Crammed with

imports, there's almost always a bargain waiting to be discovered.

If money is no object, look for glassware at **Steuben Glass,** 717 Fifth Avenue, or **Baccarat,** 625 Madison Avenue.

The rich and famous have been known to make a quick stop at **Pratesi,** 829 Madison at 69th, to stock up on bed linens. If you're looking for silver, head to **Georg Jensen,** 683 Madison Avenue.

Toys and Games

Everybody knows about **F.A.O. Schwarz,** 766 Fifth Avenue between 58th and 59th, the Music Hall of toy stores, but there are lots of others for the kid in all of us. **Penny Whistle Toys,** 448 Columbus Avenue, is an old-fashioned toy store, while **Mouse Dynasty,** 503 Columbus, is devoted to Mickey worshippers of all ages. **Go Fly a Kite,** 1201 Lexington, is filled with brilliant kites for budding Ben and Benita Franklins. **Mythology,** 370 Columbus, runs the gamut from crafts to antique wind-ups; **Dapy,** 232 Columbus and 431 West Broadway is strictly eighties kitsch; and **Think Big,** 313 Columbus and 390 West Broadway, explodes everything out of proportion with great good humor.

Leather and Luggage

New York is just the place to play hide and seek. Head for the top: **Bottega Veneta,** 635 Madison—perfect Italian craftsmanship that turns out purses, totes, and shoes as precious as jewels. **Gucci** is at 683 Fifth Avenue; **Louis Vuitton,** 51 East 57th. **La Bagagerie,** 727 Madison, is sure to have the latest in trendy French handbags. For the most delicious colors and designs in clothes, try **Loewe,** 711 Madison, Spain's foremost leathersmith. Many of the designer boutiques have fine leather goods on display, but it's at **Fine & Klein,** 119 Orchard Street, that you'll find the best uptown labels at downtown prices.

Arts and Crafts

While New Yorkers have found ways to make an art out of almost everything from hailing a cab to crossing the street against the light, there's still time to enjoy less dangerous forms of self-expression. **Erica Wilson** (717 Madison) is HQ for superb needlework patterns and completed creations. **Pearl Paint** (308 Canal Street) is where starving artists go to replenish supplies, while **Sam Flax** (various locations, including 747 Third Avenue, 25 East 28th Street, 12 West 20th Street) is for the artist with a paycheck and a penchant for fine stationery. **Tender Buttons** (123 West 57th Street) is a one-of-kind delight that's a treasure trove of antique and contemporary buttons.

Handblock (487 Columbus Avenue) has a wonderful collection of handcrafted Indian fabrics sold by the yard or made up into table linens, quilts, and clothes. African crafts, jewelry, and clothes (as well as toys) are highlighted at **Liberty House** (2389 Broadway) Mexico is handsomely represented at **Pan American Phoenix** (153 East 53rd Street) with toys, glassware, pottery, and wonderfully romantic Mexican wedding dresses. The **U.N. Gift Shop** has the most extensive collection of crafts from around the world, but check out also the shops at the **Museum of Natural History** and the **Brooklyn Museum.**

For stationery and paper devotees, one of the most unusual shops is **80 Papers** (510 Broome Street) with imports from all over the world; **ffolio** (33 East 68th) has stationery to excite all letterwriters; and **Il Papiro**'s marbelized papers (1021 Lexington) are a joy.

Astro Minerals (155 East 34th) is one of the most exotic shops in the city, with African and Indonesian crafts scattered amid geodes and jewelry that make perfect gifts.

8

RESTAURANTS

New York is the eating capital of the world. There are some 25,000 restaurants that represent virtually all known cuisines and can satisfy all palates and purses whether you have an appetite for pâté or pastrami, *haute cuisine* or hot dogs, nouvelle or nosh. There are more Szechuan restaurants per block than in Szechuan. There are better Italian restaurants on Second Avenue than in many Italian towns. Nowhere else on the entire planet will you find such a dazzling variety of choices—gastronomically, socially, and economically.

From street food (the hot dog carts and falafel vendors on the cross streets off Fifth Avenue around 50th Street) to coffee shops and small family-run ethnic restaurants, from intense minimalist vegetarian hideaways to bustling urban bistros that serve burgers as though cholesterol were going out of style. There are tummy temples where each string bean is supposed to make the earth move, and margarita mills where brunch has been elevated to an art form second only to long-distance dialing. You will find places that are impossible to get into without a reservation and impossible to get out of with both arms and legs intact. Service will range from "Hello, my name is Barry, I'm your waiter this evening" to maître d's who give you the feeling you have to send a telegram to get their attention.

We have profiled 35 restaurants that we regard as quintessentially New York: They are synonymous with the excellence, the glamour, the pulse of the city. We hasten to add that these are not the only 35 that serve good food, nor is this list meant for New Yorkers trying to figure out which is the best French restaurant in the city. We have specifically avoided all "La" comparisons (La Côte Basque vs. La Grenouille vs. La Reserve vs. La Caravelle, etc.). That wasn't our intent. This book is, first and foremost, a travel guide. And since it isn't *The Backpacker's Guide to Gotham,* we presume a certain level of sophistication, or at the very least, adventure. (Neither is this *The Paranoid's Guide to N.Y.C. Restaurants*—so we're not wasting time telling you where *not* to go.) Instead, we're drawing on years of experience to compile a primer for our hometown. We wanted to cover as many facets of the restaurant scene as possible, including the glitz factor that simply can't be overlooked in a place like

New York. If you want to focus on food criticism, read Gael Greene in *New York* magazine or Bryan Miller in the Friday *New York Times.*

In addition to the 35 restaurants featured, we have made restaurant suggestions in the preceding neighborhood sections. For your convenience, those restaurants have been indexed alphabetically following the profiles in this chapter.

Prices

Dining out in New York is expensive. There's not much leeway around the $50 per person figure (exclusive of wine, tax, and tip) that keeps cropping up at the "better" restaurants. But there is some: Lunches are generally cheaper than dinners, and many restaurants have pre-theater dinners that are anywhere from one-third to one-half the usual price. Since the object of going to a restaurant is to have a wonderful time, we've never believed in choosing one we couldn't comfortably afford. Or afford to splurge on. Generally speaking, all the restaurants mentioned in the neighborhood sections are less expensive than those profiled here.

If you're really determined to keep costs down, you'll want to explore the restaurants in ethnic areas such as Chinatown, the Lower East Side, and Little Italy. Try the Indian restaurants on and around East 6th St., and on Lexington Ave. in the lower thirties and upper twenties. You can dine fabulously (and inexpensively) by taking your fast food purchases onto Pier 17 at the South Street Seaport, having a hot dog on the Staten Island Ferry, or picnicking in Central Park.

Reservations

If possible, make restaurant reservations for your special nights out before you leave home. It's often impossible to get a table on short notice in many of the more popular restaurants. And even with a reservation, you have to be prepared to be seated in Siberia. The best tables are always held for regulars. But that doesn't mean you have to sit next to the kitchen door or the men's room if you don't want to. Be polite but firm in explaining that you do not want to be seated there. If that's the only seat in the house, and you honestly don't want it, don't make the mistake of staying. You won't enjoy yourself.

Some restaurants have the nasty habit of overbooking, so that when you do arrive on time for your reservation, you're told your table won't be ready for twenty minutes or so and would you mind waiting at the bar. You have a choice: Decide if it's worth the delay. Sometimes it is. If not, leave.

Credit cards

Unless otherwise noted, all restaurants profiled accept major credit cards (American Express, Visa, MasterCard, Diner's Club, Carte Blanche). Though it's wise to double check. Do not expect coffee shops or many of the small ethnic restaurants to take credit cards. All restaurants are keyed into the appropriate page and coordinates of the color atlas at the back of the book.

❦ THE SELECTIONS

Arizona 206
UPPER EAST SIDE, p. 7, D11

206 East 60th St.; (212) 838-0440.

The concept of Southwestern dining as dished out at Arizona 206 has created a totally "New York" restaurant. Sure it's got adobe walls, bleached floors, and straight-backed wooden chairs at wooden tables. There are even knotholes in the wood, and nubby fabric on the cushions. But, to be honest, the bar is ten deep with cowpokes from Bloomingdale's, and Yuppietalk floats around the room like urban tumbleweed. The place looks great. The people look great. And, despite the blare of country music, you just know everyone would drop dead at the thought of chicken-fried steak and burned gravy.

With good reason. Those dudes didn't come here for down-home cooking: No one in sight of the painted desert ever had tequila-basil gravlax, or escabeche of tuna with papaya relish. We sampled crab ravioli with saffron sauce and salsa picante; fresh corn and chili soup with crawfish; seared beef tenderloin with dry chili pesto; green chili tamale with black bean sauce — and that was only for starters.

Don't let the word "chili" frighten you: Remember, this is a New York restaurant where the hottest thing is gossip. The chili here is warming, spicy by innuendo, and used for flavor, not to camouflage a dish. Among the main courses we tried were corn flour pasta with seared sea scallops and smoked chili sauce; poached lobster salad with a spectacular poblano mousse; and, the one dish guaranteed to be on the menu despite seasonal changes, a superb chili-rubbed chicken with sweet corn and basil. The chicken is rubbed with a "chili cure" and marinated overnight so that the coating hangs on for dear life and crisps as it's seared. The restaurant's signature dishes created by Brendan Walsh are still on the menu, and Walsh continues on a consulting chef basis. But we're promised some twists from new chef Marilyn Frobucciano, while continuing the spirit of the team that created Arizona 206.

Desserts run the range from a killer red currant tart to espresso ice cream. The all-American wine list has a number of good selections in the $16–$18 range, and the aperitifs of choice (aside from the ubiquitous margarita) are a "lemonade" of fresh lemons, sugar, and tequila, or a peach vodka that would have made even Dostoyevski smile. Another bonus is the wait staff: They are novitiates of the highest order, clearly in love with the menu. The tab here will run about $50 per person. (If you'd like to stop in for just a taste, there's a satellite café next door that serves starters.)

Lunch: Mon.–Sat., noon–3 P.M. Dinner: Mon.–Thurs., 6 P.M.–11 P.M.; Fri.–Sat., until 11:30 P.M.; Sun., 5 P.M.–11 P.M.

The Ballroom
CHELSEA, p. 6, B14

253 West 28th St.; (212) 244-3005.

When chef-owner Felipe Rojas-Lombardi told people that he wanted to open a "tapas" bar, they looked at him strangely. Felipe speaks with a soft Spanish accent and they thought he had said "topless." An understandable mistake: His was the first bar in the country to serve those small plates of hors d'oeuvres that keep heart and soul together in Spain while waiting for the traditional 10 or 11 P.M. dinner hour. The tapas concept hit New York just as "grazing" became fashionable. But The Ballroom is far more than trendy: it is a place for serious eating. Peruvian-born Rojas-Lombardi earned his title of "master chef" by lecturing, teaching, writing, consulting, and, most of all, by virtue of his splendid cooking.

The restaurant is a sprawling, multi-level, mixed-media event. As you enter, there is a huge painting of The Ballroom at its former Soho location, tables filled with artists and art dealers. The overall effect is one of Spanish country elegance: tiled floors, bentwood chairs, potted palms, huge woven baskets filled with onions and apples. Ceiling lights are wrapped in gauze to glow throughout the evening like a soft afternoon sun. But not until you turn the corner to the long wooden tapas bar, over which hang Serrano-style hams, dried codfish, and strings of garlic and red peppers, do you understand what The Ballroom is all about.

As many as 35 huge platters are piled high with an international, very eclectic interpretation of tapas—some might be found in the Plaza Mayor, others at a bar in Lima, and still others nowhere but in Rojas-Lombardi's imagination. There are snails and red beans ("It should be white beans, but I like the red beans better. I have to please my palate"); sea scallops in curry sauce ("I don't like the taste of curry powder, it is very raw to my tongue. . . ."—and so he dissolves the powder in oil to get precisely the flavor he wants); hazelnuts and roasted peppers topping a cold pasta flavored with a typical Catalonian sauce; "Moroccan" eggplant in coriander; seviche of scallops; a fish pâté; chorizo; tortilla de patatas (a custardy potato omelet); calamari; caponata; pig's ears—and then they bring on the hot tapas which can be anything from frog's legs to spicy shrimps (*gambas*) to succulent baby lamb chops. Your tab is calculated by the tapas bartender according to the number and color of plates (white=$2.50, green=$6.50, etc.). Figuring four to six plates per person, plus wine and tip, you're close to $40 to $50 a head.

While you can sample the tapas at your table and then go on to order from the regular menu—rack of lamb, duck with figs, steamed fresh codfish—we suggest you make a meal of the tapas and sit at the bar where you can select them yourself. The Ballroom has a 200-seat theater in the back that attracts showstoppers like Peggy Lee, Blossom Dearie, and Larry Adler.

Lunch and dinner: Tues.–Fri., noon–1 A.M.; Sat. 4:30 P.M.–1 A.M.

Le Bernardin   MIDTOWN WEST, p. 6, C12
155 West 51st St.; (212) 489-1515.

The first time we ate at Le Bernardin was in Paris. Maguy Le-Coze, the distaff side of the most food-conscious brother and sister act since Hansel and Gretel, told us that she and Gilbert were looking for space in New York. In terms of historical perspective, that's roughly equivalent to Julius Caesar thinking about his trip before he came, he saw, he conquered. Virtually overnight, as though the LeCozes had invented fish, the restaurant became a sensation. And then, the unthinkable happened:

New York conquered the LeCozes. They sold the Paris property. A smart move. Now, Le Bernardin truly is incomparable.

The extraordinary success of this upscale fish house—and the reason it's had a ripple-effect on every chef in the city—is LeCoze's knight-errant determination to find only the freshest and the best; his infallible sense of how, and just how long, to cook each fish; and a palate that demands robust flavors rather than settles for the absence of negative flavor, often used to characterize fish cookery. ("Hmmm. This is good. It doesn't taste fishy.") Well, nothing tastes fishy at Le Bernardin, but the fish have lots of taste.

So does the room. However, if permitted a minor cavil, we would say the room is so huge and impersonal (despite luxurious appointments) that it has the look of a hotel lobby. A grand hotel, to be sure, but with a distinctly corporate image. That said, it is richly Continental, bordering on posh. Champagne glasses go by faster than the shopping days before Christmas.

Okay. The carpaccio of tuna is pounded petal-thin and covers the plate like a mauve blossom. It is sprinkled with chives and glossed with olive oil. Slivers of black bass (again served raw) are accompanied by basil and coriander leaves. The fricassee of shellfish (mussels, oysters, clams) prepared with cream, tomato, garlic, and parsley is addictive. Of the main courses, favorites are skate à la nage (the fish pure enough to enter a convent, blanketed in the most pristine of sauces), a tangy poached halibut with beurre blanc, and a thick cut of salmon that arrives en casserole rare as a sirloin, sprinkled with mint and coarse salt. Other choices include any fish in brown butter; red snapper with basil, pepper, and oil; or monkfish with bacon and cabbage; plus several examples of lobster à la LeCoze.

Desserts are more than an afterthought: They border on the obsessive. Banana mousse layered on chocolate mille feuille with pistachio ice cream and chocolate sauce. A coven of caramels—ice cream, flan, mousse, and melted atop a floating island. A glazed pineapple slice paired deliciously with a disk of coconut meringue.

Bernardin's splendor in the bass will run you a prix fixe $40 (without wine or tips) at lunch, $65 at dinner.

Lunch: Mon.–Sat., noon–2:15 P.M. Dinner: Mon.–Thurs., 6 P.M.–10:15 P.M., Fri.–Sat., 5:30 P.M.–10:30 P.M.

Brive
MIDTOWN EAST, p. 7, E11

405 East 58th St.; (212) 838-9393.

"I don't do safe food," chef-owner Robert Pritsker told us. "This place is all about passion." The man was not whistling "Dixie." His menu included a ham and shiitake mushroom terrine with mustard-mango compote, a three-duck trio (roast Peking with green peppercorns, Muscovy confit with roasted garlic cake, and Moulard foie gras sauté with rhubarb glaze). For dessert, milk-chocolate soup or pecan pizza.

The entrance of Brive looks something like one of those idiosyncratic London French restaurants: a tiny bar off to the side, swagged drapes, cream-colored walls stenciled with an asymmetrical pattern. All very small and perfect. Oriental rugs. Antiques. A staff that was genuinely helpful without becoming our new best friends. Nestled into a main artery off Sutton Place, Brive was suitably posh. But never cold. Always daring.

The *bouche amusée* (a tidbit to make your mouth smile) was a bouche-ful of lamb tartar on toasted brioche sprinkled with chives. Intense and garlicky. And delight followed delight. A fish soup of pan-blackened trout, fennel and tomato with a rouille that spelled out Brive. Marinated sole in lemon with a purée of spiced coriander. Sweetbreads circled with red pepper in a lobster sauce. A mille-feuille of honey-and-sage-lacquered pigeon. And his signature dish, liver coated in a crunch of mustard seed and white and black pepper in a pool of veal stock strengthened by Armagnac and crème fraîche.

Dinner, exclusive of wines and tip, will run $50 to $60 per person. But then again, this is Sutton Place. Which is why you'll also find modest wines in the $20 range for those who know how to manage their finances. Definitely not on the tourist map. Brive is for sophisticated diners seeking more than celebrities under glass or yet another designer dining room. The premises are as individual as the food.

Dinner only: 6 P.M.–10 P.M. Closed Sun. and Aug.

Café des Artistes   UPPER WEST SIDE, p. 4, B10
1 West 67th St.; (212) 877-3500.

If Mozart had gone into the restaurant business, he would have opened des Artistes. The only other person with sufficient sophistication and brilliance is George Lang, restaurant consultant to the Planet Earth. George is the genius who began at the Waldorf, ran The Four Seasons, conducts classes, writes books and articles (including the Restaurant and Gastronomy sections in the Encyclopedia Britannica).

For starters, des Artistes is located on a quintessential New York street, on the ground floor of a building in which the duplex apartments are as legendary as the people who once dined at the restaurant: Valentino, Isadora Duncan, Noel Coward, Al Jolson. Lang took over the restaurant in the mid-seventies, careful to preserve the original Howard Chandler Christy murals of buxom beauties cavorting sans couture. Lots of wood, spotlights bouncing off crystal and silver, carts filled with hors d'oeuvres and desserts, the gentle purr of cultured people enjoying the perks of civilization.

The triumph of Lang's menu lies in its being eclectic (this is not a French restaurant), dedicated to the finest ingredients (when was the last time you saw anchovies get star billing?), and most blessedly, confident enough to avoid all that is terminally trendy. Among favorite starters are salmon four ways (slices of dill-marinated gravlax, smoked salmon, perfectly poached salmon, and a hefty dollop of salmon tartar); "Snow White" anchovies with buffalo mozzarella and tomato; and home-cured bresaola with melon, parmigiana shavings, and rosemary olive oil. The oysters are sweet and fresh, the charcuterie among the best. Main courses run from pot au feu with marrow bones, braised beef with gingersnap gravy, roast baby chicken stuffed with fettuccini, a lightly grilled swordfish paillard, and a steak tartar with pine nuts that is lightly toasted and curried.

There's a prix fixe dinner for $30, but expect to spend upwards of $45 per person (without wine and tip) if you order à la carte. Wines, salads, desserts, and cheeses are selected with the same care as the bread and butter. Lang, the consummate professional, realizes that nothing is unimportant. Lang, the incurable romantic, has created the perfect restaurant in which to fall in love.

Lunch: Mon.–Fri., noon–3 P.M. Brunch: Sat., noon–3 P.M., Sun., 10 A.M.–3 P.M. Dinner: Mon.–Sat., 5:30 P.M.–midnight; Sun. till 11 P.M.

Carnegie Delicatessen
MIDTOWN WEST, p. 6, C11

854 Seventh Ave. at 55th St.; (212) 757-2245 (but don't call for reservations).

So listen. You want *the* quintessential New York meal? Park your tush at the Carnegie. Eastern European Jewish "deli" is the city's major contribution to the culinary world and shouldn't be missed. True is true: Los Angeles corned beef or London salt beef simply don't cut the mustard. According to manager Milton Parker, the secret is the New York water in which his briskets of beef are steamed after being injected with a solution of salt, garlic, thyme, allspice, coriander, and mustard seeds. Whatever.

Part of the Carnegie's charm is its total lack of charm. You line up like a Perigord goose, waiting for an empty seat at one of the long tables shared by fugitives from a Breughel painting. The noise and bright lights are almost as disconcerting as the staff, each of whom is convinced you don't know what the hell you're ordering and if you would only leave it to them . . . Nevermind. It's not for nothing that Woody Allen shot *Broadway Danny Rose* here. The corned beef and pastrami are the best in town. A sandwich ($7.45) is piled high with three-quarters of a pound of meat that sells by the pound for $16. (If you're looking for an economical nosh to have in your suite at the Pierre, buy one sandwich and two extra slices of bread. You'll still be full.)

However, we advise on-site mastication because the Carnegie is as much a "sight" as a restaurant. Here's where you'll find New Yorkers refueling their New Yorkity. It's not necessarily a pretty sight, but it's a unique one. Also, as a rule of thumb for visitors, don't order anything that's a combination (triple decker pastrami, tongue and salami with Indian relish), or anything that has a cute name (Julienne Child, Egg-quus, or Vidal Sardine), and don't lull yourself into thinking that brunch is the answer, either. Just go and bite the brisket! Think corned beef or pastrami. Period. In a pinch, maybe turkey or chopped liver.

Open daily 6:30 A.M.–3:30 A.M. No credit cards.

China Grill
MIDTOWN WEST, p. 6, C11

52 West 53rd St.; (212) 333-7788.

China Grill doesn't miss a trick. Its Oriental high-tech cuisine borrows from the best of Chinese, French, and California cooking to create dishes that are elegant without being trendy. You can tell this is a class act the moment you step into Jeffrey Beers's spacious two-story dining room: soaring windows, "flying saucer" lighting, and computer terminals at the wait stations raise your consciousness into 21st-century sleek. The piped-in

Vivaldi and soft rock seem positively, and equally, ancient. Lines from the writings of Marco Polo travel across the bleached wood floor in green and gold stripes. A long bar faces into an open kitchen with all the color and drama of a Chinese opera. This bar is China Grill's pulse point. Good news for the geriatric over-thirty set: Tables in the dining room are spaced generously. You can still feel the joint jumping, but not in your lap.

Don't make the mistake of writing off China Grill as just "another California restaurant." Chef Makoto Tanaka has devised an East meets West menu that plays havoc with traditional compass points as the definition of East alternates between New York and Beijing. For starters there are Chardonnay steamed mussels in black beans and sake, crisp calamari on potato chips with sweet and sour sauce, grilled quail in a nest of crispy noodles, and raw oysters in a plum wine and black vinegar brew. Main courses are served "family style" for ease in sharing. Grilled Szechuan beef in hot oil and cilantro is possibly one of the best dishes in town. Couple it with crispy (deep-fried) spinach and you won't even care that you're running up a $50 per person tab. Grilled is the operative word here (i.e., China Grill) and you'll find it preceding everything from free-range chicken to scallops, marinated lamb, tuna, and squab.

There's no bread and butter or salt and pepper on the table. Nothing to detract from the stark beauty of each platter. Dessert presentations are as dramatic as Garbo. The wine list is knowledgeable and with several excellent under-$20 selections.

Lunch: Mon.–Fri., noon–2 P.M. Dinner: Mon.–Wed., 5:45 P.M.–11 P.M.; Thurs.–Sat., till 11:30 P.M., Sun., 6 P.M.–10 P.M. Closed Sun. during July and Aug.

Le Cirque UPPER EAST SIDE, p. 5, D10
58 East 65th St.; (212) 794-9292.

Le Cirque is a restaurant that breaks all the rules and still comes out on top. The room is bright enough for everyone to see and be seen and still wear sunglasses. The tables are closer together than the Rockettes during a high kick, but this is one of the few places in town you might actually want to be close to the people next to you. Going to Le Cirque is like entering the winner's circle. People here aren't wishing for the stars, they're holding them.

The ringmaster at Le Cirque is Sirio Maccioni. Part lion tamer, part movie star, part drill sergeant; nothing and no one escapes his eye. Without Sirio there would be no Le Cirque: it is the best of his personality kept on its toes by the worst of his fears. "This business, 25 percent can be fantasy, 75 percent must be food. I have an agreement with my chef. I taste new dishes with my eyes closed. No matter how it looks, it must taste right." You may notice Bill Blass seated across the room with Pat Buckley. Patty Hearst, doing some P.R., at a front table. "Never take anything for granted," Sirio said, his eyes darting around the room. He gets up quickly, sensing someone about to leave. Sirio really works the door—no one he knows goes in or out without a hello and a goodbye. After all, what kind of host would he be?

Most people at Le Cirque don't come to do business. They come to enjoy themselves. Let's face it: While the $30 prix fixe lunch is "reasonable" for a restaurant of this caliber, no one who comes here on a weekday is hurrying back to punch a clock.

Incredibly, despite trellised wallpaper and murals of monkeys (Louis XIV monkeys doing all those Louis XIV things), the food arriving from Chef Daniel Boulud's kitchen is heavenly enough to be served in a less antic dining room. Yes, ye who scorn the lifestyles of the rich and famous, the food at Le Cirque, currently under license to a bespectacled young chef who looks like a clerk in a Paris bookstore, is terrific. Sometimes daring. Always top of the line. Did we tell you this place breaks all the rules?

The menu changes here three times a year, the specials change from lunch to dinner. You could probably go to Le Cirque every day for a month and never have the same dish twice. Among those we wouldn't mind having twice: a casserole of scallops "dressed in black tie" (i.e., slices of black truffle in a winey, truffle sauce); a carpaccio of red snapper over arugula; and a terrine of beef shanks and leeks in a light caper cream sauce. But there are two dozen others from which to choose. A main course of lamb stew has lamb that practically melts into the gravy and is accompanied by penne tossed in basil. The confit is perfect: a rich mahogany sauce for the duck and sautéed red potatoes to make certain not a drop is left on the plate. And need we mention the not-on-the-menu but trendiest dish of the decade that originated under Sirio's ever-watchful eye: pasta primavera (spaghetti with fresh vegetables). Try the black sea bass wrapped in paper-thin potato slices and served with a red wine sauce. Or the famous chicken roasted with lemon, garlic, herbs, and olive oil.

Of all the desserts, including the frozen strawberry mousse served between layers of thin chocolate, or the crepes with cherries and ice cream, we can never go to Le Cirque without having crème brûlée. It is the restaurant's signature sweet.

Lunch: Mon.–Sat., 11:45 A.M.–2:30 P.M. Dinner: Mon.–Sat., 5:45 P.M.–10:30 P.M.; credit cards: AE, DC, CB.

Dawat
MIDTOWN EAST, p. 7, D11
210 East 58th St. (Second and Third aves.); (212) 355-7555.

The jewel in the crown of this peaceful pastel retreat is the omnipresence of Indian food guru Madhur Jaffrey. Her specialties are sprinkled through the extensive menu adding a culinary chic to the already elegant peach, aqua, and gray quasi-deco decor. Except for a very occasional whiff of curry and a few masks on the wall (no tented ceiling here), it's hard to tell you're in one of the city's best ethnic restaurants. Certainly, there is nothing to prepare you for the fact that you can dine like a maharajah at lunch for under $10—truly an astonishing bargain. Dinner will be at least $30 per person, but well worth it.

If you know your way around an Indian menu, you're likely to come upon a number of surprises in Jaffrey's signature dishes. Since neither the descriptions on the menu nor those given by the friendly staff are sufficient for novices, stick to dishes with Jaffrey's imprimatur and you can't go wrong. For starters, try the shrimp flavored with garlic, mustard seeds, and curry; crisp spinach leaf and potato skin fritters; and the superb "snack cart" items including potato crisps and noodles in sweet, sour, and hot chutneys. Favorite main dishes are fish (whatever is available that day) covered in fresh coriander chutney and steamed in a banana leaf; chicken cubes marinated in yogurt and ginger before they're roasted in a tandoor (clay oven); shrimp in coconut milk; and lamb in a spicy spinach purée.

Vegetarians will be in seventh heaven here, as well as aficionados of specialty breads (there are varieties of *nan* stuffed with ground lamb, nuts and dried fruit, or onion and fresh coriander). *Lassi,* a sweet or salty cold yogurt drink, is the traditional beverage and, although we once actually did order such a thing ourselves, a modest white wine or imported beer is preferable.

Lunch: Mon.–Sat., 11:30 A.M.–3 P.M. Dinner: daily, 5:30 P.M.– 11 P.M.

The Four Seasons
MIDTOWN EAST, p. 7, D11

99 East 52nd St. between Park and Lexington; (212) 754-9494.

It's this simple: If you put a gun to our heads and demanded to know where to go if you had time for only one meal in New York, our answer would be The Four Seasons.

Now to explain. Like the Carnegie Deli, the Empire State Building, and Broadway, The Four Seasons could not exist anywhere else on earth. This is the quintessential New York restaurant. Period. And its celebrity and deserved success are not diminished one iota by the revelation (honk if you're surprised) that it does not have the best food in town.

We overheard a waiter one night trying to answer a diner's question as to what kind of menu they had. "Well, it's not exactly French," he said. "There are so many good French restaurants in New York." And he named them. "Our food is more continental. More New York," he explained with a smile. Actually, Chef Seppi Renggli holds the copyright on New York food. His dishes are sophisticated, adventurous without being threatening. "Threatening" is an adjective best left to the prices which are as stunning as the decor. Once you accept that this is going to be an expensive evening (entrées alone are between $35 and $40 apiece) and stop comparing the kitchen to the culinary cathedrals of France, The Four Seasons will perform for you on more levels than *Starlight Express.*

You enter on 52nd Street, check your coat and powder your nose in the marble vestibule downstairs. Then you walk up the staircase to the Grill Room, a heroic space with burled French walnut walls, Mies van der Rohe chairs, Philip Johnson tufted banquettes, the tallest twenty-foot ceilings in town, and landmark-worthy floor-to-ceiling windows curtained with swags of aluminum chain that are in constant motion. The stark modern decor is made almost embarrassingly sensuous by the brilliant use of space and texture. To wit: the Richard Lippold sculpture (3,000 suspended brass rods) over one of the best bars in town.

The Grill Room, in more ways than one, means business. Even at night, you can smell lunch deals in the air like smoke hovering after the cease fire. The shortened menu and showcase wine list are different from those in the restaurant's other dining room. The captain explained: "When we serve duck in the Pool Room, it is well cooked. In the Grill Room, it is rare." It is also rare in the Grill Room not to feel like a member of a very exclusive club where service is impeccable. Even better, it is intuitive. All you have to worry about is the menu, and with choices like carpaccio with Grana (cheese) and arugula, and baked oysters with golden caviar to start with, who's worried? We're especially fond of the truly gutsy Louisiana shrimp curry; crabmeat cakes with mustard sauce (chunky pieces of crab and no potato filler); and shad roe with crisp bacon. Everything looks perfect, and the wines by the glass ($5.75) are well chosen.

However, if you're in a romantic mood and don't mind risking well-done duck, make a reservation in the Pool Room. You'll be ushered through a cavernous travertine-lined foyer whose raison d'être (aside from the extravagant use of space that defines the restaurant) is as a gallery for Picasso's 1919 stage curtain for the ballet, *Le Tricorne*. "I could put another whole restaurant here," owner Paul Kovi told us proudly.

The Pool Room's centerpiece is a 14-foot-square white-marble reflecting pool with lush palm trees at each corner. Again, aluminum chains curtain towering windows. More wood. Quite simply, the room is majestic. And always jammed. (Only card-carrying New Yorkers select the Grill Room over the Pool Room.) It's here that every table is a party, and no matter what you order, it's festive. Some of our most successful dinners here have taken advantage of the kitchen's super savvy for roasting and grilling. Menus change seasonally (i.e., the four seasons) but there are enough daily specials to keep you on your toes. Now, however we carped about prices, the wine list is not only a course in classic wine collecting, but it has some of the best (read: least expensive) prices you'll find in *any* restaurant. There's an $11 Spanish white from Domecq, Chateau Greysac at $15, and a super Muscadet for $15.

A word about desserts. Actually two: Chocolate velvet.

Grill Room. Lunch: Mon.–Sat., noon–1:45 P.M. Dinner: Mon.–Sat., 5:30 P.M.–11:15 P.M. *Pool Room.* Lunch: Mon.–Fri., noon–2:15 P.M. Dinner: Mon.–Thurs., 5 P.M.–9:15 P.M.; Fri.–Sat., till 11:15 P.M. Pre-theater dinner ($41.50): Mon.–Sat., 5 P.M.–6:15 P.M. Post-theater dinner ($41.50): Mon.–Sat., 10 P.M.–11:15 P.M.

The Gotham Bar & Grill
GREENWICH VILLAGE, p. 7, D15

12 East 12th St.; (212) 620-4020.

Take a chef who graduated top of his class at the Culinary Institute of America, went to France to work for the legendary Troisgos brothers, Michel Guerard, Jacques Maximin, and then plunk him down in a restaurant on the edge of Greenwich Village and you suddenly understand what steroids are all about. If chefing were an olympic competition, Alfred Portale would be disqualified. The man is a consummate professional.

The Gotham is guaranteed to raise your consciousness the moment you walk through the door. It is an award-winning riot of postmodern design. Platforms, risers, levels, and angles litter the former warehouse space as though dropped by some divine architect. Parachute cloth chandeliers float like clouds above white-linen-covered tables, bright-green painted chairs, and more accented moldings and columns than in the Roman forum. In the midst of all this urbanity, there's a mini-Statue of Liberty we could swear was lit by the static electricity of the Gotham's highly eclectic clientele. You'll find people dressed to the nines or decked out in second-hand counterchic. No one cares. Certainly not the staff in their chino pants and white sneakers.

Portale once designed jewelry and he's carried his sculptural focus into the kitchen. Unlike today's fashionably flat painted platters, his food arrives at the table in 3-D. There is not only drama, but height, to the salads. A creator rather than a follower of trends, he bursts with opinion: "Food should be clever but delicious"; "I've never used a jalapeño"; "Muscovy [duck] legs don't *confit.*" The Gotham's menu does. It preserves the best of French and Italian and translates it into pure Portale. The shellfish terrine is Byzantine, a mosaic of prawns, scallops, and lobster. Tomato salad has five or six different types of tomato, the veal carpaccio with curls of Parmesan is brilliant, and the squab salad arrives with a peppery couscous and a curried vinaigrette that could drive you crazy. Oops! Did we mention the seafood salad glistening with roe? Squid, scallops, octopus, mussels, and lobster, alive, alive-o? Our hands-down favorite entrée was sautéed black bass in red wine vinegar and port with shiitake mushrooms and leeks. But it was hard to choose, considering the thick strands of pasta-shaped spatzle in mustard butter that accompanied mahogany-colored squab with wild mushrooms—and the dry-aged New York steak with crushed white peppercorns, marrow mustard custard (not our rhyme), and deep-fried shallots.

Desserts are extravagant, wines are mainly American, and the tab will run about $50 per person.

Lunch: Mon.–Fri. only, noon–2:15 P.M. Dinner: Mon.–Thurs., 6 P.M.–10:30 P.M.; Fri.–Sat., till 11:30 P.M.; Sun., 5:30–9:30 P.M.

Hard Rock Café   MIDTOWN WEST, p. 6, C11
221 West 57th St.; (212) 459-9320.

The Hard Rock Café takes neither reservations nor prisoners. This place demands total unconditional surrender. The decibel level, which discourages lingering over Clyde's Iced Tea and helps turn the tables fast, is high enough to set dogs howling. Despite all, there is something very lovable about the Hard Rock. (See what we mean about surrendering?)

For starters, there's the big fat rear end of a 1960s Cadillac suspended over the door, in front of which millions of teenagers have watched their zits come and go while they wait on line to get in. There is always a line, the same line, we suspect, that began in London in 1971 when Isaac Tigrett opened the first Hard Rock Café. The easiest times to get in are for a late lunch or early in the evening. Once inside, it's difficult to know where to look first. We are talking about a two-story-high restaurant (with a forty-foot guitar-shaped bar) that has been called "the Smithsonian of Rock 'n' Roll." A mammoth collection of musical memorabilia rotates among Hard Rocks in other cities. Among the most valuable (and interesting) items to be found on the walls are guitars that belonged to Bo Diddley, Jimi Hendrix, and Eric Clapton; David Bowie's jeans; a letter from Thomas Jefferson; the jacket Prince wore in *Purple Rain*; and, suspended from the ceiling, the throne chair from the original company of *The King and I.*

Not that Lutèce has anything to worry about, but the kitchen at the Hard Rock has a few surprises up its sleeve. The pig sandwich is a juicy hickory-smoked pulled pork concoction. B.L.T.s and burgers are served in industrial strength portions. But the giant club sandwich is the item to have gathered kudos from munch-maven Craig Claiborne who pronounced it one of the best: It is two triple-decker sandwiches—thick slices of homemade bread slathered with mayo, slabs of roast chicken, bacon, tomato, and curly leaf lettuce. Better bring your raincoat to eat this one. The dessert of choice here is a wicked hot fudge brownie (vanilla ice cream and hot fudge on a brownie, topped with nuts and whipped cream), or a banana split big enough to bring back The Grateful Dead. You ought to be able to get out of there comfortably for about $15, plus tax and tips.

Open daily 11:30 A.M.–2:30 A.M.

Hatsuhana
MIDTOWN EAST, p. 7, D12

237 Park Ave. between 45th and 46th Sts.; (212) 661-3400.

There's a casual atmosphere at Hatsuhana that belies the precise execution of Japanese food. (And, let's face it, execution is a hefty part of a Japanese chef's repertoire.) In this very relaxed dining room, ceremony is something that defines presentation; it's not anything the diner has to stand on. The sushi masters behind the counter create masterpieces of design with salmon, pike, shrimp, yellowtail, and tuna—among other fish. (Over one-third of all the fish served here is imported daily from Japan.)

This cool, elegantly intellectual cuisine is a perfect balance to the raw emotions on the sidewalk. Once past the always hyperactive sushi bar (you thought McDonald's served fast food?), you enter a very pacific room with bleached wooden tables and chairs, and a few accents of plum. One wall is glass, a greenhouse design that overlooks the Park Avenue Atrium. Tables are filled equally by Japanese businessmen and people too young to have seen *Rashomon* during its first-run showing.

You don't have to be an aficionado of sushi or sashimi to enjoy yourself: Salmon or yellowtail teriyaki is grilled moist and served with Hatsuhana's own sauce. The best of both worlds is the "Hatsuhana Special," a combination of sushi, sashimi, grilled salmon, and beef negimaki (scallion in thinly rolled beef). Dynamite starters here include *chawanmushi,* a silky steamed egg custard with shrimp, fish, and vegetables; a salad of avocado and salmon roe; and vegetarian roll sushi (vegetables in vinegared rice wrapped in dried seaweed). Broiled sea scallops are sweet and perfectly cooked.

There is another Hatsuhana at 17 East 48th St., (212) 355-3345, where the menu is the same, and the restaurant is open for dinner on Saturday. We happen to prefer the setting here. Prices for Japanese food approximate those of Western cuisines. Expect to pay close to $25 per person, plus wine and tips.

Lunch: Mon.–Fri., 11:45 A.M. to 2:30 P.M. Dinner: Mon.–Fri., 5:30 P.M.–9:30 P.M.

Joe Allen

326 West 46th St.; (212) 581-6464.

Yes, Virginia, there is a Joe Allen. Twenty years ago, as a bartender at P.J. Clarke's, he was bitten by the theater bug and decided to go west. Allen wanted a restaurant close enough to the stage doors for actors, producers, et al., to feather his nest, but his main concern was to open a "working man's" place where the backstage crew could afford to come for a burger and a beer. They've been coming ever since. Joe Allen's is always packed, as high-spirited as an opening night party. It attracts everyone from top stars to chorus liners to members of the audience at nearly every show. When you call for a reservation, and reserve you must, you're always asked what show you're going to or coming from. Joe Allen operates on Broadway time.

You walk into a long room divided by brick arches—the main dining room has a skylight in the back and an open kitchen. Hanging on the brick walls are posters from flop shows. At first, it was strictly for laughs, but now the producer of a flop would be offended not to see his poster on Joe's wall.

Joe's new chef is his daughter, Julia Lumia, responsible for the brilliant success of her own restaurant right next door, the very "in" Orso, where agents, writers, and actors can be found enjoying an Italian *piatto del giorno.* The old Joe Allen signature dishes (black bean soup, ribs, La Scala salad, and hazelnut cheesecake) are now on the printed menu, but you still have to ask for a burger. And you *should* ask for one, they're terrific. You might opt, however, for boneless fried chicken, a grilled sirloin with green peppercorn butter, or grilled lamb with tomato and eggplant. Main dishes are $16 and under, making it possible for two to dine for under $50. But to tell you the truth, we're happiest dropping in for a salad or a burger, focusing our spotlight on the obvious joy everyone has in just being there. Incidentally, beer lovers will have a field day: there are nearly 30 brews from which to choose.

Open daily, noon–midnight; Wed. and Sat., 11 A.M. on. MC and V only.

Lafayette

65 East 56th St.; (212) 832-1565.

Take a deep breath and get rid of all your prejudices against hotel dining. Lafayette may be located inside the Drake Hotel but its life support systems are hooked up to the south of France. The food here is, quite simply, superb. And that's *despite* the fact it's probably the most beautifully "designed" food in New York. Frankly, you could go into the postcard business just taking pictures of each plate as it leaves the kitchen.

The dining room has a luxurious, sink-deep-down-into-the-carpet feeling. Rich, silk fabric on the wall—"vieux rose" is the official name of the color surrounding the contemporary furnishings sprinkled with French antiques. It is a warm room filled with dressy people. A huge floral arrangement is reflected, along with the flickering of candles, in the inset ceiling mirrors. Tables are set well apart and the mauve velvet chairs are very comfortable. Not at all the kind of room in which you'd expect there to be a glass wall into the kitchen. But that about sums up Lafayette:

Nothing is what you expect it to be. Chef Jean-Georges Vongerichten constantly exceeds your expectations.

A "marble" of raw tuna and black bass has the appearance of stained glass. It is one of those presentations you think twice about disturbing, that is until you inhale the perfume of the oil with which the fish is coated. (Vongerichten, who at thirty still looks like a choirboy, smiled when we later mentioned the oil. He has it shipped in from a secret source in Santa Barbara.) Sautéed foie gras on fennel was accompanied by a small glass of sauterne. The sauce, barely sweet, was a deglaze of sugar, sauterne, and cracked pepper that sent us into orbit. Crayfish on a bed of zucchini with a tomato-basil vinaigrette was too fresh to have had time to clear customs on its way in from the Mediterranean. For starters, yet.

Yellow pike arrives after poaching in a caramelized shallot sauce—moist, laced with oil and bits of blackened shallot. Lightly sauced lobster medallions in green asparagus are showered with sparkling beads of roe. Slices of rare duck breast are robed in a rich truffle sauce with a "brick" of phyllo filled with foie gras, chicken liver, and *cèpes* (mushrooms). The perfect ending is an upside-down rhubarb tart surrounded by fresh strawberries on a blanket of strawberry purée.

Dinner is priced at $55, without wine or tips. There are tasting menus at $65 and $75 per person.

Lunch: Mon.–Fri., noon–2:30 P.M. Dinner: Mon.–Fri., 6:30 P.M.–10:30 P.M.; Sat., from 6 P.M. Closed Sun.

Lutèce MIDTOWN EAST, p. 7, D12
249 East 50th St.; (212) 752-2225.

After years of shooting the rapids of nouvelle cuisine, returning to Lutèce is like coming home. The ever-cheerful Mme. Soltner heads toward you as though she had seen your picture in the post office and is about to claim the reward. The very clubby inner salon extends into a trellised garden room that works because, like Mme. Soltner's greeting, it is from the heart.

There is a widespread perception that Lutèce is not merely the best French restaurant in New York, but the best in the entire country. Any criticism centers around its not having kept up with the latest trends or its not having created them—rather like faulting a Rolls-Royce because it doesn't fly. If instead, you focus on Lutèce as the capital of culinary déjà vu, and André Soltner as the keeper of the flame, you will be dazzled by the professionalism and passion behind this man. To have withstood nearly thirty years in the most fickle of businesses and still be considered the standard-bearer (chef after chef with whom we spoke, no matter how different their styles, accorded Soltner guru status), makes Lutèce the closest we have to a Lourdes for foodies.

Thankfully, there is nothing about a visit to Lutèce that makes one feel intimidated. Not the decor (Paris in the 1950s), the seamless service (the last time Soltner hired a waiter was five years ago), or the prices (comparatively speaking) will ruffle your Type-A personality: Lunch is a prix fixe $35, and dinner tallies in at $58, or more if you select dishes with a surcharge. The emotional climate here is set by Soltner himself, a gracious, twinkly Jack Lemmonish man who stands not only in back of, but alongside, the food he serves.

We asked him what advice to give someone coming to Lutèce for the first time. He shrugged. "Many people go to a restaurant as if it was a bullfight. But we are here to please people who have confidence in us." A polite way of saying, don't come in with a chip on your shoulder. We look around the room. Lutèce attracts a clientele significantly different from many other restaurants: lots of people are eating soup, for one thing. Think about that. Others are being served the vegetables of the day—mashed potatoes and sliced carrots. Real comfort food. Soltner believes that food is meant to be eaten, not merely admired. Coincidentally, no one is here "to be seen." There are ladies lunching, Sutton Place grandmothers with a gaggle of grandchildren, and lots of corporate types who have been coming daily for years or have arrived to celebrate a deal they made somewhere else. They are here to eat.

What to order is defined by your level of confidence in Soltner. The printed menu is extensive, but we always hold out for the daily specials. Not that you can't be gastronomically paranoid and make it through on Lutèce's herby roast chicken, or the sweetbreads with capers, or the lamb, or the fish, or almost anything that comes out of the kitchen.

Starters may include anything from a perfumy gazpacho to a terrine of smoked salmon and spinach to Alsatian onion tart. Main courses depend upon market availability ("Everyday I plan. I know that if I want a suckling pig, I must call by 9 A.M. and then I put it on the menu for the next day.") and include rabbit, frog's legs, baby bass in beurre blanc, veal shank, venison—you name it.

Desserts are taken very seriously here. Marron soufflé. A hot Grand Marnier soufflé. Homey cakes. Tarte tatin. And with coffee, a big beautiful tray of cookies that have more than one bite in them. Lutèce is an event that does not disappoint. It upholds the essence of classic French cuisine, and when the glamour-pusses have begun to age, and after the last three-cheese pizza has been eaten, there will still be a Lutèce.

Lunch: Tues.–Fri., noon–2 P.M. Dinner: Tues.–Sat., 6 P.M.–10 P.M.

Il Mulino
GREENWICH VILLAGE, p. 8, C16

86 West 3rd St. between Sullivan and Thompson sts.; (212) 673-3783.

Il Mulino is named after Fernando Masci's 145-year-old house in Italy, a mill in the Abruzzi. And it is Fernando's passion that makes his restaurant competitive with the best the city has to offer. "This place is where you make a living. You do everything with this place. You bring up your children. You pay for your car. You must show respect." Most of the staff has been there since the restaurant opened. Fernando's brother is the chef, his mother makes the pasta and the salami, his sister-in-law is the hostess.

But Il Mulino is just another Italian family restaurant the way Château Lafite-Rothschild is just another French family vineyard. Don't even think this is like one of those Greenwich Village "kiss me, I'm Italian" garlic palaces, or Upper East Side "I dress Italian" hybrids where parsley is considered ethnic. We are talking world class, perhaps the most genuinely elegant Italian service in town. Certainly, the best traditional Italian food.

No sooner are you seated than the meal begins. A plate of homemade salami. A dish of breaded, perfectly sautéed sliced zucchini. A dynamite bruschetta (chopped tomato in a garlicky vinaigrette on toasted bread). And then a piece of Parmesan cheese scooped from a wheel larger than some Italian hill towns. All of this to accompany generous drinks and a wine service that includes decanting all reds into enormous pitchers so they can really take a deep breath. The ubiquitous kir royale, elsewhere poured out like Gatorade, is an event here: fluted glasses upside down in a tub of ice, a bucket with two splits of champagne, and a bottle of cassis are brought to the table and assembled to your taste.

In the world according to Fernando, there is always a wait while the kitchen prepares your dinner. "If you cut scaloppine in the morning, it loses flavor." Everything at Il Mulino is *al dente*. Including the pasta specials that Fernando himself prepares in the dining room. No naked noodles with a dollop of sauce— each strand is properly dressed and piping hot before appearing at the table. There's an enormous menu that never changes, and a long list of daily specials according to the best the market has to offer. You will probably not have fresher, more carefully selected ingredients anywhere, nor a more dedicated ombudsman to check each plate as it's brought from the kitchen.

And what plates they are! Let Fernando talk you into a pasta special to share as an appetizer. Whether fusilli with white truffles, crème fraîche, and champagne, or pappardelle with a peppery red sauce, you cannot go wrong. Veal and seafood entrées, assertively fresh, are standouts: a veal chop, thick as a dictionary but a lot more juicy, is boutonnaired with a sprig of fresh sage; an elegantly thin, breaded chop served Abruzzi-style is topped with freshly chopped tomato and arugula; succulent scampi (flown in from Italy) fra diavolo, or clams posillipo in a broth that could be bottled and sold as the Italian "Obsession." Beef filet appears in a spicy caper sauce more suave than Fred Astaire.

Desserts are stunners. An incredibly posh orange that has been luxuriating in a bath of cognac and Grand Marnier is brought to the table to be sectioned and dressed with slivers of marinated rind. You won't soon forget the fudgy splendor of the chocolate cake. End it all with a glass of homemade grappa. Superlatives don't come cheap: expect to spend $100 per couple.

Lunch: Mon.–Fri., noon–2:30 P.M. Dinner: Mon.–Sat., 5 P.M.–11:30 P.M. Credit cards: AE only.

Oyster Bar & Restaurant   MIDTOWN EAST, p. 7, D12

Grand Central Station, Lower Level, at 42nd St. and Vanderbilt Ave.; (212) 490-6650.

When the Oyster Bar opened in 1913, it was a white-glove restaurant for formal dining: a vaulted tile ceiling above a sea of linen-covered tables filled with dressy turn of the century diners who took railway station cuisine very seriously. Today, the huge room looks almost the same and is outstanding enough as a visual presentation to be included on your sightseeing list as well.

Since its opening, nearly every president of the United States has eaten here: Jack Kennedy even had a kind word for the New England clam chowder. (Harry Truman played it safe with a piece of plain broiled fish.) Diamond Jim Brady always joked with the waiters, promising a $50 tip if he failed to identify his favorite Wellfleet oysters—even while blindfolded. Although Jim never lost, he tipped the $50 anyway. That's how good the food is.

One reason is that the fish comes from small fishing boats with small catches. The kitchen never buys from large trawlers with freezer lockers. And the menu is printed daily after the buyer comes back from the Fulton Fish Market. The guys here are very proud of the fact they were the first to serve Mako shark after the release of *Jaws:* It made them feel they were fighting back! Aside from the daily specials, there can be ten varieties of oysters (sold by the piece from $1.05 to $1.65 each), for one of the greatest oyster tastings ever. Not only is there a dazzling variety of fish and shellfish, but the methods of preparation are nearly as numerous. Reading the menu is an encyclopedic experience.

Among the most famous dishes are the oyster pan roast and oyster stew, both creamy and soup-plated, with the former a mite creamier and even spicier. You can sit at the enormous counter (perfect for travelers on their own) and watch them being made. She-crab soup and bouillabaisse are exemplary starters as well. With the quality of the fish as impeccable as it is, we'd suggest the luxury of the Truman approach: It's likely to be a while before a piece of plain fish will taste as good. Besides, then you won't feel as guilty trying one of the desserts: banana cream pie, coconut layer cake, caramel nut sundae—to name a few million calories.

Wine lovers will rejoice. There's an All-American list of some 120 white wines, plus a few reds, that's almost as much fun to read as it is to sample. Prices are within reason, and there are a number of half bottles from which to choose. It isn't difficult to have a bill of $30 to $35 per person plus wine and tips, although one can budget for less.

Open Mon.–Fri. only, from 11:30A.M.–9:30 P.M.

P.J. Clarke's   MIDTOWN EAST, p. 7, D11
915 Third Ave.; (212) 355-8857.

In 1934, P.J. (Paddy) Clarke worked in a corner saloon on Third Avenue under the El. It was just a run of the mill Irish bar, one of the many bars that gave Third Avenue its rough and tumble reputation. Today, Paddy is gone, the El is gone, but P.J. Clarke's is probably the most famous bar in New York. It reeks saloon chic. It buzzes with good stories, jokes, and gossip. It is always three-feet deep with writers, actors, account executives, and postal workers (there's a post office down the block), as well as anyone who can find the elbow room to hoist a beer.

If you saw the movie, *The Lost Weekend*, you've seen Clarke's. Hollywood copied every detail so that it could be reproduced on a sound stage. It is the quintessential New York bar: turn of the century mahogany, a pressed tin ceiling, a tile floor, bits of stained glass to help you forget the madding crowd outside. The bartenders wear long white aprons and the nonstop juke box is packed with Peggy Lee, Duke Ellington, and even Marlene Dietrich. Who needs a time machine?

The only menu at Clarke's is on the blackboard. Every table has a pad on which customers write their orders at lunch. The custom started way back when some of the waiters couldn't read or write. Clarke's specialties include beef barley soup, great steak tartare, some of the best burgers in town, and spinach and bacon salad which is said to have originated here. Prices are extremely low (most main dishes are under $10) and include enough pasta, fish, and salads to give anyone more than enough choices.

A favorite story about Clarke's—and everyone has a couple—is credited to one of the bartenders. (They're a very special breed. No identity crises here.) One night, two football superstars who had been huddling over the bar for hours left for the men's room at the same time. The bartender began cleaning off the bar and wasn't sure whether to pour another round or not. He turned to one of their friends and said, "See what the backs in the boy's room will have."

Speaking of the facilities, the stuffed dog that hangs over the women's room was a real dog, beloved by all the regulars at the bar. When it died, they chipped in and hired a taxidermist.

Open daily, 11:45 A.M. to 4 A.M. AE and DC only.

Palio
MIDTOWN WEST, p. 6, C12

151 West 51st St.; (212) 245-4850.

The Palio of Siena is a centuries-old wild and reckless horse race climaxing in a pageant-filled celebration. The Palio of New York is another kind of spectacle. You enter the ground floor bar, your eyes and emotions swept upward by one of the city's most handsome murals, a 54-by-124-foot riot of horses and color by Sandro Chia. Gothamites who have earned the right to play hard gather around the polished marble bar, or at chic little black tables to enjoy pre- or post-theater *sfiziosi* (read: the best bar food in town—baby squid casserole with polenta, duck and goose liver ravioli, buffalo mozzarella with marinated vegetables).

After your dinner reservation is checked, you enter the private elevator. You may have just come from Siena Revisited, but as you step off on the second floor, the dining room is pure Milan. It is calm, elegant. Oak paneled walls and grillwork around the windows. Multicolored silk banners hang overhead above the Calegaro silver and the Frette linens. Tables are large, well-spaced, and blessedly private for those arriving two-by-two. The chic chit-chat and horses hooves below are a mere memory as you arrive at the capital of Italian sleek. Sit back, order a Bellini, and tell the waiter to send for your clothes and pets. You are never leaving.

Chef Andrea Hellrigl is known at Palio as "Andrea da Merano" out of respect to his status as chef-proprietor of the jewel-like Villa Mozart in Merano, near the Austrian border where Andrea was born. No matter. A chef by any other name . . . The menu he has devised for Palio is a star turn: His food is not merely delicious, it represents the ultimate pairing of invention and tradition, ingredients and techniques. Air-dried roebuck (the likes of which Sears has never heard) with juniper-berry flavored olive oil. An ethreal terrine of baccala (salt cod) more glamorously plated than Sophia Loren. Comfort food for the most dedicated malcontent: fusilli in fava bean sauce with tomato cubes. And then—trust us—a spectacular risotto with blueberries and Barolo wine that puts pasta out to pasture. Easily one of the best dishes is Andrea's namesake lobster from Maine, meat moist and sweet after a swift sauté in aromatic herbs, sprinkled with glistening lobster roe and grilled radicchio. Rabbit, now appearing on menus all over town, is sauced here in hot pepper and honey. And for dessert, how about dark chocolate polenta pudding with white chocolate sauce?

The wine service, thanks to Andrea, is exceedingly knowledgeable. Exclusive of wine and tips, you can have a five-course tasting menu (from a variety of regions) for $60; otherwise à la carte entrées range from $22 to $35, which when you add on appetizers, pasta, and dessert makes for lots of lire. There is a $35 pre-theater and $45 post-theater dinner, but frankly, Palio is not a place to rush in or out of, nor should your choices be limited. If time or budget is of concern, instead of heading upstairs, have lunch (around $20 plus dessert, wine, and tips) or *sfiziosi* ($15 per plate) at the bar. At the very least, stop in for a drink: the place is dazzling.

Lunch: Mon.–Fri., noon–2:30 P.M. Dinner: Mon.–Sat., 5:30 P.M.–11 P.M. Bar: Mon.–Fri., 11:30 A.M.–midnight; Sat., 4 P.M.–midnight.

Palm
MIDTOWN EAST, p. 7, E12
837 Second Ave. between 44th and 45th sts.; (212) 687-2953.

Here's the deal: the Palm doesn't take reservations and, frankly, we wouldn't believe them if they did. Listen, these guys don't even have a menu. You have to ask the "don't-ask-me" waiter and hope to pry from his sealed lips some hint of what's cooking. Only if he knows you will he fess up about the veal, fish, and Italian specialties. But don't let this minor victory go to your head. Just try to get him to tell you what it costs! And yet, people line up for tables. Why? The Palm serves neither unusual food nor great food. The reason people line up is that they serve BIG food.

Everything about the Palm is larger than life. Including the check. However, in all fairness, the Palm is merely fulfilling one of the fantasies that card-carrying carnivores have about New York steakhouses. Some want them plush and quiet, with deference paid to the thickness of the steak and the size of the martini. But those who gravitate toward the mayhem and madness of the Palm are looking for the Great American Clubhouse Experience. A meeting place for newspaper people who use hushed tones only at funerals, the room is noisy and smoky, with sawdust on the floor.

The Palm was originally named Parma when it was opened in 1927 by two Italians from (you guessed it!) Parma. But after Prohibition, when they finally managed to get a liquor license, the examiner misunderstood the word Parma and substituted Palm. Still run by the grandchildren of the original owners, the operation spilled over across the street to a mirror image of itself at Palm Too where reservations are taken for parties of four or more.

For your first visit, don't order anything but steak or lobster. On a good night, they are cooked to perfection. The lobsters look like mutants: they weigh in at four and a half pounds and cost about $44. The size of the steaks (so what if we've never been able to figure out to the penny what they cost—it's somewhere between $1 and $100) would give a pterodactyl pause. Since you have to cross the Palm with so much silver, think seriously about sharing. No matter what the waiter says, there's plenty of food if you split a sirloin and go halfies on the onion rings and potatoes, both of which can be super-crunchy and greaseless on that same good night. Most people opt for the cottage fries, but the hash browns are better. The tab somehow always comes out close to $50 per person, plus wine and tip, even if you share.

Open Mon.–Fri., noon–11 P.M.; Sat., 4 P.M.–11:30 P.M.

Petrossian
MIDTOWN WEST, p. 6, C11

182 West 58th St.; (212) 245-2214.

Listen to this, comrades: Once upon a time, there were two Armenian brothers whose families had a fishery on the Caspian Sea where they harvested sturgeon for the Russians. Comes the revolution, they flee to Paris to escape an expected slump in the caviar market in Russia. But the Petrossian brothers (one now a lawyer and one a doctor) find to their horror that no one in Paris has even heard of caviar! They make one of the earliest deals with the new Soviet regime to export caviar to France, and then convince hotelier César Ritz to put fish eggs on his carte du jour. Ta da! A luxury is born! As one of the Petrossians said, "Caviar is not a food, it is a dream, a philosophy of life and living." Well, depending upon how philosophical you can afford to be, you're going to love this place.

The misconception about Petrossian is that it serves only caviar. Not true. Rather than put all their eggs in one basket, this is a top French restaurant that happens to specialize in some of its own products: caviar, foie gras, and smoked salmon. As for being priced out of reach for mere mortals, there's a $35 pretheater tasting (pressed caviar with blini, an assortment of "teasers" using Petrossian products, and dessert) that would see you through anything but *Nicholas Nickleby.* You can even come here for brunch at prices that wouldn't raise eyebrows on the Upper West Side, or for non-caviar dinners at rates comparable to those all over town. What is incomparable about Petrossian is not losing anything in the translation of its "philosophy" into decor and service.

The room is filled with palms, marble, pink lights, fluted champagne glasses, burled wood, flowers, etched Erté mirrors, and even the chandelier from Mme. Lanvin's bedroom. It is pure fantasy, a colorized version of an Art Deco set from an Astaire-Rogers film. The staff virtually slides across the polished granite floor, deftly holding champagne bottles as they were made to be held—four fingers around the bottom, thumb lodged in the "punt." Waiters have not merely been coached, they have been choreographed to ensure that everyone gets million-dollar service. Well, let's face it: if you're going to have a $92 appetizer, you might as well do it right. (Oh grow up! You didn't really think we were going to leave without caviar!)

The Royal Gourmet is a neat little presentation of 30 grams (just over an ounce) each of beluga, sevruga, and ossetra caviar. Your $92 also includes toast and temporary custody of a tiny gold paddle (the Petrossians say that silver imparts a taste to the caviar). Period. Maybe a wedge of lemon. But forget about onions, eggs, or sour cream. These guys play for keeps: They claim to have first dibs on the best of the Caspian crop and aren't about to let you junk it up.

Continuing to sample the house brand, we had a salad with shavings of the best foie gras we've ever tasted piled high atop beans and lettuce. Slices of smoked salmon were sheer velvet perfection: Part of the secret of its success was the "secret" wood used for smoking.

And then chef Michel Attali took full command of the menu. A daunting assignment, but one handled superbly. A terrine of sea scallops—fresh, almost creamy, enhanced by a vigorously spiced sauce. A salad of shrimp with mango, basil, and hazelnut oil. Seafood à la nage (white wine and fish stock) was incredibly delicate and flavorful. Salmon grilled in black pepper and ginger finished cooking on the plate. Pompano and lobster arrived with two sauces, lobster and beet, as well as cucumber linguini. Michel does all the pastries himself and they look as though they belong in a jeweler's case.

Lunch: Mon.–Fri., 11:30 A.M.–3:30 P.M. Brunch: Sat.–Sun., 11:30 A.M.–3:30 P.M. Dinner: Mon.–Sat., 5:30 P.M.–10:30 P.M. (pretheater 5:30 P.M.–7:30 P.M.) Supper Menu: Mon.–Sat., 10:30 P.M.–midnight; Sun., 5:30 P.M.–11:00 P.M.

Provence
SOHO, p. 8, C17

38 MacDougal St.; (212) 475-7500.

Despite her mother-in-law's prejudice against eating aioli or bourride in the evening "since everyone in Provence knows they should only be served for lunch," Patricia Jean has it on the dinner menu. After all, this Provence is in New York—far from the small French town in which Patricia and husband Michel Jean had a small inn before deciding to return to the states. (They met while both were working at Regine's. Michel later saw frontline combat as a captain at Le Cirque.) The whiff of la vie de Provence that you find in this Soho bistro is unerringly appealing. It also doesn't hurt that prices are unbelievably low: the most expensive main course (steak frites) is $17. Two can dine very well here for $50, plus wine and tips.

The decor is country French sans killer chic: flowers, greens, paneling, a washed shutter look, a wall of windows onto Mac-Dougal Street, open-air dining in the garden. This is a very relaxed restaurant, witness the staff in shirt, tie, and jeans. There's a large bar up front that attracts a post-Yuppie crowd, lots of downtown gallery people and neighborhood types. The food (drawing on Michel's family recipes and his C.I.A. cooking skills) insinuates itself mouthful by mouthful as you enjoy the appetizers with a glass of Provençal wine: brandade de morue (a purée of salt cod, potato, garlic, and olive oil), grilled goat cheese splattered with olive oil, garlicky eggplant caviar, tapenade (black olives, capers, and anchovies), and pissaladière (an onion and anchovy tart). There's also a super rabbit pâté, the gelée made with rabbit bones, the plate garnished with a pickled cherry, cornichon, and olives.

Continuing to prove that Aix marks the spot, main courses include the aforementioned bourride (poached seafood in broth with a garlic mayonnaise a.k.a. aioli), roast lotte in a saffron sauce, a first-rate grilled snapper with grapefruit and tomato, and pan-roasted lamb with ratatouille in a tomatoey sauce that's been sprinkled with fresh rosemary. For dessert, a lemon tart with raspberry sauce, a plum tart, or a "so-it's-not-Le Cirque" crème brûlée that stands up on its own.

Even though Provence totals up an impressive amount of square footage, it's the closest you'll get to that cozy little French bistro of yesteryear when people were still more excited about what they were eating than who was eating it at the next table.

Lunch: Tues. through Fri., noon–3 P.M.; Sat.–Sun., until 3:30 P.M. Dinner: Tues.–Thurs., 6 P.M.–11 P.M.; Fri.–Sat., until 11:30 P.M.; Sun., 5:30 P.M.–10:30 P.M.

The Rainbow Room

MIDTOWN WEST/NEAR FIFTH AVENUE, p. 6, C12

30 Rockefeller Plaza; (212) 632-5100.

You've heard about "restaurant as theater." Well, The Rainbow Room goes them one better: it is the restaurant as a movie. From the moment you enter the fabulous marble lobby at 30 Rock, you know this is going to be an extraordinary experience. Step onto the special express elevator to the 65th floor (the ultimate in gastronomic foreplay). Step off into the dramatic glass-and-rosewood columned chamber where you're guided along by young cutie-pies in page-boy suits (don't let Betty Friedan near this place or she'll have a fit!). A few steps up to the two-story multi-tiered room with a 32-foot revolving dance floor and you are ready to check your skepticism with the maître d'. The Latin band is playing "Guantanamera" and you surrender unconditionally. There is no way not to love this room, unless you are related by blood to the grinch who stole Christmas.

The party line is that The Rainbow Room is a restoration of the 1934 original. Don't you believe it for one second. It is nothing short of a brilliantly executed scientific experiment in déjà vu. Waiters in two-tone cutaways. Silver lamé tablecloths. Busboys with gleaming silver bowls spoon fresh ice into water goblets. Men in tuxedos dance with women in sequined gowns.

Without your even noticing it, one band has been replaced by another. Suddenly, the sounds of Gershwin and Porter. The flash of a baked Alaska flaming in the aisles. A cigarette girl with plenty of leg and a little pink hat (Is her name Trixie?) hips her way around the room. The twinkle of city lights outside the windows competes with the laughter at ringside tables. Alan Lewis, formerly head honcho at Windows on the World, now director of The Rainbow Room, smiles and says, "I love the forties." Sigh, look around the Art Moderne room and think, Where are Betty Grable and Rita Hayworth when you need them?

But man does not live by glitz alone. Rumor has it that you have come here to eat. The menu, by design, is as retro as the decor. Alligator pears. Oysters Rockefeller. (Perhaps *that's* the cigarette girl's name.) Vol-au-vent of snails. Okay: To be fair, they've also got a ravioli of sweetbreads and truffles, and a salad of warm quail and foie gras. But this is the place for famous food of the past as re-created by chef André René. Begin with champagne, otherwise you'll never forgive yourself. Head directly into the Shellfish Extravaganza. (Better they should have given *this* name to the cigarette girl rather than some poor unsuspecting crustaceans!) No matter, it is an overwhelming display of oysters, clams, mussels, lobster, shrimp, and crab with proper sauces for each. Given our druthers, we'd stay with champagne and open the time capsule for lobster thermidor, the MGM of fish courses. There's also pigeon en cocotte, tournedos Rossinni (Aha! *That* must be her name!) and lots of red meat including black Angus steak, rack of lamb, and venison. Whoever heard of cholesterol in the forties?

The frozen praline soufflé with hot chocolate sauce will produce more guilt than Kafka, that is, if you're strong enough to pass up baked Alaska lit with the eternal flame of culinary nostalgia. Speaking of strength, be prepared for the bill. While Scrooge himself might be able to get out of here for $50 per head, mere mortals should figure close to double that. Resist, if you can, the $38.50 pre-theater dinner, a false economy that doesn't allow you to linger and enjoy the last dance. Have your accountant amortize dinner over the cost of an entire lifetime. Or else promise to take back all your empty beer cans and save the deposit money. However you work it, be sure to fly somewhere over The Rainbow Room. It is a joy.

Brunch: Sat. and Sun., 11:30 A.M.–2:30 P.M. Dinner: Tues.–Sat., 5:30 P.M.–midnight. AE only.

The Russian Tea Room   MIDTOWN WEST, p.6, C11
150 West 57th St.; (212) 265-0947.

Remember the scene in the movie *Tootsie* when Dustin Hoffman first dresses up as Dorothy to meet his startled agent at a restaurant? Well, this is the restaurant, and people have been dressing up as their own personal Dorothys and coming here ever since the Tea Room was founded by expatriate members of the Imperial Russian Corps de Ballet after the Russian Revolution. Actors, dancers, writers, musicians, producers, and directors conduct more business here than at their offices. There aren't too many show biz deals made in New York that haven't been discussed over blinis and martinis in this forever-Christmas room.

The Tea Room (as it's known locally) is "Hunter" green, in deference to the color used to paint Imperial Hunting Lodges. There are Christmas ornaments and gold tinsel hanging throughout the year. Booths are bright red leather trimmed in brass and the salads aren't the only things with Russian dressing. The waiters, in red tunics that button at the neck, look like fugitives from a road company of *Uncle Vanya.* Antique samovars and a fabulous art collection complete the background against which movers and shakers shake their stuff till it hurts. No fear of a power failure at the Tea Room as long as there's one agent and one actor on the premises.

Gorbachev may not know it, but *perestroika* has had its effect here. Master chef Jacques Pepin was brought in to consult on sprucing up some of the Czar's favorite dishes. Leave it to Jacques to lighten the sauces, and add slim-skii cuisine, yet! Fear not, the blini still soak up as much butter as possible before being slathered with thick sour cream, and caviar of choice. But, most important, the vodka still flows like the Volga even though chicken kiev and beef stroganoff (sounds like a vaudeville team!) share billing with newcomers like steamed halibut with olives, capers, and horseradish on spinach; and grilled breast of chicken with parsley lemon butter. Take our advice: the moment you walk through the door, head for the borscht and blini.

Another word or two on walking through the door: turn around and walk right out if you can't get seated downstairs. Never mind that superagent Sam Cohn sometimes (the key word is sometimes) seeks solitude in Siberia (i.e., upstairs). You are not Sam Cohn and you didn't come here for solitude: The fun of going to the Tea Room is that if you hit it on a good day, you're likely to see brighter stars than those at the Hayden Planetarium. Here's how to do it: If you arrive at about 11:30 A.M., and even if you don't have a reservation, chances are you can swing a seat at one of the Tea Room's glitziest tables—providing you take a blood oath to finish your cranberry kissel (a soothing dessert of puréed cranberries served with cream) by one o'clock when all hell breaks loose.

Dinners run between $35 and $45, without wine or tips. Lunches border on a real bargain: You can get out for under $20, even with a glass of wine.

Lunch and dinner: daily, 11:30 A.M.–midnight.

Serendipity 3
UPPER EAST SIDE, p.7, D11
225 East 60th St.; (212) 838-3531.

If the Mad Hatter held his tea party in New York, this is where it would be. Half wonderland and half boutique, everything blends into a topsy-turvy environment that is totally unique. The word "serendipity" means the art of finding the pleasantly unexpected by chance. That's exactly what happens when you step through the door and find yourself surrounded with boutique-ish items such as Hebrew eye-charts, and stuffed animals cute enough to make Noah think twice. But you're afraid to linger because who knows what treats await inside. After all, this is the place Cher had her *Moonstruck* party, Barbra Streisand sang

"Happy Birthday" to her mother, and Andy Warhol once sketched at a back table. The Kennedy kids, Marilyn Monroe, Truman Capote, and even Tennessee Williams camped out under the Tiffany glass shades that hang all around the room.

The gorgeous back room is white brick, with a white tin ceiling, white oak tables, and chairs. The most expensive of the Tiffany lamps, now valued at $750,000, still illuminates the banana splits with all the high drama of Garbo's key light. When you're not looking up at the lamps, or hunting for celebs around the room, there's much food for thought. The environmental kitsch is translated into birthday party cuisine. The signature "frozen hot chocolate" is presented in a swimming-pool-size bowl. The foot-long hot dogs (they originated here) take up half the table. Burgers are festooned with red caviar and sour cream, and cappuccino is brought into the fourth dimension with a huge bonnet of whipped cream topped with a mound of shaved chocolate. Like a hyperactive kid, the menu careens from comfort food (shepherd's pie, cheese omelets, French toast) to zen hash (brown rice and veggies), a ricotta cheese sandwich with lemon curd dressing, and a frozen apricot smush.

You can come in for lunch, brunch, dinner, snacks, tea, pre- and post-theater and movies, and most important, immediately after a Spartan nouvelle dinner—just to keep your perspective. You can get out for under $10 per person: it would be difficult to spend more than $15, but not impossible.

Lunch and dinner: Mon.–Fri., 11:30 A.M.–midnight; Sat. and Sun., till 2 A.M.

The Sign of the Dove   UPPER EAST SIDE, p.5, D10
1110 Third Ave. at 65th St.; (212) 861-8080.

The bartender wears a tux. So do the waiters. There's a piano player, a tile floor, Hoffmann chairs, marble tables. And that's only the bar. Inside, the dining rooms are connected by graceful arches, brick walls, palm plants, antiques, mirrors, skylit ceilings, pink lights, and lots of flowers. This has always been a beautiful setting. Now, thanks to chef Andrew D'Amico, it is a wonderful restaurant.

Despite attracting one of the city's dressiest clienteles, D'Amico is not into designer cuisine. Food is attractive, even hearty, often with a nod to Eastern influences, and with an originality that enhances taste rather than mere reputation. D'Amico is not a self-indulgent chef; he is too good an editor. Instead of tuna, he uses skate in a salade niçoise. Sautéed sweetbreads are paired with Chinese sausage and yu-choy (a bok choy-ish green reminiscent of both broccoli and mustard greens). Pan-seared tuna (read: cooked on the outside, raw inside) has a sweet, fresh taste off which to play the accompanying taramasalata. A snapper escabéche uses ginger and cumin, items not normally found in a Spanish marinade, as well as cilantro which is more Mexican than Spanish. However, we lost our hearts to a Maine lobster and oyster pan roast.

Main courses featured a shellfish stew with saffron; grilled swordfish with caramelized scallions and lobster butter; veal medallions with braised endive, chanterelles, and wild rice pancake. Sea scallops luxuriated in a thyme and olive oil broth surrounding a tian of eggplant, tomato, and zucchini.

The $60 prix fixe dinner menu includes an excellent cheese service with which to finish off a wine selected from the truly first-rate list. Desserts are neither slivers of nonsweets nor plated as if presenting jewelry to be worn. The *real* food concept continues: tarte tatin with cinnamon ice cream, orange crème brûlée tart, and a superb sleeve of dark chocolate filled with white chocolate in a raspberry coulis.

Those addicted to love in the afternoon will adore a $35 prix fixe that includes dessert and coffee. A bonus at all times: Tables are generously spaced and the staff is smooth and professional. At the very least, stop in while you're "doing" Third Avenue for a drink and one of the terrific snacks served at the bar.

Lunch: Tues.–Sat., noon–3 P.M. Brunch: Sun., 11:30 A.M.–3 P.M. Dinner: daily, 5:45 P.M.–11 P.M.

La Tulipe
GREENWICH VILLAGE, p. 6, C15
104 West 13th St.; (212) 691-8860.

La Tulipe is very chic, very small, and very plush. It's on the ground floor of a townhouse owned by Sally and John Darr, (chef and manager, respectively) whose personal style and elegance set the tone for their bistro. You enter from the street to find yourself bellying up to the most Parisian bar this side of the Atlantic (it came from the old Les Halles). The small dining room is accented with French antiques and the mirrored reflections of well-dressed people at other tables. Be forewarned: This is not a spot for celeb watching or trendy flashes in the pan, rather it is one of those tiny jewels that inspires club-like loyalty from its regulars.

Sally Darr was the former food editor of *Gourmet* magazine and spent four years in France, with ex-headmaster John, collecting recipes for the book, *Gourmet's France.* With no previous restaurant experience, the Darrs opened La Tulipe (named after a dessert Sally once had). They had three caveats: never do lunch, serve no more than 65 people a night, and keep the menu down to seven or eight choices. Dinner is currently a prix fixe $59, not including wine or tips.

You can't go wrong with the starters: a chilled shrimp soup that has chunks of shrimp and cucumbers; fresh tomato soup with basil, mint, and a dollop of crème fraîche; smoked trout mousse (you'll want more); or a wonderfully peppery Parmesan soufflé in phyllo pastry. Standout main courses recently were the very elegant papilotte of red snapper, in which the fish and vegetables were steamed in paper and robed in a beurre blanc, and the best softshell crabs we'd ever had—perfectly moist inside, crusty outside, reclining on a bed of carmelized tomato and fresh basil leaves. The house salad is served with a wedge of cheese. Desserts are a major event at La Tulipe, including the namesake in which vanilla ice cream with hot chocolate is served in a pastry shell. However, we lost our hearts to an apricot soufflé that was more intense than a first-year medical student.

One thing. La Tulipe is not a place to go if you have to make a curtain or a train or have a baby. Everything is made to order, so expect to linger between courses rather than over coffee.

Tues.–Sun., dinner only. There are two sittings: 6:30 P.M.–7 P.M., and 9 P.M.–9:30 P.M.

"21"
MIDTOWN WEST, p. 6, C11

21 West 52nd St.; (212) 582-7200.

In the wine cellar at "21," in the private reserve section, there's a bottle of Dom Perignon '59 with Joan Crawford's name on it. Aristotle Onassis left behind a bottle of Pommard '62. The ceiling in the downstairs dining room is littered with other toys: baseball bats, ballet slippers, NFL helmets, plane models, trucks, and boats. (You know you've "arrived" in New York when The "21" Club accepts your contribution to the ceiling.) A brass plaque identifies "Bogie's Corner" where Bogart and Bacall fell in love. Let's face it, you need a machete to cut through the nostalgia in this joint.

First things first. It is untrue that "21" is a private club open only to members. Next: It is absolutely true that "21" is a private club open only to members. Oh, sure, anybody can get a reservation, and you can stamp and kick your feet until you get a table downstairs—don't you believe for one second that upstairs is as good as downstairs. Once you get in, it's as though you've wandered onto the set of *Lifestyles of the Rich and Hungry*. Young men wearing suits that cost more than your mortgage payments sip diet cokes while discussing the hardcover books they've been reading and the stocks they've been buying; elegantly turned out middle-aged women network on the high cost of body maintenance, trading names of plastic surgeons and estrogen creams with equal facility; and then you spot a movie star. Is this a place or what?

The fact that they happen to serve food at this pit stop for millionaires is real nice. Not the best food in the world, but think of it as an admission charge and it won't hurt a bit. We love "21." It's a major New York institution, and even though its values are as suspect as those of Willy Loman, "attention must be paid." The ingredients here are as impeccable as a blue-chip stock. The cuisine is "men's food" or more accurately, "*old kid's food*." Actually, "rich, old kid's food" when you think of the "21" burger costing $21.50, or the lovable chutzpah of putting a $50 caviar omelet on the menu. No matter what you order, the maître d' will congratulate you on your choice. The busboy, as though carrying fresh white truffles, brings the bottle of Heinz ketchup to the waiter who brings it to the table. The maître d' asks the sommelier if Table 46 is happy with the wine. (Try as we may, we just can't get mad at this place.)

For the record, the "in" dishes are the infamous burger (save your money), a nicely spiced chicken curry that isn't on the menu, chicken hash (talk about retro food!), and for the ladies who lunch, cobb salad. The only things richer than the rice pudding are some of the people in the room. Your tab will run an easy $50 per head, before wine or tips. Except, there is a pretheater dinner for $37.50 (seating between 5:30 and 6:30 P.M., only). If you can, do "21" for lunch rather than dinner. The "floor show" is infinitely better.

Lunch: Mon.–Fri., noon–3 P.M. Dinner: Mon.–Sat., 5:30 P.M.–midnight.

Union Square Café

NEAR GRAMERCY PARK, p. 7, D15

21 East 16th St.; (212) 243-4020.

This is the Yuppie "21." A big, open, friendly, comfortable place for the soon-to-be-rich-and-famous. A lunchtime hangout for downtown publishers and the uptown art crowd, this is not a place for the starry-eyed. You'd need a supercomputer to tally up the combined SAT scores of these dudes. Owner Danny Meyer is as bright as a penny reflection of his clientele. He wants the best and isn't prepared to settle for anything less. He was a tour guide in Europe who spent all his free time in restaurants. He kept a diary of everything he ate. "I can remember everything I put in my mouth."

The room buzzes with groups of people discussing foreign rights or prospectuses. Lots of suits. Very pragmatic conversations wafting across the room. Intense talk about jobs and futures and whether to order the pappardelle of zucchini or the risotto with escargot. Food here is nothing if not hearty. Herbs and spices are used to create robust dishes with which to quaff down some of the management's excellent wine selections. Among the main courses, grilled marinated fillet of tuna (a chunk of tuna seared on the outside but sushilike inside) is a standout. Grilled filet of Norwegian salmon was served with a chive beurre blanc and braised leeks. Again, it was perfectly prepared— slightly charred on the outside and moist within. Other choices include sea scallops in a muscat sauce, rib-eye steak with rosemary, crisp Pekin duck with mashed potatoes.

Side orders are especially appealing: hot garlic potato chips; mashed turnips with crispy shallots; and sautéed spinach with shallots and lemon. Standouts among the desserts were a ginger crème brulée, and a hot apple tart with crème fraîche. Discuss your wine selection with Danny—he roams from table to table. As usual, we're in the $50 per head ball park, plus wine and tip.

Lunch: Mon.–Sat., noon–3 P.M. Dinner: Mon.–Thurs., 6 P.M.–11 P.M.; Fri.–Sat., until midnight.

Rooms with a View
or
When Is a Restaurant Not a Restaurant?

We have five favorite restaurants for visitors that go beyond the question of food. Not that some of those listed wouldn't rate inclusion on any "best restaurant" list, but their locations are extraordinary enough to warrant being highlighted in a special category.

The River Café. 1 Water St., Brooklyn; (718) 522-5200.

This would be a dynamite restaurant no matter where it was, but it happens to be on a barge underneath the Brooklyn side of the Brooklyn Bridge. A dazzling sea-level view of the lower Manhattan skyline coupled with the soft sound of a piano bar compete for your attention with Chef David Burke's imaginative menu and equally arresting presentations. Who wins? You do. The food is as provocative as the cityscape. Main courses include roast loin of lamb and curried sweetbread ratatouille, pan-roasted squab with corn risotto and a confit of dates; and salmon steak seared with ginger and cracked pepper in a burgundy butter. Desserts are every bit as fabulous. The prix fixe dinner is $52, plus wine and tip. And a taxi back to Manhattan.

Lunch: Mon.–Fri., noon–2:00 P.M., *Brunch:* Sat. and Sun., 11:30 A.M.–2 P.M. *Dinner:* Mon.–Thurs., 6:30 P.M.–11 P.M. Fri. and Sat., 7 P.M.–11:30 P.M.

The Sea Grill. 19 West 49th St. (Rockefeller Plaza); (212) 246-9201.

Marble, brass, and cherrywood accents add to the luxury-liner luxury that makes the Sea Grill one of the city's most posh rooms. The added bonus here is that one glass wall looks out onto the Rockefeller Plaza skating rink and the golden statue of Prometheus. This is one of those quintessential New York settings. In the fall and winter, especially when the giant Christmas tree is up, there's probably no finer location in which to capture the seasonal excitement of the city. In the spring and summer, the changing colors of the waters in the fountain surrounding Prometheus provide a light show worthy of the Music Hall. It is made all the more irresistible by Chef Stefano Battistini. In the course of a single tasting, we had the best swordfish and crabcakes in town. A tartare of lobster, and a ratatouille crayfish bisque were stunning examples of Battistini's talents, as were a gratin of lobster and potato slices with parmesan cheese, and a grilled tournedos of bluefin tuna with deep-fried ginger. Grilled bittersweet orange custard, and key lime pie were favorite desserts. Fred Mills, director of the Sea Grill, has put together one of the most knowledgeable American wine lists we've seen. This is a world-class restaurant that excites the palates of jaded New Yorkers as well as visitors. An added bonus here is the price: dinners at $41.50 and pre-theater dinners (between 5:30 P.M. and 6:30 P.M.) for a very low $29.95.

Lunch: Mon.–Fri., 11:30 A.M.–3 P.M. *Brunch* on Sat. *Dinner:* Mon.–Fri., 5 P.M.–11 P.M.

Tavern on the Green. Central Park West at 67th St.; (212) 873-3200.

Imagine Catherine the Great's hunting lodge as done by Disney. Sitting in the Crystal Room at Tavern on the Green in the middle of Central Park is like being inside a kaleidoscope, looking out. Twinkling lights illuminate the trees and the city's most extravagant patio is filled with garden party furniture and a dance band. The room is filled with people out for a good time as though they had come to an amusement park. But this particular amusement park now has a Michelin-star chef in the kitchen. (Heaven knows they've needed someone for a long time!) This is the place to which grandmothers love to be taken, and guys bring their dates when they come into "the city." It is also a restaurant unafraid to challenge its own status quo by bringing in an inventive young chef like Georges Masraff who had a small restaurant in Paris. (Do you know that Tavern on the Green serves more diners than any other restaurant in America?) Masraff shrugged. "Why come to America to open another small restaurant?" Incredibly, the food I.Q. at Tavern, like Masraff himself, has taken a major leap forward. Salmon and sea bass roulade. Smoked duck salad. Grilled seafood sausage. Lobster bisque. Hmmm. And that's only for starters. Turbot with five greens: asparagus, broccoli, fava beans, spinach, and herb butter. Rack of lamb with tarragon potatoes. Sautéed veal medallions with broccoli ravioli. What are all those young guys with their dates going to eat? Or perhaps Masraff is doing just what he wanted to do. "French boys in Toulouse will eat cèpes sautée once a week. They have a history of food. I am fighting against what I call the prehistoric American. If they want a hamburger, I make it. But I would like to take them into the kitchen and show them other things, too." Dinner can easily cost (you guessed it) $50 per person, plus wine and tip. However, (now listen up!) there is a three course pre-theater menu available Monday through Friday from 5:30 P.M. to 6:45 P.M. at the truly astonishing price of $14.50. Has to be the best deal in town!

Lunch: Mon.–Fri., 11:30 A.M.–4 P.M. *Brunch:* Sat.–Sun., 10 A.M.–4 P.M. *Dinner:* Sun.–Fri., 5:30 P.M.–1 A.M. Sat. from 5 P.M.

Windows on the World. One World Trade Center, 107th floor; (212) 938-1100.

Picture yourself sitting on a cloud and having dinner. That's a little what it's like at Windows on the World. But clouds have no comfortable chairs to sink back into, no waiters to make certain your wine glass is full, and no room to stroll from window to window for a view of the entire skyline. The Restaurant, as differentiated from Cellar in the Sky (a small inner room where oenophiles are treated to exclusive dinners with hand-picked wines at $70 per person, including wine) and the Hors d'Oeuvrerie (the bar area where breakfast, Sunday brunch, tea, and drinks are served) is a sprawling, terraced room that allows everyone a spectacular view whether seated at a window table or against the wall. Our favorite time here is sunset. If you play your reservation right, you can see the city lights come on, daylight vanish, and the moon come into view. Considering the spectacular setting, the prix fixe dinners ranging from $29.95 to $33.95 are downright reasonable. Choices include appetizers such as pâté of duck liver, tortellini in cream, oysters or clams on the half shell, or corn and crab chowder with black mushrooms. For main courses, there's breast of chicken, casserole of sea scallops and shrimp, or white veal with mushroom sauce. You can spend much more ordering from the à la carte side of the menu. But the better part of valor is to select items more dependent upon quality than preparation. Even if the food isn't always as astonishing as the panorama, that's a small price to pay for sitting on top of the world.

Lunch (Grand Buffet, $21): Sat., noon–3 P.M.; Sun., till 7:30 P.M. *Dinner:* Mon.–Sat., 5 P.M.–10 P.M.

World Yacht Cruises. Pier 62, West 23rd St. and the Hudson River; (212) 929-7090.

Don't ask any questions. Just go. Like taking the bateaux mouches in Paris, and a gondola ride in Venice, you have to see New York from the water or else you just haven't seen New York. Now, make no mistake about it: this is not a Circle Line cruise. This is a yacht. People are dressed to the nines. We counted three bottles of Dom Perignon passing us in the aisle as we sat down. Dinner is an acceptable meal, albeit dangerously reminiscent of business-class airline food. But who cares? The dining room had large picture windows, starched linen napery, and enough silver and china to make you feel first class for the entire cruise. Between courses you can polish the dance floor as the orchestra plays, or else go up on deck for a stroll. The staff is friendly, service is thoughtful, and you'd have to be a real malcontent not to have a good time. We've lived in New York all our lives and found the evening totally exhilarating.

Lunch: Mon.–Sat., 11 A.M.–2 P.M., $22.

Brunch: Sun. 11:30 A.M.–2:30 P.M., $29.50. *Dinner:* Mon.–Thurs., 6 P.M.–10 P.M., $45; Fri.–Sun., $50.

RESTAURANT INDEX

This convenient alphabetical index includes our favorites from among the restaurants mentioned in the neighborhood sections. No effort has been made to compile a "telephone directory" of all the good restaurants in New York—merely those selected by us for inclusion in this edition.

Border Café West UPPER MANHATTAN, p. 4, B7
2637 Broadway; 749-8888; p. 151

Bouley TRIBECA, p. 8, C18
165 Duane St.; 608-3852; p. 134

Café Geiger UPPER EAST SIDE, p. 5, D8
206 East 86th St.; 734-4428; p. 95

Café Le Figaro GREENWICH VILLAGE, p. 8, C16
184 Bleecker St.; 677-1100; p. 123

Caffè Dante GREENWICH VILLAGE, p. 8, C16
79–81 MacDougal; 982-5275; p. 123

Caffè Reggio GREENWICH VILLAGE, p. 8, C16
119 MacDougal; 475-9557; p. 123

Canton CHINATOWN, p. 9 D18
45 Division St.; 226-4441; p. 140

Caroline's at the Seaport LOWER MANHATTAN, p. 9, D19
Pier 17, 89 South St. Seaport; 233-4900; p. 148

Chanterelle SOHO, p. 8, L17
6 Harrison St.; 966-6960; p. 131

Chez Louis MIDTOWN EAST, p. 7, E11
1016 Second Ave.; 752-1400; p. 70

Chumley's GREENWICH VILLAGE, p. 8, B16
86 Bedford St.; 675-4449; p. 123

Coastal UPPER WEST SIDE, p. 4, B9
300 Amsterdam Ave. at 74th St.; 769-3988; p. 106

Columbus UPPER WEST SIDE, p. 4, B10
201 Columbus Ave. at 69th St.; 799-8090; p. 103

Contrapunto UPPER EAST SIDE, p. 7, D11
1009 Third Ave. at 60th St.; 751-8616; p. 93

Il Cortile LITTLE ITALY, p. 9, D18
125 Mulberry St.; 226-6060; p. 141

Cupping Room Café SOHO, p. 8, C17
359 West Broadway; 925-2898; p. 129

Dallas BBQ UPPER WEST SIDE, p. 4, B9
27 West 72nd St.; 873-2004; p. 103

David K's UPPER EAST SIDE, p. 5, D10
1115 Third Ave.; 371-9090; p. 93

DDL Foodshow FIFTH AVENUE, p. 7, D11
725 Fifth Ave.; 832-1555; p. 50

Delegates' Dining Room MIDTOWN EAST, p. 7, E12
U.N. Building (U.N. Plaza at 45th St. & 1st Ave.); 963-7625; p. 71

Diane's UPPER WEST SIDE, p. 4, B9
249 Columbus Ave. near 72nd St.; 799-6750; p. 103

Dine-O-Mat MIDTOWN EAST, p. 7, D11
942 Third Ave. near 57 St.; 755-3755; p. 68

Dock's UPPER WEST SIDE, p. 4, A8
2427 Broadway; 724-5588; p. 113

Elaine's UPPER EAST SIDE, p. 5, E8
1703 Second Ave. at 88 St.; 534-8103; p. 96

Elephant and Castle SOHO, p. 8, C17
183 Prince St.; 260-3600; p. 132

Empire Diner CHELSEA, p. 6, B14
210 Tenth Ave. at 22nd St.; 243-2736; p. 118

Empire Szechuan Gourmet UPPER MANHATTAN, p. 4, B7
2574 Broadway; 663-6004; p. 151

Erminia UPPER EAST SIDE, p. 5, D8
250 East 83rd St.; 879-4284; p. 97

Ernie's UPPER WEST SIDE, p. 4, B9
2150 Broadway between 75th & 76th sts.; 496-1588; p. 111

Extra! Extra! MIDTOWN EAST, p. 7, E12
767 Second Ave.; 490-2900; p. 70

Ferrara's   LITTLE ITALY, p. 9, D17
195 Grand St.; 226-6150; p. 142

Fluties   LOWER MANHATTAN, p. 9, D19
19 Fulton, Seaport; 693-0777; p. 148

Food   SOHO, p. 8, C17
127 Prince St.; p. 129

Forest & Sea International Restaurant   UPPER WEST
477 Amsterdam Ave.; 580-7873; p. 107   SIDE, p. 4, B8

Fraunces Tavern   LOWER MANHATTAN, p. 9, D20
54 Pearl St.; 269-0144; p. 145

Fujiyama Mama   UPPER WEST SIDE, p. 4, B8
467 Columbus Ave.; 769-1144; p. 104

Genoa   UPPER WEST SIDE, P. 4, B9
271 Amsterdam Ave. 787-1094; p. 106

Ginger Man   UPPER WEST SIDE, p. 4, B10
51 West 64th St.; 399-2358; p. 110

Good Enough to Eat   UPPER WEST SIDE, p. 4, B9
424 Amsterdam Ave.; 496-0163; p. 107

Grand Dairy Restaurant   LOWER EAST SIDE, p. 9, E17
341 Grand St.; 673-1904; p. 137

Greene Street Café   SOHO, p. 8, C17
101 Greene St. near Prince St.; 925-2415; p. 132

Grotta Azzurra   LITTLE ITALY, p. 9, D17
387 Broome St.; 925-8775; p. 141

Hamburger Harry's   TRIBECA, p. 8, C18
157 Chambers St.; 267-4446; p. 134

Harbor Lights   LOWER MANHATTAN, p. 9, D19
South St. Seaport (2nd level); 227-2800; p. 148

Hong Fat   CHINATOWN, p. 9, D18
63 Mott St.; 962-9588; p. 140

Horn & Hardart Automat   MIDTOWN EAST, p. 7, D12
200 East 42 St.; 599-1665; p. 69

Ideal   UPPER EAST SIDE, p. 5, D8
238 East 86th St.; 535-0950; p. 95

Indochine   EAST VILLAGE, p. 8, C16
430 Lafayette St.; 505-5111; p. 128

J.G. Melon   UPPER WEST SIDE, p. 4, B9
340 Amsterdam Ave.; 877-2220; p. 106

J.G. Melon   UPPER EAST SIDE, p. 5, D9
1291 Third Ave. near 74th St.; 650-1310; p. 94

Jackson Hole Hamburgers   UPPER EAST SIDE, p. 5, D7
1270 Madison Ave.; 427-2820; p. 91

Jade Sea   LOWER MANHATTAN, p. 9, D19
Pier 17, South St. Seaport; 285-0505; p. 148

John Clancy's Restaurant   GREENWICH VILLAGE, p. 8, B16
181 West 10th St.; 242-7350; p. 123

John's Pizzeria   GREENWICH VILLAGE, p. 8, B16
278 Bleecker St.; 243-1680; p. 123

Katz's   LOWER EAST SIDE, p. 9, D17
205 East Houston St.; 254-2246; p. 135

Kiev Coffee Shop   EAST VILLAGE, p. 9, D16
117 Second Ave. near 7th St.; 674-4040; p. 126

Kleine Konditorei   UPPER EAST SIDE, p. 5, D8
234 East 86th St.; 737-7130; p. 95

Lenge   UPPER WEST SIDE, p. 4, B10
202 Columbus Ave.; 799-9188; p. 103

Lincoln Square Coffee Shop   UPPER WEST SIDE, p. 4, B10
2 Lincoln Sq. (Columbus Ave. near 65th St.); 799-4000; p. 110

Lion's Head   GREENWICH VILLAGE, p. 8, B16
59 Christopher St.; 929-0670; p. 122

Little Bucharest GREENWICH VILLAGE, p. 8, C16
40 Thompson St.; 529-2933; p. 123

Loeb Boathouse Café CENTRAL PARK, p. 4, C9
72 St. and Central Park; 517-2233; p. 84

Lucy's Surfeteria UPPER MANHATTAN, p. 4, B6
2756 Broadway; 222-4453; p. 151

Luna's LITTLE ITALY, p. 9, D18
112 Mulberry St.; 226-8657; p. 141

Man Ray CHELSEA, p. 6, B15
169 Eighth Ave. and 19th St.; 627-4220; p. 117

Manganaro's MIDTOWN WEST, p. 6, B13
492 Ninth Ave.; 947-7325; p. 80

Manhattan Brewing Company SOHO, p. 8, C17
40 Thompson St.; 219-9250; p. 132

Manhattan Chili Company GREENWICH VILLAGE, p. 8, B16
302 Bleecker St.; 206-7163; p. 123

Martell's UPPER EAST SIDE, p. 5, D8
1469 Third Ave. and 83rd St.; 861-6110; p. 94

Mary Ann's CHELSEA, p. 6, B15
116 Eighth Ave. and 16th St.; 633-0877; p. 117

McSorley's Old Ale House EAST VILLAGE, p. 9, D16
15 East 7th St.; 473-9148; p. 126

Memphis UPPER WEST SIDE, p. 4, B9
329 Columbus Ave.; 496-1840; p. 104

Meriken CHELSEA, p. 6, C14
162 West 21st St. and Seventh Ave.; 620-9684; p. 117

Metropolis Café GRAMERCY PARK, p. 7, D15
31 Union Square West at 16th St.; 675-2300; p. 115

Mike's American Bar and Grill MIDTOWN WEST, p. 6, B12
650 Tenth Ave.; 246-4115; p. 81

Miss Grimble UPPER EAST SIDE, p. 5, E10
1199 First Ave.; 628-5800; p. 96

Miss Ruby's Café CHELSEA, p. 6, B15
135 Eighth Ave. at 16th St.; 620-4055; p. 117

Mitali EAST VILLAGE, p. 9, D16
334 East 6th St.; 533-2508; p. 126

Mitsukoshi MIDTOWN EAST, p. 7, D11
461 Park Avenue; 935-6444; p. 65

Mocca UPPER EAST SIDE, p. 5, E8
1588 Second Ave.; 734-6470; p. 95

Montrachet TRIBECA, p. 8, C18
239 West Broadway; 219-2777; p. 134

Mortimer's UPPER EAST SIDE, p. 5, D9
1057 Lexington Ave. and 75th St.; 517-6400; p. 92

Nectar UPPER EAST SIDE, p. 5, D9
1022 Madison Ave.; 535-4115; p. 85

Odeon TRIBECA, p. 8, C19
145 West Broadway; 233-0507; p. 134

Old Town Bar GRAMERCY PARK, p. 7, D15
45 East 18th St.; 473-8874; p. 115

One Hudson Café TRIBECA, p. 8, C18
1 Hudson St.; 608-5835; p. 133

107 West UPPER MANHATTAN, p. 4, A6
2787 Broadway; 864-1555; p. 151

One If By Land, Two If By Sea GREENWICH VILLAGE, p. 8,
17 Barrow St.; 228-0822; p. 123 B16

Opera Espresso UPPER WEST SIDE, p. 4, B10
1928 Broadway; 799-3050; p. 110

Pamir · · · UPPER EAST SIDE, p. 5, E9
  1437 Second Ave.; 650-1095; p. 95
Panama City · · · UPPER EAST SIDE, p. 5, E8
  1572 First Ave.; 288-0999; p. 96
Panarella's · · · UPPER WEST SIDE, p. 4, B8
  513 Columbus Ave.; 799-5784; p. 104
Pasta Vicci · · · UPPER WEST SIDE, p. 4, B9
  410 Amsterdam Ave.; 595-7100; p. 107
Pedro O'Hara's · · · LOWER MANHATTAN, p. 9, D19
  19 Fulton, South St. Seaport; 267-7634; p. 148
Peking Duck House · · · CHINATOWN, p. 9, D18
  22 Mott St.; 227-1810; p. 140
Pete's Tavern · · · GRAMERCY PARK, p. 7, D15
  129 East 18th St.; 473-7676; p. 114
Phoenix Garden · · · CHINATOWN, p. 9, D18
  46 Bowery (in the arcade); 962-8934; p. 140
Piccolino · · · UPPER WEST SIDE, p. 4, B8
  448 Amsterdam Ave.; 873-8004; p. 107
Pig Heaven · · · UPPER EAST SIDE, p. 5, E9
  1540 Second Ave.; 744-4887; p. 95
Pink Teacup · · · GREENWICH VILLAGE, p. 8, B16
  42 Grove St.; 807-6755; p. 122
Poccino · · · UPPER WEST SIDE, p. 4, B10
  1889 Broadway; 262-2234; p. 110
Primavera · · · UPPER EAST SIDE, p. 5, E8
  1578 First Ave.; 861-8608; p. 96
Puglia · · · LITTLE ITALY, p. 9, D17
  189 Hester St.; 966-6006; p. 141
The Quilted Giraffe · · · MIDTOWN EAST, p. 7, D11
  550 Madison Ave.; 593-1221; p. 64
Rao's · · · UPPER MANHATTAN, p. 3, E5
  455 East 114th St.; 534-9625; p. 150
Ratner's · · · LOWER EAST SIDE, p. 9, E17
  138 Delancey St.; 677-5588; p. 137
Rikyu · · · UPPER WEST SIDE, p. 4, B10
  210 Columbus Ave.; 799-7847; p. 103
The Saloon · · · UPPER WEST SIDE, p. 4, B10
  1920 Broadway; 874-1500; p. 110
Sammy's Roumanian Steak House · · · LOWER EAST SIDE, p. 9, D17
  157 Chrystie St.; 673-0330; p. 136
Sarabeth's Kitchen · · · UPPER EAST SIDE, p. 5, D7
  1295 Madison Ave.; 410-7335; p. 107
Sarabeth's Kitchen · · · UPPER WEST SIDE, p. 4, B9
  423 Amsterdam Ave.; 496-6280; p. 91
Sardi's · · · MIDTOWN WEST, p. 6, B12
  234 West 44th St. between Broadway and Eighth Ave.; 221-8440; p. 80
Second Avenue Deli · · · EAST VILLAGE, p. 9, D16
  156 Second Ave. near 10th St.; 677-0606; p. 126
Shun Lee West · · · UPPER WEST SIDE, p. 4, B10
  43 West 65th St.; 769-3888; p. 103
Sidewalker's · · · UPPER WEST SIDE, p. 4, B9
  12 West 72nd St.; 799-6070; p. 103
Silver Palace Restaurant · · · CHINATOWN, p. 9, D18
  50 Bowery; 964-1204; p. 140
Soho Kitchen and Bar · · · SOHO, p. 8, C17
  103 Greene St.; 925-1866; p. 132
Le Steak · · · MIDTOWN EAST, p. 7, E11
  1089 Second Ave.; 421-9072; p. 70

Succès La Côte Basque   UPPER EAST SIDE, p. 5, D9
1032 Lexington Ave.; 535-3311; p. 92

Sugar Reef   EAST VILLAGE, p. 9, D16
93 Second Avenue between 5th and 6th sts.; 477-8427; p. 126

Supreme Macaroni Company   MIDTOWN WEST, p. 6, B13
511 Ninth Ave.; 502-4842; p. 80

Swensen's Ice Cream Factory   UPPER EAST SIDE, p. 5, E10
1246 Second Ave., between 65th & 66th sts.; 879-8686; p. 94

Sylvia's   UPPER MANHATTAN, p. 2, C4
328 Lenox Ave. near 127th St.; 996-0660; p. 154

Tai Hong Lau   CHINATOWN, p. 9, D17
70 Mott St.; 219-1431; p. 140

Teachers Too   UPPER WEST SIDE, p. 4, A8
2271 Broadway between 81st & 82nd sts.; 362-4900; p. 112

The Terrace on Five   FIFTH AVENUE, p. 7, D11
725 Fifth Ave.; 371-5030; p. 49

Trastevere   UPPER EAST SIDE, p. 5, E8
309 East 83rd St.; 734-6343; p. 97

Trastevere II   UPPER EAST SIDE, p. 5, D8
155 East 84th St.; 744-0210; p. 97

20 Mott Street   CHINATOWN, p. 9, D18
20 Mott St.; 964-0380; p. 140

Ukrainian East Village Restaurant   EAST VILLAGE, p. 9,
140 Second Ave. and 8th St.; 529-5024; p. 126   D16

Umberto's Clam House   LITTLE ITALY, p. 9, D17
129 Mulberry St.; 431-7545; p. 141

Vasata Restaurant   UPPER EAST SIDE, p. 5, E9
339 East 75th St.; 988-7166; p. 96

Viand Coffee Shop   UPPER EAST SIDE, p. 5, D9
1011 Madison Ave.; 249-8250; p. 85

Viand Coffee Shop   UPPER EAST SIDE, p. 5, D10
673 Madison Ave. and 61st St.; 751-6622; p. 85

Victor's Cuban Café   UPPER WEST SIDE, p. 4, B9
240 Columbus Ave. and 71st St.; 877-7988; p. 103

Vincent's Clam Bar   LITTLE ITALY, p. 9, D18
119 Mott St.; 226-8133; p. 141

White Horse Tavern   GREENWICH VILLAGE, p. 8, B16
567 Hudson St.; 243-9260; p. 122

Yellow Rose Café   UPPER WEST SIDE, p. 4, B8
450 Amsterdam Ave.; 595-8760; p. 107

Yellowfingers   UPPER EAST SIDE, p. 7, D11
1009 Third Ave. at 60th St.; 751-8615; p. 93

9

ENTERTAINMENT

All the world's a stage in New York City. Theater, music, opera, dance, movies, television, comedy clubs—and even sports arenas make for a city with nearly as many performers as there are people in the audience. However "up to date" things may be in Kansas City, New York is the world champ for "things to do." There's more going on here in one night than in some countries during a whole year. The problem for visitors isn't whether there's something to do, but rather how to get it all done.

Here's where you need a finely honed game plan. The days of picking up cancellations for a big Broadway hit just before curtain time are over. The same holds true for ringside seats at sporting events or in cabarets where your favorite jazz is being played. Consult a copy of the Sunday *New York Times* (Arts & Leisure Section), or *The New Yorker* or *New York* magazine as far in advance of your trip as possible. Call N.Y.C./On Stage (587-1111) (toll-free from out-of-state, 800/Stage–NY) for information on theater, music, and dance events. Decide what you want to see and either write for tickets or use one of the electronic reservation systems (Ticketron, etc.) to be certain you have seats for the event and time that you want. If you're going to be staying at a large hotel, consider calling the concierge for some pre-arrival help in getting the reservations you require.

THEATER

Broadway
The star-studded stages that make up the "Great White Way" are located in a small (and unfortunately dingy) section of the city between 41st and 53d streets and Sixth and Eighth avenues. Many theaters have been given landmark status to protect them from New York's ongoing demolition fever. The heart and soul of the area is Schubert Alley, a private connect-

ing street between 44th and 45th streets, right in front of the Schubert Theater, where *A Chorus Line* is into its second decade. You can almost smell the greasepaint as you stroll through.

Everybody wants to give their regards to Broadway. But that's not as simple as it sounds. The plays that are sure-fire hits are sold out months in advance. And then there's the price of a ticket to a Broadway show. We've already broken the $50 mark for an orchestra seat, and have even gone into three figures for a few imports from London. Still, there are ways to lower the ante, and your blood pressure, at the same time.

HALF-PRICE THEATER TICKETS

TKTS

If you don't mind standing on line for an hour or so, you can buy tickets (cash or traveler's checks only) to shows that are not entirely sold out for half the normal price, plus a $1.50 service charge. Considering that tickets are available on the same day as the performance, the selection is surprisingly large. The line moves briskly, and if you arrive about half an hour before the booth opens you'll be able to wrap things up within 45 minutes. (The TKTS line is an experience in itself with everyone chatting back and forth about what's really hot and what they've already seen. You're surrounded by countless critics, helping you make a choice.)

TKTS, 47th Street and Broadway (354-5800). Monday through Saturday: 3 P.M. to 8 P.M. for evening performances on the same day. Saturday & Wednesday: noon to 2 P.M. for matineee performances the same day. Sunday: 2 P.M.–8 P.M. for both matinee and evening, same day.

TKTS, Two World Trade Center (354-5800). Monday through Saturday: 11 A.M. to 5:30 P.M. for most evening performances, same day. *But here tickets for Wednesday, Saturday, and Sunday matinees may be purchased the day before.* Tickets for Sunday evening are also sold on Saturday. Aside from the hours being more civilized, lines are generally shorter.

Twofers

Twofers allow you to go to the box office in advance of performance date and buy tickets at half-price (two-for-the-price-of-one). The obvious advantage is that you can plan ahead, although twofers are not always available for the show of your dreams. Twofers may be picked up at the New York Convention and Visitor's Bureau (2 Columbus Circle, or 158 West 42nd Street). You can also write in advance to Hit Shows, 300 West 42d Street, N.Y., N.Y. 10036, and enclose a self-addressed stamped envelope. They'll put you on their mailing list. Twofers are also found in hotel lobbies, and at some shops and restaurants.

Off-Broadway

Because Off-Broadway productions are cheaper to mount and the pay scale is far lower than Broadway, plays are produced here that wouldn't otherwise see the light of day. Some of the most exciting plays of past seasons have originated off Broadway. This is where producers can afford to take chances that they would never take on the star-struck "Great White Way." Off-Broadway shows that are brought to Broadway arrive with a hefty increase in ticket prices. Off-Broadway tickets, significantly less expensive than Broadway, are an even bigger bargain when purchased through TKTS.

Off-Broadway began in Greenwich Village, at the Provincetown Playhouse, where Eugene O'Neill was the resident playwright. Even today most of the Off-Broadway action is in the Village: at the Lortel, the Cherry Lane, the Sullivan Street Playhouse (where *The Fantasticks* has been playing for over 25 years), Circle in the Square Downtown, etc.

Some of the best-known repertory groups are **Circle Repertory** (99 Seventh Avenue), **Negro Ensemble Company** (424 West 55th Street), **Hudson Guild** (441 West 26th Street), **The Manhattan Theater Club** (City Center, 131 West 55th Street), **Equity Library Theater** (310 Riverside Drive), and the **AMAS Repertory Theater** (1 East 104th Street).

These are perhaps the two most famous Off-Broadway theaters:

Shakespeare in the Park. Delacorte Theater, Central Park, 81st Street & Central Park West; 598-7100; 861-7277 in summer. For anyone visiting New York during the summer months, these open-air productions by Joe Papp (in association with the now world-famous Public Theater) are almost as much fun as the Old Globe used to be. Tickets are free, but the lines are as long as some of the soliloquies and begin forming well in advance of the 6 P.M. box office opening. Most New Yorkers make a "happening" out of it and bring a buddy, a blanket, and a bottle to ease the waiting. Casts are almost always top notch, composed of big names eager for a chance to tread the boards with the Bard.

Public Theater 425 Lafayette Street; 598-7100. Under the brilliant leadership of Joe Papp, this six-theater complex has launched such hits as *A Chorus Line,* and *Cuba and his Teddy Bear* with Robert De Niro. Both of them wound up on Broadway, as do many of the workshop productions originating at the Public. Ticket prices are between $20 and $25, but 25 percent of the seats are held for sale before the performances at one-half of the ticket price. This phenomenon is called "Quiktix," and tickets may be purchased from 6 P.M. before evening performances, and 1 P.M. prior to matinees.

Other Off-Broadway theaters have sprung up all over town, most notably on 42nd Street between Ninth and Tenth avenues, now called "Theater Row" and home to companies such as Playwrights Horizons.

Off-Off-Broadway

Welcome to the world of experimental theater. Performers here usually work for the credits on their résumés, and in the hopes they can attract an agent to see them on stage. Playwrights who would never be given a chance elsewhere can see their work mounted here. One of the most respected of all the stages here is Café La Mama Experimental Theater Club where Harvey Fierstein first presented *Torch Song Trilogy*. Ticket prices for Off-Off-Broadway are rock bottom and they, too, are sometimes available at TKTS.

MUSIC

For recorded information about music and dance events, call N.Y.C./On Stage (587-1111; toll-free from out-of-state, (800) STAGE–NY).

For reduced-price tickets to music and dance events, the TKTS/Bryant Park booth at 42d Street and Sixth Avenue (Avenue of the Americas), 382-2323, is open from 12:00 noon–2:00 P.M. for afternoon performances, and 3:00 to 7:00 P.M. for evening performances. Tickets are available on day of performance only.

CONCERT HALLS

Alice Tully Hall. Lincoln Center, 65th Street and Broadway; 362-1911. Located in the Juilliard School, this intimate recital hall has acoustics that best highlight chamber music groups.

Avery Fisher Hall. Lincoln Center, 65th Street and Broadway; 874-2424. Home of the New York Philharmonic under the baton of Zubin Mehta. Season runs September through May. Tickets are currently $7.50 to $40. One of the most important orchestras in the world, the New York Philharmonic, with its 150 years or so of history, is the longest-running musical hit in town. One of the best bargains around is a $4 ticket to a Philharmonic open rehearsal. Call 580-8700, ext. 202, for the rehearsal schedule. During July and August, when the Philharmonic is not in residence, the Mostly Mozart Festival fills the hall.

Brooklyn Academy of Music (BAM). 30 Lafayette Avenue, Brooklyn; (718) 636-4100

This is the oldest musical center in the country. Four separate theaters include a large concert hall for symphony orchestra series, and chamber music. The season runs from fall through the spring.

Carnegie Hall. 881 Seventh Avenue (57th Street); 247-7800 Saved from the wrecker's ball and restored to its former glory, Carnegie still offers the best acoustics in the city. Orchestras from all over the world want to appear on the stage that presented Tchaikovsky, Toscanini, and Rachmaninoff.

Town Hall. 123 West 43d Street; 840-2824. Before Lincoln Center, Town Hall was one of the few concert halls available for recitals and chamber ensembles. Since it opened 67 years ago, among those who have appeared are Richard Strauss, Duke Ellington, and Philip Glass. Prices here are far lower than at Lincoln Center.

OPERA

See note under Music for information, especially about half-price tickets.

Light Opera of Manhattan (LOOM). Playhouse 91, 316 East 91st Street; 831-2000. If you're an operetta lover, this is the company of your dreams. Lehár, Strauss, Romberg, and Gilbert & Sullivan are all in the repertoire.

Metropolitan Opera House. Lincoln Center, Broadway and 64th Street; 362-6000. Singers at the Met are, of course, world famous and set the standard for the rest of the planet. The Met also sets the standard for some of the highest priced tickets anywhere. They range from $17 to $98 depending on the day of the week and location. However, the budget approach is to arrive at least two hours before curtain and buy standing room for about $7 to $11. For a real bargain, attend one of the free concerts given by the Met in Central Park during the summer. The season is September through May.

New York City Opera. Lincoln Center, New York State Theatre, Broadway and 63d Street; 870-5570. The City Opera, until recently under the direction of Beverly Sills, has always been willing to encourage opera to take new, exciting paths. Not bound by the classicism of the Met, the City Opera has a truly eclectic repertoire, from Romberg to Rossini. Most important, it has given rise to the American opera singer. The public has been captivated by the youth and energy of the company. Ticket prices are about half of the Met's. Try to send for seats before you arrive. The season is July through November.

DANCE

See note under Music for information and half-price tickets.

American Ballet Theatre. Lincoln Center, Metropolitan Opera House, Broadway and 64th Street; 362-6000. Directed by Mikhail Baryshnikov, the ABT is a pioneer in its presentation of new ballets, both modern and classical. It also has the distinction of having attracted most of the greats who defected from Russia: Nureyev, Makarova, and Baryshnikov himself. The season is May through July.

Brooklyn Academy of Music (BAM). 30 Lafayette Avenue, Brooklyn; (718) 636-4100. Dance events go on year round, so it's a good bet something will be happening while you're in town. Martha Graham usually brings her company in, as does José Limón.

The City Center. 131 West 55th Street; 581-7907. Moorish architecture with a domed ceiling and fantasy flavor has turned this old Masonic Temple into a landmarked theater. At one time it was used for extravagant stage productions. Now it's home to various dance companies including the Joffrey Ballet, Dance Theater of Harlem, and Alvin Ailey.

Dance Theatre Workshop. 219 West 19th Street; 924-0077. A workshop in the best sense of the word: whatever new is happening it's happening here. Young choreographers and dancers become stars on this stage.

Joyce Theatre. 175 8th Avenue (19th Street); 242-0800. A new dance space that's part of the revitalization of the Chelsea area. The Joyce is home to the Eliot Feld Ballet. Other companies from around the country make stops here.

New York City Ballet. Lincoln Center, New York State Theater, Broadway and 63d Street; 870-5570. The great George Balanchine was the guiding force behind the New York City Ballet until the day he died. He, along with Jerome Robbins, created classic ballets. If you are visiting in December, write in advance for tickets to the *Nutcracker:* it's a real dazzler. Tickets are from $5 for standing room to $45 for orchestra seats. The seasons are May through June, November through February.

MOVIES

New Yorkers love all kinds of movies: old, new, cult, classic, and documentary. Many visitors find New York the perfect place to catch up on those small but perfect gems that never make it to the local mall. Check the newspapers for schedules. Plan on arriving early since movie houses around town usually have lines before show time. Most first-run houses charge $7 admission and almost that much for the popcorn.

Revival houses, showing everything from schlock horror flicks to glorious thirties musicals, are scattered around town. Schedules can be found in the newspapers.

Other places for film buffs to explore include the following:

The Museum of Modern Art. 11 West 53rd Street; 708-9490. Included in the price of admission to the museum is a ticket to a screening of a film from MOMA's vast collection of classics. There are two separate theaters. The showings are at 2:00 P.M., 2:30 P.M., 6:00 P.M., and 6:30 P.M.

The Museum of the Moving Image. 35th Avenue at 36th Street, Astoria, Queens; (718) 784-4520. While there is as yet no formal screening schedule, films are often shown here, and movie buffs should call for information.

Public Theatre. 425 Lafayette Street; 598-7150. The Little Theatre, part of the Public Theater complex, shows golden oldies and classics almost every weekend afternoon. Admission: $5.

The Whitney Museum. 945 Madison Avenue (75th Street); 570-0537. The Whitney is used as a showcase for new American filmmakers. Film shown here may be too avant-garde or experimental for standard release. Museum admission fee entitles you to see the film.

TELEVISION SHOWS

Free tickets are available from the Visitors and Convention Bureau (2 Columbus Circle; N.Y., N.Y. 10019). If you want to see some of your favorite shows that originate in New York, write ahead to the following:

ABC, Guest Relations, 36A W. 66th St., N.Y., N.Y. 10023.
CBS, Ticket Division, 524 W. 57th St., N.Y., N.Y. 10019.
NBC, 30 Rockefeller Plaza, N.Y., N.Y. 10012.

CLUBS

There's probably no more varied scene in New York than the club scene. Any bartender with a singing brother-in-law is a potential Billy Rose, and the seedy corner pub, a hot new cabaret. But we've included only those places that are fairly tried and true. (The mortality rate, as you can imagine, is high.) Before even thinking twice about going to a club, check sources: the *New York Times* (Friday and Sunday), *New York* magazine, *7 Days,* the *Village Voice,* or *The New Yorker.* You'll find out who's appearing while you're in town, and at what times.

Always call ahead. Do you need a reservation? Is there a cover charge? Is there a minimum in addition to the cover charge? If they serve food, what kind and at what time? Obviously, you're not expecting a gourmet experience when going to a club, but it's often helpful to know that you can skip dinner, go the theater, and have a light supper just before the jazz gets hot. Another point: many clubs are not located in prime real estate areas, and you'll probably be traveling at odd hours. Plan to take taxis.

Jazz

Amazonas. 492 Broome Street; 966-3371. Wild Brazilian sounds in a wild setting. Amazon decor and food to match. One of a kind.

Blue Note. 131 West 3rd Street; 475-8592. Deco setting for some of the biggest jazz names in the business. Unfortunately, it packs the crowds in wall to wall. Jazz brunches on weekends.

Fat Tuesday's. 190 Third Avenue (17th Street); 533-7902. Upstairs for drinking and mingling, downstairs for wall-to-wall jazz. Sunday brunch is very popular here.

Greene Street. 101 Greene St.; 925-2415. A smashing Soho restaurant converted from a garage. Huge leafy spaces to echo great sounds. Somewhat pricey French-American menu accompanies the music, but there is no entertainment charge.

Knitting Factory. 47 East Houston Street; 219-3055. A small room and good music all work to the listener's advantage.

Michael's Pub. 211 East 55th Street; 758-2273. Was put on the map by Woody Allen, who usually sits in with the group on Monday nights to exercise his clarinet. Even if he doesn't show up, there are top jazz acts with whom to drown your sorrow.

Red Blazer Too. 349 West 46th Street; 262-3112. Dixieland and a look into the past in this theater-district club. Lots of nostalgia and toe-tapping for a somewhat more mature crowd.

Sweet Basil. 88 Seventh Avenue South (Bleecker Street); 242-1785. Jazz in a mini-greenhouse setting. Plants, white brick walls, and some of the town's best jazz groups in a restaurant/club.

Village Gate. 160 Bleecker Street (Thompson Street); 475-5120. Among the oldest jazz clubs in N.Y.C., the Gate's current musical focus is "Salsa Meets Jazz." Definitely one of the best shows in town.

Village Vanguard. 178 Seventh Avenue South (11th Street); 255-4037. This cellar club is over 52 years old and should be designated a jazz museum. The room still echoes with the sounds of John Coltrane, Miles Davis, and Charlie Mingus.

Cabarets and Comedy Clubs

Algonquin Hotel—Oak Room. 59 West 44th Street; 840-6800. You can't get any more sophisticated than Michael Feinstein or Julie Wilson, both of whom have performed here. Veddy upper crust place to hear singers and jazz.

Café Carlyle. Carlyle Hotel, Madison Avenue at 76th Street; 744-1600. This is where Bobby Short has been singing the most romantic songs ever written for more years than anyone can remember.

Catch a Rising Star. 1487 First Avenue, at 78th Street; 794-1906. Proving ground for some of the most famous names in comedy. A traditional first stop for new young talent breaking into the business. Sometimes, a "name" act drops in to polish a new act.

Chicago City Limits. 351 East 74th Street; 772-8707. Like the Second City in Chicago, this is drill team group improvisation. The audience throws out suggestions, and the group fires away.

Chippendale's. 1110 First Avenue (61st Street); 935-6060. As you no doubt know, this is the flip side of the strip for dollars scene. The stage is chock full of Gypsy *Moe* Lee's, taking it off for an audience of cheering, leering ladies.

Dangerfield's. 1118 First Avenue (61st Street); 593-1650. Rodney himself doesn't perform here regularly, but this is where he tapes his cable TV shows. His enthusiasm for giving new comics a break is contagious. You'll sometimes find big names in the audience trying to catch the competition.

Danny's Skylight Room. Grand Sea Palace, 346 West 46th Street; 265-8130. An unlikely place for great singers and smooth music. Served up with snacks in the back of a Thai restaurant. Only in New York!

Don't Tell Mama. 343 West 46th Street; 757-0788. The piano bar in the front lets you sing along, but the comedy and revues in the back are for listeners only. Attracts a lively gay crowd.

The Duplex. 55 Grove Street; 255-5438. Joan Rivers and Woody Allen were some of the new acts who broke in here. A Greenwich Village comedy hall of fame.

Improvisation. 358 West 44th Street (Ninth Avenue); 765-8268. This is the place that sets the standards. Practically every big name comedy performer started here.

Mostly Magic. 55 Carmine Street; 924-1472. If you believe the hand is quicker than the laugh, this is the place for you.

Country, Western, Folk

Eagle Tavern. 355 West 14th Street; 924-0275. It's St. Patrick's Day 365 days a year here. Traditional Irish folk music and a stage for all manner of performers, even poets.

The Lone Star Café. 61 Fifth Avenue (13th Street); 242-1664. Forget the address—just look for the iguana on the roof. Funky Texas sounds served up with home on the range food.

Speakeasy. 107 MacDougal Street; 598-9670. New York's folk music headquarters, operated by a folk musicians co-op. They co-op seven nights a week.

Eclectic Music Clubs

The Bottom Line. 15 West 4th Street; 228-6300. A small club bursting with music acts. Check the papers to see who is appearing. Tickets are usually needed in advance—and even then you'll have to jockey for a good seat.

SOB's. 204 Varick Street at Houston Street; 243-4940. Sounds of Brazil in a big room with tastes of Brazil to round out the experience.

Trixie's. 307 West 47th Street; 582-5480. A cross between *Animal House* and *A Night at the Opera*—anything goes at Trixie's. Off-the-wall entertainment, vibrating music, and diner food.

Dance Clubs and Nightclubs

The New York dance club scene attracts an older but no less exuberant audience than a midnight screening of *The Rocky Horror Picture Show*. By and large, the decibel level and costuming are the same. The real difference is that the dance club aficionado is notoriously fickle: today's hot spot is tomorrow's flash in the pan. And since all you're paying for is the sizzle, we can virtually guarantee that this list is already out of date. Check the sources listed under Clubs to find out who's inherited the wind.

If you're determined to dance, then be prepared to run the gamut in expenses, and depending upon where you go, put yourself through the indignity of being scrutinized by some galoot at the door before you're allowed in. Obviously, there are notable exceptions to the rule, and none of that folderol applies to nightclubs or big name places like the Rainbow Room.

Au Bar. 41 East 58th Street; 308-9455. As of this writing, THE place to see and be seen. Eurochic at its most demanding. People wait months for a reservation at this dance-dinner club. Be prepared for the dressiest crowd in town.

Café Iguana. 235 Park Avenue South; 529-4770. A huge iguana hangs from the ceiling, flashing its eyes at the gringos on the dance floor of this hot hot new supper club. When you spend your night at the Iguana, the Iguanarita is the drink of choice.

CBGB. 315 Bowery (Bleecker Street); 982-4052. An institution in the new wave rock scene, CBGB's attracts kids and those who wish they still were.

China Club. 2130 Broadway (75th Street); 877-1166. China blue walls, Chinese wall hangings (and assorted dragons) make this one of the more exotic places to dance and listen to music. A favorite of those in the business. Top music stars often drop in and jam.

Edwardian Room. Plaza Hotel, Fifth Ave. at 59th Street; 759-3000. What could be more romantic than dining and dancing in a gorgeous turn-of-the-century wood-paneled room with large windows overlooking Central Park?

Fat Tuesday's. 190 Third Avenue; 533-7902. A supper club upstairs with top musicians. Very informal and laid back. Its small size makes it super cozy.

Jimmy Weston's. 131 East 54th Street; 838-8384. A dance and supper club that specializes in 1940s and 1950s déjà vu. After being around for nearly 25 years, this place has a really comfortable, lived-in feeling.

Limelight. 47 West 20th Street; 807-7850. If you're into outrageous, what could be better than a 19th-century church turned dance club. Stained-glass windows, chapels, and the original church pews surround a crowd of up to 2,000. Who said never on Sunday?

M.K. 204 Fifth Avenue (25th Street); 779-1340. Hot + trendy = hard to get into. A converted bank is the background for this name-dropper's paradise. Dance club is in the vault downstairs. Two stuffed Doberman pinschers set the scene.

Nell's. 246 West 14th Street; 675-1567. Uh oh. Doorman discretion determines who gets into this dance and supper club. Once favored by the Yuppie NY novelist crowd (Bret Easton Ellis, Jay McInerney), now is not quite what it used to be. Victorian overstuffed sofas and gilt mirrors give it a British men's club look. Still attracts a veddy dressy crowd.

The North River Bar. 145 Hudson Street; 226-9411. One of the few places to feature swing-dancing. Drop in on Wednesday nights for a dance down memory lane.

Pyramid Club. 101 Avenue A (6th Street); 420-1590. Very informal and unique. Hot bands offer rhythms so infectious that waiters dance on the bar. The East Village crowd vibrates to the music on a tiny dance floor amid animal murals and graffiti-covered walls.

The Rainbow Room. 30 Rockefeller Center; 632-5000. Do not miss it! See Restaurants.

The Ritz. 119 East 11th Street (near Third Avenue); 254-2800. A vast two-level New Wave dance club that's heavy on the video. The young crowd here takes their sound very seriously.

Roseland. 239 West 52nd Street; 247-0200. What becomes a legend most? Ballroom dancing is alive and well and polishing the parquet in the same place it's been for 65 years. A great place to carry out your Fred and Ginger fantasies.

Stringfellow's. 35 East 21st Street; 254-2444. Peter Stringfellow, who already has two top clubs in London, has brought his brand of dance club-theatrics to New York. What looks to be a very elegant restaurant turns into a dance club at the sound of the 1812 Overture as mirrored walls swing open to reveal a dance floor. Lots of show biz types here.

The Tunnel. 220 Twelfth Avenue; 244-6444. Not since *Phantom of the Opera* has there been such a spooky environment in which to have fun. It's a huge vaulted chamber that leads off into nothingness (and abandoned train tracks). Think of 15,000 square feet of tunnel with a dance floor to match. Attracts everyone from punks to Via Veneto look-alikes.

BARS

The bar scene in New York is all things to all people. There are bars for shots of whiskey, neat. There are bars for singles. There are bars for lingering over a martini. As a matter of fact, there's hardly a restaurant in town that doesn't have a bar, even if it's just to serve drinks when your reservation isn't being honored promptly. Still, as far as we can figure, no one has ever said, "Hey, I feel like a drink. Let's go to the bar at Lutèce."

The first thing to do is decide whether you'll be drinking alone, looking for company, or already be accompanied. Then, do you want entertainment, conversation, or something to eat? If you'd like to tap your swizzle stick or are in the mood for a laugh, check the list of clubs on the preceding pages. Many of them have bars as well as tables, and you might enjoy seeing the show without having to absorb a minimum imposed for being seated.

Nothing beats a hotel bar for conversation when you're alone. Everyone is accustomed to solo fliers and even if you're not a guest at the hotel, it's an easy spot to walk into unaccompanied. An increasing number of bars recognize that people may not wish to go through the formality of "dining" but still get hungry. You'll find lots of bars serving abbreviated menus. Call before you go.

And then there are some bars that are landmarks and could as easily fit on your sightseeing agenda: The Four Seasons, Hors d'Oeuvrerie (at Windows on the World), Palio, Rainbow Room, the Oak Bar at the Plaza, the White Horse, the Algonquin lobby bar, P.J. Clarke's, "21," and the Odeon. See also Restaurants, above.

Algonquin Lobby Bar. Algonquin Hotel, 59 West 44th Street; 840-6800. If there's a Brit show in town, you'll find members of the cast sitting here. Very sedate, reeks with atmosphere from a bygone era.

Bemelmans Bar. Carlyle Hotel, Madison Avenue at 76th Street; 744-1600. A small and cozy very upscale bar named for the Bemelmans murals that decorate the walls.

Chumley's. 86 Bedford Street; 675-4449. Behind an unmarked door lurks a coven of yuppies downing beer and burgers. Lots of history here.

Costello's. 225 East 44th Street; 599-9614. Proximity to the *New York Daily News* makes this a reporter's hangout. As such, for serious drinkers only.

Downtown Beirut. 158 First Avenue (9th Street); 777-9011. Depends upon your sense of humor. This place lives up to its name with barbed wire atmosphere and graffiti-covered walls.

Fanelli's. 94 Prince Street; 226-9412. It's been around for 125 years or more, and the neighborhood still isn't bored with it.

Hard Rock Café. 221 West 57th Street; 489-6565. I can't hear you! What did you say? (See Restaurants.)

Joe Allen's. 326 West 46th Street; 581-6464. A show-biz hangout with a bar that must attract almost everyone appearing on Broadway. (See Restaurants.)

King Tut's Wa Wa Hut. Avenue A at 7th Street; 254-7772. Off-the-wall bar in the East Village. Decor is early horror film, but the place is so original, it's hard to resist.

Lion's Head. 59 Christopher Street; 929-0670. Here, the lion is a literary one. Writers meet to plot the future while downing tap beer and burgers.

Manhattan Brewing Company. 40 Thompson Street; 219-9250. A working brewery that makes and serves its own beer in a huge room with the old casks in view. Good pub food.

McSorley's Old Ale House. 15 East 7th Street; 473-9148. New York's oldest bar. Reeks atmosphere and college kids.

Oak Bar. Plaza Hotel, Fifth Avenue at 59th Street; 546-5330. This is the one many New Yorkers think is the best hotel bar in town. Jam packed most of the time but worth the crush if you get near a window.

Odeon. 145 West Broadway; 233-0507. A long bar from which to watch the quintessential Tribeca scene.

P.J. Clarke's. 915 Third Avenue (55th Street); 355-8857. If you had to pick one New York bar. . . . (See Restaurants.)

Pete's Tavern. 129 East 18th Street; 473-7676. Pete's was doing business back in 1864. O. Henry was a regular.

Prince Street Bar. 125 Prince Street; 228-8130. This Soho spot is a favorite with art dealers and shoppers alike. Lots of kitsch to go with the food and drink.

Redbar. 116 First Avenue. A new waveish hangout near St. Marks Place that's recently been discovered by preppies and Yuppies.

Top of the Sixes. 666 Fifth Avenue; 757-6662. Spectacular views from the bar. Just the right balm after a hard day's shopping.

White Horse Tavern. 567 Hudson Street (11th Street); 243-9260. A landmark pub thanks to Dylan Thomas.

Sports

Aside from the daily decathalon most New Yorkers participate in just trying to get across town, New York is a sports lover's dream come true.

Spectator Sports
Baseball. New York's two clubs that seem to create endless "do or die" pennant races every year are the Mets and the Yankees. The baseball season runs from April through Octo-

ber with enough home games scheduled to ensure most visitors a chance to say, "Take me out to the ballgame."

The Yankees, of course, date back to the golden years of baseball when teams were made up of legendary superstars such as Joe DiMaggio and Mickey Mantle. The Yankees' home base is **Yankee Stadium** in the Bronx; call 293-6000 for information. Sadly, the area around the stadium has deteriorated through the years, so it's best not to explore or linger after the crowds have left. (Sadly, too, the Yankee spirit has taken a beating as George Steinbrenner's continual trading of players infuriates fans who just want their team to be left alone!) Tickets can be purchased at the stadium or through Ticketron outlets. The stadium can be reached by subway: take either the IRT No. 4 train to 161st Street station, or the IND D or C to 161st Street station.

The Mets, who were born much later than the Yankees, have captured New Yorkers' hearts as the "underdogs," fighting their way to the top of the heap. They appear at **Shea Stadium** in Queens; call (718) 507-8499 for information. The stadium can be reached by the IRT No. 7 Flushing Line to Willets Point, Shea Stadium station.

Football. In the "nothing is ever simple in New York" tradition, both of New York's football teams, the N.Y. Jets and the N.Y. Giants, are based in New Jersey at the **Meadowlands Sports Complex;** call (201) 935-8222 for information. Not people to hold a grudge, New York football fans trek across the river loyally. The football season is from September through January. The best way to reach the Meadowlands, if you're not driving, is to take a bus from the Port Authority Bus Terminal, Eighth Avenue at 42nd Street; call 564-8484 for information.

Basketball. The home team is the N.Y. Knickerbockers (the Knicks) who play at Madison Square Garden. The season runs from October to April. College basketball tournaments are also held at the Garden in November and March. **Madison Square Garden** (32nd Street and Seventh Avenue; 563-8000) is easily reached by subway or bus.

Boxing. The stellar attraction for New Yorkers is the Golden Gloves Amateur Tournament, usually held in March of each year. But there are also bouts that go on a couple of times a month, usually on a Thursday, at Madison Square Garden (32nd Street and Seventh Avenue; 563-8000).

Hockey. One thing you have to say about the Islanders and the Rangers, New York's hockey jockeys, is that they never skate on thin ice. The Rangers do their figure eights at Madison Square Garden (32d and Seventh Avenue; 563-8000). The Islanders team up on the ice at the **Nassau Coliseum,** Hempstead Turnpike, Uniondale, N.Y. (516-587-9222). You can get there via the Long Island Railroad (718-454-5477) to Hempstead, and a short bus ride to the Coliseum.

Tennis. The U.S. Open Tennis Championship is the superstar event of the year. Originally played in Forest Hills, it has been moved to the **National Tennis Center** (718-592-8000) in Flushing Meadows, Queens. The championship takes place in September, and most of the "greats" of the game appear. Tickets become harder and harder to get as the final rounds approach. You can reach the center by taking the IRT No. 7 Flushing train to the Shea Stadium stop.

Horseracing. Thoroughbred racing is one of the most popular spectator sports in New York and attracts hordes of people on a regular basis.

Aqueduct, in Ozone Park, Queens (718-641-4700), is the largest thoroughbred track in the country. It can be reached by subway: just take the A train (IND line) to the Aqueduct stop. The season runs from October through April.

Belmont Park Racetrack (718-641-4700) in Elmont, N.Y., on Long Island, has its season from May through Oct. This is where the last race of the "Triple Crown," the Belmont Stakes, is run. Belmont can be reached by the Long Island Railroad (718-454-5477), which goes directly there.

A day at the races can also be arranged by contacting the **New York Racing Association** (718-641-4700) for directions and racing schedules.

Thoroughbred harness racing is held at **Yonkers Raceway** (914-968-4200) in Westchester County (just outside the city limits), and also at the **Meadowlands** in East Rutherford, New Jersey (201-935-8500). Both of these can be reached by bus from the Port Authority Bus Terminal (564-8484), Eighth Avenue at 42nd Street.

If by some chance you wish to make a small wager on the outcome of one of these events and can't be at the track personally, New York City is all too happy to help out. There are over 150 OTB (Off-Track Betting) branches all over the city. You can participate in the "sport of kings" without even leaving the city streets. Call OTB (221-5624) for locations, or check the phone book.

Participant Sports

A few specific activities are suggested here because to experience these in N.Y. is unlike the same activity anywhere else.

Bicycling. There are bike rental stores sprinkled throughout the city that can be found in the *New York Yellow Pages,* but for a central location that can't be beat, the **Loeb Boathouse** in Central Park (861-4137) has bikes at an hourly or daily rate.

Ice Skating. For sheer drama and romance, the skating rink at **Rockefeller Center** (Fifth Avenue at 50th Street; 757-5731), offers an incredible setting from October to April. The picture-postcard time to be here is over the holidays with the giant Christmas tree in the background. Skates are available for rental.

Central Park has its own skating rink that's a bit more casual and relaxed. **Wollman Rink** at 63rd and the East Drive is open from November to April. Rental skates are also available here.

Horseback Riding. You won't have to give your kingdom for a horse at the **Claremont Riding Academy,** 175 West 89th Street, 724-5100. You can rent one from them for about $27 an hour. The bridle paths in Central Park are just a few blocks away.

10

EXCURSIONS

That's a New Yorker for you. No sooner do you get here than we're telling you how to get out. The reason for this is simple: The Northeast corridor of this country offers everything from restorations to roulette.

This is probably the only time during your trip to New York that a car might come in handy. Check with the desk at your hotel about rental agencies.

New York

The **Sleepy Hollow Restorations** include Washington Irving's home, **"Sunnyside"** in the town of Sleepy Hollow. The house is filled with memorabilia belonging to Irving. If *The Headless Horseman* was your favorite ghost story, then you probably would love to explore the area where Rip Van Winkle took a nap.

Two miles away on Route 9 is **Philipsburg Manor** near Tarrytown. It was built by a Dutch family in the 1700s who chose to root for the British in the Revolution and subsequently lost their home and land. Everything has been perfectly preserved including a grist mill attached to the house. The kitchen is Dutch Colonial in every detail and a guide dressed in 17th-century costume leads the tour.

Van Cortlandt Manor farther up on Route 9 is close to the town of Croton-on-Hudson. This is a far more extensive restoration than Philipsburg. There's an 18th-century Dutch manor house, a tavern, gardens, fruit orchards, etc. In addition to tours of the house and gardens there are also craft demonstrations.

All three Sleepy Hollow Restorations are about an hour and a half drive from New York City and have a combined ticket price of $12 for adults, $10.50 for seniors, and $7 for children aged 6 to 17. Tickets may be purchased separately for each restoration for about $5 to $4.50 for seniors, and $3 for kids. Call (914) 631-8200 for driving instructions.

Hyde Park has been the Roosevelt family home since 1867. FDR was born there in 1882 and returned frequently during his presidential years. The house has been maintained exactly as it was when he was alive. It's full of family memorabilia and the library houses FDR's presidential papers. He and Eleanor are buried in the rose garden. The house is now a national monument. Admission is $2 (there is a small extra charge for the library). For hours and driving instructions call (914) 229-9115.

Nyack is the perfect example of a Hudson River village that came into its own around the turn of the century. Large Victorian houses were built to overlook the river, and the town became a favorite for prosperous New Yorkers who were captivated by the charm of Nyack's setting. (Helen Hayes still lives there.) Today, its streets are filled with antique and craft shops. Artist Edward Hopper was born in Nyack and his boyhood home (Hopper House) is now an art gallery and museum. There are also street fairs held in mid-May, mid-July, and mid-October. Call the Nyack Chamber of Commerce (914-353-2221) for information and driving instructions.

Bethel was actually the site of that infamous **Woodstock** concert in the sixties. Today, Woodstock has become a crafts center for artists from all over the country. There are numerous crafts shops in the village and also tours of some studios. For information call (914) 337-4836.

LONG ISLAND

True to its name, Long Island stretches 120 miles from the very edge of New York City out into the Atlantic. The South Shore of the island has become *the* summer destination for New Yorkers to play, be chic, and rub elbows with writers, filmmakers, and other movers and shakers from the city. The most popular of the summer colonies are the Hamptons (East, South, and West). Narrowing it down even further, **East Hampton** is where the summer scene is hottest.

This tiny 19th-century village can hardly hold all the restaurants, antique shops, craft shops, and boutiques that are crammed into its charming streets and lanes. One of the most famous summer theaters in the area, the John Drew Theater, presents first-rate productions that draw actors from Broadway as well as California. The drive from New York takes you past miles of beaches, little fishing ports, and fabulous estates right out of the *The Great Gatsby.* The easiest way to reach the Hamptons is via the Queens-Midtown Expressway, then onto the Long Island Expressway (1-495, N.Y. 495) and then onto N.Y. 24 and N.Y. 27 following the signs to Montauk

Point. For visitor information, write ahead to the Long Island
Tourism and Convention Commission, 213 Carlton Ave., Central Islip, N.Y. 11722.

New Jersey

Atlantic City. Las Vegas with salt water taffy. Who amongst
us is strong enough to withstand the temptation of ocean
views, a boardwalk, miles of good beaches, endless slot machines, and the place where Miss America is crowned? That's
what the casino operators said before they decided to resusci-
tate a down-in-the-dumps seaside resort by making it the le-
galized gambling capital of the East Coast.

The easiest and most accessible way to travel here is by
bus from the Port Authority Bus Terminal (42nd Street and
Eighth Avenue, 564-8484). The trip takes about 2 ½ hours.
Round-trip tickets cost under $25. But there are special bus
tours that go directly to specific casinos. Greyhound-Trailway
handles them (971-6363). The price of a round-trip ticket,
$23.75, includes $5 in gambling vouchers and $17 refunded
on the ticket by the casino. That makes the fare practically
free! If you're going by car, begin at the Lincoln Tunnel, get
on the New Jersey Turnpike until it leads into the Garden
State Parkway. Get off at exit 38 and follow the Atlantic City
Expressway into town.

Secaucus. New York's newest, hottest, not-so-secret place
for discount shopping. Unlike the usual shopping mall, Secaucus has a series of factory outlets and warehouses with
discounted clothes, housewares, china, and even gourmet
foods.

Designers like Gloria Vanderbilt, Calvin Klein, Anne Klein,
Harvé Benard, and many more are crammed into places that
look like airplane hangers. Since everything is so spread out,
having a car is the most convenient way of getting around.
Take the Lincoln Tunnel to New Jersey and pick up Route
3 to the Meadowlands Parkway. There will be signs directing
you from there. If you don't want to drive, there are shoppers'
buses that leave from the Port Authority Bus Terminal (42nd
Street and Eighth Avenue; 564-8484) and take you back to
Manhattan. They make the trip out from 6:30 A.M. to 9:30
A.M. You can return in the afternoon from 3:30 P.M. to 6:10
P.M. The ride takes about 20 minutes, and the fare is $1.85
in exact change.

11

CITY LISTINGS

All sights are keyed to their appropriate neighborhoods and the pages and coordinates of the color atlas in the back of the book. Page references within the listings refer to the book page(s) on which the sight is discussed.

CHURCHES

Abyssinian Baptist Church　　　　　UPPER MANHATTAN, p. 2, C3
132 West 138 St.; 862-7474; p. 154

Cathedral of St. John the Divine　　UPPER MANHATTAN, p. 2,
Amsterdam Ave. at 112th St.; 316-7400; p. 151　　　　　　B5

Riverside Church　　　　　　　　UPPER MANHATTAN, p. 2, A4
490 Riverside Dr.; 222-5900; p. 152

St. Bartholomew's Church　　　　　MIDTOWN EAST, p. 7, D12
109 East 50th St.; 751-1616; p. 65

St. Mark's Church in the Bowery　　EAST VILLAGE, p. 9, D16
131 East 10th St.; 674-6377; p. 125

St. Patrick's Cathedral　　　　　FIFTH AVENUE, p. 7, D12
Fifth Ave. at 50th St.; 753-2261; p. 52

Trinity Church　　　　　LOWER MANHATTAN, p. 8, C19
Broadway at Wall St.; 602-0800; p. 146

MUSEUMS

Abigail Adams Smith Museum　　　UPPER EAST SIDE, p. 7, E11
421 East 61st St.; 838-6878; Mon.–Fri. 10 A.M.–4 P.M.; p. 97

American Museum of the Moving Image　　　　　　QUEENS
35th Ave. at 36th St., Astoria; (718) 784-0077; Mon.–Thurs., 1–5 P.M.; Fri. 1–8 P.M.; Sat. 10 A.M.–8 P.M.; Sun., 10 A.M.–5 P.M.; p. 159

American Museum of Natural History　　UPPER WEST SIDE,
Central Park West at 79th St.; 769-5100;　　　　　　p. 4, B9
Mon.–Sat. 10 A.M.–5:45 P.M.; Wed., Fri., Sat. to 9 P.M.; p. 101

American Numismatic Society　　　UPPER MANHATTAN, p. 2,
Broadway at West 155th St.; 234-3130;　　　　　　　B1
Tues.–Sat. 9 A.M.–4:30 P.M., Sun. 1–4 P.M.; p. 155

Asia Society Gallery UPPER EAST SIDE, p. 5, D10
725 Park Ave.; 288-6400; Tues.–Sat. 10 A.M.–5 P.M., Thurs. to 8 P.M., Sun. 1–5 P.M.; p. 91

Aunt Len's Doll and Toy Museum UPPER MANHATTAN, p. 2, B2
6 Hamilton Ter.; 281-4143; hours by appt. only; p. 154

Black Fashion Museum UPPER MANHATTAN, p. 0, xx
155 West 126th St.; 666-1320; Mon.–Fri. 12–8 P.M.; p. 154

Brooklyn Children's Museum BROOKLYN
145 Brooklyn Ave.; (718) 735-4432; Mon., Wed., Fri. 2–5 P.M., Sat., Sun. 10 A.M.–5 P.M.; p. 158

Brooklyn Museum BROOKLYN
200 Eastern Pky.; (718) 638-5000; Wed.–Mon. 10 A.M.–5 P.M.; p. 158

The Cloisters UPPER MANHATTAN
Fort Tryon Park; 923-3700; Tues.–Sun. 10 A.M.–4 P.M.; p. 155

Cooper-Hewitt Museum FIFTH AVENUE, p. 5, D8
2 East 91st St.; 860-6868; Tues.–Sat. 10 A.M.–5 P.M., Tues. to 9 P.M., Sun. 12–5 P.M.; p. 56

Fire Department Museum SOHO, p. 8, B17
278 Spring St.; 691-1303; Tues.–Sat. 10 A.M.–4 P.M.; p. 134

Fraunces Tavern Museum LOWER MANHATTAN, p. 8, C20
54 Pearl St.; 425-1778; Mon.–Fri. 10 A.M.–4 P.M.; p. 145

Frick Collection FIFTH AVENUE, p. 5, D10
1 East 70th St.; 288-0700; Tues.–Sat. 10 A.M.–6 P.M., Sun. 1–6 P.M.; p. 58

Guggenheim Museum FIFTH AVENUE, p. 5, D8
1071 Fifth Ave. (at 88th St.); 360-3513; Wed.–Sun. 11 A.M.–4:45 P.M., Tues. to 7:45 P.M.; p. 57

Hayden Planetarium UPPER WEST SIDE, p. 4, B9
Central Park West at 81st St.; 769-5920; Mon.–Fri. 1:30–3:30 P.M., Sat.–Sun. 1–4 P.M.; p. 102

Hispanic Society of America UPPER MANHATTAN, p. 2, B1
Audubon Terrace, Broadway at 155th St.; 926-2234; Tues.–Sat. 10 A.M.–4:30 P.M., Sun. 1–4 P.M.; p. 155

International Center for Photography FIFTH AVENUE, p. 5, D7
1130 Fifth Ave (at 94th St.); 860-1777;
Tues.–Fri. 12–5 P.M., Tues. to 8 P.M., Sat.–Sun. 11 A.M.–6 P.M.; p. 56

Intrepid Museum MIDTOWN WEST, p. 6, A12
Pier 86, Twelfth Ave. at 46th St.; 245-0072; Wed.–Sun. 10 A.M.–5 P.M.; p. 81

Jacques Marchais Center of Tibetan Art STATEN ISLAND
338 Lighthouse Ave.; 718-987-3478; Apr.–Oct., Fri.–Sun. 1–5 P.M., May–Sept., Thurs.–Sun. 1–5 P.M., closed Dec.–Mar.; p. 160

Jewish Museum FIFTH AVENUE, p. 5, D7
1109 Fifth Ave.; 860-1888; Mon.–Thurs. 12–5 P.M., Tues. to 8 P.M., Sun. 11–6 P.M.; p. 56

Metropolitan Museum of Art FIFTH AVENUE, p. 5, D8
Fifth Ave. at 82nd St.; 535-7710; Wed.–Sun. 9:30 A.M.–5:15 P.M., Tues. to 8:45 P.M.; p. 57

Morris-Jumel Mansion UPPER MANHATTAN, p. 2, B1
Edgecombe Ave. at West 160th St.; 923-8008; Tues.–Sun. 10 A.M.–4 P.M.; p. 155

El Museo del Barrio FIFTH AVENUE, p. 5, D6
1230 Fifth Ave.; 831-7272; Wed.–Sun. 11 A.M.–5 P.M.; p. 55

Museum of the American Indian UPPER MANHATTAN, p. 2, B1
Broadway at West 155th St.; 283-2420; Tues.–Sat. 10 A.M.–5 P.M., Sun. 1–5 P.M.; p. 155

Museum of Broadcasting MIDTOWN EAST (NEAR FIFTH AVENUE), p. 0, xx
1 East 53rd St.; 752-7684; Tues. noon–8 P.M., Wed.–Sat. to 9 P.M.; p. 51

Museum of the City of New York FIFTH AVENUE, p. 5, D6
1220 Fifth Ave. (at 103rd St.); 534-1672; Tues.–Sat. 10 A.M.–5 P.M., Sun. 1–5 P.M.; p. 55

Museum of Holography SOHO, p. 8, C17
11 Mercer St.; 925-0526; Tues.–Sat. 12–6 P.M.; p. 133

Museum of Modern Art FIFTH AVENUE, p. 6, C11
11 West 53rd St.; 708-9500; Fri.–Tues. 11 A.M.–6 P.M., Thurs. to 9 P.M.; p. 50

New York Historical Society UPPER WEST SIDE, p. 4, B9
170 Central Park West (at 77th St.); 873-3400; Tues.–Sat. 10 A.M.–5 P.M.; p. 101

Pierpont Morgan Library MIDTOWN EAST, p. 7, D13
29 East 36th St.; 685-0008; Tues.–Sat. 10:30 A.M.–4:45 P.M., Sun. 1–4:45 P.M.; p. 73

South Street Seaport Museum LOWER MANHATTAN, p. 9, D19
Front St., South Street Seaport; 669-9424; daily 10 A.M.–5 P.M.; p. 147

Studio Museum in Harlem UPPER MANHATTAN, p. 0, xx
144 West 125th St.; 865-2450; Wed.–Fri. 10 A.M.–5 P.M., Sat.–Sun. 1–6 P.M.; p. 154

Trinity Church Museum LOWER MANHATTAN, p. 8, C19
Broadway at Wall St.; 285-0872; daily 9 A.M.–3:45 P.M.; p. 146

Whitney Museum of American Art UPPER EAST SIDE, p. 5, D9
945 Madison Ave. (at East 75th St.); 570-3676; Tues. 1–8 P.M., Wed.–Sat. 11 A.M.–5 P.M., Sun. 12–6 P.M.; p. 90

Whitney Museum at the Equitable Center MIDTOWN WEST, p. 6, C11
757 Seventh Ave. (at West 51st St.); 554-1113; (Mon.–Fri. 11 A.M.–6 P.M.; also to 7:30 P.M. Thurs; Sat. noon–5 P.M.

Whitney Museum of American Art at Philip Morris MIDTOWN EAST, p. 7, D12
120 Park Ave. (at East 42nd St.); 880-5000; Mon.–Sat. 11 A.M.–6 P.M.; p. 66

LANDMARKS AND HISTORIC SITES

Brooklyn Bridge LOWER MANHATTAN, p. 9, D/E 19
Reached from Frankfort St. and Park Row; p. 147

Castle Clinton National Monument   LOWER MANHATTAN,
Battery Park; 344-7220; p. 143   **p. 8, C20**

Chrysler Building   MIDTOWN, p. 7, D12
405 Lexington Ave.; 682-3070; p. 67

City Hall   LOWER MANHATTAN, p. 8, C18
Broadway at Murray St.; 566-8681; p. 149

Empire State Building   FIFTH AVENUE, p. 6, C13
Fifth Ave. at 34th St.; 736-3100; 9:30 A.M.–midnight; p. 53

Federal Hall National Memorial   LOWER MANHATTAN, p. 8,
   C19
26 Wall St.; 264-8711; Mon.–Fri. 9 A.M.–5 P.M.; p. 146

Flatiron Building   FIFTH AVENUE, p. 7, D14
175 Fifth Ave.; 477-0947; p. 54

General Grant National Memorial   UPPER MANHATTAN,
Riverside Dr. at 122nd St.; 666-1640;   p. 2, A4
Wed.–Sun. 9 A.M.–4:30 P.M.; p. 152

Grand Central Station   MIDTOWN EAST, p. 7, D12
Park Ave. at 42nd St.; p. 67

Lincoln Center for the Performing Arts   UPPER WEST
Broadway at 65th; 877-1800; p. 108   SIDE, p. 4, B10

New York Public Library   FIFTH AVENUE, p. 6, C12
Fifth Ave. at 42nd St.; 221-7676; Mon.–Wed. 10 A.M.–9 P.M., Thurs.–Sat.
10 A.M.–6 P.M.; p. 53

New York Stock Exchange   LOWER MANHATTAN, p. 8, C19
20 Broad St.; 656-3000; Mon.–Fri. 9 A.M.–3 P.M.; p. 146

Poe Cottage   THE BRONX
East Kingbridge Rd. and Grand Concourse; 881-8900. Wed.–Fri., 9 A.M.–5
P.M., Sat., 10 A.M.–4 P.M., Sun. 1–5 P.M.; p. 157

Richmondtown Restoration   STATEN ISLAND
441 Clarke Ave.; (718) 351-1611; Mon.–Fri. 10 A.M.–5 P.M., Sat., Sun. 1–5
P.M.; p. 160

Rockefeller Center   FIFTH AVENUE, p. 6, C12
Fifth Ave. at 47–50th sts.; 246-4600; p. 52

South Street Seaport   LOWER MANHATTAN, p. 9, D19
Fulton and Water sts., Piers 15, 16, 17; p. 147

Staten Island Ferry   LOWER MANHATTAN, p. 9, D20
Whitehall St. near Battery Park; 806-6940; p. 145

Statue of Liberty   LOWER MANHATTAN, p. 8, C20
Liberty Island; 363-3200; daily 9 A.M.–4 P.M. Take ferry from Battery
Park.; p. 143

United Nations   MIDTOWN EAST, p. 7, E12
First Ave. from 42nd St. to 49th St.; 963-1234; daily 9:15 A.M.–4:45 P.M.;
p. 71

Van Cortlandt Mansion
See Van Cortlandt Park.

Wave Hill   THE BRONX
249th St. and Independence Ave., Riverdale; 549-2055. Daily 10 A.M.–4:30
P.M.; p. 157

World Trade Center   LOWER MANHATTAN, p. 8, C19
  2 World Trade Center; 466-7377; daily 9:30 A.M.–9:30 P.M.; p. 143

PARKS, GARDENS, ZOOS

Aquarium   BROOKLYN
  West 8th St. and Surf Ave., Coney Island; (718) 265-3474; daily 10
A.M.–4:45 P.M.; p. 157

Bronx Zoo   THE BRONX
  Fordham Rd. and Bronx River Pkwy.; 367-1010; daily 10 A.M.–4:30 P.M.,
to 5:30 P.M. on Sun.; p. 156

Brooklyn Botanic Garden   BROOKLYN
  1000 Washington Ave; (718) 622-4433; Tues.–Fri. 8 A.M.–6 P.M., Sat.,
Sun., and holidays 10 A.M.–6 P.M.; p. 158

Central Park   CENTRAL PARK, p. 4 and 6, C6–10
  59th to 110th sts., Fifth Ave. to Central Park West; p. 47

Central Park Zoo   CENTRAL PARK, p. 4, C9
  Fifth Ave. and 64th St. Mon.–Fri. 10 A.M.–5 P.M., to 8 P.M. Tues.; weekends and holidays to 5:30 P.M.; Nov.–March to 4:30 P.M.; p. 83

Jamaica Bay Wildlife Refuge   QUEENS
  Broadchannel West; (718) 474-0613; 8:30 A.M.–5 P.M.; p. 160

New York Botanical Gardens   THE BRONX
  Southern Blvd., north of Fordham Rd.; 220-8700; daily dawn–dusk; p. 156

Prospect Park   BROOKLYN
  Grand Army Plaza; (718) 788-0055; p. 159

Van Cortlandt Park (and Van Cortlandt Mansion)   THE
                                                         BRONX
  246th St. and Broadway; 543-3344; Mansion open Tues.–Sat., 10 A.M.–4
P.M., Sun. noon–5 P.M.; p. 157

Washington Square Park   GREENWICH VILLAGE, p. 8, C16
  MacDougal St. to University Place, at lower end of Fifth Ave.; p. 124

12

TRAVEL ARRANGEMENTS

For Information. . .

Once your travel reservations are confirmed, get a copy of the Sunday *New York Times, The New Yorker,* and/or *New York* magazine. Go to the library and find out what articles have appeared recently on New York. Contact the **New York Convention and Visitors Bureau,** 2 Columbus Circle, New York, NY 10019, 212–397–8222, for brochures. In short, bone up for your trip. We promise that advance planning will pay off by allowing you to arrive in town with reservations at Lutèce and tickets to *Phantom of the Opera*—well, maybe.

The Seasons in New York

The only thing predictable about New York's weather is its unpredictability. In general the climate is surprisingly moderate, but there are the occasional subzero days in winter, along with the rare, but not unheard of, 100-degree-plus summer days. In addition, New York is unfortunately one of those cities for which a fraction of an inch of snow or a small amount of rain spells disaster. It takes very little to incapacitate New York, especially where mass transit is concerned.

Weather Information

	Avg. Max. Temp.	Avg. Min. Temp.	Avg. Precip.
Jan	38° (4)	25.5° (−3)	3.21 in.
Feb.	40.1° (4)	26.6° (−3)	3.13
March	48.6° (9)	34.1° (1)	4.22
April	61.1° (16)	43.8° (7)	3.75
May	71.5° (22)	53.3° (12)	3.76
June	80.1° (27)	62.7° (18)	3.23
July	85.3° (29)	68.2° (20)	3.77
Aug.	83.7° (28)	67.1° (19)	4.03
Sept.	76.9° (25)	60.1° (16)	3.66
Oct.	65.6° (19)	49.9° (11)	3.41
Nov.	53.6° (12)	40.8° (5)	4.14
Dec.	42.1° (5)	30.5° (−1)	3.81
Annual	62.2° (16)	46.9° (8)	44.2

Note: Centigrade temperature is given in parens.

Probably the very best times to be in New York, if you have any choice in the matter, are Oct. and May. The former has crisp, brisk days, and the latter offers the full pleasures of spring. The next-best time, despite the incredible crowds, is between Thanksgiving and New Year's. New York puts on quite a show: The buildings on Fifth Avenue are decorated, shop windows are filled with marvelous displays, and somehow the crosstown traffic is no longer a major topic of conversation. If you have no other choice but to come during summer, don't let the weather stop you, but be forewarned: the combination of heat and humidity in New York can dampen the most ardent sprits.

1989 EVENTS

January
"The Changing Image of George Washington," Jan. 30 (through May 28), 1989, Fraunces Tavern Museum, Broad and Pearl sts.

February
"Academy Nominated Films," Feb. (through March), 1989, Museum of Modern Art, 11 W. 53d St.

"Refigured Painting: The German Image, 1960–1988," Feb. 11 (through Apr. 23) Guggenheim Museum, Fifth Ave. at 88th St.

"Andy Warhol," Feb. 5 (through May 2), 1989, Museum of Modern Art, 11 W. 53d St.

Chinese New Year Celebrations—4687, Year of the Snake, Feb. 6, 1989, Chinatown

Marcel Marceau, Feb. 7–26, 1989, City Center, 37 W. 65th St.

"Yoko Ono," Feb. 8 (through Apr. 16), 1989, Whitney Museum of American Art, 945 Madison Ave. at 75th St.

"From Africa to America: Black Roots Sampler," Feb. 10, 17, Town Hall, 123 W. 43d St.

"Frederic Remington: The Masterworks," Feb. 11 (through Apr. 16), 1989, Metropolitan Museum of Art, Fifth Ave. and 82d St.

Paul Taylor Dance Company, Feb. 25–26, 1989, Brooklyn Center for the Performing Arts, Brooklyn College, Campus Rd. and Hillel Place

Merce Cunningham Dance Company, Feb. 28 (through March 12), 1989, City Center, 37 W. 65th St.

March
St. Patrick's Day Parade, March 17, Fifth Ave.

Ringling Bros. and Barnum & Bailey Circus, March 23 (through Apr. 23), 1989, Madison Square Garden, 32d St. and Seventh Ave.

Easter Parade, March 26, 1989, Fifth Ave.

"L'Art de Vivre: Decorative Arts and Design in France 1789–1989, March 30 (through Aug. 6), 1989, Cooper-Hewitt Museum, 2 E. 91st St. at Fifth Ave.

April
"French Film Festival: Perspectives on French Cinema," the entire month, Museum of Modern Art, 11 W. 53d St.

American Ballet Theatre, Apr–June, 1989, Metropolitan Opera House, Lincoln Center

The Paul Taylor Dance Company, Apr. 11 (through May 7), 1989, City Center, 37 W. 55th St.

Itzhak Perlman, Pinchas Zukerman, and Lynn Harrell, Apr. 16, 1989, 92nd St. Y

Celebration of the Bicentennial of George Washington's Inauguration, including a flotilla in New York Harbor, dedication of a new museum at Federal Hall, parade, concerts, and fireworks, Apr. 30, 1989

May

"Directed by Vincente Minnelli," May 5 (through June 18), 1989, Museum of Modern Art, 11 W. 53d St.

Alvin Ailey American Dance Theater, May 6, 1989, Lehman Center for Performing Arts, the Bronx

Cherry Blossom Weekend, May 6–7, 1989, Brooklyn Botanic Garden, 1000 Washington Ave.

"Goya and the Spirit of Enlightenment," May 6 (through July 16), 1989, Metropolitan Museum of Art, Fifth Ave and 82d St.

Ninth Avenue International Food Festival, May 20–21, 1989, 35th–57th sts.

"Helen Frankenthaler," May 25 (through Aug. 8), 1989, Museum of Modern Art, 11 W. 53d St.

June

Free Metropolitan Opera Concerts, throughout the month, in the parks, all five boroughs

Puerto Rican Day Parade, Fifth Ave.

Gay Pride Day Parade, Fifth Ave.

Salute to Israel Parade, June 4, 1989, Fifth Ave.

Belmont Stakes, June 10, 1989, Belmont Racetrack, Hempstead Turnpike and Plainfield Ave., Queens

"Hispanic Art in the United States: Thirty Contemporary Painters and Sculptors, June 10 (through Sept. 4), 1989, The Brooklyn Museum, Eastern Pkwy. and Washington Ave.

Flag Day Celebration and Open House, June 14, 1989, Fraunces Tavern Museum, corner of Broad and Pearl sts.

"Andrew Wyeth: The Helga Pictures," June 16 (through Sept. 18), 1989, The Brooklyn Museum, Eastern Pkwy. and Washington Ave.

July

Macy's Fourth of July Fireworks, July 4, 1989, over the East River

Fraunces Tavern Museum Open House, July 4, 1989, corner of Broad and Pearl sts.

Free Summerpier concerts, July and Aug., 1989, at South Street Seaport

Free Summergarden concerts, July and Aug., 1989, Museum of Modern Art, 11 W. 53d St.

Free Shakespeare Festival, July and Aug., 1989, Central Park

August
Free New York Philharmonic concerts, the entire month, in the parks, all five boroughs

"Views of Rome: Drawings and Watercolors from the Collection of the Biblioteca Apostolica Vaticana, Aug. 8 (through Oct. 29), 1989, Cooper-Hewitt Museum, 2 E. 91st St. at Fifth Ave.

U.S. Open Tennis Championships, Aug. 28 (through Sept. 10), 1989 Flushing Meadows, Queens

Fall
Ellis Island reopens to public

September
Feast of San Gennaro, Mulberry St., Little Italy

Schooner Regatta, South Street Seaport

"Unique Collaboration: Picasso and Braque, 1907–1914," Sept. 24, 1989 (through Jan. 16, 1990), Museum of Modern Art, 11 W. 53d St.

October
Columbus Day Parade, Fifth Ave.

Pulaski Day Parade, Oct. 1, 1989, Fifth Ave.

Halloween Parade, Oct. 31, 1989, Greenwich Village

November
NYC Marathon, Nov. 5, 1989, five-borough run

Magnificent Christmas Spectacular, Mid-Nov. 1989 (through early Jan. 1990), Radio City Music Hall, 50th St. and Sixth Ave.

Animated Store Window Displays, late Nov. 1989 (through early Jan. 1990), Fifth Ave.

Macy's Thanksgiving Day Parade, Nov. 23, 1989, Central Park West from 77th St.–59th St., down Broadway to 34th St.

December
Giant Christmas Tree, Rockefeller Center

"The Nutcracker," The entire month, New York City Ballet, Lincoln Center, Broadway and 65th St.

Fifth Avenue Holiday Mall, Dec. 17, 1989, 34th–57th sts.

Giant 32-ft. Hanukkah Menorah, Dec. 22–29, 1989, Grand Army Plaza, Fifth Ave. at 59th St.

New Year's Eve Celebrations: Fireworks and midnight run in Central Park; lighted Big Apple atop Times Square; fireworks in Prospect Park, Brooklyn

WHAT TO PACK

Some New Yorkers like to dress up; others like to dress down. You'll go to the theater and see people in formal attire sitting next to a couple that's casual with a capital K. Frankly, that's okay for New Yorkers who don't think twice about such things, but you, as a visitor, might not feel at ease with either extreme. Generally speaking, New York is still a place where ties and dresses are the most acceptable form of attire (at least, north of 14th Street). It's not that you won't be admitted into many restaurants and practically all theaters in more casual attire; you just might be more comfortable if you dress up a little. Remember, New York is the fashion capital of the country. Upscale restaurants are filled with beautifully dressed "beautiful people."

There's a wonderful new phrase, "designer casual," and it applies to many New York situations. As long as what you're wearing looks expensive, it doesn't necessarily have to be formal. As a rule, jeans in the evening are strictly verboten unless you're hanging out in Soho or heading for the Bronx Zoo. While locals have a sixth sense about what to wear where, if you're going to err, better to err "up" instead of "down."

From Oct. through April you'll need sweaters, parkas, or topcoats depending on the weather. Even in summer, because everything is air conditioned (except the taxis and some buses and trains), you'll want a shawl or sweater. Otherwise, summer is a time for your lightest clothes. Unlike many other cities, New York doesn't cool down considerably at night.

Since walking is often the preferred method of locomotion around the city, it's imperative that your shoes be comfortable.

Formalities for Foreign Visitors

If New York is your port of entry into the U.S., you'll need a valid passport and visa. Check with your local travel agent, airline, or closest U.S. Embassy. Vaccination certificates are not required. You should also check on customs regulations since they are quite specific.

If you have currency other than U.S. dollars, do *not* expect it to be accepted anywhere except a bank. New York is not sophisticated in terms of foreign currencies. Even your traveler's checks should be in U.S. dollars. Check with your local bank, before you leave home, for exchange rates and branches close to your hotel. Plan to convert enough money so that you will arrive in New York with U.S. $100. This amount should see you through all entry situations and well into your first day so that you're not pressed to exchange money immediately.

Hotel exchange rates are never as good as those at a bank. However, New York banks are open generally only Mon.–Fri., 9:00 A.M.–3:00 P.M. Even worse, most banks are not equipped to handle foreign currency transactions. In addition to banks, exchange facilities are offered by **Deak Perera International** (29 Broadway, 635–0540; 41 E. 42d St., 883–0400; 630 Fifth Ave., 757–6915) and **Thomas Cook** (18 E. 48th St., 310–9400; 5 World Trade Center, 938–0950; 25 Tudor City Plaza, 661–4750). But the best place for currency exchange is **Checque Point USA** (551 Madison Ave. at 55th St., 980–6443) because it's open seven days a week: Mon.–Fri., 8:00 A.M.–6:00 P.M.; Sat.–Sun., 10:00 A.M.–6:00 P.M.

Another important consideration for foreign visitors has to do with medical services, which in the U.S. are private and not government subsidized. You may wish to check with your local brokers concerning the purchase of medical insurance while in New York. While the quality of medical care in NY is high, so is the cost.

In the event that you are homesick, try **Hotalings** (142 W. 42d St., 840–1868) for out-of-town newspapers and magazines.

Money Matters

While most places accept credit cards and/or traveler's checks, be certain to inquire in advance. Policies change, shops may not accept the particular card you had in mind, etc. Increasingly, New York shops accept checks with proper identification. Before you swoop down to the Lower East Side on a

Sunday morning when all the banks are closed, be sure you know how you're going to pay, and that you have a safe place to carry your money.

Automated teller machines, usually attached to a bank, which will dispense cash at any hour of the day or night if you possess but one of a myriad of acceptable cards, are never more than a block away from almost anywhere in New York. Just take extra precautions if you need to use them in questionable areas, or at night.

You never have to worry about tipping in a restaurant if you adopt the system used by many New Yorkers: simply, double the tax (.0875) and round it off. It works out to 17 ½%, which is perfectly fine if the service was up to par.

Cab drivers expect 15 to 20 percent of the fare. Porters and bellmen usually get $.75 to $1.00 per bag, but no less than $1.00 at any time. You may wish to be more generous if the bags are heavy or the distance far.

Tours

As important as it is to make your own discoveries when visiting New York, considerations of time (and reality) often turn a carefully chosen tour into one of the best discoveries of all. Chances are that a tour may be your only way to take a dinner cruise, sightsee in Harlem, or go backstage at Radio City Music Hall. Put aside your fears about an "If this is Tuesday, we must be in Belgium" situation. Many of the tours listed here are taken by New Yorkers themselves.

If you are coming to New York for the first time from overseas, we strongly urge that you take at least a half-day city tour to orient yourself as quickly as possible. Check at your hotel for tour information, as well as with the New York Convention & Visitors Bureau (2 Columbus Circle, 397-8222). Special-interest tours are listed in *The New York Times,* The *New Yorker,* and *New York* magazine. Unless noted, tour prices are under $10 per person.

Adventure on a Shoestring, 300 West 53rd St.; 265-2663. Adored by New Yorkers as well as visitors, this group always comes up with a fascinating new angle on the city. The tours usually include a visit to an area like Gramercy Park, Chinatown, or the Lower East Side, and a chat with a resident of the community about the history and folklore of the area. The walks are given only on weekends and usually take about an hour and a half. Write ahead for their schedule.

Art Tours of Manhattan, Princeton, NJ; (609) 921-2647. East Village, Soho and Madison Avenue galleries are included as well as visits to artist's studios. Since tours are customized for the individual or small groups, prices vary. They start at $35 and go to $75 depending upon time and admission costs. Some include lunch.

Backstage on Broadway, 228 West 47th St.; 575-8065. Takes you behind the scenes for a one-hour visit backstage at a Broadway show. A must for theater buffs. Mon.–Fri. at 10:30 A.M.

Circle Line around Manhattan, Pier 83 at West 43rd St.; 563-3200. Three-hour look at Manhattan from the rivers that surround it. A guide points out the sights. April through Nov. Daily at 9:30 A.M., 10:30 A.M., 11:30 A.M., 1:15 P.M., 2:15 P.M., and 3:15 P.M. $15.

Circle Line Statue of Liberty, Battery Park South; 269-5755. Leaves from Battery Park to Liberty Island. Tour the Statue of Liberty and then visit the American Museum of Immigration. Daily, every hour on the hour, 9 A.M.–4 P.M., year round.

Doorway to Design. 1441 Broadway; 221-1111, and (718) 339-1542. Custom tours of New York's art, antiques, fashion, and theater worlds. An expert in each takes you on an in-depth tour behind the scenes to see professionals at work. $150 per person for a half-day tour.

Fulton Fish Market. 171 John St.; 669-9416. Given by the South Street Seaport Museum on the first and third Thurs. of the month. Breakfast with clam chowder and a tour of the market. Given in the spring and summer until Oct. 20. For early birds only. 6 A.M.–7:30 A.M. $15. Even if the fish market tour is not available, others are given in the area daily. One includes a visit to the *Peking* and the *Ambrose*, old sailing ships docked at Pier 16. Others visit the back streets of the neighborhood to talk about some of the houses that date from the 1770s and 1780s.

Gray Line Tours. 247-6956. A wide range to choose from, including day tours around the city, harbor cruises, shorter harbor tours, birds-eye views of the city from a helicopter. Also foreign language tours.

Harlem Spirituals, Inc. 1457 Broadway; 302-2594. Tours of churches in Harlem (where gospel music and spirituals are sung) as well as visits to jazz spots. Sun. Spirituals and Gospel Tour, 9 A.M.–12:45 P.M., $25. Wed. Gospel Weekday Tour, 9 A.M.–1 P.M., $28. Thurs. tour includes a soul food lunch, 9 A.M.–1:30 P.M., $32. Harlem by Night (Thurs.–Sat., 7 P.M.–midnight) includes jazz and soul food, $60.

Harlem, Your Way! Tours Unlimited, 129 West 130th St.; 866-6997. A 2 ½–3-hour walking tour of Central Harlem that includes the Schomberg Center, Abyssinian Baptist Church, Strivers' Row, and the Apollo Theater. Daily from 12:30 P.M. $25.

Horse-drawn Carriages Fifth Avenue at 59th St. A horse-drawn carriage is a terrific way to see the park. You can also arrange rides to short destinations around the downtown area. $17 for the first half hour. $5 for each additional quarter of an hour. (But confirm price in advance.)

Hungry Peddlers. 559-5542, 222-2243. Unique full-day gourmet bicycle tours. You buy your own food at places like La Marqueta in Spanish Harlem, or the Greek food shops in Astoria, Queens. Tours start early in the morning so that you have time to work up an appetite for lunch. $12 per person, or $20 for couples. Tours are given from April to Nov.

Inside New York. 203 East 72nd St.; 861-0709. Touring the fashion, art and interior design worlds. Half- or full-day, $17 and $25.

Island Helicopter Sightseeing. 34th Street at the East River; (718) 895-1626. Day and evening flights over Manhattan. Spectacular views provide "forever" memories of the city. Prices range from $30 to about $140.

Jewish New York. (718) 951-7072. Oscar Israelowitz, author of *Guide to Jewish New York City,* takes you to the Lower East Side, including a stop at a pickle barrel. Usually Sun. at 1:30 P.M. Two hours. $10.00.

The Museum of the City of New York Walking Tours. 534-1672, ext. 236. An overview of NYC's past. Walks have covered two centuries on the Lower East Side, the financial district, the East and West Villages, etc. Tours last about 4 hours. Sun. $10.

New York Big Apple Tours. 22 West 23rd St.; 691-7866. This tour takes you to a church in Harlem to hear Gospel singing as well as a visit to Sugar Hill, Strivers' Row, the Morris-Jumel Mansion and, if time permits, the Cathedral of St. John the Divine. Every Sun. morning from 9:30. The tour takes about 3 ½ hours. $25 (includes Jumel Mansion admission).

The New York Historical Society. 170 Central Park West; 873-0125. Two-hour tours of historic locations around the city are given once a month. Mon.–Sat. at 2 P.M. $10.

Peddler's Pack Walking Tour. 413-0233. A colorful look at the Lower East Side and its history led by a costumed actor-guide. Sponsored by the Lower East Side Historic Conservancy, it includes Hester St., the public baths, a yeshiva, and a Yiddish theater. Tours are given from March through Nov. and start at 1 P.M. $12.

River to River Walking Tours. Ruth Alscher-Green, 375 South End Ave.; 321-2823. You can count on Ruth Alscher-Green for one of the most customized and personal views of lower New York. You are given an in-depth look at the seaport, the financial center, and everything in between, river to river. A tour averages two hours but can continue much longer, depending on the enthusiasm of the group. $35 per person, $50 for a couple.

Sidewalks of New York. 517-0201. Sam Stafford conducts theme tours of New York. His "Hollywood on the Hudson" is one of the most popular: he leads his group to apartment buildings and town houses (outside only) of stars living in Manhattan. Two hours. $10.

Lou Singer's Tours. 130 St. Edwards St., Brooklyn; (718) 875-9084. Tours have exotic names like "Fabulous Flatbush," "Noshing on the Lower East Side," and "Little Old New York." They are conducted by Lou Singer who gets a terrific kick out of showing off the city. $25.

Sound Publishers, Inc. 30 Riverside Plaza; 686-0356. You can "do it yourself" with one of these cassettes covering various sights in the city. Just snap one into your Walkman and you're ready to go. Write for a list of the sightseeing tapes available.

Urban Park Rangers. 397-3081. One-hour wildlife walks in the parks of each of the five boroughs. There's even a horseback tour of Prospect Park. Call a couple of weeks in advance for a schedule. All tours are free with the exception of the mounted ones, which are $20. Sat.–Sun. only, 1 P.M. or 2 P.M.

"Wildman" Steve Brill. (718) 291-6825. "Wildman" Steve Brill, an expert on edibles growing in the city parks, takes you on nature walks that last about four hours with a lunch break. (That includes nuts, berries, mushrooms, etc., ripe for the picking.) Sat.–Sun. and holidays, March to Dec. Free.

The World of Samuel Fraunces. 54 Pearl St.; 425-1778. Under the auspices of the Fraunces Tavern Museum, the one-hour tour will guide you around some of the famous landmarks of pre-Revolutionary New York, in which Fraunces lived and worked.

Business Brief

Business and pleasure come together at their finest in New York City. A power lunch at the 21 Club, an evening with clients at Lincoln Center, and a continuous series of business meetings beginning early in the morning make up a typical day for many Power Brokers who make New York their center of the universe. To New Yorkers time is money and when it comes to making money almost nothing else matters. If you are looking for a business challenge, the Big Apple is for you.

The following are tips on the business protocols of New York that will assist you in the successful conduct of business with New Yorkers:

- Do not be surprised if a New Yorker asks you, "What's in this deal for me?" or, "What will I get out of this?" Just make sure that you are prepared to answer the question.

- New Yorkers rarely work as a team in business. Individual performance is what counts and officers are rewarded according to their individual contribution to an organization. Rank and status are not acquired at birth or with age; they are given to the individual who proves to be the best.

- Be very punctual with any appointment you make. Executives often schedule appointments within twenty minutes of each other. If you are late you may have missed an opportunity to meet with the necessary party. Schedules are planned weeks in advance and it may be difficult to reschedule on short notice.

- In business, New Yorkers do not spend much time on pleasantries. Once you shake hands and exchange business cards get right to the point of your visit. Within the first five minutes, an executive will determine whether or not your proposal has merit, is right for the company, or is interesting enough to pursue further.

- Business is often discussed socially: at breakfast, lunch, dinner, cocktail parties, golf outings, on the tennis courts, or at the health club. New Yorkers believe that in every situation there is a potential deal.

- In many cases, personal relationships have little or no bearing on business. When a New Yorker is selling something, it goes to the highest bidder not to the seller's friend. When a New Yorker is buying something, he or she usually buys from the person who has the best for the least.

- It is not considered impolite for an executive to take calls while you are having a meeting in his or her office. In addition, many executives either carry beepers, which signal they should call in, or inform their offices of their every move in case someone needs to reach them. Even restaurants provide their clients with plug-in telephones for use at their tables.

- New Yorkers love to conduct business over meals. It is very fashionable to have meetings over a "power breakfast" from 7:30 to 9 A.M. Business lunches usually begin at 12:30 P.M. and end no later than 2 P.M. Business dinners are usually scheduled early, around 7 P.M., since many New Yorkers commute to the city from surrounding suburbs and wish to return home in time to be with their families before it gets too late.

- Schedule your appointments in proximity to each other. For example, try not to make appointments on Wall Street the same day you have meetings in Midtown. Separate the two if at all possible to avoid being rushed or delayed.

- Gifts are usually not exchanged when conducting business. Strict rules and policy in American corporations may prohibit or discourage the exchange of gifts. An executive must report any gift received and, in most cases, will not be allowed to accept those valued over $20.

—Sondra Snowdon

CULTURAL TIMELINE

1000	Manhattan, Canarsee, Hackensack, and Rockaway Indians occupy the area now known as New York City.
1524	Giovanni da Verrazano (sailing for France) enters the Narrows and discovers New York bay.
1526	Estevan Gomez (sailing for Spain) explores the shoreline.
1609	Henry Hudson (sailing for the Netherlands) lands on Manhattan and heads up the river that will bear his name.
1625	The town of Nieuw Amsterdam (near the Battery) is named as seat of government for Nieuw Netherlands (Manhattan).
1626	Peter Minuit buys **Manhattan** from the Algonquin Indians for 60 guilders (approximately $24).
1636	Settlers buy "Breukelen" **(Brooklyn)** from the Indians.
1639	Jonas Bronck buys land from the Indians **(the Bronx)**. But settlers are driven out of what is now Staten Island.
1643	The area population is about 500, with some 18 languages being spoken.
1645	The first permanent settlement in what is now **Queens** is at "Vissingen" (Flushing).
1653	City receives its charter establishing the municipal government. Nieuw Amsterdam's first tavern (at what is now 73 Pearl Street) becomes its first city hall. Peter Stuyvesant, now governor, builds a wall from river to river **(Wall Street)** to protect against the British who were trading rivals.
1661	First permanent settlement is built on **Staten Island:** Oude Dorp.
1664	The British capture the city without a fight and rename it in honor of the Duke of York.
1673	Dutch recapture New York, renaming it Nieuw Orange.
1674	British recapture Nieuw Orange, taking permanent control via the Treaty of Westminster. The "province" and the city are renamed **New York.** (Whew!)
1725	*New-York Gazette,* the city's first newspaper, is founded by William Bradford.
1732	First theater is opened near Maiden Lane.
1733	John Peter Zenger publishes an anti-British newspaper, the *New-York Weekly Journal.*
1735	Zenger's acquittal after being jailed for slander establishes the concept of freedom of the press.
1765	Colonial Congress meets in New York to denounce the Stamp Act and other British taxation policies.
1770	Battle of Golden Hill, first conflict of the Revolution.

1776	After Declaration of Independence is signed on July 4th, New York City is occupied by the British. Battles rage and by November, the British have beaten Washington and take control of Manhattan.
1783	British sign the Treaty of Paris, recognizing the independence of the colonies.
1785	New York becomes capital of the state (until 1789) and the nation (until 1790).
1789	U.S. Constitution is ratified. George Washington takes oath as first president at Federal Hall.
1790	First official census puts population of Manhattan at 33,000.
1792	Forerunner of **New York Stock Exchange** is formed.
1807	Robert Fulton demonstrates his steamboat, *Clermont,* in the Hudson River.
1812	U.S. declares war on Britain. New York harbor is blockaded until war ends in 1814.
1820	New York's population reaches 123,706, making it the country's largest city.
1834	The City of Brooklyn is established.
1856	Land purchased for **Central Park.**
1860	Population reaches nearly 815,000 due to influx of immigrants (caused by 1846 potato famine in Ireland and 1848 political uprisings in Germany).
1861	New York is one of 23 states fighting the South as the Civil War begins.
1867	Single-track elevated railroad runs from Battery to 13th Street. **Prospect Park** opens in Brooklyn.
1868	First wave of Italian and East European immigrants arrive.
1869	**Rutherford Stuyvesant** builds the city's first apartment house on East 18th Street.
1882	Thomas Edison opens the first generating plant to make electricity commercially available in the city.
1883	**Brooklyn Bridge** and the **Metropolitan Opera** open.
1886	**Statue of Liberty** is unveiled.
1892	**Ellis Island** immigration station opens.
1898	The five boroughs are joined under a single municipal government. Their combined population of 3.4 million makes this the world's second-largest city (only London, with 4 million inhabitants, is larger). New York City is officially born.
1904	The first line of the **subway,** the underground railway, opens.
1930	The Art Deco **Chrysler Building,** briefly the tallest building in the world, opens.
1931	The **Empire State Building,** becomes the world's tallest building, finished after two years' work.
1940	The **Rockefeller Center** complex opens.
1952	The **United Nations** meets for the first time in its new headquarters overlooking the East River.
1973	The twin towers of the **World Trade Center** open in lower Manhattan.
1986	The **Statue of Liberty** is restored for its centennial.

Emergencies

In case of a **life-threatening emergency** call **911.**

Sex Crimes Report Line: 267-7273

For specific complaints:

Crime Victims Hotline: 577-7777

Hospitals

With 24-hour emergency rooms:

Beth Israel Medical Center, First Ave. and 16th St., 420-2840

Cabrini Medical Center, 227 East 19th St., 725-6620

Montefiore Medical Center, 111 E 210 St., 920-5731

Mount Sinai Medical Center, 100th St. and Fifth Ave., 650-7171

New York Infirmary-Beekman Downtown Hospital, 170 William St., 312-5070

If You Lose Your Passport

Contact your consulate immediately:

Australian Consulate General, 636 Fifth Ave., 245-4000

British Consulate General, 845 Third Ave., ninth floor, 888-2112

Canadian Consulate General, 1251 Sixth Ave., 586-2400

New Zealand Consulate General, 630 Fifth Ave., 698-4650

If Your Traveler's Checks Are Lost Or Stolen

Contact the office of the bank or company from which you bought the checks. Take along the list of check numbers (which you still have because you kept them separate from your checks) and a piece of identification.

If Your Credit Cards Are Lost Or Stolen

American Express (800) 528-2121

Diners Club (800) 525-9150

Mastercard (800) 627-8372

Visa (800) 336-8472

Visitor Information

For the most up-to-date information on the city's activities and seasonal events, contact:

New York Convention & Visitors Bureau, 2 Columbus Circle, New York, NY 10019; (212) 397-8222.

Post Offices

The main post office at Eighth Ave. and 33rd St. (967-8585) is open 24 hours a day to receive letters and packages; other services available daily 8 A.M.–6 P.M. Other larger branches (Times Square Station, 340 W. 42nd St.; Grand Central Station, 450 Lexington Ave.): Mon.–Fri. 9 A.M.–6 P.M., Sat. 10 A.M.–1 P.M.; smaller stations: Mon.–Fri. 9 A.M.–5 P.M., closed Sat.

Telephones

Hotels add a surcharge to your phone bill for calls made from the room.

Manhattan and the Bronx are in the 212 area code; Brooklyn, Queens, and Staten Island are 718.

To make a local call from a phone booth (within the 212 area code) insert 25 cents. Calls to Brooklyn, Queens, Staten Island, and the rest of the outside world can be made two ways:

1. Insert 25 cents, dial 1 plus the number. A recorded voice will then tell you how much more change to deposit. The voice will also tell you when to deposit more change to continue your conversation.
2. Dial 0 plus the number. The recorded voice will ask for your calling card number. If you have an AT&T calling card, enter the number after the tone. Otherwise, wait for the operator to come on the line.

For New York City directory assistance dial 411. Even though Brooklyn and Queens are in a different area code, you can get directory assistance for the boroughs by dialing 411.

For direct dial international calls dial 011 plus the country code. For our visitors from other English-speaking countries, country codes are:

Australia, 61
Canada, 1
New Zealand, 64
Great Britain, 44

Useful Phone Numbers

Weather: 976-1212
Time and temperature: 976-1616

Electricity

Contrary to the local belief that the Big Apple is the most energetic city around, requiring more energy than its Macintosh counterpart, the voltage in New York is the same as that throughout the U.S.—110–120 volts, 60 cycles. Since much of the world runs on 220–240 volts, 50 cycles, foreign visitors should bring an adaptor plug and converter or purchase them here at a hardware store or a variety store (such as Woolworth's or Lamston's).

—Charlotte Savidge

Index

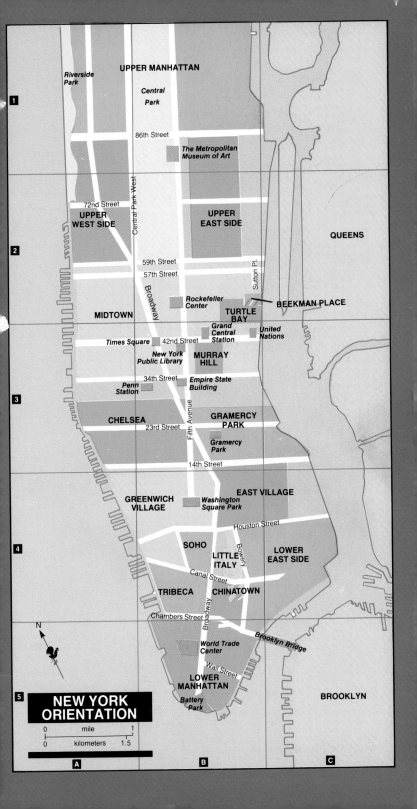

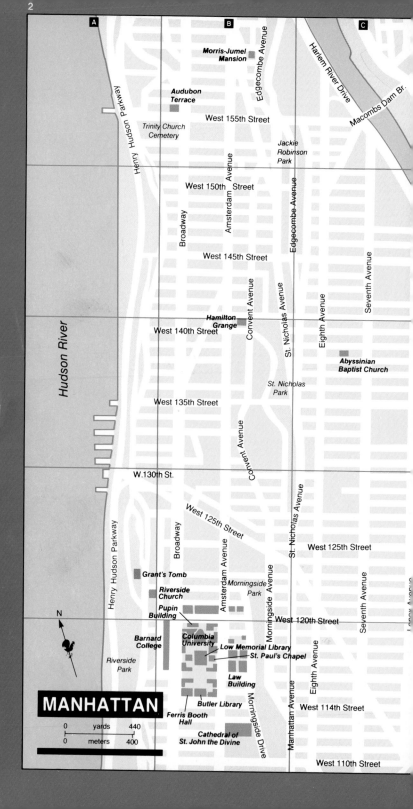

2

A **B** **C**

Harlem River Drive

Macombs Dam Br.

Morris-Jumel Mansion

Edgecombe Avenue

Audubon Terrace

West 155th Street

Trinity Church Cemetery

Jackie Robinson Park

Hudson River

West 150th Street

Henry Hudson Parkway

Broadway

Amsterdam Avenue

West 145th Street

Edgecombe Avenue

Seventh Avenue

Convent Avenue

Hamilton Grange

West 140th Street

St. Nicholas Avenue

Eighth Avenue

Abyssinian Baptist Church

St. Nicholas Park

West 135th Street

Convent Avenue

W.130th St.

West 125th Street

Broadway

Amsterdam Avenue

St. Nicholas Avenue

West 125th Street

Seventh Avenue

N

Henry Hudson Parkway

Grant's Tomb

Riverside Church

Morningside Park

Morningside Avenue

Pupin Building

West 120th Street

Barnard College

Columbia University

Low Memorial Library
St. Paul's Chapel

Eighth Avenue

Riverside Park

Law Building

Morningside Drive

MANHATTAN

Butler Library

Ferris Booth Hall

Manhattan Avenue

West 114th Street

0 yards 440
0 meters 400

Cathedral of St. John the Divine

West 110th Street

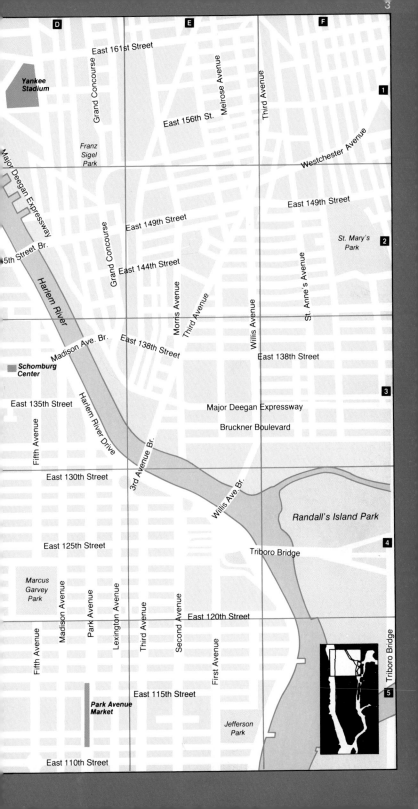

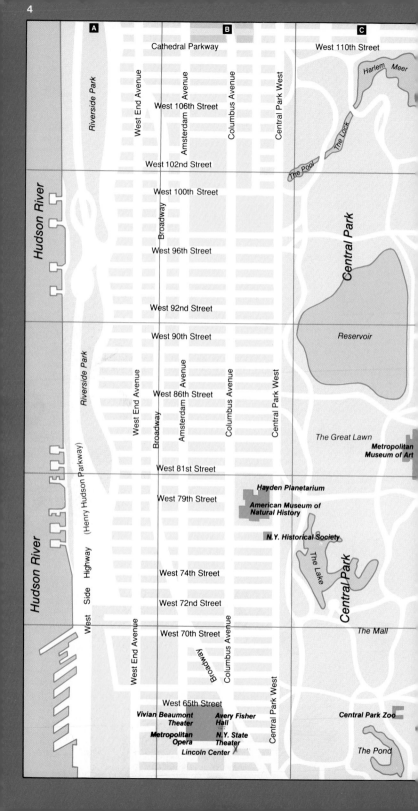

D

East 110th Street

E

F

MANHATTAN

6

Madison Avenue

Park Avenue

Lexington Avenue

Third Avenue

East 106th St.

Second Avenue

First Avenue

N

Museo del Barrio

useum of the
ty of New York

East 102nd Street

0   yards   440

0   meters   400

Wards Island

East 100th Street

East River

East 96th Street

nternational
center of
hotography

Franklin D. Roosevelt Drive

7

ewish Museum

East 92nd Street

ooper-Hewitt
useum

East 90th Street

uggenheim Museum

Madison Avenue

Park Avenue

Lexington Avenue

Third Avenue

East 86th St.

Second Avenue

First Avenue

York Avenue

Carl Schurz Park

8

East 81st Street

East 79th Street

East River

Whitney Museum of
American Art   East 74th Street

East 72nd Street

9

rick Collection

East 70th Street

Roosevelt Island

emple
manu-El

Park Avenue

Lexington Avenue

Third Avenue

East 65th St.

Second Avenue

First Avenue

York Avenue

10

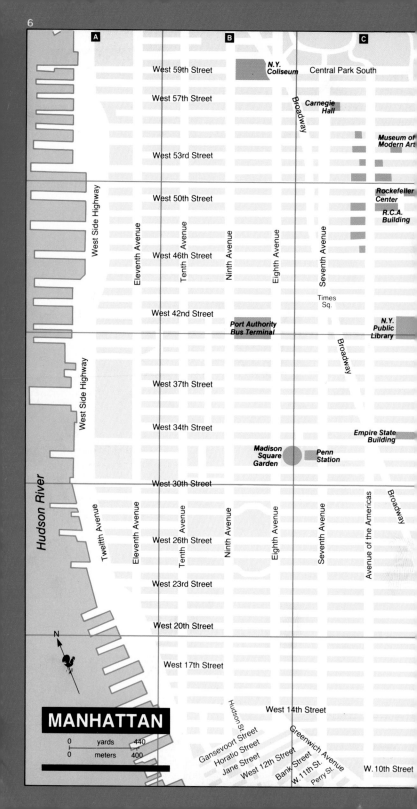

D

E

F

Queensboro Bridge

East 59th Street

**General Motors
Building**

East 57th Street

mp Tower

11

Park Avenue

East 53rd Street

Franklin D. Roosevelt Drive

East River

Roosevelt Island

Patrick's
thedral ■ **St. Bartholomew's Church**
East 50th Street

Waldorf Astoria

12

Madison Avenue

Lexington Avenue

Third Avenue

Second Avenue

First Avenue

**Pan Am
Building**
East 46th St.

Vanderbilt Ave.

**Grand Central
Station** ■ **Chrysler Building**

United Nations

East 42nd Street

**Manhattan
Air Terminal**

East River

**Pierpont
Morgan
Library**
East 37th Street

13

East 34th Street

East 30th Street

Madison Avenue

Park Avenue South

Lexington Avenue

Third Avenue

Second Avenue

First Avenue

Franklin D. Roosevelt Drive

East 26th St.

14

*adison Sq.
rk*

East 23rd Street

*Gramercy
Park*
East 20th Street

Irving Place

East 17th Street

Stuyvesant
Sq.

Union Sq.

Avenue A

Avenue B

Avenue C

15

Fourth Avenue

Broadway

East 14th Street

East 12th Street

East 10th Street

Third Ave.

D
East 11th Street
East 10th Street
East 9th Street

Cooper Union St. Marks Pl.

East 7th Street

East 6th Street

E
Tompkins Sq. Park
East 8th Street

F

Franklin D. Roosevelt Drive

East River Park

East River

16

Bowery

East 5th Avenue Street

Second Avenue

First Avenue

East 4th Street

East 3rd Street

East 2nd Street

eat Jones St.

Avenue A

Avenue B

Avenue C

Avenue D

East 1st Street

East Houston Street

Stanton Street

Rivington Street

Norfolk Street

Suffolk Street

Clinton Street

Ridge Street

Pitt Street

Attorney Street

Columbia Street

Williamsburg Bridge

17

enmare St.

Chrystie Street

Broome Street

Bowery

Eldridge Street

Forsythe Street

Ludlow Street

Delancey Street

Grand Street

Park

Willet St.

Lewis St.

Jackson Street

Gouvernor St.

Corlears Hook Park

Street

Mott Street

Hester Street

Elizabeth St.

Canal Street

Rutgers Street

Jefferson Street

Clinton Street

Montgomery St.

Mulberry St.

CHINATOWN

East Broadway

Henry Street

Madison Street

Market St.

Pike St.

South Street

East River

18

Baxter St.

Park Row

Madison Street

Catherine St.

Cherry Street

Water Street

Manhattan Bridge

Governor Smith Houses

Frankfort St.

Spruce St.

eekman Street

Cliff St.

Fulton St.

Pearl St.

Water Street

South Street

Fulton Street

Elevated Highway

South Street Seaport

Fletcher St.

Brooklyn Bridge

Brooklyn Queens Expressway

Fulton Street

Henry Street

Brooklyn

Clinton Street

19

t

Water Street

Front Street

South Street

East River

Old Slip

raunces Tavern

Tillary Street

20

Staten Island Ferry Terminal

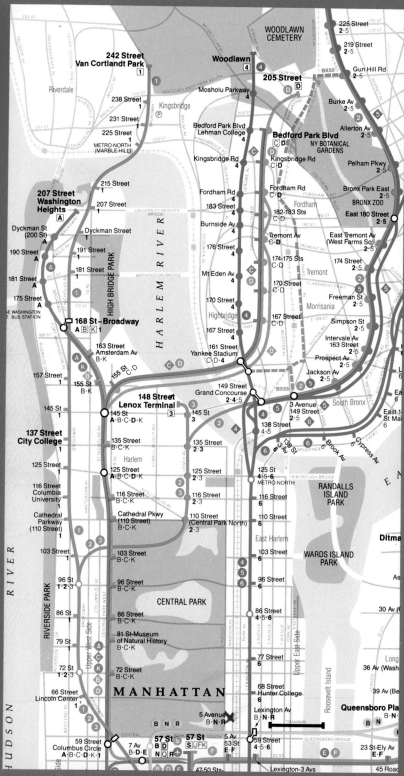

CENTRAL PARK

MANHATTAN

HUDSON

EAST RIVER

Riverside P.

86 St
B·C·K

79 St

72 St
1·2·3

66 Street
Lincoln Center
1

59 Street
Columbus Circle
A·B·C·D·1

50 Street
C·E·K

42 Street
A·C·E·K

42 Street
Times Sq

34 Street
Penn Station
A·C·E·K

Chelsea

23 Street
C·E·K

14 Street
A·C·E·K

8 Av
L

Christopher St
Sheridan Square

Greenwich
Village

Houston St

Canal St
Tribeca
Franklin St

Chambers St
A·C·JFK

Chambers St
1·2·3

World Trade Center
E·K

WORLD
TRADE
CENTER
PATH

Cortlandt St
N·R

Cortlandt St
1

Rector St
1

Upper West Side

86 Street
B·C·K

81 St-Museum
of Natural History
B·C·K

72 Street
B·C·K

7 Av
B·D·E

57 St
B·D
N·Q·R

E 50 St
49 St
B·N·R

47-50 Sts-
Rockefeller
Center
B·D·F·S·JFK

42 St
B·D·F
S·JFK

34 St
B·D·F

28 St
N·R·Q

23 St
F·S

18 St
L

6 Av

14 St
F·S

West 4 St
Washington Sq
A·C·E·F
K·S·JFK

Prince
N·R

Spring St
C·E·K

Canal St
A·C·E·K

Park
Place
2·3

City
Hall
N·R

6 Av
S

5 Av
B·N·R

57 St
S·JFK

5 Av
7

42 St
5 Av
7

33 Street

28 Street

23 Street

14 Street-Union Sq
4·5·6

Astor
Place
6

Bleecker St
6

Broadway-
Lafayette St
F·S

Spring
6

Bowery
J·M

Canal
B·D·J
M·N·Q
R·6

Chambers
J·M·R

Brooklyn Bridge-City Hall
4·5·6

Broadway-Nassau St
A·C·JFK

Fulton St
J·M·R·2·3·4·5

Wall
St
4·5

Wall Street
2·3

Broad Street
J·M·R

Rector
N·R

Bowling
Green
4·5

Whitehall St
South Ferry
N·R

South Ferry
1

Little
Italy

Grand
East Broadway

Lower East Side
F

Chinatown

Coast Guard only

Governors
Island

86 Street
4·5·6

77 Street
6

68 Street
Hunter College
6

Lexington Av
B·N·R

59 St
4·5·6

51 St
6

42 St-Grand Central
S·4·5·6·7 METRO-NORTH

Lexington-3 Avs
E·F

UN

Queensboro Plaza
B·N

23 St-Ely Av
E·F

21 Street (Van Alst)

Vernon-
Jackson Avs
7

Court House S

45 Roa

Roosevelt Island

TRAMWAY

Queensboro Bridge

Long

36 Av (Was

39 Av (B

30 Av

At press time the Mass Transit Authority decided to make changes in the New York City subway system. Fortunately, trains running within Manhattan are not dramatically affected. Here are the changes you'll need to know about: Manhattan "B" and "D" trains will connect to "B" and "D" trains in Brooklyn; the Grand Street station will be served by the "B," "D," and "Q" trains; and, the "B," "D," and "Q" trains running on Broadway will be temporarily replaced by the "N" and the "R." Please keep in mind that the above map does not show these changes.

HUDSON RIVER

HARLEM RIVER

THE BRONX

EAST HARLEM

RANDALLS ISLAND

WARDS ISLAND

CENTRAL PARK

UPPER EAST SIDE

YORKVILLE

UPPER WEST SIDE

INWOOD HILL PARK

Places to Visit

American Academy of Arts and Letters, M-2
Bus: M2, M3, M4, M5, M18, M100, M101
Subway: 1 to 157th Street

American Craft Museum, G-4
40 West 53rd Street
Bus: M1, M2, M3, M4, M5, M27, X25*, X90*
Subway: 2, 3, 4, 5 to West 50th St
M2, M3, M4, M5 to 53rd Street

Carnegie Hall, G-4
881 Seventh Avenue
Bus: M5, M6, M7, M10, M30, M31, M104
Subway: N, R to 57th Street; Columbus Circle; B, D, E to Seventh Avenue

Cathedral of St. John the Divine, J-3
Amsterdam Avenue at 112th Street
Bus: M4, M7, M11, M104
Subway: 1 to 110th Street/Cathedral Parkway

Citicorp Center, D-5
153rd Street at 53rd Street
Bus: M15, M27, M30, M101, M102
Subway: E, F, 6 to Lexington Avenue, 6 to 51st Street

City Hall, B-5
Bus: M1, M6, M15, M101, M102
Subway: 4, 5, 6 to Brooklyn Bridge;
R to City Hall, A, C, E, J, M to Chambers Street

The Cloisters, A-1
Fort Tryon Park
Bus: M4

Columbia University, K-2
Broadway at 116th Street
Bus: M4, M5, M11, M104
Subway: 1 to 116th Street/Columbia University

Cooper-Hewitt Museum, H-5
Fifth Avenue at 91st Street
Bus: M1, M2, M3, M4, M19
Subway: 4, 5, 6 to 86th Street

Dyckman House, A-3
Broadway at 204th Street
Bus: M100
Subway: A to 207th Street

Ellis Island, A-5
Bus (to Ferry): M1*, M6, M15, X25*, X90*
Subway: 1, 9, N, R to Whitehall Street;
Bowling Green; N, R to Whitehall Street

Empire State Building, E-4
Fifth Avenue at 34th Street
Bus: M1, M2, M3, M4, M5, M16, M34
Subway: B, D, F, N, Q, R to 34th Street

Frick Collection, F-5
Fifth Avenue at 70th Street
Bus: M1, M2, M3, M4
Subway: 6 to 68th Street

George Washington Bridge Bus Station, N-2
Broadway at 178th Street
Bus: M4, M5, M100
Subway: A, 1 to 175th Street/177th Street

Gracie Mansion, I-7
East End Avenue at 88th Street
Bus: M15, M18, M31, M86
Subway: 4, 5, 6 to 86th Street

Grand Central Terminal, F-5
42nd Street at Park Avenue
Bus: M1, M2, M3, M4 to Grand Central
M101, M102, M104, X25
Subway: 4, 5, 6, 7, S to Grand Central

Guggenheim Museum, H-5
Fifth Avenue at 88th Street
Bus: M1, M2, M3, M4, M19
Subway: 4, 5, 6 to 86th Street

Hispanic Society, M-2
Broadway at 155th Street
Bus: M4, M5, M100, M101
Subway: 1 to 157th Street

Intrepid Sea-Air-Space Museum, E-2
34th Street, Twelfth Avenue
Bus: M16, M34, 12th Avenue/Pier 86
Subway: A, C, E to 34th Street

Jacques Marchais Museum of Tibetan Art, J-5
New York's first and only Museum of
Tibetan Art

Jewish Museum, I-5
Fifth Avenue at 92nd Street
Bus: M1, M2, M3, M4
Subway: 4, 5, 6 to 86th Street

Lincoln Center for the Performing Arts, G-3
Broadway at 64th Street
Bus: M5, M7, M10, M11, M104
Subway: 1 to 66th Street/Lincoln Center

Madison Square Garden, E-4
Seventh Avenue at 32nd Street
Bus: M4, M5, M6, M7, M10, M16, M34
Subway: A, C, E, 1, 2, 3 to 34th Street

Metropolitan Museum of Art, H-4
Fifth Avenue at 82nd Street
Bus: M1, M2, M3, M4, M18, M79
Subway: 4, 5, 6 to 86th Street

Museum of American Folk Art, G-4
See American Craft Museum

Museum of Broadcasting, G-4
See American Craft Museum

Museum of Holography, C-5
See American Craft Museum

Museum of Modern Art, G-4
See American Craft Museum

Museum of the American Indian, M-2
Broadway at 155th Street
See American Academy of Arts and Letters

New-York Historical Society, H-3
Central Park West at 77th Street
Bus: M7, M10, M11, M79
See American Museum of Natural History

New York Public Library, F-4
Fifth Avenue at 42nd Street
Bus: M1, M2, M3, M4, M5, M104
Subway: 7 to Fifth Avenue

New York Stock Exchange, A-5
Bus: M1, M6, M15
Subway: 1, 2, 3, 4, 5, N, R to Wall Street

New York University, D-4
Washington Square
Bus: M1, M2, M3, M5, M6, M8
Subway: A, C, E, F, S to West 4th Street;
N, R to 8th Street

Pace University, B-5
41 Park Row. See City Hall

Port Authority Bus Terminal, F-3
Eighth Avenue at 41st Street
Bus: M6, M10, M11, M16, M27, M42, M104
Subway: A, C, E, 1, 2, 3, 7, N, Q, R to Times Square

Radio City Music Hall, G-4
Sixth Avenue at 50th Street
Bus: M5, M6, M7
Subway: B, D, F to 47th/50th Streets;
E, F to Fifth Avenue; D, E, B, N, R

Rockefeller Center, G-4
See American Craft Museum

Roosevelt Island Tramway, G-4
Second Avenue at 60th Street
Bus: M15, M28, M31, M32, M103

St. Patrick's Cathedral, F-5
Fifth Avenue at 50th Street
Bus: M1, M2, M3, M4, M5, M27, M50
See Rockefeller Center

South Street Seaport Museum, B-6
Bus: M15
Subway: 2, 3, 4, 5, A, C, J, M, Z to Fulton Street

Statue of Liberty, A-5
Bus (to Ferry): M1*, M6, M15. See Ellis Island
Subway: Battery Park. South Ferry; See Ellis Island

Studio Museum in Harlem, J-5
Subway: 2, 3 to 125th Street

Temple Emanu-El, G-5
Fifth Avenue at 65th Street
Bus: M1, M2, M3, M4, M30, M66
Subway: 6 to 68th Street

United Nations, F-4
First Avenue at 45th Street
Bus: M15, M27, M42, M104
Subway: 4, 5, 6, 7, S to Grand Central

Whitney Museum of American Art, H-5
Madison Avenue at 75th Street
Bus: M1, M2, M3, M4
Subway: 6 to 77th Street

World Trade Center, B-5
Church Street at Vesey Street
Bus: M6, M9, M10, M15, M22
Subway: A, C, E, N, R, 1, 2, 3, 4, 5, J, M, Z to
Chambers St/WTC

Yeshiva University, M-1
Amsterdam Avenue at 185th Street
Bus: M3, M100, M101
Subway: 1 to 181st Street

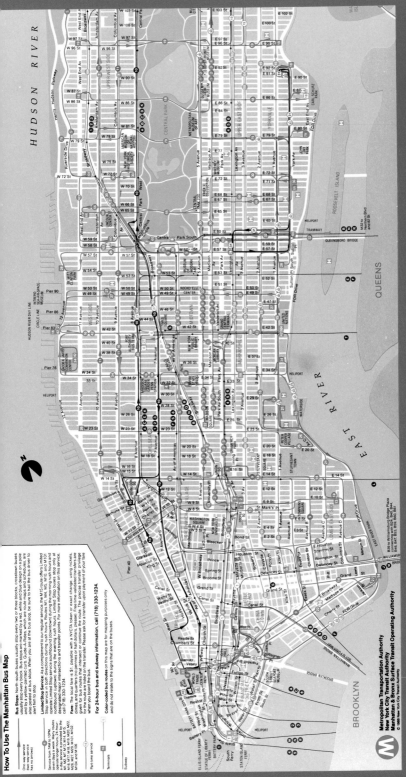

How To Use The Manhattan Bus Map

Bus Stops: North-south buses usually stop every two or three blocks; crosstown buses usually stop every block. Bus stops are marked by a red, white and blue sign on a pole and by a yellow painted curb. Guide-A-Rides, which are route maps and schedules, are also posted at bus stops. When you are at the bus stop, be sure to hail the bus driver to alert him to stop.

Limited Stop Service: As a complement to our regular service, the M15 route offers Limited Stop service in both directions during rush hours. Routes M1, M4, M5, M10, and M101 operate Limited Stop service southbound (downtown) during the morning rush hours and northbound (uptown) during the evening rush hours. Limited Stop buses stop only at designated major intersections and transfer points. For more information on this service, call (718) 330-1234.

Fare: The local fare is $1, payable with a NYCTA token or exact change, using nickels, dimes, quarters or dollars (no pennies or half dollars, please). Free transfers are given for bus routes that intersect or continue one route. The precise transfer privilege for the route are listed on the transfer. Please ask for a transfer upon payment of your fare when you board the bus.

For 24-hour bus and subway information, call (718) 330-1234.

Color-coded bus routes on this map are for mapping purposes only and do not relate to the signs that are on the buses.

One-way service
Two-way service

Service from 7AM to 10PM
usually seven days a week; some routes
operate longer hours; 24-hour
service is available for
M1, M2, M7, M15, M14, M15,
M21, M22, M27, M60, M22,
M26, M27, M60, M101, M102,
M104, and M106.

Part-time service

Terminals

Subway

Metropolitan Transportation Authority
New York City Transit Authority
Manhattan & Bronx Surface Transit Operating Authority

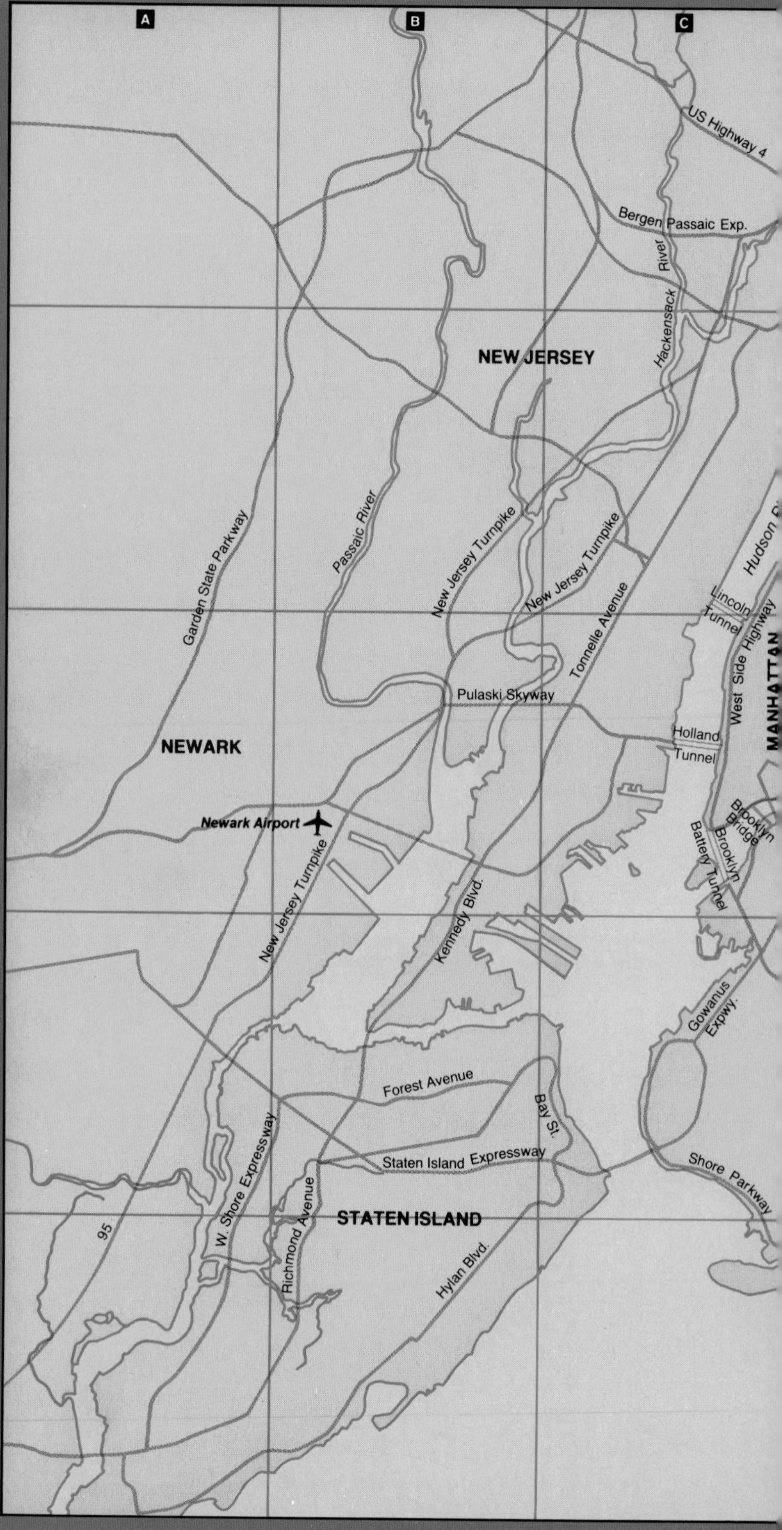
A
B
C
US Highway 4
Bergen Passaic Exp.
Hackensack River
NEW JERSEY
Passaic River
Garden State Parkway
New Jersey Turnpike
New Jersey Turnpike
Tonnelle Avenue
Hudson R
Lincoln Tunnel
West Side Highway
MANHATTAN
Pulaski Skyway
Holland Tunnel
NEWARK
Newark Airport
Brooklyn Bridge
Brooklyn Battery Tunnel
New Jersey Turnpike
Kennedy Blvd.
Gowanus Expwy.
Forest Avenue
Bay St.
Staten Island Expressway
W. Shore Expressway
Richmond Avenue
STATEN ISLAND
Shore Parkway
95
Hylan Blvd.

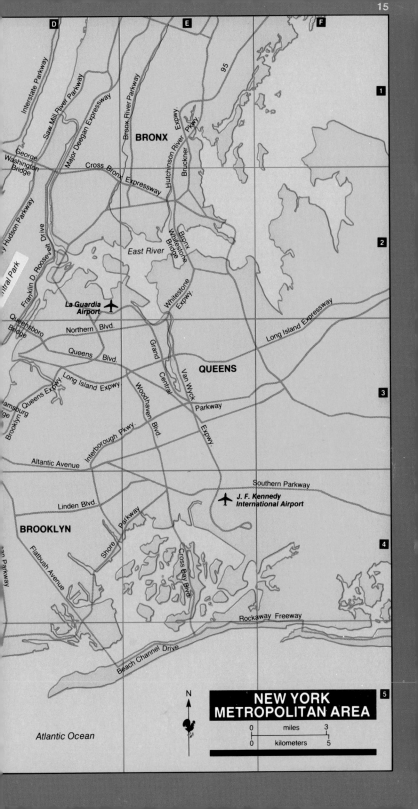

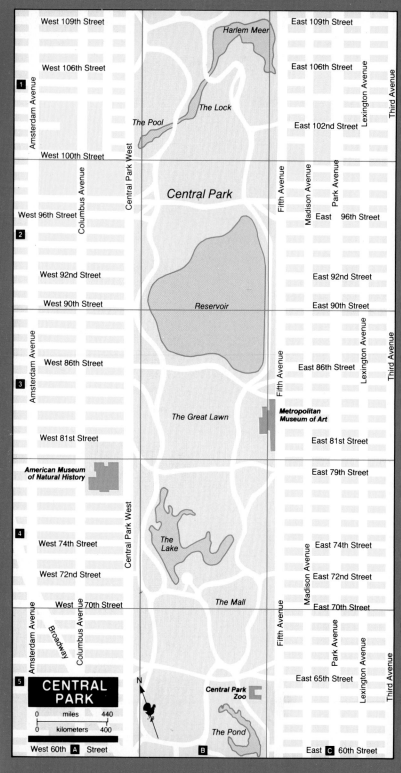

16

West 109th Street

Harlem Meer

East 109th Street

West 106th Street

East 106th Street

Amsterdam Avenue

Lexington Avenue

Third Avenue

1

The Lock

The Pool

East 102nd Street

West 100th Street

Central Park West

Central Park

Columbus Avenue

Fifth Avenue

Madison Avenue

Park Avenue

West 96th Street

East 96th Street

2

West 92nd Street

East 92nd Street

West 90th Street

Reservoir

East 90th Street

Amsterdam Avenue

West 86th Street

East 86th Street

Fifth Avenue

Lexington Avenue

Third Avenue

3

The Great Lawn

Metropolitan Museum of Art

West 81st Street

East 81st Street

American Museum of Natural History

East 79th Street

Central Park West

The Lake

4

West 74th Street

Madison Avenue

East 74th Street

West 72nd Street

East 72nd Street

West 70th Street

The Mall

East 70th Street

Amsterdam Avenue

Broadway

Columbus Avenue

Fifth Avenue

Park Avenue

Madison Avenue

Lexington Avenue

Third Avenue

5

CENTRAL PARK

N

Central Park Zoo

East 65th Street

0 miles 440

0 kilometers 400

The Pond

West 60th **A** Street

B

East **C** 60th Street